Torah Down Under

Observations and insights on the weekly sedrah

from

The Land Down Under

by

Pinchos Chalk

FIRST EDITION: December 2020

Cover design and contents © Pinchos Chalk, Melbourne, 2020

ISBN-10 : 0-64821-319-6 / ISBN-13 : 978-0-64821-319-2

Dewey Decimal classification 220.6

Please address any questions or comments regarding this book to the author: torahdownunder@gmail.com

A catalogue record for this work is available from the National Library of Australia

Approbation from Rabbi C. Feldman, Golders Green Beis Ha'medrash

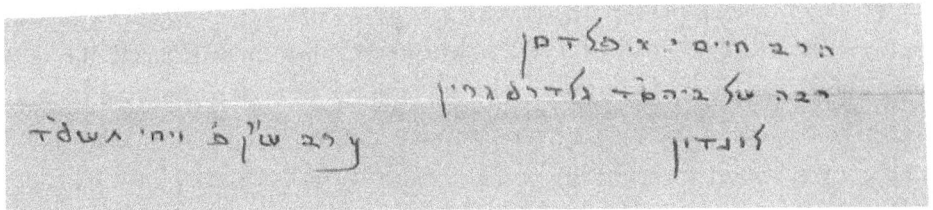

Last week I had the pleasure to meet once again with Rabbi Pinchos Chalk. He told me that he had written *divrei torah* both on the *sidros* of the year and also for the *chagim* and I studied some of his commentary.

He is a very serious student of Torah and he has collated into each piece of his writing some important thoughts. Without the usual linguistic embellishment, he delivers the explanations concisely and precisely.

I sincerely trust that these briefly annotated thoughts will find favour with the readers, who will appreciate the great sincerity of the deliberations.

Approbation from Rabbi D. Nojowitz, Torah U'Mesorah

To my dear friend Rabbi Pinchos Chalk *shlit"a*,

I read with interest parts of your manuscript "Torah Down Under" on Sefer Bereishis. I found it to be both instructive and enjoyable and certainly worthy of being in every Jewish home. It is not an easy read and requires much thought and concentration on the part of the reader. But it is certainly worth the effort.

I read Rav Wurzberger's shlit"a approbation and was inspired by his mentioning that you wrote these *droshos* as a way of keeping in touch with your dear parents through Torah learning. This is of itself a most worthy effort and achievement.

I look forward to receiving the completed work on the other four *chumashim*.

Continued Hatzlocho in your labor of love, *limud ha'Torah*.

Sincerely,

Dovid Nojowitz

Approbation from Rabbi Y. A. Oppenheimer, Gateshead Yeshiva

חודש אלול, תשע"ט לפ"ק

לכבוד ידידי הדגול הרב ר' פנחס טשאלק שליט"א

It gave me great pleasure to read some of your דברי תורה on ספר בראשית, which are so clearly written, so well documented, and of such real and meaningful content!

You should continue to have the זכות for many, many years to come to give such wonderful quality satisfaction and נחת to your dear Parents שיח' – to whom we owe much from bygone years, and they too should have the great זכות of motivating you to spend time and effort on presenting your beautiful דברי תורה so well and making them available to כלל ישראל!

בברכת כתיבה וחתימה טובה ושנת ברכה והצלחה מרובה בכל עבודתכם הק' ורוב נחת דקדושה ממשפחתכם היקרה שיח',

ברוב כבוד והוקרה,

יוסף אהרן אופנהיימר

פה גייטסהעד, יצ"ו

Approbation from Rabbi O. Z. Rubenstein, Yeshivas Toras Simcha

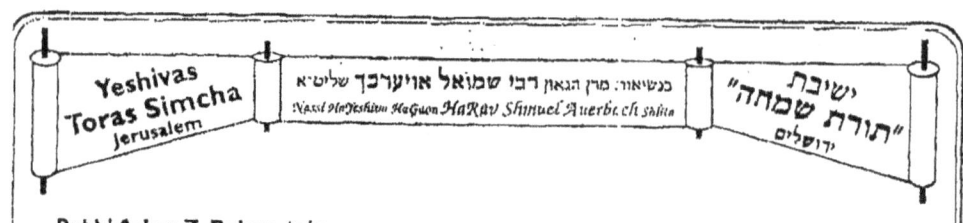

יום רביעי ח׳ אייר תשס״ג

בס״ד

באתי בזה להמליץ על ידידי הרב פנחס טשאלק שליט״א ממלבורן, אוסטרליה שהנני מכירו כבר שנים רבות. עוד בהיותו תלמיד ישיבת מיר המעטירה בירושלים עיה״ק ראיתי בו שאיפות להבין ולהשכיל כל דבר על מכונו ועוד יותר כשתחתן ועבר לגור באוסטרליה ולמד בכולל החשוב שם, פעמים רבות קבלתי טלפונים ממנו לשוחח על סוגיות קשות במחשבה ומוסר ברצותו להגיע להבנת עומק הדברים. הוא בן תורה אמיתי וגם ידיו רב לו בעסקי צדקה וחסד. אבל עם כל מה שהכרתי רוב עמלו ובירור סוגיות, הופתעתי לטובה כששלח לי כמה ממאמריו שחבר בלשון האנגלית והפיץ ברבים. נהניתי מאוד לראות שנתברך בלשון לימודים והצליח להסביר עניינים עמוקים בלשון צח וברור ששוים לכל נפש ולכן ראיתי להיות חפקים על ספר דגם בני תורה ימצאו בהם הסברים ערבים שלא ידעו, וגם אלו שעוד לא נתקרבו אם רק שכל ובינה להם, יהנו מדבריו המשכנעים לקרב לבותם לאבינו שבשמים. ואני מברכו שיזכה להמשיך לעלות בתורה ולחבר חבורים נחמדים לזכות את הרבים.

Approbation from Rabbi B.Z. Wurtzberger, Kollel Beis Ha'Talmud, Melbourne

בס"ד

בהקדמת המו"ל לשו"ת מלמד להועיל כתב, מרגלא היה בפומו של אבי מורי זצ"ל, אל יעבור עליך יום בלי חידוש בכתב, ומאמרו זו נראה שהוא ע"פ מש"כ במשלי, וקובץ על יד ירבה. והן הראה לי תלמידי החביב פינחס טשאלק נ"י את קונטרסו של דברי תורה על פרשיות השבוע, והוא חיבור של דברי תורה ששלח להוריו שיחיו באנגליא דבר שבוע בשבועתו לכבוד שבת קודש. ועיקר ענינו הוא לפרש דרשות חז"ל בדרך מוסרי הקרוב אל הפשט, לעורר לבבות להבין ולהשכיל דברי חכמים וחידותם בעומק קריצת רמיזותיהם של חז"ל.

ואני אומר יישר חיליה לאורייתא, ובאתי לברכו שיפוצו מעיינותיו חוצה, ויתבדרון דבריו בבי מדרשא, ויזכה להגדיל תורה ולהאדירה.

בברכת התורה

בנימין זאב ווירצבורגער
פה מלבורן, יע"ו

וְנָתַתִּי לָהֶם בְּבֵיתִי וּבְחוֹמֹתַי יָד וָשֵׁם (ישעיה נ"ו)

לזכרון עולם בהיכל ה'

לעילוי נשמת

מרת חוה רפאלה קרמר - מילר ע"ה

בת הר"ר יעקב יוסף הי"ו

נקטפה בשנת הכ"א לחייה

ב' חשון תשס"א

במדרש תנחומא פרשת כי תשא (סימן ג'), כי תשא את ראש בני ישראל. כך פתח רבי תנחומא בר אבא, מתוקה שנת העובד אם מעט אם הרבה יאכל, והשבע לעשיר איננו מניח לו לישון (קהלת ה' י"א). אמרו לו לשלמה, אלו אחר אמר הפסוק הזה, היינו שוחקין עליו. אתה שכתוב בך ויחכם מכל האדם (מלכים א' ה' י"א), תאמר, מתוקה שנת העובד אם מעט אם הרבה יאכל. אין הדבר כך. שכל מי שהוא רעב, אכל קמעא, שנתו מתנדדת ממנו. אכל הרבה, שנתו מתוקה.

אמר להם, איני מדבר אלא בצדיקים ובעמלי תורה. כיצד. אדם שכל שנותיו שלשים שנה, ומעשר שנים ואילך הוא עמל בתורה ובמצות, ומת לשלשים שנה. ואדם אחד חיה שמונים שנה, ומעשר שנים ואילך עמל בתורה ובמצות עד שמת. את אומר, הואיל ולא יגע הראשון אלא עשרים שנה בתורה, וזה שיגע שבעים שנה, שהקדוש ברוך הוא מרבה לזה שכר יותר ממי שעסק בתורה עשרים שנה. לפיכך אני אומר אם מעט אם הרבה יאכל, שיכול בן עשרים שנה לומר לפני הקדוש ברוך הוא, אלולי שסלקתני מן העולם בחצי ימי, הייתי מאריך שנים ומרבה בתורה ובמצות. לפיכך אני אומר אם מעט אם הרבה יאכל, שמתן שכרו של זה כמתן שכרו של זה.

ת.נ.צ.ב.ה.

Table of Contents

Introduction
   A *dvar torah* for Shabbos   15

Bereishis
   Monetary law for *benei noach*   18
   Clarity and responsibility   24

Noach
   Meriting rescue   29

Lech lechah
   The Great Name of Hashem   37
   Avraham's choice   42

Vayera
   How Avraham taught *emunah* to his guests   46
   Praying for Sedom   50

Chaye Sarah
   Sarah and Esther   54

Toldos
   Why Yitzchak resembled Avraham   58
   The surprising *madregah* of Yitzchak   65
   Yaakov and Cana'an   68

Vayetze
   Escaping Lavan   74
   Exile and self-sacrifice   78
   The dream of the ladder   83

Vayishlach
   And Yaakov remained alone   93
   Fighting Esav's *malach*   100

Vayeshev

The split between Yosef and the brothers	105
Yosef's survival in the pit	110

Miketz

The *bitachon* and wisdom of Yosef	116
Yosef and the butler	121
Interpreting Pharoh's dream	125

Vayigash

The truth of *lashon ha'kodesh*	129
The Oneness of Hashem	132

Vayechi

The eternal blessing	139
Ephraim's *berachah*	146

Shemos

Redemption for all generations	152

Va'era

The power of Hashem	157
The plague of pestilence	161

Bo

The plague of locusts	167

Beshalach

Yosef and *krias yam suf*	172
Krias yam suf	177

Yisro

Yisro's blessing	183
Avodah zarah	189
The *mitzva* to believe in Hashem	196
Havdalah	202

Mishpatim
- Foundation through justice — 207

Terumah
- Donating to the *mishkan* — 211

Tetzaveh
- The Western Lamp of the menorah — 217
- The greatness of Aharon — 222

Ki Sisa
- Moshe's loan to the *benei yisrael* — 227

Vayakhel
- Perpetuating *kedushah* — 235

Pekudei
- Avoiding the *ayin ha'ra* — 243

Vayikra
- Calling Moshe — 247

Tzav
- Spiritual ascendancy — 255

Shemini
- The atonement of the *benei yisrael* — 259

Tazria
- Rising above *tzara'as* — 265

Metzora
- The order of *tzara'as* — 272

Acharei mos
- The timelessness of Yom Kippur — 278

Kedoshim
- The gift of holiness — 285

Emor
    The balance of the *kohanim*   291

Behar
    The holiness of *she'mitah*   296

Bechukosai
    Complete blessing   304

Bamidbar
    Declaring the oneness of Hashem   310

Naso
    Eretz Yisrael and *galus*   314

Beha'alosechah
    The light of the *menorah*   318

Shelach lechah
    The trees of Eretz Yisrael   324

Korach
    Unity in service of Hashem   328

Chukas
    The purity of the *parah adumah*   332

Balak
    Balak's *korbanos*   338

Pinchas
    Kehunah and vengeance   344

Matos

Masei
    The travels of the *benei yisrael*   356

Devarim
    The healing power of the Torah   362

Va'eschanan

    The cities of refuge   367

Ekev

    Miracles through water   372

Re'eh

    The protection of the Torah   377

Shoftim

    Judging truthfully   382

Ki Setze

    One *mitzva* leads to another *mitzva*   389

Ki Savo'u

    The holiness of *bikkurim*   394

Nitzavim

    The covenant of Hashem   399

Vayelech

    Moshe's legacy   405

Ha'azinu

    The dedication of the *avos*   411

Ve'zos he'berachah

    Finding Hashem in *galus*   417

Simchas Torah

    Completing the Torah   424

Appendix

    Glossary of Hebrew terms   432
    Bibliography   438

Introduction

A *dvar torah* for Shabbos

When we were young, we were always expected to have a *dvar torah* to say on Shabbos. When we went to *yeshiva*, this *minhag* continued by proxy, and we spent Friday afternoon writing a *dvar torah*, which the postman would deliver next morning to be read at the Shabbos table.

Our favourite *seforim* were the *Koheles Yitzchak* (Vilna, 1900) and, of course, the *Mayanah shel Torah* (Torah Wellsprings, Warsaw, 1938). These *seforim* were easy enough for us to understand but involved enough to make for an interesting *dvar torah*.

Most of the *divrei torah* in these *seforim* fall into the category of *derush*. These are ideas and thoughts based on a gemara or a medrash that cannot be conclusively proven, but that express the timeless spirit and strength of the *benei yisrael*, as they travel through the sea of *galus* towards their final goal.

The gemara says in Taanis (5b)

הכי א"ר יוחנן יעקב אבינו לא מת א"ל וכי בכדי ספדו ספדנייא וחנטו חנטייא וקברו קברייא א"ל מקרא אני דורש שנאמר (ירמיהו ל', י') ואתה אל תירא עבדי יעקב נאם ה' ואל תחת ישראל כי הנני מושיעך מרחוק ואת זרעך מארץ שבים מקיש הוא לזרעו מה זרעו בחיים אף הוא בחיים

Rabbi Yitzchak said to Rav Nachman that Rabbi Yochanan said as follows, "Yaakov Avinu did not die."

Rav Nachman asked him, "And was it for naught that the eulogisers eulogised him and the embalmers embalmed him and the buriers buried him?"

Rabbi Yitzchak replied to Rav Nachman, "I am interpreting a *passuk*, as it says, "Therefore do not fear, My servant Yaakov, says Hashem, neither be dismayed, oh Yisrael, for I will save you from afar, and your children from the land of their captivity" (Yirmiyah 30:10). The *passuk* compares Yaakov to his children. Just as his children are alive when redeemed, so too, Yaakov himself is alive.

Rabbi Yitzchak Hutner z"l (Pachad Yitzchak, Pesach, 52.6) asks that it would seem difficult to understand how Rabbi Yitzchak answered Rav Nachman's question. Rav Nachman asked that the Torah relates how Yaakov was embalmed, eulogised and buried. So, despite Rabbi Yitzchak's *derashah*, it would seem an indisputable fact that Yaakov did indeed die.

He answers that the key to understanding Rabbi Yitzchak's answer lies in the words מקרא אני דורש, "I am relating how these *pessukim* may be understood from the perspective of *derush*."

This means to say that Rabbi Yitzchak responded to Rav Nachman as follows. "Yes, in the world of *peshat*, the obvious meaning, Yaakov Avinu did die. But in the world of *derush*, in which lives the hopes, the striving, the tears and the joy of the *benei yisrael*, Yaakov Avinu is alive, together with all of his children who derive strength and succour from the elusive but eternal spirit of life that is concealed within the words of the Torah.

When *mashiach* comes, these echoes of hope will take shape in the return of Yaakov, together with his children, to Eretz Yisrael."

Through the words of the Torah, we hear the *tefillos*, the strivings and the joys of the previous generations. As Rabbi Boruch Ber Lebovitz z"l said (The Jewish Observer, December 1989, page 23), "The *maskilim* (intellectuals) know when and where Abaye was born, and when and where Abaye died. We know where Abaye lives! Right before our eyes in the *heilige* (holy) gemara!"

May we merit to imbibe of the Torah's stream of life whose source lies in the lives of our *avos* and which flows ever onwards towards the sea of knowledge of Hashem, as the *passuk* says (Yeshaya 11.9)

לֹא יָרֵעוּ וְלֹא יַשְׁחִיתוּ בְּכָל הַר קָדְשִׁי כִּי מָלְאָה הָאָרֶץ דֵּעָה אֶת ה' כַּמַּיִם לַיָּם מְכַסִּים

They shall not do evil or destroy in all My sacred mount, for the land shall be filled with knowledge of Hashem as water covers the sea.

Pinchos Chalk, Melbourne
6th of Kislev, 5781

Bereishis

Monetary law for *benei noach*

It says in this week's *sedrah* (Bereishis 2:16)

וַיְצַו ה' אֱלֹקִים עַל הָאָדָם לֵאמֹר מִכֹּל עֵץ הַגָּן אָכֹל תֹּאכֵל

And Hashem commanded the man saying, "You may eat from all of the trees of the garden."

The gemara in Sanhedrin (56a) derives the obligation of non-Jews to observe the *sheva mitzvos benei Noach* (the seven Noachide commandments) from this *passuk*:

תנו רבנן שבע מצות נצטוו בני נח, דינין וברכת השם ע"ז גילוי עריות ושפיכות דמים וגזל ואבר מן החי... מנהני מילי אמר ר' יוחנן דאמר קרא (בראשית ב', ט"ז) ויצו ה' אלקים על האדם לאמר מכל עץ הגן אכל תאכל ויצו אלו הדינין... ה' זו ברכת השם... אלקים זו עבודת כוכבים... על האדם זו שפיכות דמים... לאמר זו גילוי עריות... מכל עץ הגן ולא גזל אכל תאכל ולא אבר מן החי

The *chachamim* have taught: The descendants of Noach were commanded seven *mitzvos*; to uphold the law, not to blaspheme, not to serve *avodah zarah*, concerning immorality, murder, theft and concerning not eating the limb of a live animal.

[The gemara continues to explain how Rabbi Yochanan derived all of these *mitzvos* from the *passuk* of וַיְצַו ה' אֱלֹקִים עַל הָאָדָם לֵאמֹר מִכֹּל עֵץ הַגָּן אָכֹל תֹּאכֵל.]

Which laws are non-Jews obliged to judge?

One of the *sheva mitzvos benei noach* is that non-Jews should uphold the law, that means that they should setup courts that will enforce the law. There is a disagreement between the Ramban and the Rambam concerning which laws these courts are required to enforce.

According to the Rambam in Hilchos Melachim (9:14), non-Jewish courts need only uphold the observance of the other *sheva mitzvos benei noach*:

וכיצד מצווין הן על הדינין, חייבין להושיב דיינין ושופטים בכל פלך ופלך לדון בשש מצות אלו ולהזהיר את העם

> How are non-Jews commanded concerning applying judgement? They are obliged to set up judges and law enforcers in every city to judge and to enforce the observance of the other six *mitzvos* concerning which they are commanded, and to warn the people to observe them.

The Ramban (Bereishis 34:13) however, argues with the Rambam and says:

ועל דעתי, הדינין שמנו לבני נח בשבע מצות שלהם אינם להושיב דיינין בכל פלך ופלך בלבד, אבל צוה אותם בדיני גנבה ואונאה ועושק שכר שכיר ודיני השומרים כענין הדינין שנצטוו ישראל

> My opinion is that the law concerning which the *benei noach* were commanded, does not only entail setting up courts in each city (to enforce the other six *mitzvos benei noach*). Rather Hashem commanded them to observe the

laws of stealing, over-charging, not paying workers, guarding items and so on just like the monetary laws that Hashem commanded the *benei yisrael*.

According to the Ramban, the *benei noach* are commanded to apply all monetary laws, and not just to enforce the other 6 *mitzvos benei noach*.

Nevertheless, the Meshech Chachmah (Bereishis 18.19) explains that there is still a difference between the way that Jews and non-Jews are required to apply monetary law.

Compromise in court

The gemara in Sanhedrin (6a) brings a dispute concerning whether a judge should make a compromise in monetary cases. According to one opinion it is forbidden for a judge to make a compromise, according to another opinion, it is a *mitzva* for a judge to make a compromise:

> רבי אליעזר בנו של רבי יוסי הגלילי אומר אסור לבצוע וכל הבוצע הרי זה חוטא... אלא יקוב הדין את ההר שנאמר (דברים א', י"ז) כי המשפט לאלקים הוא...רבי יהושע בן קרחה אומר מצוה לבצוע שנאמר (זכריה ח', ט"ז) אמת ומשפט שלום שפטו בשעריכם והלא במקום שיש משפט אין שלום ובמקום שיש שלום אין משפט אלא איזהו משפט שיש בו שלום הוי אומר זה ביצוע..

Rabbi Eliezer the son of Rabbi Yossi HaGlili says that it is forbidden for a judge to reach a compromise and anyone who makes a compromise is a sinner... Rather "the law should pierce the mountain" as the *passuk* says כי המשפט לאלקים הוא – judgement belongs to Hashem (and therefore it is not up to the judge to alter the course of the law).

Rabbi Yehoshua ben Karchah says it is a *mitzva* to make a compromise, as the *passuk* says in Zecharia "You should judge truth and justice and peace in your gates." If there is justice, there is no peace (because the contending parties have not been reconciled) and in a place where there is peace there is no judgement? Rather which judgement is it that brings peace? That is compromise.

The court of Avraham

The Meshech Chachmah points out that concerning the way in which Avraham enacted justice, the *passuk* (Bereishis 18.19) says:

כִּי יְדַעְתִּיו לְמַעַן אֲשֶׁר יְצַוֶּה אֶת בָּנָיו וְאֶת בֵּיתוֹ אַחֲרָיו וְשָׁמְרוּ דֶּרֶךְ ה' לַעֲשׂוֹת צְדָקָה וּמִשְׁפָּט לְמַעַן הָבִיא ה' עַל אַבְרָהָם אֵת אֲשֶׁר דִּבֶּר עָלָיו

[Hashem said,] "For I have favoured him because he commands his children and his household to continue in his way, by guarding the way of Hashem to do charity and justice, in order that Hashem should bring on Avraham that [blessing] which he spoke concerning him."

Since the *passuk* says צְדָקָה וּמִשְׁפָּט – charity and [then] justice, it is evident that in the court of Avraham, compromise was preferred to strict judgement.

- We see from this *passuk* that compromise is preferred to strict justice. How then can Rabbi Eliezer say that it is forbidden for a judge to make a compromise?

The Meshech Chachmah answers as follows:

The reason that Rabbi Eliezer says that it is forbidden to reach a compromise is because המשפט לאלקים הוא – justice belongs to Hashem.

The judge has an obligation to enforce the strict letter of the law because he is merely the messenger of Hashem to apply His judgement. However, this is only true concerning the laws of the Torah, which are precisely detailed in *halachah*. But concerning the laws of the *benei noach*, which are determined by society, it is preferable to reach a compromise.

In other words, the *benei noach* are commanded to compile a code of law and to enforce monetary judgements in order to ensure that society operates in a fair and pleasant manner. Therefore, in a case where making a peaceable compromise between the litigants will benefit society more than a strict decision (which would cause further strife), it is appropriate for the judge to seek a compromise.

Since Avraham judged prior to the giving of the Torah, it would appear that he judged according to the laws of the *benei noach*. Therefore, it was preferable for Avraham to make a compromise, rather than to enforce a strict ruling.

This does not pose a contradiction to the opinion of Rabbi Eliezer who says that after the giving of the Torah, it is forbidden to make a compromise[1].

In summary, the requirement for *benei noach* to apply monetary law is derived from the *passuk* that says וַיְצַו ה' אֱלֹקִים עַל הָאָדָם, "And Hashem commanded concerning the man". We can only derive from here, that Hashem commanded that a system of law should be implemented, such as would enable the descendants of Adam to achieve peaceful co-existence.

Therefore, regarding monetary law for the *benei noach*, in a case where application of the strict letter of the law would cause dispute, it is better to reach a compromise. This differs from the monetary laws of the Torah (according to Rabbi Eliezer) which are mandated unequivocally in all their details, by Hashem.

---

[1] Based on this explanation, the Meshech Chachmah explains the *passuk* (שמואל ב', ח', ט"ו) that describes the way in which Dovid Ha'melech decided judgements

וַיִּמְלֹךְ דָּוִד עַל כָּל יִשְׂרָאֵל וַיְהִי דָוִד עֹשֶׂה מִשְׁפָּט וּצְדָקָה לְכָל עַמּוֹ

Dovid ruled over the whole of the Jewish people and Dovid did justice and *tzedakah* for all his people.

Why is it that regarding Dovid Ha'melech, the *passuk* says first מִשְׁפָּט (judgement) and then וּצְדָקָה (compromise), whereas regarding Avraham the *passuk* first says צְדָקָה (compromise) and then וּמִשְׁפָּט (judgement)?

The Meshech Chachmah explains that for Dovid Ha'melech, who judged according to the law of the Torah, it was preferable to do precise judgement (מִשְׁפָּט) before making a compromise (צְדָקָה). Whereas for Avraham who judged according to the laws of the *benei noach* which are based on social convention, it was preferable to try and arrange a compromise before imposing a strict ruling.

Clarity and responsibility

It says in this week's *sedrah* (Bereishis 3:8)

וַיִּשְׁמְעוּ אֶת קוֹל ה' אֱלֹקִים מִתְהַלֵּךְ בַּגָּן לְרוּחַ הַיּוֹם וַיִּתְחַבֵּא הָאָדָם וְאִשְׁתּוֹ מִפְּנֵי ה' אֱלֹקִים בְּתוֹךְ עֵץ הַגָּן

They heard the sound of Hashem moving about in the garden to the breeze of the day; and the man and his wife hid from Hashem among the trees of the garden.

The medrash says (Bereishis Rabbah 19.8)

וישמעו, אל תקרי וישמעו, אלא וישמיעו. שמעו קולן של אילנות שהיו אומרים הא גנבא דגנב דעתיה דברייה.

Do not read וַיִּשְׁמְעוּ (and they heard), rather read וַיַּשְׁמִעוּ (and they gave out a sound). They heard the voice of the trees which were saying, "Here is the thief who has cheated the mind of his creator."

- In what way did Adam cheat Hashem?

It would seem that we can explain as follows:

Breaking the *luchos*

The *passuk* says in Ki Sisa (Shemos 32.19)

וַיְהִי כַּאֲשֶׁר קָרַב אֶל הַמַּחֲנֶה וַיַּרְא אֶת הָעֵגֶל וּמְחֹלֹת וַיִּחַר אַף מֹשֶׁה וַיַּשְׁלֵךְ מִיָּדָיו אֶת הַלֻּחֹת וַיְשַׁבֵּר אֹתָם תַּחַת הָהָר.

And it was when he came near the camp and he saw the *egel ha'zahav* and the dancing, he became enraged and he hurled the *luchos* from his hands and shattered them at the foot of the mountain.

The *medrash* (Shemos Rabbah 43) explains why Moshe broke the *luchos*

למה הדבר דומה, לשר ששלח לקדש אשה עם הסרסור, הלך וקלקלה עם אחר. הסרסור שהיה נקי, מה עשה, נטל את כתובתה, מה שנתן לו השר לקדשה, וקרעה. אמר מוטב שתדון כפנויה ולא כאשת איש... ועוד אמר משה, מוטב נידונין כשוגגין ואל יהו מזידין, למה שהיה כתוב בלוחות אנכי ה' אלקיך, ועונשו אצלו זובח לאלקים יחרם, לפיכך שבר את הלוחות.

To what is this matter comparable? To a prince who sent a messenger to betroth a woman to him, and the woman was unfaithful. The messenger tore the marriage contract in order that she should be judged as an unmarried woman...

[Similarly, Moshe broke the *luchos* which were like a marriage contract between Hashem and the *benei yisrael*, in order to lighten the punishment for the *benei yisrael* having been unfaithful by serving *avodah zarah*.]

And further Moshe said, "It is better that they should be judged as having sinned accidentally and not deliberately. For it says in the *luchos*, 'I am Hashem your G-d.' And the punishment for transgressing this *mitzvah* and serving *avodah zarah* is written adjacent to it, 'One who sacrifices to other gods will be destroyed.'"

- How could breaking the *luchos* retroactively change the intentions of the *benei yisrael* when they served the *egel ha'zahav*?

Remembering Torah

The gemara says in Eruvin (54a)

ואמר רבי אליעזר מאי דכתיב (שמות ל"ב, ט"ז) חרות על הלוחות אלמלי לא נשתברו לוחות הראשונות לא נשתכחה תורה מישראל

Rabbi Eliezer said: What is the meaning of that which is written, "And the *luchos* were the work of Hashem, and the writing was the writing of Hashem, engraved upon the *luchos*"? This teaches us that had the first *luchos* not been broken, the Torah would never have been forgotten from the *benei yisrael* [as the Torah would have been engraved upon their hearts].

The Medrash Tanchuma (Ekev, 11) adds

אמר הקדוש ברוך הוא, בעולם הזה, על ידי יצר הרע, היו למדין ומשתכחין. אבל לעולם הבא, אני עוקר יצר הרע מכם ואינכם משתכחים, שנאמר, והסרותי את לב האבן מבשרכם ונתתי לכם לב בשר (יחזקאל ל"ו כ"ו). ולא עוד, אלא שאינכם צריכים לאדם שילמדם שנאמר, ולא ילמדו עוד איש את רעהו ואיש את אחיו לאמר דעו את ה' כי כלם ידעו אותי למקטנם ועד גדולם (ירמיה ל"א ל"ד).

Hashem said, "In this world, because of the *yetzer hara*, they used to learn and forget. But in *olam habah*, I will uproot the *yetzer hara* from your hearts and you will not forget, as the *passuk* says, 'And I will remove the heart of stone from your flesh and I will give you a heart of flesh.' And not only that but it will not be necessary for anyone to teach them, as the *passuk* says, 'And they will not teach anymore, one man his friend and a man his brother, saying, "Know Hashem." For they will all know Me from their smallest to their greatest.'"

It is evident from the medrash, that the same *yetzer ha'ra* that causes us to forget Torah, is that *yetzer ha'ra* that causes us not to know Torah naturally, without being taught.

In other words, when the Torah is a natural way of life, it is not necessary for us to be taught the Torah since we are able to naturally intuit the ways of the Torah. However, when the *yetzer ha'ra* presents other possible ways of living, the Torah is no longer natural and must be learnt. Once the Torah is no longer natural to us, it is given to be forgotten.

Receiving the *luchos*

When the *benei yisrael* were given the first *luchos*, the *yetzer ha'ra* was uprooted from their hearts and the Torah became the natural way of life for them. In this mode of living, the *benei yisrael* would never have forgotten the Torah, since nothing in the Torah was alien to them.

Had the *benei yisrael* been on this level when they were judged for serving the *egel ha'zahav*, they would have been judged as having sinned deliberately. Notwithstanding that the mistake of serving the *egel ha'zahav* was subtle and elusive, since the *benei yisrael* could have intuitively known that this was not the Will of Hashem had they wanted to, they would have been judged as having sinned willfully.

In order to avoid this harsh judgement, Moshe broke the *luchos*. The *benei yisrael* were no longer now at the level on which the Torah was intuitive to them, and therefore they could be judged as having served the *egel ha'zahav* in error.

Similarly, when Adam ate from the Tree of Knowledge he descended to the level where the Torah was something external to him, that he now had to learn and remember[2].

Once he descended to this level, the words of the Torah were no longer so clear to him, and he could not be held culpable of sinning wilfully against Hashem. Just as Moshe saved the benei yisrael by breaking the luchos, so too Adam saved himself by excluding himself from the level of clarity he attained in Gan

---

[2] See Nefesh Hachaim 1.6

Eden.

Hence the trees of Gan Eden rebuked him and said, "Here is the thief who has cheated the mind of his creator."

Noach

Meriting rescue

It says in this week's *sedrah* (6.12)

וַיַּרְא אֱלֹקִים אֶת הָאָרֶץ וְהִנֵּה נִשְׁחָתָה כִּי הִשְׁחִית כָּל בָּשָׂר אֶת דַּרְכּוֹ עַל הָאָרֶץ

And Hashem saw the earth and behold it was corrupted, for all flesh had corrupted its way on the earth.

Rashi comments

כי השחית כל בשר: אפילו בהמה חיה ועוף נזקקין לשאינן מינן

> **For all flesh had corrupted its way**: Even domesticated animals, non-domesticated animals and birds would mate with different species.

It seems that according to Rashi, the animals and birds were destroyed because they too became corrupt.

However, the gemara says in Sanhedrin (108a)

> וימח את כל היקום אשר על פני האדמה אם אדם חטא בהמה מה חטאה תנא משום רבי יהושע בן קרחה משל לאדם שעשה חופה לבנו והתקין מכל מיני סעודה לימים מת בנו עמד (ובלבל) [ופזר] את חופתו אמר כלום עשיתי אלא בשביל בני עכשיו שמת חופה למה לי אף הקב"ה אמר כלום בראתי בהמה וחיה אלא בשביל אדם עכשיו שאדם חוטא בהמה וחיה למה לי

The *passuk* says, "And He obliterated every living thing that was upon the face of the ground" (Bereishis 7:23). The Gemara asks, "If man sinned, in what way did the animals sin, so that they too, warranted destruction?"

The Gemara answers: It was taught in the name of Rabbi Yehoshua ben Korcha, "This is analogous to a man who fashioned a *chuppah* for his son and prepared all sorts of food for the wedding feast. Sometime later, before the wedding, his son died. What did the man do? He arose and scattered his son's wedding canopy.

He said, 'Did I do this for any reason other than for my son? Now that my son has died, why do I need a *chupah*?'

So too, Hashem said, 'Did I create domesticated animals and non-domesticated animals for any reason other than for man? Now that man has sinned and is sentenced to destruction, what need do I have of them?"

- It seems that according to the gemara, the animals were destroyed because they had no purpose now that man was to be destroyed. If so why does Rashi imply that the animals were destroyed because they became corrupted?

The next *passuk* says (6.13)

וַיֹּאמֶר אֱלֹקִים לְנֹחַ קֵץ כָּל בָּשָׂר בָּא לְפָנַי כִּי מָלְאָה הָאָרֶץ חָמָס מִפְּנֵיהֶם וְהִנְנִי מַשְׁחִיתָם אֶת הָאָרֶץ

And Hashem said to Noach, "The end of all flesh has arisen before me for the earth is filled with violence before them and behold I am about to destroy them together with the earth."

Rashi comments

קֵץ כָּל בָּשָׂר: כל מקום שאתה מוצא זנות ועבודת אלילים אנדרלמוסיא באה לעולם והורגת טובים ורעים

The end of all flesh: Every place where you find immorality and idolatry, total destruction comes to the world and it kills the good together with the bad.

כִּי מָלְאָה הָאָרֶץ חָמָס: לא נחתם גזר דינם אלא על הגזל

For the earth is filled with violence before them: Their judgement was only sealed because of robbery.

- These two statements of Rashi appear to be contradictory. First Rashi says that the people were killed because of immorality and idol worship, then Rashi says that they were killed because of robbery?

Later in the *sedrah* it says (7.2)

מִכֹּל הַבְּהֵמָה הַטְּהוֹרָה תִּקַּח לְךָ שִׁבְעָה שִׁבְעָה אִישׁ וְאִשְׁתּוֹ וּמִן הַבְּהֵמָה אֲשֶׁר לֹא טְהֹרָה הִוא שְׁנַיִם אִישׁ וְאִשְׁתּוֹ

Of every pure animal you shall take seven pairs, males and their mates, and of every animal that is not pure, two, a male and its mate.

Rashi comments

הטהורה: העתידה להיות טהורה לישראל, למדנו שלמד נח תורה

Pure: It means those animals which will in future be permitted to the *benei yisrael*, we learn from here that Noach studied Torah.

However, the gemara says in Zevachim (116a)

טהורין אבל לא טמאין: ומי הוו טמאין וטהורין בההיא שעתא... רבי אבהו אמר אמר קרא (בראשית ז', ט"ז) והבאים זכר ונקבה הבאין מאיליהן

[The *baraisa* teaches that even before the *mishkan* was built, *korbanos* were brought from animals and birds that were kosher, but not from non-kosher species. This is based on the *passuk* that describes the *korbanos* that Noach brought when he came out of the *tevah*, "And he took of every pure animal and of every pure bird and offered *olos* on the *mizbeach*" (Bereishis 8:20). The Gemara asks...]

And were there pure and impure species at that time, at the time of Noach?

Rabbi Avahu says, "The *passuk* states, 'And they that went in, went in male and female of all flesh' (Bereishis 7:16). This means, 'Those that went in on their own.' Consequently, Noach did not need to distinguish between pure and impure animals, as only the pure ones approached."

- According to the gemara, the kosher animals were determined by the *tevah*. If so, why does Rashi say that Noach knew which animals were kosher, because he learnt Torah?

It would seem that we can explain as follows[3]:

The Yalkut Shimoni says

רבי לוי אמר כל מי שנאמר בו היה, ראה עולם חדש. אמר רבי שמואל חמשה הן. נח, אתמול אבנים שחקו מים, דאמר רבי לוי בשם רבי יוחנן אפילו אצטרובולין של רחים נמחה במים, והכא את אמר ויהיו בני נח היוצאים מן התיבה אתמהא. אלא ראה עולם חדש...

---

[3] עיין בספר דברי יואל

Rabbi Levi said, "[The Torah uses the word היה (נֹחַ אִישׁ צַדִּיק תָּמִים הָיָה) – "he was", with regards to Noach.] Whenever the Torah uses the word היה this signifies that the person saw a new world (i.e. a new world order)."

Rabbi Shmuel said, "There are five people concerning whom the Torah uses the word היה and who say a new world. Noach – yesterday even the millstones were dissolved in the water of the *mabul*, and now you say, 'And the sons of Noach who came out of the *tevah* were Shem, Cham and Yaphes'? This is so incompatible that you must say that he saw a new world.

It would seem that according to the Yalkut Shimoni, two types of judgement took place before the *mabul*. One judgement was that the entire world was sentenced to be ended. The other judgement was whether or not anyone would escape from the old world, which was to be entirely destroyed, to the new world, which began when Noach and his sons came out of the *tevah*.

Hence we can understand as follows:

The reason for the destruction

When Rashi says "Every place where you find immorality and idolatry, total destruction comes to the world and it kills the good together with the bad," Rashi is explaining why the old world was entirely destroyed.

But when Rashi says, "Their judgement was only sealed because of robbery," Rashi is explaining why none of the people merited to escape, together with Noach, to the new world. That means to say, their judgement was sealed to remain within the old world with which they had inextricably entangled themselves by stealing and taking advantage of whatever was to be had within that world.

The fate of the animals

Regarding the animals, when Rashi says, "[And Hashem saw the earth and behold it was corrupted, for all flesh had corrupted its way on the earth.] Even domesticated animals, non-domesticated animals and birds would mate with different species," he is explaining why the old world was swept away.

However, when the gemara says, "Hashem said, 'Did I create domesticated animals and non-domesticated animals for any reason other than for man? Now that man has sinned and is sentenced to destruction, why do I need domesticated animals and non-domesticated animals?'," it is explaining why even the non-corrupted animals were not transported to the new world, together with Noach.

Identifying the *kosher* animals

When Rashi says, "**Pure**: It means those animals which will in future be permitted to the *benei yisrael*, we learn from here that Noach studied Torah," Rashi means that a proportionally greater presence of kosher animals was required in the new world, because the *benei yisrael* were to accept the Torah, and kosher animals are given preference in the Torah.

However, when the gemara says, "And were there pure and impure species at that time, at the time of Noach? Rabbi Avahu says, 'The *passuk* states, "And they that went in..." This means, "Those that went in on their own,"'" the gemara means that due to the *taharah* of the kosher animals they were able to naturally leave the old corrupt world, with which they had not become entangled.

According to this, we can explain the first *passuk* in the *sedrah* (6.9) as follows:

אֵלֶּה תּוֹלְדֹת נֹחַ נֹחַ אִישׁ צַדִּיק תָּמִים הָיָה בְּדֹרֹתָיו אֶת הָאֱלֹקִים הִתְהַלֶּךְ נֹחַ

These are the happenings of Noach. Noach was a *tzadik* and a wholesome person in his generations. Noach went with Hashem.

When the *passuk* says that Noach was a *tzadik* it means that he had not become corrupted together with the rest of the world. When the *passuk* says that Noach was a wholesome person, it means that he was not a cheat, thereby he escaped becoming entangled with the world that was to be destroyed.

Through the combination of both of these virtues, Noach merited to see the new mended world in which the *benei yisrael* would eventually accept the Torah.

Lech lechah

The Great Name of Hashem

The passuk says at the beginning of this week's sedrah (12.1)

וַיֹּאמֶר ה' אֶל אַבְרָם לֶךְ לְךָ מֵאַרְצְךָ וּמִמּוֹלַדְתְּךָ וּמִבֵּית אָבִיךָ אֶל הָאָרֶץ אֲשֶׁר אַרְאֶךָּ

And Hashem said to Avram, "Go forth from your native land and from your father's house to the land that J will show you."

The medrash comments on this passuk

וַיֹּאמֶר ה' אֶל אַבְרָם לֶךְ לְךָ מֵאַרְצְךָ וְגוֹ', ר' יצחק פתח (תהלים מ"ה, י"א) שִׁמְעִי בַת וּרְאִי וְהַטִּי אָזְנֵךְ וְשִׁכְחִי עַמֵּךְ וּבֵית אָבִיךְ, אמר רבי יצחק משל לאחד שהיה עובר ממקום למקום וראה בירה אחת דולקת אמר תאמר שהבירה זו בלא מנהיג הציץ עליו בעל הבירה אמר לו אני הוא בעל הבירה כך לפי שהיה אברהם אבינו אומר תאמר שהעולם הזה בלא מנהיג הציץ עליו הקב"ה ואמר לו אני הוא בעל העולם

Rabbi Yitzchak gave the following introduction: The *passuk* says in Tehillim, "Listen, daughter, and see, and incline your ear and forget your people and your father's house." Rabbi Yitzchak said, "It is analogous to one who was passing from place to place and he saw a tower burning. He said, 'Is it possible that this tower does not have someone in charge of it?' The owner of the tower looked out at him and said to him, 'I am the owner of the tower.' So too, since Avraham used to say, 'Is it possible that this world does not have someone conducting its affairs, Hashem looked out on him and said, 'I am the master of the world.'"

- What is the connection between the *passuk* in Tehillim, which refers to Avraham forgetting his father's house, and the story of the man who saw the burning tower?

- Why is the tower said to be burning, in the *mashal*?

In פסוק ד' it says

וְאַבְרָם בֶּן חָמֵשׁ שָׁנִים וְשִׁבְעִים שָׁנָה בְּצֵאתוֹ מֵחָרָן

And Avraham was 75 years old when he left Charan.

The medrash (בראשית רבה, ס"ד, ד') comments

רבי יוחנן ורבי חנינא תרוויהון אמרי בן ארבעים ושמונה שנה הכיר אברהם את בוראו ריש לקיש אמר בן שלש שנים הכיר אברהם את בוראו

Rabbi Yochanan and Rabbi Chanina says that Avraham was 48 years old when he recognised Hashem. Reish Lakish says that Avraham was 3 years old when he recognised Hashem.

At any rate, according to all opinions Avraham recognised Hashem prior to the beginning of Lech Lechah.

- If so, what was the new level of recognition of Hashem that Avraham now achieved?

It would seem that we can explain as follows[4]:

The Yerushalmi in Yuma (פרק ג', הלכה ז) says

חד אסי בציפורין אמר לרבי פינחס בר חמא איתא ואנא מסר ליה לך אמר ליה לית אנא יכיל אמר למה אמר ליה דאנא אכיל מעשר ומאן דרגיל ליה לא יכיל מיכול מבר נש כלום

A physician in Tzipporin said to Rabbi Pinchos bar Chama, "Come and I will hand over the secret pronunciation of the Great Name of Hashem [that the *kohen gadol* used to say on Yom Kippur] to you." He replied, "I am not able to be a recipient of this knowledge." He said, "Why?" He said, "Because I [take from others and] eat *maaser*, and one who is familiar with the Great Name of Hashem may not eat anything from anybody."

- Why is it not permissible for one who knows the Great Name of Hashem to benefit from anyone else?

The *sefer* Sha'arei Orah says (שער ג', ד)

ואחר שהודענוך כל אלו העקרים הגדולים התבונן ודע כי השם הגדול הנכבד והנורא... הוא השם הכולל כל השמות כולן בכל שמות הקודש הנזכרים בתורה

---

[4] עיין בספר כסף נבחר

Know and understand that the Great Name of Hashem is the name that incorporates all the other names of Hashem that are mentioned in the entire Torah.

In other words, each discrete name of Hashem represents the way in which Hashem may be most easily understood according to the particular time and place in which a person finds themselves. The Great Name of Hashem (that was used by the *cohen gadol* on Yom Kippur) includes all the understandings that it is possible to have of Hashem, that are represented by the other names of Hashem.

If someone benefits from other people, then he comes under their influence, and thus is liable to only be able to perceive Hashem in the way that their benefactors understand Hashem. Therefore one who benefits from others cannot be taught the Great Name of Hashem.

This is why the *passuk* says in Tehillim (9.11)

וְיִבְטְחוּ בְךָ יוֹדְעֵי שְׁמֶךָ

Those who know Your name will trust in You.

In order to come to a comprehensive and all-encompassing understanding of Hashem, and the way in which He conducts the world, it is necessary to benefit from no-one. Therefore a person who wants to come to this understanding must excel in the trait of trusting Hashem, because they have no-one else on whom to rely.

Initially Avraham Avinu understood the localised way of understanding Hashem, when he was 3 years old, or 48 years old. Then Avraham Avinu saw the tower burning, this means to say that it seemed to him that Hashem was presented differently in different times and places, and that Hashem conducted the world differently in different times and places. So the world appeared to be on fire, as different parts of the world were run in a contradictory manner.

Avraham Avinu then reached a higher *madregah* of *emunah*, and he said, "Is it possible the tower does not have someone controlling all its affairs?" meaning to say, "Surely there must be a higher level of knowledge of Hashem, which will allow me to reconcile all the different emanations of Hashem that I see in the world."

Hashem then looked out at Avraham and told him His Great Name, with which Avraham could reconcile all the apparent contradictions in the world. However, in order to reach this understanding, Avraham had to be reliant on nothing at all, and he had to leave his father's house and all that was familiar to him.

Only by achieving the level of understanding and dedication described in Tehillim (45.11), could Avraham come to understand the Great Name of Hashem.

שִׁמְעִי בַת וּרְאִי וְהַטִּי אָזְנֵךְ וְשִׁכְחִי עַמֵּךְ וּבֵית אָבִיךְ

Listen, daughter, and see, and incline your ear and forget your people and your father's house.

Avraham's choice

It says in this week's *sedrah* (בראשית ט"ו י"ז)

וַיְהִי הַשֶּׁמֶשׁ בָּאָה וַעֲלָטָה הָיָה וְהִנֵּה תַנּוּר עָשָׁן וְלַפִּיד אֵשׁ אֲשֶׁר עָבַר בֵּין הַגְּזָרִים הָאֵלֶּה

The sun set and there was thick darkness, and behold a smoking furnace and a flaming fire passed between the halves of the animals.

The Medrash Rabbah comments on this *passuk*

... והנה תנור עשן ולפיד...אמר לו במה אתה רוצה שירדו בניך, בגיהנם או במלכיות, רבי חנינא בר פפא אמר אברהם ברר לו את המלכיות, רבי יודן ורבי אידי ורבי חמא בר חנינא אמרו אברהם ברר גיהנם, והקב"ה ברר לו את המלכיות, הדא הוא דכתיב (דברים ל"ב) אם לא כי צורם מכרם זה אברהם, וה' הסגירם מלמד שהסכים הקב"ה לדבריו

Hashem asked Avraham, "Do you want your descendants to be descend to *gehinnom* (purgatory) or to be subjected to servitude in exile?"

Rabbi Chanina bar Pappa said that Avraham chose servitude in exile. Rabbi Yuden and Rabbi Idi and Rabbi Chama the son of Chanina said that Avraham chose *gehinnom* but Hashem advised him to choose servitude in exile.

This is the meaning of the *passuk* which says (דברים ל"ב, ל')

אֵיכָה יִרְדֹּף אֶחָד אֶלֶף וּשְׁנַיִם יָנִיסוּ רְבָבָה אִם לֹא כִּי צוּרָם מְכָרָם וַה' הִסְגִּירָם

How can one pursue a thousand and two pursue ten thousand, if not that their rock sold them and Hashem imprisoned them?

"If not that their rock had sold them," this refers to Avraham, who selected servitude in exile. "And Hashem imprisoned them," this refers to Hashem's agreement with Avraham's choice.

Based on this medrash, the Meshech Chachmah explains the gemara in Eruvin (19a) that says

אלא הא דכתיב עוברי בעמק הבכא ההוא דמחייבי ההיא שעתא בגיהנם ואתי אברהם אבינו ומסיק להו ומקבל להו בר מישראל שבא על בת עובד כוכבים דמשכה ערלתו ולא מבשקר ליה

The *passuk* says in Tehillim (84:7)

עֹבְרֵי בְּעֵמֶק הַבָּכָא מַעְיָן יְשִׁיתוּהוּ

Those who pass into the valley of tears (a reference to *gehinnom*) will create a well with their tears.

This refers to someone who enters *gehinnom* for only one moment and is then extricated by Avraham. However if a Jewish man married a non-Jewish woman then Avraham does not extricate him from *gehinnom*.

- Why does Avraham specifically not extricate someone who married a non-Jewish woman from *gehinnom*?

The Meshech Chachmah explains as follows:

The *passuk* in Eichah (1:3) says

גָּלְתָה יְהוּדָה מֵעֹנִי וּמֵרֹב עֲבֹדָה

Yehudah went into *galus* from poverty and over work.

The Medrash Rabbah (Eichah, 1:28) asks why the *passuk* in Eichah uses the term *galus* regarding the *benei yisrael*, whereas we do not find this term used regarding the exile of other nations. The Medrash Rabbah explains as follows:

אומות העולם אינן גולים, אלא אע"פ שגולים אין גלותם גלות, אומות העולם שאוכלים מפתם ושותים מיינם אין גלותם גלות, אבל ישראל שאין אוכלין מפתם ואין שותין מיינם גלותם גלות, אומות העולם שהן מהלכין באסקפטיות שלהם אין גלותם גלות, אבל ישראל שהן מהלכין יחפין גלותם גלות, לכך נאמר גלתה יהודה

Do the other nations not go into *galus*? Rather, even though they do go into *galus*, this is not a hard *galus*, because they eat the bread, drink the wine and wear the clothes of the nations among whom they are exiled.

Since they are similar to the nations among whom they are exiled, these nations are kind to them. However when the *benei yisrael* go into *galus* they differentiate themselves from the nations among whom they are exiled, and therefore they are not kind to them.

Subsequently we can understand that Avraham is able to extricate someone who goes to *gehinnom*, because Avraham chose servitude in exile as the atonement for the *benei yisrael*, instead of *gehinnom*. Since the person who entered *gehinnom* has already endured suffering in exile, he need not suffer again.

However if someone marries a non-Jewish woman, whereby he made himself at home in *galus*, then his exile is no longer that difficult *galus* which comes of being different, which was chosen by Avraham.

Since he has rejected Avraham's choice of servitude in exile, he is only left with the choice of *gehinnom* in order to attain atonement.

How Avraham taught *emunah* to his guests

It says in this week's *sedrah* (בראשית י"ח ב')

וַיִּשָּׂא עֵינָיו וַיַּרְא וְהִנֵּה שְׁלֹשָׁה אֲנָשִׁים נִצָּבִים עָלָיו וַיַּרְא וַיָּרָץ לִקְרָאתָם מִפֶּתַח הָאֹהֶל וַיִּשְׁתַּחוּ אָרְצָה

And he lifted his eyes and he saw and behold there were three men standing close to him, and he ran to meet them from the entrance of the tent and he bowed down to the ground.

The Medrash Rabbah (מדרש רבה, מ"ח, ט') comments on this *passuk*

אמר ר' לוי, שלשת האנשים שנראו לאברהם אבינו אחד נדמה לו בדמות סרקי, ואחד בדמות נווטי ואחד בדמות ערבי

Rabbi Levi said, "One of the *malachim* appeared to Avraham as a thief[5], one of the *malachim* appeared to Avraham as a sailor and one of the *malachim* appeared to Avraham as an Arab."

The Chasam Sofer explains the intention of this *medrash* as follows:

---

[5] This is the translation of the Chasam Sofer, the Matnos Kehunah however quotes the Aruch who translates סרקי as a baker.

The Arab

The Arabs served idolatry, as Rashi says (בראשית י"ח ד')

> **ורחצו רגליכם**: כסבור שהם ערביים שמשתחוים לאבק רגליהם
> והקפיד שלא להכניס ע"א לביתו (ב"מ פ"ו)

Avraham asked the guests to wash their feet because he thought that they were Arabs who worshipped the dust on their feet, and he was particular not to allow idolatry into his house.

Avraham's lesson for the Arab was that he should believe in Hashem instead of believing in idols.

The thief

A thief is on a higher level than an idolater, since he believes in Hashem, as the gemara says

> גנבא אפום מחתרתא רחמנא קרי (ברכות ס"ג)

A thief calls out to Hashem before he breaks into a house.

Nevertheless a thief does not trust that Hashem will provide him with a livelihood, because otherwise he would not steal. Therefore Avraham's lesson for the thief was that he should trust Hashem to provide for him.

The sailor

Sailors place their trust solely in Hashem, as the gemara says at the end of Kiddushin (קידושין פ"ב א') הספנין רובן חסידים, most sailors are *tzaddikim*, because they *daven* to Hashem to save them during storms. Therefore Avraham only had to teach the sailor the *mitzvos* of the Torah.

Subsequently we can understand Avraham's conversation with the *malachim* as follows:

וַיֹּאמַר אֲדֹנָי אִם נָא מָצָאתִי חֵן בְּעֵינֶיךָ אַל נָא תַעֲבֹר מֵעַל עַבְדֶּךָ

And he said, "My master, if I have please found favour in your eyes, please do not pass on from your servant."

First Avraham asked the most senior of the group (the sailor), not to leave while Avraham explained the principles of *emunah* and *bitachon* to the Arab and to the thief.

יֻקַּח נָא מְעַט מַיִם וְרַחֲצוּ רַגְלֵיכֶם

Let there be taken a small amount of water so that you may wash your legs.

Avraham told the Arab that through that aspect of the Torah which is compared to water, he would be able to come to *emunah* in Hashem (who is the living G-d and is therefore alluded to by water, which is vital for life) and thus remove the dust of idolatry (which is considered as a dead thing) from his legs.

וְהִשָּׁעֲנוּ תַּחַת הָעֵץ

And rest under the tree.

Avraham told both the Arab and the thief that through that aspect of the Torah which is compared to a life-giving tree, they would come to trust that Hashem would provide them with their livelihood, and so rest under the tree of trust in Hashem.

Then Avraham told his guests

וְאֶקְחָה פַת לֶחֶם וְסַעֲדוּ לִבְּכֶם

And let me fetch a morsel of bread that you may feast yourselves

We find that the Torah is compared to bread, as the *passuk* says in Mishlei (9:5 - 6)

לְכוּ לַחֲמוּ בְלַחֲמִי וּשְׁתוּ בְּיַיִן מָסָכְתִּי. עִזְבוּ פְתָאיִם וִחְיוּ וְאִשְׁרוּ בְּדֶרֶךְ בִּינָה.

Come, eat my food and drink the wine that I have mixed. Give up simpleness and live, walk in the way of understanding.

Avraham concluded that through the wisdom of the Torah, which is compared to bread, they would come to understand the wondrous ways of Hashem, and observe His *mitzvos*.

Praying for Sedom

It says in this week's *sedrah* (18:17 - 18)

וַה' אָמָר הַמְכַסֶּה אֲנִי מֵאַבְרָהָם אֲשֶׁר אֲנִי עֹשֶׂה. וְאַבְרָהָם הָיוֹ יִהְיֶה לְגוֹי גָּדוֹל וְעָצוּם וְנִבְרְכוּ בוֹ כֹּל גּוֹיֵי הָאָרֶץ.

Now Hashem had said, "Shall I hide from Avraham what I am about to do? But Avraham is to become a great and populous nation and all the nations of the earth will bless themselves by him."

Rashi comments:

ואברהם היו יהיה: מדרש אגדה, זכר צדיק לברכה הואיל והזכירו ברכו ופשוטו וכי ממנו אני מעלים והרי הוא חביב לפני להיות לגוי גדול ולהתברך בו כל גויי הארץ

> **But Avraham shall surely become**: The Midrash applies to this the *passuk* in Mishlei (10:7), "The mention of the *tzaddikim* shall be for a *berachah*". Therefore, since He mentioned him He blessed him (Bereishis Rabbah 49:1). But its literal meaning is: "Shall I conceal it from him, seeing that he is so beloved by Me as to become a great nation and cause that all the nations of the earth shall bless themselves through him."

- Why was the rule of זכר צדיק לברכה applied specifically when Hashem revealed the fate of Sedom to Avraham, and not in any other place?

The gemara says in Yuma (28b)

> דתניא (ויקרא י"ב, ג') וביום השמיני ימול בשר ערלתו מלמד שכל היום כשר למילה אלא שהזריזין מקדימין למצות שנאמר (בראשית כ"ב, ג') וישכם אברהם בבקר ויחבוש וגו'

It was taught in a *beraisa* concerning the *passuk*: "And on the eighth day he should give his son a ברית." This *passuk* teaches that the entire day is suitable for the mitzva of *bris milah*. However, the eager are early in their performance of *mitzvos* and would perform a *bris* in the morning, as it is stated with regard to the Akeida: "And Avraham rose early in the morning and saddled his donkey."

Tosafos comments on this gemara:

> **שנאמר וישכם אברהם בבקר**: בפ"ק דפסחים (דף ד. ושם) פריך וניבדוק מצפרא מי לא תניא כל היום כשר למילה אלא שהזריזין מקדימין שנאמר וישכם אברהם וגו' ותימה היכי גמר מהכא דאין זריזין מקדימין מאורתא דלמא מה שאברהם לא עמד בלילה משום דת"ח לא יצא יחידי בלילה כדאמר בפרק גיד הנשה (חולין דף צא.).

> וי"ל דמש"ה לא היה אברהם נמנע מלהשכים בלילה כיון דשלוחי מצוה אינן ניזוקין מיהו קשה דהיא גופה דלא יצא יחידי בלילה מוישכם אברהם בבקר יליף התם ועוד קשיא כיון דשלוחי מצוה אינן ניזוקין למה נמנע מלהשכים בלילה מתוך דת"ח אל יצא יחידי.

> וי"ל דתרי וישכם כתיבי חד בעקידה וחד כשהתפלל על סדום והכא מייתי קרא דעקידה הלכך פריך שפיר מינה בפסחים דאי זריזין מקדימין למצות מאורתא א"כ אברהם נמי לקדום באורתא שהרי לא היה ירא כלום חדא דשלוחי מצוה אינן ניזוקין ועוד דשני נעריו עמו הוו

ובפרק גיד הנשה (שם) מייתי קרא דסדום דהתם יחידי הוה שלא יראו במפלתה של סדום כדאשכחן באשתו של לוט ולא הוה נמי שליח מצוה כי לא היה חפץ הקב"ה שישא בעדם רנה ותפלה

...the *halacha* that a person should get up early to perform a *mitzva* only applies once it is the morning, there is no preference given to getting up while it is still night. That is why Avraham only got up early in the morning to go to do the Akeidah and did not get up in the night. It could not be that the reason he did not start off in the night is because he was afraid of the dangers of the night, because he was a שליח מצוה and we have a rule that שלוחי מצוה אינן ניזוקין. Furthermore, he was accompanied by his two lads.

However, when Avraham got up early to daven a second time for Sedom, he was unaccompanied, because it was not fitting that anyone else should see the punishment of Sedom, and he was also not protected as a שליח מצוה because he was not doing a *mitzva*, since Hashem did not want him to daven for Sedom. Therefore, in that case we derive from the fact that Avraham did not get up while it was still night that a *talmid chacham* should not go out alone at night due to the danger involved.

- If Hashem did not want Avraham to *daven* for the people of Sedom, then why indeed did he daven for them?

The influence of *tefillah*

It would appear difficult to understand altogether why Avraham, who taught the importance of *chesed*, davened so hard that the people of Sedom, who indulged in cruelty and avariciousness, should be saved.

Rabbi Mordechai Miller z"l explained that had the people of Sedom been saved through the *tefillos* of Avraham, then they would have done *teshuvah*. Since their continued lives would only have been due to the *tefillos* of Avraham, this would have created an influence of purity and kindness, that would have washed away their desire to do evil.

Based on this thought, it seems that we can understand as follows:

The reason that Avraham *davened* for the people of Sedom, even though it was not then the רצון ה' that he should *daven* for them, is that had Avraham been able to save Sedom through his *tefillos*, that would have influenced the people in Sedom to follow in the ways of Avraham. Because Avraham's *tefillos* would have caused the people of Sedom to do *teshuvah*, it would have been retroactively apparent that it was appropriate for Avraham to have *davened* for them.

The reason why the rule of זכר צדיק לברכה is applied specifically when Avraham davened for Sedom is because Avraham sought to use his own fame as a means to save Sedom. Had he succeeded in saving Sedom through this *tefillos*, then his fame in Sedom would have caused the people of Sedom to do *teshuvah* and retroactively cause them to be worthy of being saved.

The reason that the mention of a צדיק is a ברכה is because the צדיק wishes that whatever fame he has, should be itself a source of ברכה.

Chaye Sarah

Sarah and Esther

It says at the beginning of this week's *sedrah* (23:1)

וַיִּהְיוּ חַיֵּי שָׂרָה מֵאָה שָׁנָה וְעֶשְׂרִים שָׁנָה וְשֶׁבַע שָׁנִים שְׁנֵי חַיֵּי שָׂרָה

And the lifetime of Sarah was one hundred and twenty-seven years, this was the span of Sarah's life.

The Medrash Rabbah (58:3) comments on this *passuk*:

> רבי עקיבא היה יושב ודורש והצבור מתנמנם בקש לעוררן אמר מה ראתה אסתר שתמלוך על שבע ועשרים ומאה מדינה אלא תבא אסתר שהיתה בת בתה של שרה שחיתה מאה ועשרים ושבע ותמלוך על מאה ועשרים ושבע מדינות

> Rabbi Akiva was giving a *derasha* and the people listening were falling asleep. He sought to wake them up and he said,

"Why did Esther merit to rule over 127 provinces? Because we say – Esther who was descended from Sarah, who lived for 127 years, should come and rule over 127 provinces."

- Why did Rabbi Akiva draw a connection between the time for which Sarah lived, and the area over which Esther ruled?

It would seem that we can explain as follows:

The *passuk* says in Megillas Esther (4:14) that Mordechai told Esther:

כִּי אִם הַחֲרֵשׁ תַּחֲרִישִׁי בָּעֵת הַזֹּאת רֶוַח וְהַצָּלָה יַעֲמוֹד לַיְּהוּדִים מִמָּקוֹם אַחֵר וְאַתְּ וּבֵית אָבִיךְ תֹּאבֵדוּ וּמִי יוֹדֵעַ אִם לְעֵת כָּזֹאת הִגַּעַתְּ לַמַּלְכוּת

For if you keep silent at this time, relief and deliverance will come to the *benei yisrael* from another quarter, while you and your father's house will perish. And who knows, perhaps you have attained a royal position for just such a time.

The Maharal expounds on the choice of the words רוח (literally salvation, but can also mean broadening) and מקום (place) (אור חדש, פרק ד'):

ר"ל ריוח והצלה יעמוד ליהודים ממקום אחר כי הוא יתברך נקרא מקום בשביל שהוא יתברך מקיים הכל ונותן מקום, על כן המלך ג"כ יש לקרא מקום בשביל שהוא מקיים על אומה שהוא מלך, וכאשר אתה

מלכה גם כן עליך יש לקיים את אומתך ואם אין אתה עולה זה ריוח והצלה יעמוד ליהודים ממקום אחר, הוא הש"י אשר הוא מקום אל הכל בשביל שהוא מקיים הכל, כי עתה ראוי לך שתהיה את מקום לישראל כאשר את מלכה ולתת להם קיום מפני האויב, והבן הדברים האלו מאוד כי הוא יתברך מעמיד ומקיים הכל לכך מקום הוא אל הכל.

Hashem is called מקום because he sustains all and provides a place for all (and the place of a thing is that which allows it to exist, which is why מקום, which is related to the word מקיים, means place). Therefore we refer to a king using the term מקום, since he sustains the nation over which he is king (by providing a place in which that nation can exist).

Mordechai told Esther as follows: Since you are the queen it is incumbent on you to provide a place for your nation, the *benei yisrael*, so that they should not be driven out of existence by Haman (who wishes to deny them any place in which to live). If you do not act as Hashem's emissary (to provide a place for the *benei yisrael* in this world), then the salvation of the *benei yisrael* will come directly from Hashem (who gives place to all), without the need for yourself as an intermediary.

Based on this idea, we can explain that according to Rabbi Akiva, Esther acquired the ability to provide the spiritual space in which the *benei yisrael* could exist, from Sarah. This is because Sarah, through her wisdom and kindness, created a household in which Avraham could pursue his service of Hashem. Avraham's deeds and accomplishments were performed and acquired meaning in the context of the elevated household that Sarah built. In this way, Sarah became the prototype of Jewish women who create a sublime and elevated atmosphere, in which their husbands' service of Hashem acquires meaning and context.

When Haman sought to deny the *benei yisrael* a place in which they could continue in their service of Hashem, it was Esther, a descendant and spiritual heir of Sarah, who elevated the entire world into a place in which the *benei yisrael* could continue flourish in their observance of the Torah.

Since Sarah pursued her *avodah* of creating an elevated household for Avraham for 127 years, Esther acquired the ability to convert 127 provinces into a sanctified dwelling place for the *benei yisrael*.

Toldos

Why Yitzchak resembled Avraham

It says at the beginning of this week's *sedrah* (25:19)

וְאֵלֶּה תּוֹלְדֹת יִצְחָק בֶּן אַבְרָהָם אַבְרָהָם הוֹלִיד אֶת יִצְחָק

And these are the events that happened to Yitzchak - Avraham bore Yitzchak.

Rashi comments on this *passuk*:

אברהם הוליד את יצחק:... ע"י שכתב הכתוב יצחק בן אברהם הוזקק לומר אברהם הוליד את יצחק לפי שהיו ליצני הדור אומרים מאבימלך נתעברה שרה שהרי כמה שנים שהתה עם אברהם ולא נתעברה הימנו מה עשה הקב"ה צר קלסתר פניו של יצחק דומה לאברהם והעידו הכל אברהם הוליד את יצחק וזהו שכתב כאן יצחק בן אברהם היה שהרי עדות יש שאברהם הוליד את יצחק

Since the *passuk* said יִצְחָק בֶּן אַבְרָהָם (Yitzchak the son of Avraham), therefore the *passuk* had to say אַבְרָהָם הוֹלִיד אֶת יִצְחָק (Avraham begot Yitzchok). Because the scoffers of the generation said that Avimelech was the father of Yitzchak, because she was married to Avraham for many years and did not become expectant. What did Hashem do? He carved the appearance of Yitzchak's face to be similar to that of Avraham and everyone testified that Avraham bore Yitzchak. Therefore the *passuk* says יִצְחָק בֶּן אַבְרָהָם meaning to say we know that Yitzchak was the son of Avraham because there was testimony that Avraham bore Yitzchak.

Uniqueness

The Noda Biyehuda (אה"ע סימן ס"ה) discusses the following case:

A man came to a town where he was identified as the husband of an *agunah* by both the *agunah* and the townspeople, and he subsequently gave the *agunah* a *get*. The man then went to the next town where he was identified as the husband of a different *agunah* and the townspeople, and he gave the second *agunah* a *get*. The man said that he was not really the husband of the first *agunah* and had given her a *get* only because someone had paid him to do so. However the *agunah* from the first town gave *simanim* that he was her husband and argued that the *get* was *kosher*, and her townspeople agreed with her.

The Noda Biyehuda *paskens* that neither *get* is valid, and bases his *pesak* on the Mishnah in Sanhedrin (4:5) which says:

לפיכך נברא אדם יחידי... ולהגיד גדולתו של הקדוש ברוך הוא, שאדם טובע כמה מטבעות בחותם אחד וכולן דומין זה לזה, ומלך מלכי המלכים הקדוש ברוך הוא טבע כל אדם בחותמו של אדם הראשון לו ואין אחד מהן דומה לחבירו.

Only one man (Adam) was created originally... to teach you the greatness of Hashem, because a person stamps many coins with one stamp and all the coins are the same, however Hashem stamped every person with the stamp of Adam Harishon and there is not one person who looks like anyone else.

Since the Mishnah says that it is impossible for two people to look identical, therefore if both the townspeople from the first town and also from the second town identified one person as different people, then this is a proof that neither testimony is valid. In other words, if it was indeed possible for one person to look exactly like someone else, then it could have been possible that the man came from the first town, nevertheless he was mistakenly identified as the husband from the second town. Or it could be that the man came from the second town, but nevertheless he was mistakenly identified as the husband from the first town.

However since it is impossible for two different people to look absolutely identical, therefore it must be that one of the set of townspeople had simply not paid sufficient attention to accurately identifying the man, and since we do not know which set of townspeople had been careless in this regard, therefore the testimony of both sets of townspeople is considered to be baseless.

The reason that it is impossible for two people to look exactly the same is because the appearance of a person reflects the פנימיות of the person (which is why the word פנים – face – also means the inside). The פנימיות (inner nature) of every person is different, in order so that each person can have a unique share in making a *kiddush Hashem* by serving Hashem in their own unique way and by understanding the Torah in their own unique way.

- If so, it is difficult to understand how Yitzchak and Avraham could look identical. Avraham served Hashem predominantly with the *middah* of *chesed* (loving kindness), and Yitzchak served Hashem predominantly with the *middah* of *gevurah* (strength and fortitude). Therefore, according to the above idea, it should have been impossible for them to look the same?

The gemara says in Shabbos (89b)

א"ר שמואל בר נחמני א"ר יונתן מ"ד (ישעיה ס"ג, ט"ז) כי אתה אבינו כי אברהם לא ידענו וישראל לא יכירנו אתה ה' אבינו גואלנו מעולם שמך לעתיד לבא יאמר לו הקב"ה לאברהם בניך חטאו לי אמר לפניו רבש"ע ימחו על קדושת שמך אמר אימר ליה ליעקב דהוה ליה צער גידול בנים אפשר דבעי רחמי עלייהו אמר ליה בניך חטאו אמר לפניו רבש"ע ימחו על קדושת שמך אמר לא בסבי טעמא ולא בדרדקי עצה

אמר לו ליצחק בניך חטאו לי אמר לפניו רבש"ע בני ולא בניך בשעה שהקדימו לפניך נעשה לנשמע קראת להם (שמות ד', כ"ב) בני בכורי עכשיו בני ולא בניך ועוד כמה חטאו כמה שנותיו של אדם שבעים שנה דל עשרין דלא ענשת עלייהו פשו להו חמשין דל כ"ה דלילותא פשו להו כ"ה דל תרתי סרי ופלגא דצלויי ומיכל ודבית הכסא פשו להו תרתי סרי ופלגא אם אתה סובל את כולם מוטב ואם לאו פלגא עלי ופלגא עליך ואת"ל כולם עלי הא קריבית נפשי קמך פתחו ואמרו אתה אבינו

In the time to come Hashem will say to Avraham, "Your children have sinned against Me." Avraham will say before Him, "Master of the Universe, if so, let them be eradicated to sanctify Your name."

Hashem said, "I will say this to Yaakov. Since he experienced the pain of raising children, perhaps he will ask for mercy on their behalf." He said to Yaakov, "Your children have sinned." Yaakov said before Him, "Master of the Universe, if so, let them be eradicated to sanctify Your name." Hashem said, "There is no reason in elders and no wisdom in youth."

He said to Yitzchak, "Your children have sinned against Me." Yitzchak said before Him, "Master of the Universe, are they my children and not Your children? At Sinai, when they said, 'We will do' before 'We will listen', didn't You call them, 'My son, My firstborn son Yisrael'? Now that they have sinned, are they my children and not Your children?

And furthermore, how much did they actually sin? How long is a person's life? Seventy years. Subtract the first twenty years of his life. One is not punished for sins committed then, as in the heavenly court, a person is only punished from the age of twenty. Fifty years remain for them. Subtract twenty-five years of nights, and twenty-five years remain for them. Subtract twelve and a half years during which one *davens* and eats and uses the bathroom, and twelve and a half years remain for them.

If You can endure them all and forgive the sins committed during those years, excellent. And if not, half of the sins are upon me to bear and half upon You. And if You say that all of them, the sins of all twelve and a half years that remain, are upon me, I sacrificed my life before You and You should forgive them in my merit."

The Jewish people then began to say to Yitzchak, "You are our father."

- It seems difficult to understand this gemara. Normally we understand that Yitzchak represents the *middas ha'din* (Divine attribute of strict judgement), Avraham represents the *middas ha'chesed* (Divine attribute of kindness), and Yaakov represents the *middas ha'rachamim* (Divine attribute of mercy). If so, Avraham should have been the first to defend the *benei yisrael* and Yitzchak should have been most strict with their judgement?

It would appear that we can understand as follows:

One of the differences between the *middas ha'chesed* and the *middas ha'din* is that when a person is judged according to the *middas ha'chesed* then he is recognised and rewarded for every accomplishment and for every level that he accomplishes. On the other hand, when a person is judged according to the *middas ha'din*, he is only recognised and rewarded when he reaches the end goal, and until then he is considered deficient.

When a person sets out initially to grow in their observance of Torah and *mitzvos*, the *middas ha'chesed* is appropriate for his condition, as thereby he is encouraged and rewarded for each initial accomplishment. However, when a person draws near to reaching his final goal, then he must consider himself deficient relative to that which he knows he can accomplish, in order to force himself to climb to that pinnacle which requires his entire fortitude and perspicacity[6].

---

[6] עיין מכתב מאליהו, ח"ב, עמוד 122

Hence, as the *benei yisrael* draw close to the completion of their task in *olam ha'zeh*, it is specifically the attribute of Yitzchak, the *middas ha'din*, that will draw the *benei yisrael* towards the final culmination of their *kiddush Hashem* and conquest of the *yetzer ha'ra*.

At that time, the *benei yisrael* will recognise that the *middas ha'din* of Yitzchak, which initially seemed harsh and foreboding, was nevertheless that attribute and approach which ultimately guaranteed their final success.

The scoffers of the generation were those people who believed that everything should be measured according to their yardstick. If something did not appear practical and long-lasting according to their perception, then they scoffed at it as something unfeasible and void.

Because the scoffers were locked into the limitations of their own perceptions, they claimed that Yitzchak was not a continuation of Avraham. They could not imagine that the *benei yisrael* could ever reach a level at which the *middas ha'chesed* of Avraham would merge with the opposite *middas ha'din* of Yitzchak in order to bring the entire world to its fruition and final purpose.

Therefore Hashem made Yitzchak's appearance the same as Avraham's, in order to demonstrate that although Avraham and Yitzchak had opposite approaches, both approaches were born of the same ultimate purpose, and will in the end unite.

The surprising *madregah* of Yitzchak

It says in this week's *sedrah* (25.19)

וְאֵלֶּה תּוֹלְדֹת יִצְחָק בֶּן אַבְרָהָם אַבְרָהָם הוֹלִיד אֶת יִצְחָק

And these are the generations of Yitzchak the son of Avraham, Avraham bore Yitzchak.

The Medrash Rabbah comments on this *passuk*.

ואלה תולדות יצחק בן אברהם, (משלי כ"ג) גיל יגיל אבי צדיק ויולד חכם ישמח בו. גילה אחר גילה, בזמן שהצדיק נולד.

The *passuk* says in Mishlei (23:24), גִּיל יָגִיל אֲבִי צַדִּיק וְיוֹלֵד חָכָם יִשְׂמַח בּוֹ. The father of a *tzaddik* has great joy; a man who has a wise son rejoices. When the *tzaddik* is born there is rejoicing after rejoicing.

- What does the medrash add by saying that there is rejoicing after rejoicing, when a *tzaddik* is born?

When Yitzchak gave a *berachah* to Yaakov he said (Bereishis, 27.28)

וְיִתֶּן לְךָ הָאֱלֹקִים מִטַּל הַשָּׁמַיִם וּמִשְׁמַנֵּי הָאָרֶץ וְרֹב דָּגָן וְתִירֹשׁ

May Hashem give to you of the dew of the heavens, and of the fatness of the earth, and an abundance of corn and wine.

Since the word וְיִתֶּן is the beginning of the *beracha*, it is again difficult to understand why a *vav* is used, which implies ויו מוסיף על ענין ראשון. Subsequently Rashi explains

ויתן לך: יתן ויחזור ויתן

Hashem should give to you and then give to you again.

However, when Yitzchak gave Esav a *berachah*, he said

וַיַּעַן יִצְחָק אָבִיו וַיֹּאמֶר אֵלָיו הִנֵּה מִשְׁמַנֵּי הָאָרֶץ יִהְיֶה מוֹשָׁבֶךָ וּמִטַּל הַשָּׁמַיִם מֵעָל

And Yitzchak, his father, answered and said to him, "Behold from the fat places of the earth will be your dwelling, and of the dew of the heavens from above."

The word הִנֵּה has an opposite implication to יתן ויחזור ויתן. The word הִנֵּה means, "Behold, this is how it will be," as opposed to יתן ויחזור ויתן which means that Hashem will continually give.

- Why did Yitzchak grant to Yaakov a continually given *berachah*, and to Esav a complete and final *beracha*?

It would seem that we can explain as follows:

The Malbim says in Tehillim (89:17) that the word *gilah* refers to the happiness related to a new event.

ויש הבדל בין שמחה וגיל, ששמחה היא השמחה התמידית, וגיל הוא על דבר מתחדש כמו מציאה בשורה טובה ודומיה

There is a difference between שמחה and גיל, the word שמחה refers to constant happiness, whereas the word גיל refers to something new that happened, such as finding something or hearing good news.

According to the Malbim, it would seem difficult to understand why the Medrash Rabbah says גילה אחר גילה בזמן שהצדיק נולד? Since גילה is the fleeting happiness you experience on hearing good news, how can there be another גילה after the first גילה, seeing as no further good news has arrived?

Based on this question, it seems evident from the medrash that there is more than one item of news when a *tzadik* is born. For initially, there is the news of the birth of the *tzadik*. But subsequently, there is the news of the great person that the *tzadik* has now become.

This means to say, it is in the nature of a *tzadik* to exceed any expectations of him. The greatness that a *tzadik* can accomplish, is not something that could have been foreseen given his previous attainments. Therefore, because it is not easily possible to explain how the *tzadik* reached his current *madregah*, his accomplishments of are a constant source of surprise.

This is the intention of the medrash when it says גילה אחר גילה בזמן שהצדיק נולד, "When the *tzaddik* is born there is rejoicing after rejoicing." The first rejoicing concerns the birth of the *tzadik*, the subsequent rejoicing concerns the greatness accomplished by the *tzadik*, that could not have been foreseen by considering who he was previously.

Because Yaakov constantly grew and advanced to new levels that were not contiguous with the previous level that he had attained, the *berachah* that Yitzchak gave him, יתן ויחזור ויתן, was also that Hashem should constantly give him a greater *berachah*, that could not have been foreseen from the *berachah* that he had previously received.

Yaakov and Cana'an

The *passuk* says in this week's sedrah (28.1)

וַיִּקְרָא יִצְחָק אֶל יַעֲקֹב וַיְבָרֶךְ אֹתוֹ וַיְצַוֵּהוּ וַיֹּאמֶר לוֹ לֹא תִקַּח אִשָּׁה מִבְּנוֹת כְּנָעַן. קוּם לֵךְ פַּדֶּנָה אֲרָם בֵּיתָה בְתוּאֵל אֲבִי אִמֶּךָ וְקַח לְךָ מִשָּׁם אִשָּׁה מִבְּנוֹת לָבָן אֲחִי אִמֶּךָ. וְקֵל שַׁדַּי יְבָרֵךְ אֹתְךָ וְיַפְרְךָ וְיַרְבֶּךָ וְהָיִיתָ לִקְהַל עַמִּים. וְיִתֶּן לְךָ אֶת בִּרְכַּת אַבְרָהָם לְךָ וּלְזַרְעֲךָ אִתָּךְ לְרִשְׁתְּךָ אֶת אֶרֶץ מְגֻרֶיךָ אֲשֶׁר נָתַן אֱלֹקִים לְאַבְרָהָם.

So Yitzchak sent for Yaakov and blessed him. He instructed him, saying, "You shall not take a wife from among the women of Cana'an. Get up, go to Padan Aram, to the house of Besuel, your mother's father, and take a wife there from among the daughters of Lavan, your mother's brother. May Hashem (Keil Shakkai) bless you, make you many and numerous, so that you become an assembly of peoples. May He grant the blessing of Avraham to you and your offspring, that you may possess the land where you are sojourning, which Hashem assigned to Avraham.

The Medrash Rabbah (67.12) explains

> אָמַר רַבִּי אֶלְעָזָר אֵין קִיּוּם הַגֵּט אֶלָּא בְּחוֹתְמָיו, שֶׁלֹּא תֹאמַר אִלּוּלֵי שֶׁרִמָּה יַעֲקֹב בְּאָבִיו לֹא נָטַל בִּרְכוֹתָיו, תַּלְמוּד לוֹמַר וַיִּקְרָא יִצְחָק אֶל יַעֲקֹב וַיְבָרֶךְ אֹתוֹ

Rabbi Elazar said, "A *get* is only upheld through those that sign it. [This means to say that] you should not say that had Yaakov not cheated his father then he would not have taken his *berachos*. Therefore the *passuk* teaches you, "And Yitzchak called Yaakov and he blessed him."

The simple meaning of the *passuk*, is that Yitzchak blessed Yaakov regarding his finding a wife in Padan Aram and that he should not marry a wife from Cana'an. It would therefore seem that not marrying a wife from Cana'an and meriting the *berachos* were synonymous.

- Why was meriting the *berachos* dependent on not marrying a wife from Cana'an?

It would appear that we can explain as follows[7].

Challenge and growth

The *passuk* says in Miketz (43.14)

> וְקֵל שַׁדַּי יִתֵּן לָכֶם רַחֲמִים לִפְנֵי הָאִישׁ וְשִׁלַּח לָכֶם אֶת אֲחִיכֶם אַחֵר וְאֶת בִּנְיָמִין וַאֲנִי כַּאֲשֶׁר שָׁכֹלְתִּי שָׁכָלְתִּי

---

[7] מיוסד על שיחה ששמעתי מהגר"מ מילר זצ"ל

[Yaakov said to the brothers,] "And may Hashem dispose the man to mercy toward you, that he may release to you your other brother, as well as Binyamin. As for me, if I am to be bereaved, I shall be bereaved."

Rashi comments

וקל שדי: ...ומדרשו מי שאמר לעולם די יאמר די לצרותי

> Why did Yaakov use the name of Shakai? This is because he said, "He who said to his world, 'It is enough!' should also say 'Enough!' to my sorrows."

When did Hashem say "Enough!" to the world?

The gemara in Chagigah (12a) says

דאמר ריש לקיש מאי דכתיב (בראשית ל"ה, י"א) אני קל שדי אני הוא שאמרתי לעולם די

> Reish Lakish said, "Why does the *passuk* say, 'I am *Keil Shakai*'?" This means, "I am Hashem who said to the world, 'It is enough!' [Because when the world was created it expanded continuously until it reached the right size, whereupon Hashem halted the world from expanding further.]

Rabbi Mordechai Miller z"l explained this matter as follows:

The world in which we live is called *olam ha'zeh* (literally, this world). The word עולם – world, is related to the word העלם - hiddenness. This is because the purpose of this world is to provide a place where the open hand of Hashem is hidden. Only in such a place can man have free will, because he not coerced to recognise the omniscience of Hashem.

As the world expanded, the immediate and obvious presence of Hashem was reduced more and more. Eventually Hashem said, "It is enough!" This means that Hashem said that the difficulty of serving Hashem in *olam hazeh* has come to a sufficient stage for people to be able to justly merit reward should they choose to recognise Hashem and serve Him.

In the same way that the hiddenness of Hashem serves the purpose of providing a challenge to those who wish to serve Him, so too do the travails that come upon a person provide the wherewithal for that person to grow specifically from meeting the challenges provided by those troubles. This is why there is a relationship between the words צרה – travail, and צורה – stature.

Yaakov said, "Hashem said 'It is enough!' to the expansion of the world because He determined that the difficulties that would now present themselves to those who serve Hashem were sufficient, and that any further hiddenness and difficulty would pose an excessive challenge.

Similarly, may Hashem say, 'It is enough!' to these travails that are sent to challenge me and allow me to grow in stature."

Eretz Yisrael

The gemara in Yuma (54b) discusses how the world was created. According to one opinion, Hashem initially created the *even ha'shesiya* (the Foundation Stone that was situated in the *kodesh ha'kedashim*), and the rest of the world expanded out from the *even ha'shesiya*.

> **ושתיה היתה נקראת**: תנא שממנה הושתת העולם תנן כמאן דאמר מציון נברא העולם דתניא... וחכמים אומרים מציון נברא...

The rock in the *kodesh ha'kedashim* was called the *Even ha'Shesiyah* (the foundation stone). We have learnt, this is because the world was established from it. This is in accordance with the opinion that the world was created from Yerushalayim[8]... As we have learnt... and the *chachamim* say that the world was created from Yerushalayim

Because the world expanded from the place of the *kodesh ha'kedashim*, the whole world contains the potential to be imbued with the *kedushah* of the *kodesh ha'kedashim*. Yaakov, through his personal *avodas Hashem*, cleaved to the *middah* of finding *kedushah* within hiddenness and challenge.

Hence Yaakov inherited Eretz Yisrael, because through his meeting the challenge of finding Hashem within hiddenness, he was able to bring the purpose of *olam hazeh* to fruition, wherein the presence of Hashem would be revealed in the vast expanse of the world's expansion.

---

[8] See other opinions there in the gemara

However, just as Yaakov possessed the ability to constantly expand and grow, so too did Cana'an, since he possessed Eretz Yisrael prior to the *benei yisrael*. There was a fundamental difference between these two modes of growth, however. When Yaakov grew, he became greater and increased in stature. On the other hand, the growth of Cana'an was growth which swallowed uprightness and cast it into gloom, as the gemara says in Pesachim (113b)

חמשה דברים צוה כנען את בניו אהבו זה את זה ואהבו את הגזל ואהבו את הזמה ושנאו את אדוניכם ואל תדברו אמת

Cana'an commanded his sons with regard to five matters, "Love one another, love robbery, love immorality, hate your masters, and do not speak the truth."

The *middah* of Cana'an was to grow in an exuberant but deleterious manner, through swallowing all uprightness in his path.

Because of the dialectical opposition between the *middah* of Yaakov, which caused him to correctly inherit Eretz Yisrael, and the *middah* of Cana'an, which embodied the way in which he misused the power of Eretz Yisrael, it was necessary for Yaakov to divorce himself from and his ideas, in order to merit the *berachos* of Yitzchak and inherit Eretz Yisrael.

Escaping Lavan

The *passuk* says at the beginning of this week's sedrah (28.10)

וַיֵּצֵא יַעֲקֹב מִבְּאֵר שָׁבַע וַיֵּלֶךְ חָרָנָה

And Yaakov went out from Be'er Sheva and he set out for Charan.

The Medrash Rabbah comments

רבי שמואל בר נחמן פתח (תהלים קכ"א, א') שיר למעלות אשא עיני אל ההרים. אשא עיני אל ההורים, למלפני ולמעבדני. מאין יבוא עזרי, אליעזר בשעה שהלך להביא את רבקה מה כתיב ביה (בראשית כ"ד, י') ויקח העבד עשרה גמלים וגו' ואני לא נזם אחד ולא צמיד אחד. רבי חנינא אמר גדוד שלחו רבי יהושע בן לוי אמר שילח עמו אלא שעמד עשו ונטלה ממנו. חזר ואמר מה אנא מובד סברי מן ברייִ חס ושלום לית אנא מובד סברי מן ברייִ אלא עזרי מעם ה'.'

Rabbi Shmuel bar Nachman gave the following introduction. The passuk says in Tehillim, "A song of ascents, I will raise my eyes to the mountains." This can be read, "I will raise my eyes to my mentors, [meaning] to my teachers and to my instructors."

"From where will my assistance come?" Concerning when Eliezer went to bring Rivka, it is written, "And the servant took 10 camels etc.," whereas I have not even one nose-ring and not one bracelet.

Rabbi Chanina said that Yitzchak sent Yaakov with no money (so that Esav should not run after him and take it). Rabbi Yehoshua ben Levi said that he did send him with money but Esav chased him and took it away from him.

He relented and he said, "Will I then abandon my hope in my Creator. Heaven forfend, I will not abandon my hope in Hashem, rather, 'My salvation will come from Hashem.'"

- If Yaakov did not practically follow in the way of Eliezer (since Eliezer had 10 laden camels when he went to bring Rivka, and Yaakov had nothing), why did he refer to him as his teacher in this matter?

- It appears that Yaakov was not scared of Lavan, due to his trust in Hashem. If so, why was he concerned about his lack of money, which was a smaller problem?

Later in the sedrah, the *passuk* says (28.17)

וַיִּירָא וַיֹּאמַר מַה נּוֹרָא הַמָּקוֹם הַזֶּה אֵין זֶה כִּי אִם בֵּית אֱלֹקִים וְזֶה שַׁעַר הַשָּׁמָיִם

And he feared and he said, "How awesome is this place! This is nothing but the House of Hashem, and this is the gateway to heaven."

- Why did Yaakov use a negative expression, "This is nothing but..." Apparently he could have used a positive expression and said, "This is the House of Hashem"?

It would appear that we can explain as follows[9].

The Zohar (Vayishlach) says

> ובכל עשרת מיני כשפים וקסמים מהארת הכתרים התחתונים עשה לבן כנגד יעקב ולא יכול לו. כי כולם עשה לבן לנגדו ולא עלה בידו להרע לו כמ"ש ותחלף את משכורתי עשרת מונים ולא נתנו אלקים להרע עמדי

And with all the ten different types of witchcraft and divination from the light of the lower crowns [which are the ten *sefiros* (Divine emanations) that correspond to the ten Divine statements with which the world was created], Lavan wrought against Yaakov, but he was not able to overcome him. For all of these Lavan perpetrated against Yaakov and he was unable to do evil to him as it says, "[And your father tricked me] and he changed my wages 10 times but Hashem did not allow him to do evil to me."

Through his witchcraft and trickery, Lavan sought to give the impression that everything which he provided was as wholesome and beneficial as that which comes through the 10 utterances with which Hashem created the world. However, everything that Lavan provided was really devoid of goodness and sustenance and was based on magical imagery and illusion. Yaakov was able to see through Lavan's falsehood, and therefore every time that Lavan tried to foist an insubstantial trick through his magic, in place of real wages, on to Yaakov, Yaakov saw through the falseness of that which he was being offered.

---

[9] עיין בספר חסד שמואל

Subsequently, Yaakov's survival in the house of Lavan depended on Yaakov constantly perceiving not that which was there, because that which appeared to be there was a trick of the eye. Rather Yaakov had to constantly train himself to see that which was not there, but that should rightfully have been present. Hence, it was important for Yaakov to determine what really should have been occurring, so that he could compare that to that which was actually occurring.

The first thing that happened to Yaakov on his way to Lavan's house was that he found himself in the position of looking for a wife with nothing to offer. Yaakov understood from his teacher, Eliezer, that this was inappropriate, and that the correct way to bring a wife would have been to have had something to offer his prospective wife. Yaakov understood that missing this wholesomeness in the manner in which matters should have proceeded, was a portent of the *nisayon* that he would face in the house of Lavan, and so he changed his approach in *avodas Hashem* to perception from within the negative.

That is why he said, "Will I then abandon my hope in my Creator. Heaven forfend, I will not abandon my hope in Hashem, rather, 'My salvation will come from Hashem.'" In other words, he first considered the negative option of not trusting in Hashem, and then decided against this negative (instead of saying simply, "I will trust in Hashem"). By adopting this approach of nullification of falsehood, Yaakov adopted a mode of *bitachon* that would protect him against Lavan's tricks.

Similarly he said, negatively, "This is nothing but the House of Hashem." By seeing through the falsehood and *tumah* in the situation that he was about to enter, he was able to exclude everything that was not the House of Hashem, and through this *bitul* perceive the *kedushah* of the place in which the *beis ha'mikdash* would be built.

Exile and self-sacrifice

It says at the beginning of this week's *sedrah* (28:10)

וַיֵּצֵא יַעֲקֹב מִבְּאֵר שָׁבַע וַיֵּלֶךְ חָרָנָה. וַיִּפְגַּע בַּמָּקוֹם וַיָּלֶן שָׁם כִּי בָא הַשֶּׁמֶשׁ וַיִּקַּח מֵאַבְנֵי הַמָּקוֹם וַיָּשֶׂם מְרַאֲשֹׁתָיו וַיִּשְׁכַּב בַּמָּקוֹם הַהוּא. וַיַּחֲלֹם וְהִנֵּה סֻלָּם מֻצָּב אַרְצָה וְרֹאשׁוֹ מַגִּיעַ הַשָּׁמָיְמָה וְהִנֵּה מַלְאֲכֵי אֱלֹקִים עֹלִים וְיֹרְדִים בּוֹ.

And Yaakov went out from Be'er Sheva and he set out for Charan. He came to a certain place and he stopped there for the night, for the sun had set. And he took of the stones of that place, he placed them around his head and he slept in that place. And he dreamt; and behold a ladder was set on the ground and its top reached to the sky, and *malachim* of Hashem were going up and down on it.

Rashi explains

עולים ויורדים: עולים תחלה ואח"כ יורדים מלאכים שליווהו בארץ אין יוצאים חוצה לארץ ועלו לרקיע וירדו מלאכי חוצה לארץ ללוותו

The *malachim* went up first and then came down. The *malachim* that accompanied him in ארץ ישראל would not go to חוץ לארץ so they went up to the *shamayim*, and then *malachim* of חוץ לארץ came down to accompany him.

The Medrash Rabbah provides an alternative explanation:

ר' יהושע בן לוי פתר קרייה בגלות. ויצא יעקב מבאר שבע, היך מה דאת אמר (ירמיה ט"ו, א') שַׁלַּח מֵעַל פָּנַי וְיֵצֵאוּ. וילך חרנה, היך מה דאת אמר (איכה א', י"ב) אֲשֶׁר הוֹגָה ה' בְּיוֹם חֲרוֹן אַפּוֹ. ויפגע במקום וכו' וישכב במקום ההוא, (ירמיה ג', כ"ה) נִשְׁכְּבָה בְּבָשְׁתֵּנוּ וּתְכַסֵּנוּ כְּלִמָּתֵנוּ.

ויחלום והנה סולם, זה חלומו של נבוכדנצר. והנה סולם, זה צלמו של נבוכדנצר, הוא סמל, הוא סלם אותוי דדין, הוא אותוי דדין. מוצב ארצה, (דניאל ג', א') אֲקִימֵהּ בְּבִקְעַת דּוּרָא. וראשו מגיע השמימה, (שם) רוּמֵהּ אַמִּין שִׁתִּין פְּתָיֵהּ אַמִּין שֵׁת. והנה מלאכי אלקים, זה חנניה מישאל ועזריה. עולים ויורדים בו, מעלים בו ומורידים בו, אפזים בו, קפזים בו, שונטים בו, (שם) וְהֵן לָא יְדִיעַ לֶהֱוֵא לָךְ מַלְכָּא דִּי לֵאלָהָיִךְ לָא אִיתַנָא פָלְחִין וּלְצֶלֶם דַּהֲבָא דִּי הֲקֵימְתָּ לָא נִסְגֻּד.

והנה ה' נצב עליו, אמר להם לחנניה מישאל ועזריה עָנֵה וְאָמַר שַׁדְרַךְ מֵישַׁךְ וַעֲבֵד נְגוֹ עַבְדוֹהִי דִּי אֱלָקָא עִלָּאָה פֻּקוּ וֶאֱתוֹ.

Rabbi Yehoshua ben Levi interpreted the *pessukim* concerning *galus*. And Yaakov went out from Be'er Sheva, this refers to the *passuk* that says, "Send them from before My Presence and let them go out." And he went to Charan, this refers to the *passuk* that says, "That Hashem thought on the day of His burning anger." And he came to the place, and he slept in that place, this refers to the *passuk* that says, "We will sleep in our embarrassment and our humiliation shall cover us."

And he dreamt and behold there was a ladder, this refers to the dream of Nevuchadnezzar. And behold there was a ladder, this refers to the idol that was built by Nevuchadnezzar... Standing on the ground, this refers to the *passuk* that says, "He placed the idol in the Valley of Durah." And its top reached to the sky, this refers to the *passuk* that says, "It was 60 *amos* high..."

"And behold there were *malachim* of Hashem" – this refers to Chananya, Mishael and Azaryah. "Were going up and down on it," because Chananya, Mishael and Azaryah were elevated through their encounter with the idol and they denigrated the idol and they made fun of the idol to Nevuchadnezzar, for they said to him, "But even if He does not [save us], be it known to you, O king, that we will not serve your god or worship the statue of gold that you have set up."

And behold Hashem was standing over him, as the *passuk* says, "Nevuchadnezzar then approached the hatch of the burning fiery furnace and he called, 'Shadrach, Meshach and Aved-nego, servants of the Most High G-d, come out!'"

- What is the connection between the *malachim* who accompanied Yaakov going up and down on the ladder and the story of Chananya, Mishael and Azaryah?

It would seem that we can explain as follows:

Rashi comments on the words וַיָּלֶן שָׁם כִּי בָא הַשֶּׁמֶשׁ as follows:

היה לו לכתוב ויבא השמש וילן שם כי בא השמש משמע ששקעה לו חמה פתאום שלא בעונתה כדי שילין שם

The *passuk* should have said and the sun set and he slept there. From the fact that the *passuk* says, "because the sun had set", it is implied that the sun set suddenly, not at the right time, in order so that he should sleep there.

The light of the sun represents the light of the Torah[10]. When the sun set early for Yaakov, this signified that the light of the Torah would shine less brightly for Yaakov, in *galus*. Subsequently, Yaakov had to grapple with Lavan's trickery and deceit, in the straightened spiritual circumstances and the reduced inspiration of *galus*. Nevertheless, instead of resigning himself to descending to Lavan's level of dishonesty, Yaakov redoubled his commitment to integrity and honesty, in the service of Lavan.

Thus Yaakov rebuked Lavan and said (31.38-42)

זֶה עֶשְׂרִים שָׁנָה אָנֹכִי עִמָּךְ רְחֵלֶיךָ וְעִזֶּיךָ לֹא שִׁכֵּלוּ וְאֵילֵי צֹאנְךָ לֹא אָכָלְתִּי. טְרֵפָה לֹא הֵבֵאתִי אֵלֶיךָ אָנֹכִי אֲחַטֶּנָּה מִיָּדִי תְּבַקְשֶׁנָּה גְּנֻבְתִי יוֹם וּגְנֻבְתִי לָיְלָה. הָיִיתִי בַיּוֹם אֲכָלַנִי חֹרֶב וְקֶרַח בַּלָּיְלָה וַתִּדַּד שְׁנָתִי מֵעֵינָי. זֶה לִּי עֶשְׂרִים שָׁנָה בְּבֵיתֶךָ עֲבַדְתִּיךָ אַרְבַּע עֶשְׂרֵה שָׁנָה בִּשְׁתֵּי בְנֹתֶיךָ וְשֵׁשׁ שָׁנִים בְּצֹאנֶךָ וַתַּחֲלֵף אֶת מַשְׂכֻּרְתִּי עֲשֶׂרֶת מֹנִים.

These twenty years I have spent in your service, your ewes and she-goats never miscarried, nor did I feast on

---

[10] עיין בספר פחד יצחק, חנוכה, רשימה שבסוף הספר, אות ז'

rams from your flock. That which was torn by beasts I never brought to you; I myself made good the loss; you exacted it of me, whether snatched by day or snatched by night.

Often, scorching heat ravaged me by day and frost by night; and sleep fled from my eyes. Of the twenty years that I spent in your household, I served you fourteen years for your two daughters, and six years for your flocks; and you changed my wages time and again.

Because Yaakov was deprived of the full spiritual strength of his Torah learning in the house of Lavan, he had no choice but to sacrifice his very health and wellbeing, in order to simultaneously fulfill his obligations to Lavan, maintain his standards of integrity and build the household that would become the foundation of the *benei yisrael*.

Therefore, although the *malachim* descended the ladder, which signified that Yaakov's spiritual insight would be reduced in *galus*, Yaakov nevertheless ascended the ladder, because he stayed true to his principles, no matter the personal cost.

Yaakov's descendants, Chananya, Mishael and Azaryah also found themselves cast out of Eretz Yisrael, after the destruction of the *Beis Ha'Mikdash*, and in a situation in which they did not know if Hashem would help them. Nevertheless, they stayed true to the Torah, and did not bow to Nevuchadnezzar's idol. This situation required them to sacrifice their very bodies in order to be true to their principles, just as Yaakov had sacrificed his body in order to maintain his integrity in the house of Lavan.

Because they emulated the self-sacrifice of Yaakov, notwithstanding the reduced circumstances in which they found themselves, they too ascended the ladder of integrity and truth, just as Yaakov did before them. That is why the medrash says that Chananya, Mishael and Azaryah climbed the ladder of Yaakov's dream and thereby merited to sanctify the Name of Hashem.

The dream of the ladder

It says in this week's *sedrah* (28:12):

וַיַּחֲלֹם וְהִנֵּה סֻלָּם מֻצָּב אַרְצָה וְרֹאשׁוֹ מַגִּיעַ הַשָּׁמָיְמָה וְהִנֵּה מַלְאֲכֵי אֱלֹקִים עֹלִים וְיֹרְדִים בּוֹ

And he dreamt and behold there was a ladder standing on the ground and its top reached the heavens and *malachim* of Hashem were going up and down on it.

The Medrash Tanchuma (Vayetze 2) comments:

א"ר שמואל בר נחמן אלו שרי אומות העכו"ם דא"ר שמואל בר נחמן מלמד שהראה לו הקב"ה לאבינו יעקב שרה של בבל עולה שבעין עוקים ויורד, ושל מדי חמשים ושנים, ושל יון מאה ויורד, ושל אדום עלה ולא ידע כמה, באותה שעה נתירא יעקב אבינו ואמר שמא לזה אין לו ירידה, א"ל הקדוש ברוך הוא (ירמיה, ל') ואתה אל תירא עבדי יעקב ואל תחת ישראל כביכול אפילו אתה רואהו עולה אצלי משם אני

מורידו שנאמר (עובדיה, א') אם תגביה כנשר ואם בין כוכבים שים קנך משם אורידך נאם ה'

Rabbi Shmuel said, "The *malachim* are the geniuses of the nations of the world." For Rabbi Shmuel said, "This teaches you that Hashem showed Yaakov the genius of Bavel climb 70 rungs (corresponding to 70 years of ascendancy) and then descend. He showed Yaakov the genius of Madai climb 250 runs and then descend. He showed Yaakov the genius of Yavan climb 100 rungs and then descend. He showed him the genius of Esav climbing onwards and there did not seem to be any end to his ascent.

In that moment, Yaakov became scared and he said, 'Maybe this one will never fall?'

Hashem said to him, 'Do not fear my servant Yaakov and do not tremble Yisrael. Even if the genius of Esav were to ascend to be with Me, as if it were, from there I will bring his downfall. As the *passuk* says, "If you will rise as high as an eagle and if amongst the stars you place your nest, from there I will bring your downfall, says Hashem."'"

The medrash continues:

א"ל הקדוש ברוך הוא ליעקב למה אין אתה עולה, באותה שעה נתירא אבינו יעקב ואמר כשם שיש לאלו ירידה, כך אני יש לי ירידה, א"ל הקב"ה אם אתה עולה אין לך ירידה, ולא האמין ולא עלה...א"ל הקדוש ברוך הוא אלו עלית והאמנת לא היתה לך ירידה לעולם, אלא הואיל ולא האמנת הרי בניך משתעבדין בהללו ד' מלכיות בעה"ז במסים ובארנוניות ובגולגליות.

א"ל יעקב יכול לעולם א"ל אל תירא עבדי יעקב אל תחת ישראל... כי
אעשה כלה בכל הגוים אשר הפיצותיך שם באומות העולם שהן מכלין
את שדותיהן אבל ישראל שאין מכלין את שדותיהן ואותך לא אעשה
כלה אלא מיסרך ביסורין בעולם הזה בשביל לנקותך מעונותיך לעתיד
לבא ...

Hashem said to Yaakov, "Yaakov, why do you not go up?"

At that time Yaakov was afraid and said, "Just as these fall so too I will fall if I go up."

Hashem said to him, "If you go up you will not fall."

Yaakov did not believe and did not go up.

Hashem said to him, "Had you gone up and believed you would never have come down, however because you did not believe your children will be subjugated to these four kingdoms in *olam ha'zeh* through profit taxes, land tax and skull tax."

Yaakov asked Hashem, "Is this forever?"

Hashem replied, "Do not be afraid my servant Yaakov and do not tremble Yisrael...because I will destroy all the nations amongst which I scattered you.

[This means, I will destroy] the nations that finish off their fields. But regarding Yisrael who do not finish off their fields [because they keep *shemitah* and rest their fields every seven years and in *yovel*] – I will not destroy you. Rather I will chastise you in *olam ha'zeh* in order to cleanse you from your *aveiros* for the future..."

- Why was Yaakov afraid to go up the ladder?

- In what way should Yaakov have believed in Hashem in order to ascend the ladder?

- What is the connection between the nations finishing off their fields and their ultimate downfall?

It would seem that we can explain as follows:

The gemara says in Shabbos (31a)

> אמר ריש לקיש מאי דכתיב (ישעיהו ל"ג, ו') והיה אמונת עתיך חוסן ישועות חכמת ודעת וגו' אמונת זה סדר זרעים עתיך זה סדר מועד חוסן זה סדר נשים ישועות זה סדר נזיקין חכמת זה סדר קדשים ודעת זה סדר טהרות ואפ"ה (ישעיהו ל"ג, ו') יראת ה' היא אוצרו

Reish Lakish said, "What is the meaning of that which is written 'And the faith of your times shall be a strength of salvation, wisdom, and knowledge, the fear of Hashem is his treasure' (Yeshaya 33:6)?

Faith: This refers to the order of *Zeraim* in the Mishnah (the laws of growing food).

Your times: This refers to the order of *Moed* (the laws of the festivals).

Strength: This refers to the order of *Nashim* (the laws that relate to women).

Salvation: This refers to the order of *Nezikin* (the laws of damages).

Wisdom: This refers to the order of *Kodashim* (the laws of consecrated items).

And knowledge: This refers to order of *Taharos* (the laws of purity).

But even so, 'The fear of Hashem is His treasure house.'"

Rashi explains:

סדר זרעים: שעל אמונת האדם סומך להפריש מעשרותיו כראוי

Faith refers to the order of *Zeraim*: A person relies on his trust in Hashem when he separates tithes from his produce (since he believes that no shortage will befall him through his giving tithes to the *cohen*, to the *levi* and to the poor.)

Tosafos, on the other hand, explains:

אמונת זה סדר זרעים: מפרש בירושלמי שמאמין בחי העולמים וזורע

Faith refers to the order of *Zeraim* (which deals with agricultural law): The Talmud Yerushalmi explains that a man's belief in Hashem is demonstrated when he sows in this ground (and he trusts that Hashem will make a crop grow from the seeds that he has planted).

According to Rashi, the allusion of "Faith refers to the order of *Zeraim*" is similar to the other allusions in the *passuk*, which refer to the orders of the Mishnah. It is the observance of the *halachos* of *zeraim* that demonstrates the farmer's faith in Hashem. However, it would appear difficult to understand how Tosafos translates the gemara.

If the farmer's faith in Hashem is demonstrated when he plants seeds because he believes Hashem will make the plants grow, then this demonstration of faith occurs independently of the farmer's observance of the laws of *zeraim*. Even were the laws of *zeraim* not to apply, we could still observe the farmer's faith in Hashem's care when he sows his crop. Why then does the gemara imply that the farmer's faith is illustrated by his observance of the *halachos* of *zeraim*?

It seems evident from Tosafos that observing the laws of *zeraim* opens the eyes of the farmer to realise that his sowing seeds in the ground is indeed an act of trust in Hashem. Were the farmer to become brutish and overbearing, he would feel that the land belongs to him, comprises part of his capital and would be expected to automatically produce a crop as a consequence of his labours.

In order to prevent the development of this boorish attitude, the farmer is instructed to observe the *halachos* of *zeraim* which limit his use of the land and which oblige him to share the harvest with the needy. Observing these *halachos* makes the farmer aware that (Vayikra 25:23)

כִּי לִי הָאָרֶץ כִּי גֵרִים וְתוֹשָׁבִים אַתֶּם עִמָּדִי

For the land is Mine (says Hashem), for you are sojourners and tenants with Me.

By recognising that Hashem is the true master of his land, and by acting as the emissary of Hashem to provide food to the needy, the farmer remains alert to the gift that Hashem gives him when He makes the crop grow and flourish.

Climbing the ladder

As nations develop sophisticated and influential civilisations, they become removed from the belief in Hashem that was inculcated into them when they subsisted on the land. As a nation climbs the ladder of wealth and influence, it begins to believe that its own efforts, cleverness and adroitness have fueled its success. Eventually the nation becomes entirely devoid of recognition of Hashem and begins to worship itself as the source of its own greatness.

When this happens, the nation loses any right it may have once had to Hashem's bountifulness, as is illustrated in the following anecdote (Bereishis Rabbah 33:1)

אלכסנדרוס מוקדן אזל לגבי מלכא קציא לאחורי הרי חשך ושלח ליה... א"ל לא אתית אלא בעיא למידע היך אתון דייניץ. יתיב גביה, יומא חדא אתא חד בר נש קבל על חבריה, אמר הדין גברא זבן לי חדא קילקלתא ואשכחית בגוה סימתא, ההוא דזבין אמר קילקלתא זבנית סימתא לא זבנית והההוא דזבן אמר קילקלתא ומה דבגוה זבנית, אמר לחד מנייהו אית לך בר דכר א"ל הין ואמר לאוחרני אית לך ברתא נוקבא א"ל הין

אמר להון זיל אסיב דין לדין והוי ממונא לתרויהון.

חמתיה יתיב תמה, א"ל מה לא דיינית טב, א"ל אין, אמר ליה אלו היה גבכון היך הויתון דייניון, א"ל קטלין דין ודין ומלכותא נסבא ממונא דתרוויהון, א"ל אית גבכון מטר נחית א"ל הין, א"ל אית גבכון שמשא דנח א"ל הין, א"ל אית גבכון בעיר דקיק א"ל הן, א"ל תיפח רוחיה דההוא גברא לא בזכותכון נחית מטר ולא בזכותכון שמשא דנחה עליכון אלא בזכותיה דבעירא דכתיב "אדם ובהמה תושיע ה'" אדם בזכות בהמה תושיע ה'.

Alexander [the Great] of Macedonia once came to the land beyond the Dark Mountains and sent for the King of Katzia... "I have only come here to learn how you judge disputes," Alexander said.

He waited beside King Katzia.

One day a man came before the King with a complaint against his fellow. He said, "This man sold me a dung-heap in which I found [hidden] treasure. I bought the dung-heap, not the treasure." (The purchaser wished to be able to return the treasure to the vendor.)

The other man said, "I sold him the dung-heap and all of its contents." (The vendor refused to accept the treasure.)

King Katzia asked one of the disputants, "Do you have a son?" The man replied affirmatively.

"And do you have a daughter?" he asked the other, who again replied affirmatively. The King then declared, "Let them marry one another, and divide the treasure between them."

King Katzia noticed that Alexander seemed astonished. "Did I not rule well?" he asked.

"Yes," replied Alexander.

"If this case came before the court in your country, how would it be adjudicated?"

"The judge would condemn them both to death, and the king would keep the treasure," Alexander replied.

"Does the rain fall in your country?" King Katzia asked.

"Yes."

"Does the sun shine upon it?"

"Yes."

"Do you have young cattle?"

"Yes."

"Cursed be that man [who would render such evil judgments]!" [the King of Katzia] declared. "It is only due to the merit of the young cattle that the sun shines and the rain falls upon your country. For the sake of the small cattle you are saved!"

Thus the *passuk* says, "[Your righteousness is like the mighty mountains, Your judgments like the great deep;] man and animal You save, Hashem" (Tehillim 36:7). That is, "You save man for the sake of the animals."

The King of Katzia exhorted Alexander that if he was incapable of understanding that the blessing of Hashem can be revealed through a treasure found in a dung-heap, then perforce he must also have no recognition of the goodness of Hashem in the bounty of the sun and the rain that fell on his country.

Yaakov's fear

Yaakov was afraid that if the *benei yisrael* were allowed to occupy a position of prominence in *olam ha'zeh*, then the same fate would befall them as befalls all other nations. Their stature would become their downfall, as it would cause them to forget that it is the constant goodness of Hashem that makes them strong and affluent.

Hashem told Yaakov that he should have believed that Hashem Himself would be the guarantor that this attitude would not overcome the *benei yisrael*.

Hashem promised Yaakov however that in the end, the merit of the observance of the *halachos* of *shemitah* would give the *benei yisrael* the self-effacing *emunah* that enables them to outlast those nations who become self-intoxicated by success, and to merit to see the days of *mashiach* and of *olam habah*.

And Yaakov remained alone

The *passuk* says in this week's sedrah (32.17)

וַיִּתֵּן בְּיַד עֲבָדָיו עֵדֶר עֵדֶר לְבַדּוֹ וַיֹּאמֶר אֶל עֲבָדָיו עִבְרוּ לְפָנַי וְרֶוַח תָּשִׂימוּ בֵּין עֵדֶר וּבֵין עֵדֶר

And he placed the livestock in the charge of his servants, drove by drove, and he told his servants, "Go on ahead, and keep a distance between the droves."

The medrash comments

מהו ורוח תשימו, אמר יעקב לפני הקב"ה רבונו של עולם אם יהיו צרות באות על בני לא תביא אותם זו אחר זו אלא הרווח להם מצרותיהם. באותה שעה נשא יעקב את עיניו וראה את עשו שהוא בא מרחוק ותלה עיניו למרום. בכה ובקש רחמים מלפני הקב"ה ושמע תפלתו והבטיחו שהוא מושיעו מכל צרותיו בזכותו של יעקב שנאמר (תהלים כ', ב') יענך ה' ביום צרה ישגבך שם אלקי יעקב.

What does "And keep a distance between the droves" refer to? Yaakov said before Hashem, "Master of the Universe, if troubles befall my descendants, do not bring them one after the other, but rather give them respite between them."

At that time Yaakov lifted his eyes and saw Esav coming from afar. He lifted his eyes on high he wept and he asked for mercy from Hashem and He heard his tefillah and He promised him that he would save him from all his travails in the merit of Yaakov, as the *passuk* says in Tehillim, "May Hashem answer you on the day of travail, the name of the G-d of Yaakov should exalt you."

- Since Hashem was talking to Yaakov, why does the medrash say that Hashem would save him in the merit of Yaakov, seemingly it should have said that Hashem would save him in his own merit?

Later in the *sedrah* it says (32.25-26)

וַיִּוָּתֵר יַעֲקֹב לְבַדּוֹ וַיֵּאָבֵק אִישׁ עִמּוֹ עַד עֲלוֹת הַשָּׁחַר. וַיַּרְא כִּי לֹא יָכֹל לוֹ וַיִּגַּע בְּכַף יְרֵכוֹ וַתֵּקַע כַּף יֶרֶךְ יַעֲקֹב בְּהֵאָבְקוֹ עִמּוֹ.

And Yaakov was left alone, and a man wrestled with him until the break of dawn. When he saw that he could not prevail against him, he wrenched Yaakov's hip at its socket, so that the socket of his hip was dislocated as he wrestled with him.

The Medrash Rabbah comments (77.1)

אתה מוצא כל מה שהקב"ה עתיד לעשות לעתיד לבוא, הקדים ועשה על ידי הצדיקים בעוה"ז. הקב"ה מחיה המתים ואליהו מחיה את המתים, הקב"ה עוצר גשמים ואליהו עוצר גשמים, הקב"ה מברך את המועט ואליהו מברך את המועט, הקב"ה מחיה את המתים ואלישע מחיה את המתים, הקב"ה פוקד עקרות ואלישע פוקד עקרות, הקב"ה מברך את המועט ואלישע מברך את המועט, הקב"ה ממתיק את המר ואלישע ממתיק את המר, הקב"ה ממתיק את המר במר ואלישע המתיק

את המר במר. ר' ברכיה בשם ר' סימון אמר אין כאל ומי כאל ישורון, ישראל סבא, מה הקב"ה כתוב בו (ישעיהו ב') ונשגב ה' לבדו אף יעקב ויותר יעקב לבדו.

You will find that for everything that Hashem will do directly, He pre-empted and did similarly by means of the *tzadikim*, in *olam ha'zeh*. Hashem will resuscitate the dead and Eliyahu resuscitated the dead.... Hashem remembers the barren and Elisha remembered the barren... Hashem sweetens that which is bitter and Elisha sweetened that which is bitter... Rabbi Berachya said in the name of Rabbi Simon said... just as concerning Hashem it says, "And Hashem will be exalted alone on that day," so too concerning Yaakov it says, "And Yaakov was left alone."

- It would appear difficult to understand the last comparison of the medrash. All of the other comparisons are of great things that are done both directly by Hashem and also through *tzadikim*. But when Yaakov was left alone he was vulnerable and in danger. Why is this compared to that which it says, "And Hashem will be exalted alone"?

After Yaakov struggled with the *malach* it says (32.29)

וַיֹּאמֶר לֹא יַעֲקֹב יֵאָמֵר עוֹד שִׁמְךָ כִּי אִם יִשְׂרָאֵל כִּי שָׂרִיתָ עִם אֱלֹקִים וְעִם אֲנָשִׁים וַתּוּכָל

And he said, "Your name shall no longer be Yaakov, but Yisrael, for you have striven with divine beings and with people and you have prevailed."

Rashi comments

לא יעקב: לא יאמר עוד שהברכות באו לך בעקבה ורמיה כי אם בשררה וגלוי פנים וסופך שהקב"ה נגלה עליך בבית אל ומחליף שמך ושם הוא מברכך ואני שם אהיה לך עליהן ואודה וזהו שכתוב (הושע י"ב) וישר אל מלאך ויוכל בכה ויתחנן לו, בכה המלאך ויתחנן לו, ומה נתחנן לו, בית אל ימצאנו ושם ידבר עמנו, המתן לי עד שידבר עמנו שם, ולא רצה יעקב ועל כרחו הודה לו עליהן, וזהו ויברך אותו שם שהיה מתחנן להמתין לו ולא רצה.

Not Yaakov: It shall no longer be said that the *berachos* came to you through supplanting and trickery but rather through noble conduct and in an open manner. Because later on Hashem will reveal Himself to you at Beis El and will change your name. There He will bless you, and I shall be there and admit your right to the *berachos*.

It is to this event that the *passuk* refers (Hoshea 12.5), "And he strove with a *malach* and prevailed, he wept and made supplication to him." This means that the *malach* wept and made supplication to Yaakov. What was his supplication? This is stated in the next *passuk*, "At Beis El He will meet us and there He will speak with us." The *malach* requested, "Wait until he will speak with us there, and then I will admit your right to the *berachos*."

Yaakov, however, would not agree to this, and against his own wish the *malach* had to admit his right to the *berachos*. That is what is meant when it states (in the next *passuk*) "And he declared him blessed there," because the *malach* begged him to wait and he did not agree to do so.

- What difference did it make if the *malach* of Esav acknowledged the *berachos* immediately after the struggle and not later in Beis El?

It would seem that we can explain as follows:

It says in *passuk* 26

וַיַּרְא כִּי לֹא יָכֹל לוֹ וַיִּגַּע בְּכַף יְרֵכוֹ וַתֵּקַע כַּף יֶרֶךְ יַעֲקֹב בְּהֵאָבְקוֹ עִמּוֹ

When he saw that he could not prevail against him, he wrenched Yaakov's hip at its socket, so that the socket of his hip was dislocated as he wrestled with him.

The Yalkut Reuvaini says

וירא כי לא יכול לו ויגע בכף יריכו וגו'. כשראה סמאל שלא יכול להזיק ליעקב נתן עיניו ביוצאי ירכו והם נדב ואביהוא וכו'. לכן והוא צולע על יריכו נצטער על נדב ואביהוא.

When the *malach* of Esav saw that he was unable to harm Yaakov he set his eyes on his descendants, specifically on Nadav and Avihu. That is why it says that Yaakov was limping on his thigh, because he was pained because of Nadav and Avihu.

Many of the reasons given for the punishment of Nadav and Avihu, relate to the fact that Nadav and Avihu were פורש מן הצבור - they separated themselves from the community. For example, reasons given for their punishment are that they were not married, that they decided the *halacha* in front of Moshe and that they did not take council from each other. According to all of these reasons, Nadav and Avihu were punished because they acted in an excessively individual manner.

If the error of Nadav and Avihu originated in Yaakov's struggle with the *malach*, this indicates that Yaakov also deliberately separated himself from the rest of the community, namely from the rest of the camp, prior to his struggle with the *malach* of Esav.

It would appear that Yaakov did so because had Yaakov faced the *malach* while he was together with the rest of the camp, he could indeed have drawn strength from his family in order to gain the fortitude he needed to face the *malach* of Esav. By doing this, Yaakov would have saved himself, but he would have inadvertently given the *yetzer hara* (the *malach* of Esav) direct access to his family. This means to say, since Yaakov would have drawn the strength he needed for the struggle, from his family, the *yetzer hara* would also have been able struggle against his family, from whom he had drawn his strength.

Yaakov chose to separate himself and stand alone in his fight, thereby placing himself in greater danger of being hurt, but insulating his family from the struggle with the *yetzer ha'ra*.

As a result of this decision, the *yetzer ha'ra* was able to later make Nadav and Avihu mistakenly follow the same course of action, and incorrectly separate themselves from the rest of the *benei yisrael*, in their *avodas Hashem*.

The reason that it was important for the *malach* of Esav to acknowledge Yaakov's right to the *berachos* immediately, was that this was an acknowledgement that Yaakov, in his own right, and without any consideration of his being the father of the *shevatim*, had beaten the *yetzer ha'ra*. Had the *malach* of Esav only acknowledged the *berachos* later at Beis El, this would only have been an acknowledgement that Yaakov was meritorious against the *yetzer ha'ra* in combination with the merits of the rest of his family, which would have yet implied that Yaakov had drawn the rest of his family into his struggle against the *yetzer ha'ra*.

Since Yaakov's decision to remain alone was a deliberate self-sacrifice to preserve the purity of the *benei yisrael*, he merited through this that, in the end, the *benei yisrael* will witness when Hashem is exalted alone, *le'asid lavo*.

This is also why the medrash says, "He promised him that he would save him from all his travails in the merit of Yaakov." This is because when Yaakov separated himself from the camp, he fought the *malach* as a discrete individual, and not as part of *klal yisrael*.

Thus the medrash means to say, "Hashem promised Yaakov that after he would rejoin his family as Yaakov Avinu, his descendants would always be able to call on the merit of him having separated himself from the *klal* for their benefit, when he was only Yaakov by himself."

Fighting Esav's *malach*

It says in this week's *sedrah* (32:27)

וַיֹּאמֶר שַׁלְּחֵנִי כִּי עָלָה הַשָּׁחַר וַיֹּאמֶר לֹא אֲשַׁלֵּחֲךָ כִּי אִם בֵּרַכְתָּנִי

And he said, "Send me, because the morning has dawned." And he said, "I will not send you unless you give me a *berachah*."

Rashi explains:

כי עלה השחר: וצריך אני לומר שירה ביום

Because the morning has dawned: And I need to say *shirah* by day.

ברכתני: הודה לי על הברכות שברכני אבי שעשו מערער עליהם

Unless you give me a *berachah* (the word ברכתני really means "unless you will have blessed me", this is because Yaakov said to the *malach*) – Acknowledge that the *berachos* that Yitzchak gave me are rightfully mine, because Esav is complaining about them.

- Why did Yaakov insist that the *malach* should acknowledge that the *berachos* were his before allowing him to say *shirah*?

The *sedrah* continues (32:29)

וַיֹּאמֶר לֹא יַעֲקֹב יֵאָמֵר עוֹד שִׁמְךָ כִּי אִם יִשְׂרָאֵל כִּי שָׂרִיתָ עִם אֱלֹקִים וְעִם אֲנָשִׁים וַתּוּכָל

And he said, "It will not be said anymore that you name is Yaakov, rather your name will be Yisrael. Because you struggled with *malachim* and with people and you overcame."

Rashi explains:

לֹא יַעֲקֹב: לֹא יֵאָמֵר עוֹד שֶׁהַבְּרָכוֹת בָּאוּ לְךָ בְּעָקְבָה וּרְמִיָּה כִּי אִם בִּשְׂרָרָה וְגִלּוּי פָּנִים וְסוֹפְךָ שֶׁהַקָּבָּ"ה נִגְלֶה עָלֶיךָ בְּבֵית אֵל וּמַחֲלִיף שִׁמְךָ וְשָׁם הוּא מְבָרֶכְךָ וַאֲנִי שָׁם אֶהְיֶה וְאוֹדֶה לְךָ עֲלֵיהֶן. וְזֶהוּ שֶׁכָּתוּב (הושע י"ב) וַיָּשַׂר אֶל מַלְאָךְ וַיֻּכָל בָּכֹה וַיִּתְחַנֶּן לוֹ, בָּכֹה הַמַּלְאָךְ וַיִּתְחַנֶּן לוֹ, וּמַה נִּתְחַנֵּן לוֹ בֵּית אֵל יִמְצָאֶנּוּ וְשָׁם יְדַבֵּר עִמָּנוּ, הַמְתֵּן לִי עַד שֶׁיְּדַבֵּר עִמָּנוּ שָׁם, וְלֹא רָצָה יַעֲקֹב וְעַל כָּרְחוֹ הוֹדָה לוֹ עֲלֵיהֶן, וְזֶהוּ וַיְבָרֶךְ אוֹתוֹ שָׁם שֶׁהָיָה מִתְחַנֵּן לְהַמְתִּין לוֹ וְלֹא רָצָה

Your name will no longer be Yaakov: It will not be said that the *berachos* came to you through trickery and deceit, rather it will be said that they came to you through uprightness and honesty. In the end Hashem will appear to you in Beis Keil and He will change your name and there He will give you a *berachah*, and I will be there and I will acknowledge that the *berachos* belong to you.

This is the meaning of the *passuk* (הושע י"ב ה')

וַיָּשַׂר אֶל מַלְאָךְ וַיֻּכָל בָּכָה וַיִּתְחַנֶּן לוֹ בֵּית קֵל יִמְצָאֶנּוּ וְשָׁם יְדַבֵּר עִמָּנוּ

And he conquered the *malach* and overcame him, he cried and pleaded to him, "He will find us in Beis Keil and there he will speak with us."

The *passuk* means that the *malach* cried and pleaded to Yaakov to wait till Hashem would speak to them in Beis Keil. Yaakov did not want to wait and the *malach* was forced to acknowledge that the *berachos* were rightfully his, this is why the *passuk* says ויברך אותו שם – the *malach* gave him a *beracha* there where they had struggled, since Yaakov would not wait till later.

- Why did the *malach* want to wait to acknowledge that the *berachos* rightfully belonged to Yaakov till they would meet in Beis Keil?

The Medrash Rabbah says (77, 2)

אמר רב הונא בסוף אמר המלאך אני מודיעו עם מי הוא עוסק, מה עשה נתן אצבעו בארץ התחילה הארץ תוססת אש, אמר ליה מן דא את מדחיל לי אנא כוליה מינה הה"ד (עובדיה א') וְהָיָה בֵית יַעֲקֹב אֵשׁ וּבֵית יוֹסֵף לֶהָבָה וּבֵית עֵשָׂו לְקַשׁ וְדָלְקוּ בָהֶם וַאֲכָלוּם וְלֹא יִהְיֶה שָׂרִיד לְבֵית עֵשָׂו כִּי ה' דִּבֵּר

Rav Huna said, in the end, the *malach* said, "I'll let him know who he is dealing with."

What did he do? He placed his finger in the earth and fire poured out.

Yaakov said to him, "Is that how you are going to frighten me? I am made entirely from fire."

As the *passuk* says, "And the House of Yaakov will be fire, and the House of Yosef will be flame and the House of Esav will be straw. And they shall burn among them and they shall eat them and there shall not be a remnant from the House of Esav, because Hashem has spoken."

- Why was the conflict between the *malach* and Yaakov represent by fire?

It would seem that we can explain as follows[11]:

The conflict between the *malach* and Yaakov was whether Yaakov or Esav should have received the *berachos*. Yaakov claimed that he had a greater ability to lead the world in the service of Hashem, and therefore he should have taken the *berachos*. The *malach* on the other hand claimed that Esav's worldly way of serving Hashem would result in a greater *kiddush Hashem*, and therefore Esav should receive the *berachos*.

Furthermore, the *malach* claimed that Yaakov had not taken the *berachos le'shem shamayim*, but that the trickery which he had employed to gain the *berachos* showed that he had taken the *berachos* for his own personal benefit.

---

[11] עיין בספר אור גדליהו

Concerning the *malach*'s claim that Esav's worldly way of serving Hashem would result in a greater *kiddush Hashem*, the *malach* showed Yaakov fire coming from the earth which indicated that Esav had the potential ability to uplift the most earthy things in the service of Hashem.

However Yaakov responded by showing the *malach* that he had the ability to unify both the earthy and the spiritual aspects of creation in the service of Hashem, and that he was entirely made of fire.

Concerning the *malach*'s claim that Yaakov had not taken the *berachos le'shem shamayim*, Yaakov showed the *malach* that his heart was always and consistently unified in the service of Hashem. Subsequently even if there appeared to be something contradictory in the way that he acted, this apparent discrepancy could be explained by the end result of *kiddush Hashem* which he sought.

As acknowledgement that Yaakov was correct on both accounts, the *malach* changed Yaakov's name to Yisrael, to denote that Yaakov ruled and was able to use both the *yetzer ha'tov* and also the *yetzer ha'ra*, *le'shem shamayim*. That is why the gematria of the name Yisrael (541) has the same *gematria* as Yaakov (182) + Satan (359).

Had the *malach* only acknowledged in Beis Keil, the place of the *beis ha'mikdash*, that Yaakov deserved the *berachos*, then the *malach* would only have been admitting that Yaakov was able to serve Hashem with the *kedushah* of the *beis ha'mikdash*. Yaakov forced the *malach* to acknowledge that he was equally capable of serving Hashem and of creating a *kiddush*

Hashem using worldly matters.

Therefore Yaakov only let the *malach* go and say *shirah* once he acknowledged that Yaakov would be able to use the *berachos* in the right way under all circumstances, and that he had taken the *berachos le'shem shamayim*, for pure motives.

Vayeshev

The split between Yosef and the brothers

The *passuk* says at the beginning of this week's sedrah (37.2)

אֵלֶּה תֹּלְדוֹת יַעֲקֹב יוֹסֵף בֶּן שְׁבַע עֶשְׂרֵה שָׁנָה הָיָה רֹעֶה אֶת אֶחָיו בַּצֹּאן וְהוּא נַעַר אֶת בְּנֵי בִלְהָה וְאֶת בְּנֵי זִלְפָּה נְשֵׁי אָבִיו וַיָּבֵא יוֹסֵף אֶת דִּבָּתָם רָעָה אֶל אֲבִיהֶם

These are the generations of Yaakov. Yoseph was 17 years old, he tended the flocks with his brothers, he was a youth and he associated with the children of his father's wives Bilhah and Zilpah.

And Yoseph brought bad reports of them (his other brothers) to their father.

Rashi comments

את דבתם רעה: כל רעה שהיה רואה באחיו בני לאה היה מגיד לאביו

Bad reports of them: Any bad thing that he saw in his brothers the sons of Leah, he would relate to his father.

The medrash comments (Shemos 30.3)

בכל מקום שכתוב אלה פוסל את הראשונים... אלה תולדות יעקב פסל לאלופי עשו

Wherever it says אלה – this means to invalidate that which comes beforehand. So when the passuk says אלה – these are the generations of Yaakov, it means to invalidate the chieftains of Esav which are enumerated beforehand.

- Why did the *machlokess* between Yosef and his brothers invalidate the chieftains of Esav?

The next *passuk* says

וְיִשְׂרָאֵל אָהַב אֶת יוֹסֵף מִכָּל בָּנָיו כִּי בֶן זְקֻנִים הוּא לוֹ וְעָשָׂה לוֹ כְּתֹנֶת פַּסִּים

And Yaakov loved Yoseph best of all his sons, for he was the child of his old age; and he had made him an ornamented tunic.

The medrash comments

> דבר אחר פַּסִים, רשב"ל בשם ראב"ע (תהלים ס"ו, ה') לכו וראו מפעלות אלקים, וכתיב בתריה הפך ים ליבשה. למה וישנאו אותו בשביל שיקרע הים לפניהם פסים פס ים

Another explanation: פסים - Reish Lakish said in the name of Rabbi Elazar ben Azariah, "Go and see the acts of Hashem." (Tehillim 66:5) And in the next *passuk* it says, "He turned sea to dry land." Why did [Hashem cause that] they [should] hate him? In order that the sea would be torn before them. פסים can be read, פס – a strip, ים – of the sea.

- Why did Hashem cause there to be a rift between Yosef and the brothers?

- How did the hatred of the brothers towards Yosef cause the sea to be split?

It would seem that we can explain as follows[12]:

Yosef and his brothers each had capabilities that were required by the other, in order to be complete. However, once a rift occurred between Yosef and his brothers, it was impossible for each to complete the other, because of the divisions that separated between them. Subsequently, each one of them was forced to excel in his own particular *middah*, in order that the excellence that they achieved in their own *middah* would compensate for the complementary *middah* that they were

---

[12] עיין בספר בן הא הא

lacking. Only once they had each reached the ultimate possible *madregah* of their own *middah*, were they reunited.

Had they been able to unite at a lower *madregah*, each one would never have been forced to reach the highest possible *madregah* of their own *middah*. Only by being forcibly separated through *machlokess* and then reunited, were they able to subsequently unite as the foundation of the *benei yisrael*.

Thus, the Medrash Tanchuma (46.6) says

אמר רבי שמעון בר יוחאי, אמר הקדוש ברוך הוא לישראל, היו מכבדין את המצוות, שהן שלוחי ושלוחו של אדם כמותו, אם כבדת אותן כאילו לי כבדתני, ואם בזית אותן כאילו לכבודי בזית. אין לך אדם שכבד את המצות ועשה את התורה כיעקב, שנאמר (בראשית כ"ה, כ"ז) ויעקב איש תם יושב אהלים, ונתייסר בבנו. אמר לו הקב"ה, חייך, אבדת אחד תמצא ג', יוסף, מנשה ואפרים. כיון שבאו בשרו אותו שיוסף חי, שלח יהודה פרוזבטים אצלו, ואת יהודה שלח לפניו, זה שאמר הכתוב המשל ופחד עמו עושה שלום במרומיו (איוב כ"ה, ב'). המשל, זה מיכאל. ופחד, זה גבריאל. מיכאל מן המים וגבריאל מן האש, והן עומדין לפני השכינה ואינן מזיקין זה את זה, הוי אומר עושה שלום במרומיו... יהודה ויוסף, זה ארי וזה שור אתמול מתנגחין זה עם זה, ועכשיו הוא משלחו אצלו, שנאמר: ואת יהודה שלח לפניו הוי, עושה שלום במרומיו

Rabbi Shimon bar Yochai said, "Hashem said to the *benei yisrael*, 'Honour the *mitzvos*, for they are my messengers and the messenger of a person is like himself. If you honour them it is as if you have honoured Me, and if you denigrate them it is as if you have denigrated My honour.'"

There is no-one who honoured the *mitzvos* and who kept the

Torah like Yaakov, as the *passuk* says, "And Yaakov was a wholesome man who dwelt in the tents." And yet he was anguished through his son.

Hashem said to him, "By your life, you lost one and you will find three. Yosef, Menashe and Ephraim."

Once they came to him and announced to him that Yosef was alive, he sent Yehudah as an ambassador to Yosef, as it says, "And he sent Yehudah before him."

This is as the *passuk* says, "Sovereignty and awe are with him, He makes peace in his heights." "Sovereignty," refers to Michael. "And awe," this refers to Gavriel. Michael is made from water and Gavriel is made from fire, yet they stand before the shechinah and do not harm each other. So you see how Hashem makes peace in his heights.

Similarly, Yehudah is compared to a lion and Yosef is compared to an ox, yesterday they were goring each other, and now Yaakov sent Yehudah specifically before him to Yosef. As it says, "And he sent Yehudah before him." So you see how Hashem makes peace in his heights.

Because Yosef excelled in his own *middah* when cut off from his brothers, Yosef's two sons continued exactly in his way. Hence Hashem said, "You lost one and you found three," from which it is evident that the three were identical to the one. Only once Yosef and Yehudah had achieved the highest possible *madregah* in their own *middah*, were they then reunited before the *shechinah*, to form the foundation of *klal yisrael*.

In this way, the *machlokess* between Yosef and his brothers invalidated the chieftains of Esav who were able to conveniently complement each other's strengths without having to excel their own personalities at all.

And it was this division, elevation and subsequent reunification that caused the *benei yisrael* to reach a *madregah* where the sea, representing all indifference, was split before them.

Yosef's survival in the pit

It says in this week's *sedrah* (37:24)

וַיִּקָּחֻהוּ וַיַּשְׁלִכוּ אֹתוֹ הַבֹּרָה וְהַבּוֹר רֵק אֵין בּוֹ מָיִם

And they took him and they threw him into the pit and the pit was empty, it had no water in it.

The Medrash Tanchuma comments on this *passuk*

אמר רב כהנא, דרש רב נתן בר מניומי משמיה דרב תנחום מאי דכתיב (בראשית ל"ז) וְהַבּוֹר רֵק אֵין בּוֹ מָיִם. ממשמע שנאמר וְהַבּוֹר רֵק איני יודע שאין בו מים? אלא מה תלמוד לומר אֵין בּוֹ מָיִם, מים אין בו, אבל נחשים ועקרבים יש בו.

If the *passuk* says, the pit was empty, we know it contained no water. Why does the *passuk* say "It had no water in it"? This teaches you that it contained no water, but it did contain snakes and scorpions.

Thus it was a *nes* that Yosef survived in the pit.

The Medrash Rabbah says (100:8)

וַיָּשָׁב יוֹסֵף מִצְרַיְמָה הוּא וְאֶחָיו וְכָל הָעֹלִים אִתּוֹ לִקְבֹּר אֶת אָבִיו אַחֲרֵי קָבְרוֹ אֶת אָבִיו. וַיִּרְאוּ אֲחֵי יוֹסֵף כִּי מֵת אֲבִיהֶם וַיֹּאמְרוּ לוּ יִשְׂטְמֵנוּ יוֹסֵף וְהָשֵׁב יָשִׁיב לָנוּ אֵת כָּל הָרָעָה אֲשֶׁר גָּמַלְנוּ אֹתוֹ. וגו' רבי יצחק אמר הלך והציץ באותו הבור א"ר תנחומא הוא לא נתכוון אלא לשם שמים והם לא אמרו כן אלא לו ישטמנו יוסף ויצוו לאמר אל יוסף אביך צוה וגו'

"When Yosef and the brothers returned to Mitzrayim, the brothers were afraid that Yosef would hate them and take revenge for selling him. Why did they think this? Rabbi Yitzchak and Rabbi Tanchum explained that when Yosef was returning to Mitzrayim he looked into the pit that the brothers had thrown him into. The brothers thought that he was remembering what they had done to him, however Yosef had looked into the pit in order to make the *berachah* of שעשה לי נס במקום הזה."

- Why did the brothers not understand that Yosef looked into the pit in order to make a *berachah*?

It would seem that we can explain as follows:

The Avudraham says (ספר אבודרהם פרק שמיני ברכת הראיה, השבח והההודאה)

הרואה מקום שנעשו בו נסים לישראל כגון מעברות ים סוף ומעברות הירדן... צריך ליתן שבח והודאה למקום בא"י אמ"ה שעשה נסים לאבותינו במקום הזה...
כתב ה"ר אשר מלוניל הא דמברכין בין אניסא דרבים בין אניסא דיחיד דוקא בנס שהוא יוצא ממנהג העולם או מדרך התולדה כגון מעברות

הים ומעברות הירדן והדומה להם... אבל נס שהוא מנהג העולם ותולדתו כגון שבאו עליו גנבים בלילה ובא לידי סכנה וניצל וכיוצא בזה אינו חייב לברך שעשה לי נס במקום הזה... ובחנוכה לאו משום מעשה דיהודית מברכין שעשה נסים אלא משום פך השמן שהיה חתום בחותמו של כהן גדול ולא היה להדליק אלא יום אחד ונעשה בו נס והדליקו ממנו ח' ימים...

The mishna says, "If someone sees a place where miracles were performed for klal yisrael such as the crossing of the Yam Suf and the crossing of the Yarden, he has to make a *beracha* of שעשה נסים."

Rabbeinu Asher from Lunil says that you only make a *beracha* on a miracle when the miracle went against the laws of nature[13], like the crossing of the Yam Suf and the crossing of the Yarden, and similar occurrences. However for a miracle which occurred within the laws of nature, such as where he was attacked by bandits and he was saved, or he came into some other danger and he was saved, he does not make a *berachah*.

The reason that we make a *beracha* on the miracle of Chanukah is not because of the miracle of Yehudis (in which she managed to kill the Greek governor) but is rather because of the miracle of the jug of oil that was sealed with the seal of the *kohen gadol* which only contained enough oil to burn for one day and a miracle occurred and they lit from it for eight days.

---

[13] עיין שו"ע או"ח ס' רי"ח, סע' ט' ובמ"ב ס"ק ל"ב

Although the Avudraham differentiates between a miracle that occurs within the laws of nature and a miracle that occurs outside of the laws of the nature, it would appear that there is a grey area which is not covered by this differentiation.

For example, the Avudraham says that in a case where someone was saved from bandits, presumably by soldiers or other rescuers, that this not an open miracle, because the events occurred within the boundaries of what we call "nature".

However, what would the *halacha* be if someone was attacked by bandits, and he was then saved by the bandits being hit by lightning?

Should we say that since lighting strikes are a naturally occurring phenomenon, and people are sometimes hit by lightning, therefore this is a *nes* that occurred within the boundaries of "nature".

Or should we say that since there is highly improbable that lightning should attack so fortuitously, that we see the revealed Hand of Hashem, and he should make a *beracha* on the miracle?
It would seem that the *halacha* in this case should depend on the person's level of *bitachon* (trust in Hashem). If the person had concluded that, considering all options, they had come to the end of their life, and then an event occurred which saved them, this is classified as an open miracle on which they can make a *beracha*.

However if a person was in a difficult situation and still trusted that Hashem would save them, and then they were saved, this is not classified as an open miracle on which they can make a *beracha*. Since the person maintained, through their *bitachon*, the possibility of their being saved (despite the fact that they may not have known how this could possibly occur) therefore their being saved is not construed to be an open miracle.

Hence it is possible that the same event could occur to two people, and for one person, who trusted less in Hashem, it would be possible to make the *beracha* on an open miracle, whereas for the other person, who was on a greater level of *bitachon*, it would not be possible to make a *berachah*, since for them it was not exceptional that Hashem should have intervened in such a manner.

Thus, with regards to Yosef and the brothers, it is possible to explain as follows:

The brothers had never been exposed to the dangers of Mitzrayim, and who were therefore on a lower level of *bitachon* than Yosef, who had lived in constant danger. Therefore, for the brothers it was an open miracle that Yosef had survived and become a king in Mitzrayim. According to the brothers, therefore, Yosef could have made a *berachah* on any of the *nissim* that occurred to him in Mitzrayim.

However, for Yosef, who was constantly aware of the helping presence of Hashem it was perfectly reasonable that Hashem should have saved him and made him king.

Therefore, according to the brothers, there was no difference between the miracle of Yosef having been saved in the pit, and the miracle of Yosef having been saved in Mitzrayim. There could therefore be no halachical reason for Yosef to look in the pit (in order to make a *berachah* on the *nes*), because he could have made a *nes* on the miracles he experienced in Mitzrayim. Subsequently they concluded that the reason he looked in the pit was because he was reminiscing and planning revenge.

However Yosef himself, due to his great level of *bitachon*, could not make a *beracha* on being saved and becoming king. He therefore looked into the pit where he had indeed been miraculously saved from snakes and scorpions, so he could make a *berachah*.

Which is why the brothers misunderstood Yosef's intentions in looking into the pit.

The *bitachon* and wisdom of Yosef

The *passuk* says at the beginning of this week's sedrah (41.1)

וַיְהִי מִקֵּץ שְׁנָתַיִם יָמִים וּפַרְעֹה חֹלֵם וְהִנֵּה עֹמֵד עַל הַיְאֹר

And it was at the end of two years, and Pharaoh dreamed that he was standing by the Nile.

The Yalkut Reuvaini comments

> ויהי מקץ שנתים ימים ופרעה חולם והנה עומד על היאור זהו שאמר המשורר טוב לחסות בה' מבטוח באדם אפילו באדם עליון שעל המרכבה ומחמת זה לקה יוסף שבטח ברהבים ושטי כזב

> This is as Dovid *ha'melech* said, "It is better to hope in Hashem than it is to trust in man." When the *passuk* says "man", it refers even to the vision of the supernal Man that Yechezkel saw on the *merkavah*. [Rather one should place one's trust in Hashem without the aid of any imagery at all.] And because of this shortcoming Yosef was punished because he trusted in arrogant people steeped in deceit.

It would appear difficult to understand the Yalkut Reuvaini. Yosef did not place his trust in the image of the Man on the *merkavah*, rather he placed his trust in the butler.

- What proof then is there from the story of Yosef, that one may not place one's trust even in the vision of the *merkavah*? Maybe it is permissible to think of the vision of Yechezkel when placing one's trust in Hashem, but still Yosef erred because he placed his trust in the butler?

The passuk says later in the sedrah (41.33-36)

וְעַתָּה יֵרֶא פַרְעֹה אִישׁ נָבוֹן וְחָכָם וִישִׁיתֵהוּ עַל אֶרֶץ מִצְרָיִם. יַעֲשֶׂה פַרְעֹה וְיַפְקֵד פְּקִדִים עַל הָאָרֶץ וְחִמֵּשׁ אֶת אֶרֶץ מִצְרַיִם בְּשֶׁבַע שְׁנֵי הַשָּׂבָע. וְיִקְבְּצוּ אֶת כָּל אֹכֶל הַשָּׁנִים הַטֹּבֹת הַבָּאֹת הָאֵלֶּה וְיִצְבְּרוּ בָר תַּחַת יַד פַּרְעֹה אֹכֶל בֶּעָרִים וְשָׁמָרוּ. וְהָיָה הָאֹכֶל לְפִקָּדוֹן לָאָרֶץ לְשֶׁבַע שְׁנֵי הָרָעָב אֲשֶׁר תִּהְיֶיןָ בְּאֶרֶץ מִצְרָיִם וְלֹא תִכָּרֵת הָאָרֶץ בָּרָעָב.

And now, let Pharaoh find a discerning and wise man, and set him over the land of Mitzrayim. Let Pharaoh take steps to appoint overseers over the land, and prepare the land of Mitzrayim in the seven years of plenty. Let all the food of these good years that are coming be gathered, and let the grain be collected under Pharaoh's authority as food to be stored in the cities. Let that food be a reserve for the land for the seven years of famine which will come upon the land of Egypt, so that the land may not perish in the famine.

- If Yosef advised Pharoh what to do, why was it necessary for Pharoh to find a wise man, he could simply have found someone to carry out Yosef's instructions?

The *passuk* continues (41.38)

וַיֹּאמֶר פַּרְעֹה אֶל עֲבָדָיו הֲנִמְצָא כָזֶה אִישׁ אֲשֶׁר רוּחַ אֱלֹקִים בּוֹ

And Pharaoh said to his servants, "Could we find another like him, a man in whom is the spirit of G-d?"

- Why difference did it make to Pharoh and his servants that Yosef had *ruach ha'kodesh*?

It would seem that we can explain as follows[14]:

The *passuk* says in Shmuel Alef (1.11)

וַתִּדֹּר נֶדֶר וַתֹּאמַר ה' צְבָאוֹת אִם רָאֹה תִרְאֶה בָּעֳנִי אֲמָתֶךָ וּזְכַרְתַּנִי וְלֹא תִשְׁכַּח אֶת אֲמָתֶךָ וְנָתַתָּה לַאֲמָתְךָ זֶרַע אֲנָשִׁים וּנְתַתִּיו לַה' כָּל יְמֵי חַיָּיו וּמוֹרָה לֹא יַעֲלֶה עַל רֹאשׁוֹ

And she made this vow, "O Lord of Hosts, if You will look upon the suffering of Your maidservant and will remember me and not forget Your maidservant, and if You will grant Your maidservant a male child, I will dedicate him to Hashem for all the days of his life, and no razor shall ever touch his head."

---

[14] עיין בספר דברי שמואל

The gemara in Berachos (31b) comments

> ורבנן אמרי זרע אנשים זרע שמובלע בין אנשים כי אתא רב דימי אמר לא ארוך ולא גוץ ולא קטן ולא אלם ולא צחור ולא גיחור ולא חכם ולא טפש

And the *chachamim* say, "An offspring of men." Channah prayed for an offspring who would be inconspicuous among men, that he would not stand out in any way.

When Rav Dimi came from Eretz Yisrael to Bavel, he said in explanation, "Channah prayed that her son would not be conspicuous among men; neither too tall nor too short; neither too small nor too fat; neither too white nor too red; neither too clever nor too stupid."

Rashi explains

> **ולא חכם**: יותר מדאי שלא יהיה תימה בעיני הבריות ומתוך שנדברין בו שולטת בו עין הרע

Neither too clever: Not excessively clever so that people should not be astonished by him and because they will talk about him the *ayin ha'ra* will gain power over him.

If so, it would appear that Pharoh should have been concerned to say that Yosef was the wisest and most exceptional person that he could find, because that could have caused the *ayin ha'ra* to rule over Yosef and foil his efforts.

However, because Yosef had perfect *bitachon* in Hashem, he did not take the wisdom that had been given to him through *ruach ha'kodesh* for himself, but rather he self-effacingly acknowledged constantly that he merely a purveyor of the wisdom that had been granted to him, hence he was not susceptible to jealousy and *ayin ha'ra*.

The reason that it was necessary for Pharoh to place a wise and understanding man over Mitzrayim was because it was only by the inculcation of this wisdom that had been granted by Hashem, into Mitzrayim, that it would be possible for the Mitzrim collectively, to overcome the prediction of famine in Pharoh's dream. That inculcation could only come through Yosef, who never claimed his wisdom as his own or for himself.

Even when Yosef had requested the butler to remember him, he had only done so as a *tefillah* to Hashem, so that Yosef spoke to the butler as a representative of Hashem's corporeal representation of a possible salvation to him, while he was in jail.

When Yosef did *teshuvah* even on this smallest lack in *bitachon*, he reached a *madregah* on which all human endeavour became transparent to him as a representation of Hashem's aid and *hashgachah pratis*. This enabled the whole of Mitzrayim jointly to overcome the prediction of Pharoh's dream by accepting Hashem's guidance as revealed through the *bitachon* and humility of Yosef.

Yosef and the butler

It says in this week's *sedrah* (41:12)

וְשָׁם אִתָּנוּ נַעַר עִבְרִי עֶבֶד לְשַׂר הַטַּבָּחִים וַנְּסַפֶּר לוֹ וַיִּפְתָּר לָנוּ אֶת חֲלֹמֹתֵינוּ אִישׁ כַּחֲלֹמוֹ פָּתָר

A Hebrew lad was there with us, a servant of the chief executioner; and when we told him our dreams, he interpreted them for us, telling each of us the meaning of his dream.

Rashi comments on this *passuk*:

נער עברי עבד: ארורים הרשעים שאין טובתם שלמה מזכירו בלשון בזיון

Cursed be the *reshaim* for the favours they do are never really complete. He mentions him in disparaging language:

נער: שוטה ואין ראוי לגדולה

A lad, unwise and unfitting for a high position.

עברי: אפילו לשוננו אינו מכיר

A Hebrew, who does not even know our language.

עבד: וכתוב בנמוסי מצרים שאין עבד מולך ולא לובש בגדי שרים

A slave — and it is written in the laws of Egypt that a slave may neither become a ruler nor dress in princely robes.

The Medrash Rabbah (פרשת נשא, י"ד, י"ח) expounds further:

הֲדָא הוּא דִכְתִיב (קהלת ח, ה): שׁוֹמֵר מִצְוָה לֹא יֵדַע דָּבָר רָע, מַהוּ לֹא יֵדַע דָּבָר רָע, שֶׁאוֹתוֹ דָּבָר רָע שֶׁאָמַר שַׂר הַמַּשְׁקִים, כְּמָה דְתֵימָא (בראשית מא, יב): וְשָׁם אִתָּנוּ נַעַר עִבְרִי עֶבֶד לְשַׂר הַטַּבָּחִים וגו', דִּבֵּר כָּאן בְּנָגְעֵת יוֹסֵף שְׁלֹשָׁה דְבָרִים: נַעַר, שֶׁהוּא שׁוֹטֶה, כְּמָה דְתֵימָא (משלי כב, טו): אִוֶּלֶת קְשׁוּרָה בְלֶב נָעַר, עִבְרִי, שׂוֹנֵא, עֶבֶד, שֶׁאֵינוֹ רָאוּי לְמַלְכוּת, אַף עַל פִּי כֵן לֹא יֵדַע יוֹסֵף אוֹתוֹ דָּבָר רָע, כְּלוֹמַר שֶׁלֹּא נָגַע בּוֹ הַדָּבָר, שֶׁמָּלַךְ. (קהלת ח, ה): וְעֵת וּמִשְׁפָּט יֵדַע לֵב חָכָם, זֶה הָיָה יוֹסֵף שֶׁנִּקְרָא חָכָם, כְּמָה דְתֵימָא (בראשית מא, לט): אֵין נָבוֹן וְחָכָם כָּמוֹךָ.

The *passuk* says שׁוֹמֵר מִצְוָה לֹא יֵדַע דָּבָר רָע, "One who keeps a mitzva shall know no evil thing." This refers to Yosef, because he kept the *mitzvos* when he was in Mitzrayim, therefore those evil things that the head butler said about him, had no effect on him. Although the head butler said that Yosef was a fool, this had no effect on him, and he became a wise king.

- In what way would it have been possible for Yosef to be affected by the statement of the head butler?

The *sedrah* continues (41:14):

וַיִּשְׁלַח פַּרְעֹה וַיִּקְרָא אֶת יוֹסֵף וַיְרִיצֻהוּ מִן הַבּוֹר וַיְגַלַּח וַיְחַלֵּף שִׂמְלֹתָיו וַיָּבֹא אֶל פַּרְעֹה

Pharoh sent for Yoseph, and he was rushed from the dungeon. He had his hair cut and changed his clothes, and he appeared before Pharoh.

The Yalkut Reuvaini comments on this *passuk*:

הא דכתיב וישלח פרעה ויקרא את יוסף לקרא ליוסף מב"ל. אלא לפי שהשכינה קרא ליוסף, כתיב הכא ויקרא את יוסף וכתיב התם ויקרא אל משה.

The *passuk* should not say that Pharoh called to Yosef, rather the *passuk* should say that Pharoh sent for Yosef to be called? Rather the *passuk* means that the *shechinah* called Yosef, for we find that here the *passuk* says ויקרא את יוסף, and later the *passuk* says ויקרא אל משה.

- Why was it only possible for Yosef to exit from the dungeon after being called by the *shechinah*?

It would seem that we can explain as follows:

Had Pharoh expected Yosef to have the demeanour of a lowly slave who happened to know how to interpret dreams, then it would have been inappropriate for Yosef to draw himself up to his full stature before Pharoh.

Since Pharoh would have addressed Yosef as a slave, it would have been unexpected and untoward for Yosef to respond back to Pharoh as a freeman and as a nobleman. Had Yosef thus behaved, he would merely have appeared as a slave who was putting on airs, before Pharoh.

For this reason, Yosef was hesitant to come out of the dungeon. Since the שר המשקים had given Pharoh an incorrect and lowly assessment of Yosef, it would now be dangerous for Yosef to stand before with his true royal bearing, because this would be construed to be disrespectful vis-à-vis Pharoh's expectation of him.

Only when Yosef realised that Hashem was calling him to come out of the dungeon, then he knew that no harm would befall him. Yosef solved his dilemma by disclaiming any part that he would have in helping Pharoh (41:16):

וַיַּעַן יוֹסֵף אֶת פַּרְעֹה לֵאמֹר בִּלְעָדָי אֱלֹקִים יַעֲנֶה אֶת שְׁלוֹם פַּרְעֹה

And Yoseph answered Pharoh, saying, "It is not I! Hashem will see to the welfare of Pharoh."

Yosef disclaimed any personal potency he had or that he could apply in helping Pharoh, and he declared that he was simply a messenger of Hashem. Therefore it was irrelevant with what bearing and demeanour Yosef responded to Pharoh, because he was only acting as a messenger of Hashem.

By declaring his בטחון to Pharoh, Yosef evaded the trap that had been laid for him by the שר המשקים and he merited that Pharoh should acknowledge the truth of his words (41:38).

וַיֹּאמֶר פַּרְעֹה אֶל עֲבָדָיו הֲנִמְצָא כָזֶה אִישׁ אֲשֶׁר רוּחַ אֱלֹקִים בּוֹ

And Pharoh said to his courtiers, "Could we find another like him, a man in whom is the spirit of Hashem?"

Interpreting Pharoh's dream

It says in this week's *sedrah* (41:25)

וַיֹּאמֶר יוֹסֵף אֶל פַּרְעֹה חֲלוֹם פַּרְעֹה אֶחָד הוּא אֵת אֲשֶׁר הָאֱלֹקִים עֹשֶׂה הִגִּיד לְפַרְעֹה

And Yosef said to Pharoh, "Both of Pharoh's dreams are one. That which Hashem is doing He has told to Pharoh."

- The word עֹשֶׂה - "doing", is in the present tense. This is seemingly incongruous as the *passuk* should better have said, "That which Hashem will do [in the future] he has told to Pharoh"?

Three *pessukim* later, Yosef repeated (41:28)

הוּא הַדָּבָר אֲשֶׁר דִּבַּרְתִּי אֶל פַּרְעֹה אֲשֶׁר הָאֱלֹקִים עֹשֶׂה הֶרְאָה אֶת פַּרְעֹה

This is the matter which J said to Pharoh, that which Hashem is doing He has shown to Pharoh.

- In the first *passuk*, Yosef said that Hashem has related (הִגִּיד) to Pharoh. In the second *passuk*, Yosef said that Hashem has shown (הֶרְאָה) to Pharoh. Why did Yosef change from הִגִּיד to הֶרְאָה?

Yosef continued to advise Pharoh that the grain from the good years should be stored for the years of famine (41:36)

וְהָיָה הָאֹכֶל לְפִקָּדוֹן לָאָרֶץ לְשֶׁבַע שְׁנֵי הָרָעָב אֲשֶׁר תִּהְיֶיןָ בְּאֶרֶץ מִצְרָיִם וְלֹא תִכָּרֵת הָאָרֶץ בָּרָעָב

And the food will be a deposit for the land for the years of famine which will be in the land of Mitzrayim, and the land will not be exterminated in the famine.

- Why did Yosef offer his advice to Pharoh, seeing as he was only asked to interpret the dream?

The Tzaphnas Pa'aneach explains as follows:

The Medrash Rabbah says (Parshas Va'era)

וַיֹּאמֶר ה' אֶל מֹשֶׁה נְטֵה יָדְךָ עַל הַשָּׁמַיִם, הדא הוא דכתיב (תהלים קל"ה, ו') כל אשר חפץ ה' עשה וגו' אמר דוד אף על פי שגזר הקדוש ברוך הוא (שם קט"ו ט"ז) השמים שמים לה' והארץ נתן לבני אדם

משל למה הדבר דומה למלך שגזר ואמר בני רומי לא ירדו לסוריא ובני

סוריא לא יעלו לרומי, כך כשברא הקדוש ברוך הוא את העולם גזר ואמר השמים שמים לה' והארץ נתן לבני אדם, כשבקש ליתן התורה בטל גזירה ראשונה ואמר התחתונים יעלו לעליונים והעליונים ירדו לתחתונים ואני המתחיל שנאמר (שמות י"ט כ') וירד ה' על הר סיני וכתיב (שם כ"ד א') ואל משה אמר עלה אל ה' הרי כל אשר חפץ ה' עשה בשמים ובארץ וגו'

When Hashem created the world, He said, 'השמים שמים לה והארץ נתן לבני אדם, "Those who are in *shamayim* (the heavens) may not descend to the earth, and those who are on the earth may not rise to *shamayim*." This is comparable to a king who made a decree and said, "The people in Rome may not go down to Syria and the people in Syria may not ascend to Rome."

However when the Torah was given, Hashem annulled that decree, as the *passuk* says, and Hashem descended on to Har Sinai, and to Moshe He said, "Go up to Hashem."

The first direct and open intervention by Hashem that prepared the way to *matan torah* (the giving of the Torah on *Har Sinai*) was Pharoh's dream. Subsequently, just as at Har Sinai, Hashem "came down to the earth" and Moshe "went up to *shamayim*", so too in Pharoh's dream, Hashem brought Pharoh into the realm of *shamayim* and showed him what was happening there.

Since the concept of time is not significant in the realm of Hashem, Pharoh was able to see the years of plenty and the years of famine as they were happening, even though these would only occur 7 and 14 years in the future. That is why the *passuk* uses the present tense (עֹשֶׂה) concerning Pharoh's dream, and not the future tense.

Initially Yosef used the term הִגִּיד because Pharoh thought that Hashem had merely told him a message. However, after Yosef explained that Pharoh had risen to the realm of *shamayim* and had seen first-hand the ebb and flow of sustenance that Hashem would effect, he used the word הֶרְאָה, so that Pharoh should understand that he had actually seen what Hashem was doing in the future, and had not merely been told about it.

Furthermore, since Pharoh had been brought into the realm of *shamayim*, this meant that Pharoh himself had become a part of Hashem's plan. Subsequently Yosef explained that this meant that Pharoh was responsible for storing the flow of plenty that would come from *shamayim* during the first seven years, and for the release of this plenty during the years of famine, to counterbalance the extreme conditions that had been decreed by Hashem.

Since this advice was part of the interpretation of Pharoh's dream, Yosef did not tell Pharoh anything that he had not been asked.

The truth of lashon ha'kodesh

The *passuk* says in this week's sedrah (45.12)

וְהִנֵּה עֵינֵיכֶם רֹאוֹת וְעֵינֵי אָחִי בִנְיָמִין כִּי פִי הַמְדַבֵּר אֲלֵיכֶם

And behold you can see for yourselves, and my brother Benjamin for himself, that it is indeed I who am speaking to you.

Rashi comments on this *passuk*

והנה עיניכם רואות: בכבודי ושאני אחיכם שאני מהול ככם ועוד כי פי המדבר אליכם בלשון הקודש

And behold your eyes see my glory, and that I am your brother because I have a *bris* as you do, and further that it is my mouth that speaks to you in *lashon ha'kodesh*.

According to Rashi, Yosef pointed out that he was speaking *lashon ha'kodesh* as a proof of his own identity.

Additionally, the gemara says in Megillah (16b)

כי פי המדבר אליכם, כפי כן לבי

[The words כי פי can be read כפי – like my mouth. Yosef said to them,] "As my mouth is, so is my heart."

- It would seem difficult to understand this gemara. If the brothers of Yosef felt that Yosef was speaking what was in his heart, then he would not have had to say anything. And if they did not, then saying anything would not have helped?

It would seem that we can explain as follows[15]:

In the last *passuk* in the previous *sedrah* it says (44.17)

וַיֹּאמֶר חָלִילָה לִּי מֵעֲשׂוֹת זֹאת הָאִישׁ אֲשֶׁר נִמְצָא הַגָּבִיעַ בְּיָדוֹ הוּא יִהְיֶה לִּי עָבֶד וְאַתֶּם עֲלוּ לְשָׁלוֹם אֶל אֲבִיכֶם

And he replied, "Far be it from me to act thus! Only the man in whose possession the goblet was found shall be my slave, as for the rest of you, go back in peace to your father."

The Medrash Rabbah comments on this passuk:

ויאמר חלילה לי וגו' רבי הונא בשם רבי אחא נער פורפוריה האיש אשר נמצא הגביע בידו הוא יהיה לי עבד ואתם עלו לשלום אל אביכם אמרין ליה השלום דכוליה נשפה ורוח הקודש צווחת (תהלים קי"ט) שלום רב לאוהבי תורתך

And he said, "Far be it from me to act thus!" Rabbi Huna said in the name of Rabbi Achah, [Yosef said,] "You royal fool. The man in whose hand the goblet was found shall be my slave,

---

[15] עיין בספר דברי יואל

and you may go in peace back to your father."

They said to him, "This is a peace of darkness and gloom."

But the *shechinah* cried out, "[No.] There is abundant peace to those who love Your Torah."

The Zohar (Korach, 176b) explains the reason the Torah brings peace is as follows

רבי יוסי אמר כתיב שלום רב לאוהבי תורתך וגו'. אורייתא הוא שלום דכתיב וכל נתיבותיה שלום

Rabbi Yosi said that there is abundant peace to those who love the Torah is because the Torah itself is peace as it says in the *passuk*, "And all its pathways are peace."

This means that when a person loves the Torah, then they are forced to reconcile all of their divergent thoughts in order to be able to reach a true understanding of the Torah. Since it is only possible to reach a true understanding of the Torah by reconciling all of the different pathways of understanding the Torah, it is necessary for the person who wishes to correctly understand the Torah to also reconcile their own divergent thoughts and thereby attain peace.

Similarly, Yosef hinted to the brothers that they would only be able to reach the truth of the situation in which they found themselves if they were willing to consider the worst possible outcome, which was that they would go in peace to Yaakov and Binyamin would remain behind as a slave in Mitzrayim, since this is exactly what they had done to Yosef. By forcing the brothers to think through the impossibility of the correctness of Yosef's conclusion, Yosef brought the brothers to the realisation of the impossibility of the correctness of their conclusion concerning him.

The only language that encompasses every possible different nuance is *lashon ha'kodesh*, since this is the language that Hashem used to create the world. On the other hand, all other languages describe the world from one particular perspective. That is why when Yosef showed the brothers כפי כן לבי – that his heart was as his mouth and that all of his contradictory actions towards them had had the purpose of educating them towards *teshuvah*, and had not been from malign intent, he spoke in *lashon ha'kodesh*.

The Oneness of Hashem

It says in this week's *sedrah* (46.29)

וַיֶּאְסֹר יוֹסֵף מֶרְכַּבְתּוֹ וַיַּעַל לִקְרַאת יִשְׂרָאֵל אָבִיו גֹּשְׁנָה וַיֵּרָא אֵלָיו וַיִּפֹּל עַל צַוָּארָיו וַיֵּבְךְּ עַל צַוָּארָיו עוֹד

Yoseph ordered his chariot and went to Goshen to meet his father Yisrael; he appeared to him and he embraced him around his neck, and he wept on his neck a good while.

Rashi comments on this *passuk*

ויבך על צואריו עוד: ...אבל יעקב לא נפל על צוארי יוסף ולא נשקו ואמרו רבותינו שהיה קורא את שמע

(Yosef wept on Yaakov's neck,) but Yaakov did not fall on Yosef's neck and did not kiss him. And our teachers said that he was reading *Shema*.

- Why did Yaakov read *Shema* when he met Yosef?

The first *passuk* in *Shema* says (Devarim 6.4)

שְׁמַע יִשְׂרָאֵל ה' אֱלֹקֵינוּ ה' אֶחָד

Hear, oh *benei yisrael*, Hashem is our G-d, Hashem is One.

Rashi comments as follows

ה' אלקינו ה' אחד: ה' שהוא אלקינו עתה ולא אלקי האומות ע"א הוא עתיד להיות ה' אחד שנאמר (צפניה ג') כי אז אהפוך אל עמים שפה ברורה לקרוא כולם בשם ה' ונאמר (זכריה י"ד) ביום ההוא יהיה ה' אחד ושמו אחד

This means, Hashem who is now our G-d and not the G-d of the other peoples of the world, He will in the future be the One (sole) G-d, as it is said, (Tzephaniah 3:9) "For then I will turn to the peoples a pure language that they may all call upon the name of Hashem", and it is further said, (Zechariah 14:9) "On that day shall the Hashem be One (אחד) and His name One."

- Why does Rashi equate the nations using a pure language, with the nations accepting the oneness and the sovereignty of Hashem?

The gemara says in Sotah (36b):

א"ר חייא בר אבא אמר רבי יוחנן בשעה שאמר לו פרעה ליוסף (בראשית מ"א, מ"ד) ובלעדיך לא ירים איש את ידו וגו' אמרו איצטגניני פרעה עבד שלקחו רבו בעשרים כסף תמשילהו עלינו אמר להן גנוני מלכות אני רואה בו אמרו לו א"כ יהא יודע בשבעים לשון בא גבריאל ולימדו שבעים לשון לא הוה קגמר הוסיף לו אות אחת משמו של הקב"ה ולמד שנאמר (תהלים פ"א, ו') עדות ביהוסף שמו בצאתו על ארץ מצרים (שפת לא ידעתי אשמע)

Rabbi Chiyah bar Abba said in the name of Rebbi Yochanan, when Pharoh said to Yosef, 'Without you no-one shall lift his hand..', the astrologers of Pharoh said, 'Are you going to appoint over us a slave whose master bought him for 20 silver coins?'

He replied, 'I see royalty in him.'

They said to him, 'If so, he should know the 70 languages.'

Gavriel came and taught Yosef the 70 languages. Yosef could not understand them, so Gavriel added a letter from Hakadosh Baruch Hu's Name to Yosef's name and then he was able to learn them. As the *passuk* says 'עדות ביהוסף שמו בצאתו על ארץ מצרים' – 'Testimony when he was made Yehosef (with an extra *heh*), when he went out over the land of Mitzraim."

- In what merit was Yosef taught the 70 languages?

It seems that we can explain as follows:

Rabbi Tzadok Ha'Cohen from Lublin says (צדקת הצדיק, פרק מ"ז)

כל הכוחות הנטועות בכל נפש מישראל אין לחשוב שהוא רע גמור ושצריך להיות הפכו, כי אין לך שום מדה וכח שאין בה צד טוב גם כן, רק צריך שישתמש בה כפי רצון הש"י... ולהיפך אמרו ז"ל (שבת סג.) אם ראית תלמיד חכם נוקם ונוטר כנחש חגרהו כו'. ונחש הוא שורש הרע בכעס, ובתלמיד חכם רצו לומר אשר כל מגמותיו רצון הש"י אדרבה הוא טוב מאוד, על דרך שאמרו ז"ל (ברא"ר ט') טוב מאוד זה יצר הרע...

רק ידוע כל אומה הוא כח מיוחד, שבעים אומות ושבעים כוחות בנפש...

Concerning all of the strengths that are embedded in every soul of the *benei yisrael*, you should never think that any of these strengths is intrinsically evil and that really the opposite strength is required. For there is no leaning or strength that does not also have a good aspect to it. Just that the person should use it according to the will of Hashem.

For example, the gemara says (שבת ס"ג ע"א), "If you see a *talmid chacham* who is as vengeful and begrudging as a snake, wrap him tightly around your waist (i.e., keep him close, because you will benefit from his Torah). And when the gemara uses the term *talmid chacham* it refers to one whose sole purpose is to serve Hashem (and therefore serves Hashem by utilising all of his inner strengths, in whatever way is appropriate).

However it is known that every [one of the 70 nations] has one particular strength of the 70 strengths of the soul...

According to Reb Tzadok, when Hashem divided the world into 70 nations and 70 languages, at the time of the דור הפלגה, Hashem also divided the world into the 70 strengths of the soul (the שבעים כחות הנפש). Instead of each person containing within themselves all 70 strengths of the soul, each nation would specialise in one of these 70 strengths.

While each person contained within themselves all of the possible strengths of soul, the possibility for destruction was all the greater, because there was nothing that could stop any individual from achieving all that he desired. To safeguard against this situation, Hashem distributed the strengths of mankind across all the 70 nations, in order that each nation should be limited in what it could either accomplish, or destroy.

On the other hand, someone whose entire purpose is only to serve Hashem, is given access to all of the 70 strengths of the soul. Because this person has the integrity to only use their personal power in the service of Hashem, it is safe for Hashem to entrust them with such ability.

The integrity of Yosef

Yosef was a true and trustworthy guardian of the power with which he was entrused. As Yosef said to his brothers (Bereishis 50, 15 – 21)

וַיִּרְאוּ אֲחֵי יוֹסֵף כִּי מֵת אֲבִיהֶם וַיֹּאמְרוּ לוּ יִשְׂטְמֵנוּ יוֹסֵף וְהָשֵׁב יָשִׁיב לָנוּ אֵת כָּל הָרָעָה אֲשֶׁר גָּמַלְנוּ אֹתוֹ. וַיְצַוּוּ אֶל יוֹסֵף לֵאמֹר אָבִיךָ צִוָּה לִפְנֵי מוֹתוֹ לֵאמֹר. כֹּה תֹאמְרוּ לְיוֹסֵף אָנָּא שָׂא נָא פֶּשַׁע אַחֶיךָ וְחַטָּאתָם כִּי רָעָה גְמָלוּךָ וְעַתָּה שָׂא נָא לְפֶשַׁע עַבְדֵי אֱלֹקֵי אָבִיךָ וַיֵּבְךְּ

יוֹסֵף בְּדַבְּרָם אֵלָיו. וַיֵּלְכוּ גַּם אֶחָיו וַיִּפְּלוּ לְפָנָיו וַיֹּאמְרוּ הִנֶּנּוּ לְךָ לַעֲבָדִים. וַיֹּאמֶר אֲלֵהֶם יוֹסֵף אַל תִּירָאוּ כִּי הֲתַחַת אֱלֹקִים אָנִי. וְאַתֶּם חֲשַׁבְתֶּם עָלַי רָעָה אֱלֹקִים חֲשָׁבָהּ לְטֹבָה לְמַעַן עֲשֹׂה כַּיּוֹם הַזֶּה לְהַחֲיֹת עַם רָב. וְעַתָּה אַל תִּירָאוּ אָנֹכִי אֲכַלְכֵּל אֶתְכֶם וְאֶת טַפְּכֶם וַיְנַחֵם אוֹתָם וַיְדַבֵּר עַל לִבָּם.

When Yoseph's brothers saw that their father was dead, they said, "What if Yoseph still bears a grudge against us and pays us back for all the wrong that we did him!"

So they sent this message to Yoseph, "Before his death your father left this instruction. So shall you say to Yoseph, 'Forgive please, the offense and guilt of your brothers who treated you so harshly.' Therefore, please forgive the offense of the servants of the G-d of your father." And Yoseph wept as they spoke to him.

His brothers went to him, flung themselves before him, and said, "We are prepared to be your slaves".

But Yoseph said to them, "Have no fear! Am I a substitute for Hashem? Although you intended me harm, Hashem intended it for good, so as to bring about the survival of many people. And so, fear not. I will sustain you and your children."

Thus he reassured them, speaking kindly to them.

Yosef did not take any of his powers for his own personal use, but instead attributed all his power to Hashem, and used his power in the service of Hashem.

When Gavriel taught Yosef the 70 languages, he did not just teach him the tongue of the 70 nations. Rather, he endowed Yosef with the 70 strengths of the soul of the 70 nations.

This was because just as (later) Yosef used his imperial power solely in the service of Hashem, so too he had the personal integrity to only use his personal strengths and כחות הנפש in the service of Hashem, and therefore such great strength could be entrusted to him.

Mashiach

Through the personal עבודת ה' of a *talmid chacham*, wherein he combines and unifies all of the 70 strengths of the nations in the service of Hashem, the *talmid chacham* prepares for that day on which the nations themselves will unite all of their abilities in the service of Hashem. The clear tongue of serving Hashem to which Rashi refers, is that clear tongue that will resonate with all of the 70 strengths of the soul, reunited in the service of Hashem.

When Yaakov met Yosef, he saw that Yosef had become the archetype of the *talmid chacham* who, through his Torah learning, combines all of the 70 strengths of the soul in the service of Hashem.

Therefore Yaakov read Shema, as a portend of that day in which the whole world will reunite, with a clear tongue, in serving Hashem.

Vayechi

The eternal blessing

The *passuk* says in this week's sedrah (48.15-20)

וַיְבָרֲכֵם בַּיּוֹם הַהוּא לֵאמוֹר בְּךָ יְבָרֵךְ יִשְׂרָאֵל לֵאמֹר יְשִׂמְךָ אֱלֹקִים כְּאֶפְרַיִם וְכִמְנַשֶּׁה וַיָּשֶׂם אֶת אֶפְרַיִם לִפְנֵי מְנַשֶּׁה.

And he blessed them on that day, saying, "Through you shall the benei yisrael give blessings and say, "May Hashem make you like Ephraim and Menasheh." And he placed Ephraim before Menasheh.

- The *passuk* says וַיְבָרֲכֵם בַּיּוֹם הַהוּא לֵאמוֹר, "And he blessed them on that day, saying." Apparently the *passuk* could simply have said וַיְבָרֲכֵם לֵאמוֹר - "And he blessed them saying." What do the words בַּיּוֹם הַהוּא – "on that day", add to the meaning of the *passuk*?

- Why is the first לֵאמוֹר spelt with a full spelling, with a *vav*, and the second לֵאמֹר spelt with a truncated spelling, without a *vav*?

- Apparently the *passuk* should say בָּכֶם יְבָרֵךְ יִשְׂרָאֵל – "Through you (plural) shall the *benei yisrael* give blessings," since Yaakov was giving a *beracha* to both Ephraim and Menashe?

The Divrei Shmuel explains as follows:

The Zohar says (זהר חלק א' רל"ג א')

פתח רבי יהודה ואמר, ויברכם ביום ההוא לאמור בך יברך ישראל וגו', ויברכם ביום ההוא, מאי ביום ההוא, דהא סגי דקאמר ויברכם. ותו, כל לאמר כתיב חסר, והכא לאמר בוי"ו כתיב, מאי שנא. אלא רזא איהו, ויברכם ביום ההוא, מאי ביום ההוא, רזא דדרגא דאתמנא על ברכאן לעילא.

Rabbi Yehudah explained as follows: The *passuk* says, "And he blessed them on that day saying, 'Through you shall the *benei yisrael* give blessings.'" Why does it say, "On that day", it could just have said, "And he blessed them"? And furthermore, whenever it says לאמר it is written without a *vav*, but here the word לאמור is written with a *vav*, why is this?

Rather this alludes to a secret, the *passuk* means that he blessed them with the blessing of בַּיּוֹם הַהוּא. [According to this explanation, וַיְבָרֲכֵם בַּיּוֹם הַהוּא does not mean that he blessed them on that day, rather it means that he blessed them with the *berachah* of "on that day".]

And what is the *berachah* of בַּיּוֹם הַהוּא – "on that day"? This is the secret level that is appointed over all *berachos*.

In order to explain the Zohar, the *sefer* Divrei Shmuel quotes the Bach in Tur Orach Chaim (292). The Tur (ibid.) comes to explain why it is that at Shabbos minchah we say the passuk (Tehillim 69.14)

וַאֲנִי תְפִלָּתִי לְךָ ה' עֵת רָצוֹן אֱלֹקִים בְּרָב חַסְדֶּךָ עֲנֵנִי בֶּאֱמֶת יִשְׁעֶךָ

As for me, may my prayer come before You Hashem at a favourable time. Hashem, in Your abundant kindness, answer me with Your trustworthy salvation.

The Tur says

סדר מנחה אומר שליח ציבור אשרי ובא לציון וקדיש ואומר פסוק ואני תפלתי לך ה' עת רצון על פי המדרש כי ישיחו בי ישבי שער ונגינות שותי שכר וכתיב בתריה וַאֲנִי תְפִלָּתִי לְךָ יְהֹוָה עֵת רָצוֹן וגו' אמר דוד לפני הקב"ה רבש"ע אע"פ ששתינו ואני תפלתי לך ה'

At mincha on Shabbos the shliach tzibbur says Ashrei, Uva le'tziyon and kaddish. And then he says the passuk of וְאֲנִי תפלתי לך ה' עת רצון. The reason for this is that the medrash says as follows:

The *passuk* says in Tehillim (69.14)

יָשִׂיחוּ בִי יֹשְׁבֵי שָׁעַר וּנְגִינוֹת שׁוֹתֵי שֵׁכָר

Those who sit in the gate talk about me, I am the taunt of drunkards.

And the subsequent passuk says

וַאֲנִי תְפִלָּתִי לְךָ ה' עֵת רָצוֹן

As for me, may my prayer come to You, Hashem, at a favourable moment.

[Dovid contrasted the behaviour of the idlers and drunkards with the behaviour of the Jewish people.] Dovid said, "Hashem! Even though we eat and drink at lunch time on Shabbos, still we come before You to daven at minchah, therefore accept our tefillos with good will."

This means to say that Shabbos *minchah* is a time of favour because by davening *mincha* on Shabbos after having a large *seudah*, we differentiate ourselves from people who eat and drink and then forget about Hashem.

However, according to this explanation, it would seem that we should also say וַאֲנִי תְפִלָּתִי at *minchah* time on Yom Tov, since on Yom Tov we also have a large *seudah* and then go to *minchah*. The Beis Yosef explains that the reason we only say וַאֲנִי תְפִלָּתִי on Shabbos and not on Yom Tov is because on Shabbos *minchah* we have *krias ha'torah*. The fact that we have *krias ha'torah* combined with the fact that we come to *shul* after a large *seudah* make this a time of good will from Hashem, and therefore we say the *passuk* of וַאֲנִי תְפִלָּתִי.

The Bach asks why these two factors combine together. What is the combination of *krias ha'torah* together with the fact that we come to *shul* after a *seudah*, that allows each of these factors to strengthen each other and make this an עֵת רָצוֹן - a time of good will from Hashem?

The Bach explains as follows:

כתב בית יוסף בשם שבולי הלקט דהא דלא נהגינן לאמרו ביום טוב מפני שתיקן עזרא שיהו קורין בתורה בשבת במנחה ולא תיקן כן ביום טוב ע"כ. ונראה דטעם דכיון שקורין בתורה נופל הלשון לומר אז עת רצון כמ"ש רז"ל בספרי ומביאו רש"י ז"ל בסדר עקב דביה"כ כשכלים מ' יום האחרונים נתרצה הקב"ה בשמחה ואמר למשה סלחתי כדבריך לכך הוקבע למחילה ולסליחה ומנין שנתרצה ברצון שלם וכו' מה הראשונים ברצון אף אחרונים ברצון.

השתא ניחא דאמר ישיחו בי יושבי שער דהנכרים היו שותין ומשכרין ופוחזין ומשיחין בי ומלעיגין עלי על שאנו היו שומרים את השבתות כדאיתא בפתיחתא דאיכה רבה ר' אבא פתח ישיחו בי יושבי שער אבל ואני תפלתי לך ה' בשבתות שהוא עת רצון כיון שאנו קורין בתורה שהוריד משה לישראל בו ביום שנתרצה לישראל

The Beis Yosef writes in the name of the Shibolei Ha'leket that that which we do not say ואני תפילתי on Yom Tov is because Ezra instituted that they should read in the Torah on Shabbos at *minchah* time and he did not institute so on Yom Tov.

And it would appear that the reason that it is an עת רצון when we read the Torah is because on Yom Kippur when Moshe's final stay on Har Sinai was completed Hashem was appeased with joy and He said to Moshe סלֹחתי כדבריך, and therefore Yom Kippur was fixed as a day of forgiveness and atonement. And how do we know that Hashem was appeased with complete good will, and that it was an עת רצון, because we learn that just as the first set of 40 days were an עת רצון so too were the last set of 40 days an עת רצון.

And now we can understand [the combination of these two reasons], because the previous *passuk* says, "Those who sit in the gate talk about me," meaning that the non-Jews would drink and get drunk and talk about me and jeer about me because we kept Shabbos, as it says in the introduction to the medrash on Eichah, "Rabbi Abba gave the following introduction. 'Those who sit in the gate talk about me, but as for me, let my *tefillah* come before You at a time of good will.'" Which means to say, "Let my *tefillah* come before you on Shabbos, which is a time of good will, since we read the Torah that Moshe brought down to the *benei yisrael* on the day that Hashem was reconciled to the *benei yisrael*."

It would appear that the intention of the Bach is that since we keep Shabbos despite the taunts of the non-Jews, we strengthen our connection to the passage of time as defined by the Torah. In other words, we enter into the sanctity of the Torah's notion of the passage of time. Thus, once we are in this state, when we do *krias ha'torah*, we are able to make a connection to the Yom Kippur in the *midbar* on which Hashem forgave the *benei yisrael* joyously and with goodwill, even although according to mundane notions it would seem we are separated from that event by a vast and unbridgeable gulf of time.

The Divrei Shmuel says that we can understand the Zohar in a similar vein. When the Zohar says that Yaakov gave Ephraim and Menashe the berachah of בַּיּוֹם הַהוּא, the Zohar means to say that Zohar means that Yaakov blessed Ephraim and Menashe with such grace and goodwill that for all generations, when we want the time at which we bless children to be a time of grace and goodwill, we reconnect to the day on which Yaakov gave a *berachah* to Ephraim and to Menashe.

Subsequently, the *passuk* reads as follows. "And Yaakov blessed Ephraim and Menashe with the essential precursor to all *berachos*, which is grace and goodwill. [This level of goodwill was so great that that day itself became a reference point to which the *benei yisrael* would always refer and connect to, when they would want the time at which they would bless their own children to be a time of grace and goodwill.]"

According to this we can understand that the reason that the first לֵאמוֹר is spelt with a full spelling, with a *vav*, and the second לֵאמֹר is spelt with a truncated spelling, without a *vav*, is because the first לֵאמוֹר of Yaakov, was a "saying" that would cause other "sayings" of *berachah*, for all generations, when parents give a *berachah* to their children.

And the reason that the *passuk* says בְּךָ יְבָרֵךְ יִשְׂרָאֵל, in the singular, and not בָּכֶם יְבָרֵךְ יִשְׂרָאֵל, in the plural, is because despite the fact that Yaakov gave precedence to Ephraim, the younger, over Menashe, the older, because of his *berachah* of goodwill, they were still as one and there entered no discord or argument between them.

Ephraim's *berachah*

It says in this week's *sedrah* (48.13 - 18):

וַיִּקַּח יוֹסֵף אֶת שְׁנֵיהֶם אֶת אֶפְרַיִם בִּימִינוֹ מִשְּׂמֹאל יִשְׂרָאֵל וְאֶת מְנַשֶּׁה בִשְׂמֹאלוֹ מִימִין יִשְׂרָאֵל וַיַּגֵּשׁ אֵלָיו. וַיִּשְׁלַח יִשְׂרָאֵל אֶת יְמִינוֹ וַיָּשֶׁת עַל רֹאשׁ אֶפְרַיִם וְהוּא הַצָּעִיר וְאֶת שְׂמֹאלוֹ עַל רֹאשׁ מְנַשֶּׁה שִׂכֵּל אֶת יָדָיו כִּי מְנַשֶּׁה הַבְּכוֹר. ... וַיַּרְא יוֹסֵף כִּי יָשִׁית אָבִיו יַד יְמִינוֹ עַל רֹאשׁ אֶפְרַיִם וַיֵּרַע בְּעֵינָיו וַיִּתְמֹךְ יַד אָבִיו לְהָסִיר אֹתָהּ מֵעַל רֹאשׁ אֶפְרַיִם עַל רֹאשׁ מְנַשֶּׁה. וַיֹּאמֶר יוֹסֵף אֶל אָבִיו לֹא כֵן אָבִי כִּי זֶה הַבְּכֹר שִׂים יְמִינְךָ עַל רֹאשׁוֹ.

Yosef took both his sons, Ephraim to his right, to the left of Yisroel, and Menashe in his left, to the right of Yisroel, and he drew close to him.

And Yisroel (another name for Yaakov) stretched out his right hand and he placed it on the head of Ephraim, although he was the younger one, and he placed his left hand on the head of Menashe. He did intelligently with his hands, because Menashe was the first-born...

And Yosef saw that his father had placed his right hand on the head of Ephraim and it was bad in his eyes and he supported the hand of his father to remove it from the head of Ephraim onto the head of Menashe.

And Yosef said to his father, "This is not correct, my father, because this one is the first-born, place your right hand on his head."

- Why did Yaakov cross his hands, why did he not just tell Menashe and Ephraim to change places?

Yaakov answered Yosef that he had changed round his hands because Ephraim would become greater than Menashe (48:19)

וַיְמָאֵן אָבִיו וַיֹּאמֶר יָדַעְתִּי בְנִי יָדַעְתִּי גַּם הוּא יִהְיֶה לְּעָם וְגַם הוּא יִגְדָּל וְאוּלָם אָחִיו הַקָּטֹן יִגְדַּל מִמֶּנּוּ וְזַרְעוֹ יִהְיֶה מְלֹא הַגּוֹיִם

And his father refused, and he said, "I know my son, I know, Menashe will also become a people and he will also become great. However, his younger brother will become greater than him and his descendants will become the fullness of nations."

Rashi comments:

ואולם אחיו הקטן יגדל ממנו: שעתיד יהושע לצאת ממנו שינחיל את הארץ וילמד תורה לישראל

Yehoshua will come from Ephraim, who will bequeath Eretz Yisrael to the *benei yisrael* and who will teach them Torah.

Since Ephraim's descendants included Yehoshua, Ephraim deserved to receive Yaakov's *berachah* in a more significant manner than Menashe.

Another greatness of Yehoshua was demonstrated in the war against Amalek:

It says in Beshalach (Shemos 17.9)

וַיֹּאמֶר מֹשֶׁה אֶל יְהוֹשֻׁעַ בְּחַר לָנוּ אֲנָשִׁים וְצֵא הִלָּחֵם בַּעֲמָלֵק מָחָר אָנֹכִי נִצָּב עַל רֹאשׁ הַגִּבְעָה וּמַטֵּה הָאֱלֹקִים בְּיָדִי

And Moshe said to Yehoshua, choose for us men and go and fight with Amalek. Tomorrow I will stand on the top of the hill with the staff of Hashem in my hand.

The Ramban explains:

ויתכן שפחד משה פן יתגבר בחרבו מפני היותו עם נוחל החרב מברכת הזקן שאמר לו ועל חרבך תחיה (בראשית כ"ז מ') כי המלחמה מן המשפחה הזאת היא הראשונה והאחרונה לישראל כי עמלק מזרע עשו (שם ל"ו י"ב) וממנו באה אלינו המלחמה בראשית הגוים ומזרעו של עשו היה לנו הגלות והחרבן האחרון כאשר יאמרו רבותינו (ע"ז ב') שאנחנו היום בגלות אדום וכאשר ינוצח הוא ויחלש הוא ועמים רבים אשר אתו ממנה נושע לעולם כאשר אמר (עובדיה א' כ"א) ועלו מושיעים בהר ציון לשפוט את הר עשו והיתה לה' המלוכה, והנה כל אשר עשו משה ויהושע עמהם בראשונה יעשו אליהו ומשיח בן יוסף עם זרעם על כן התאמץ משה בדבר

And it is possible that Moshe was afraid that Amalek would overpower the *benei yisrael* with his sword, because he is a people that inherits the sword according to the *beracha* of Yitzchak, who said to him, "By your sword you shall live."

For war from this family is the first and the last that the *benei yisrael* will experience. For Amalek is a descendant of Esav, and from him came the first war of the nations against the *benei yisrael*, and from the descendants of Esav came the destruction of the second *beis hamikdash*...

And when he is defeated, together with those nations that gather to him, the *benei yisrael* will be saved forever... And just as Moshe and Yehoshua began the fight against Amalek, so too will Eliyahu and Mashiach ben Yosef (the *mashiach* who is descended from Ephraim) complete the fight in which Amalek will be eradicated. Therefore Moshe exerted himself to the utmost in the matter.

According to the Ramban, victory in the fight against Amalek can only be achieved by descendants of Ephraim. Yehoshua began the fight against Amalek and another descendant of Ephraim, Mashiach ben Yosef, will complete the victory.

Yaakov saw that Ephraim's descendant Yehoshua, would teach Torah to the *benei yisrael*, bequeath *Eretz Yisrael* to them and begin the war against Amalek.

- What is the common denominator of these strengths?

It would seem that we can explain as follows[16]:

Yaakov's thigh was dislocated when he fought with Esav's *malach*.

The Benei Yisaschar (בני יששכר מאמרי חודש כסלו טבת מאמר ב' - אור תורה, אות ל"ז) explains the significance of this event:

ותדע מה שאמרו רז"ל בזהר (ח"ג רמ"ג, א', הובא לעיל אות כ"ג) שהס"מ שנגע בכף ירך יעקב, היינו שנגע בתמכין דאורייתא

And you should know that that which *chazal* said in the Zohar that the Satan damaged Yaakov's thigh, means to say that the Satan damaged the supporters of the Torah.

Esav's *malach* could not attack Yaakov directly, because he was a *talmid chacham*. However, he was able to attack the support of Torah learning, so that it would become challenging and impractical to live a life of Torah learning. Thereby, Esav's *malach* sought to seize *olam ha'zeh* for his own nefarious purposes.

Yosef is the nemesis of Esav[17]. This is because Yosef has the ability to channel the wealth of *olam ha'zeh* for purposes of *kedushah*.

---

[16] See Pachad Yitzchak, Purim, 28

[17] בבא בתרא, קכ"ג ע"ב, בעא מיניה ר' חלבו מר' שמואל בר נחמני כתיב (בראשית ל', כ"ה) ויהי כאשר ילדה רחל את יוסף וגו' מאי שנא כי אתיליד יוסף אמר ליה ראה יעקב אבינו שאין זרעו של עשו נמסר אלא ביד זרעו של יוסף שנאמר (עובדיה א', י"ח) והיה בית יעקב אש ובית יוסף להבה ובית עשו לקש וגו'

Ephraim and his descendants promulgated this strength of Yosef, this means to say that through their great *kedushah*, Ephraim's descendants are able to rule *olam ha'zeh* and to channel the plenty of *olam ha'zeh* for the purposes of *avodas Hashem*.

That is why Yehoshua, a leader descended from Ephraim was able to:

- Fight Amalek, who oppose the *benei yisrael* on the grounds that the *benei yisrael* channel the goodness of *olam ha'zeh* for the purposes of *avodas Hashem*.

- Teach the Torah, which illustrates how to combine *avodas Hashem* with all aspects of *olam ha'zeh*, to the *benei yisrael*.

- Bequeath Eretz Yisrael, which is the pre-eminent enabler of *avodas Hashem*, to the *benei yisrael*.

Since Ephraim was the main spiritual heir of Yosef, it was appropriate for Yaakov to give preference to Ephraim, in the *berachah* that he gave to Yosef's children[18].

---

[18] The Pachad Yitzchak (Purim, 28) points out that Yaakov only put his right hand on Ephraim's head, but he did not ask Ephraim to stand on Yaakov's right hand side (so that Yaakov would not have had to cross his hands).

He explains that as long as we are in *galus*, Yaakov's limp (meaning, his inability to fully channel the wherewithal of *olam ha'zeh* to purposes of *kedushah*) is not fully healed.

Ephraim fights with his hands, with which he performs *mitzvos*, to wrest *olam ha'zeh* bit-by-bit (*mitzvah* by *mitzvah*) from Esav. But Ephraim will only stand on the right, which signifies the final healing of Yaakov's limp, with the coming of *mashiach*.

Shemos

Redemption for all generations

The *passuk* says in this week's *sedrah* (2.12)

וַיִּפֶן כֹּה וָכֹה וַיַּרְא כִּי אֵין אִישׁ וַיַּךְ אֶת הַמִּצְרִי וַיִּטְמְנֵהוּ בַּחוֹל

And he turned this way and that and he saw that no one was about, and he struck down the Egyptian and he hid him in the sand.

The medrash comments

> רבי יהודה אומר כי אין איש שיקנה להקדוש ברוך הוא ויהרגנו רבי נחמיה אומר ראה שאין מי שיזכיר עליו את השם ויהרגנו ורבנן אמרי ראה שאין תוחלת של צדיקים עומדות הימנו ולא מזרעו עד סוף כל הדורות כיון שראה משה כך נמלך במלאכים ואמר להם חיב זה הריגה אמרו לו הן

Rabbi Yehudah says, "He saw that there was no one else to avenge the honour of Hashem's name, so he killed him."

Rabbi Nechemiah says, "He saw that there was no one else to invoke the explicit name of Hashem on him, so he killed him."

The *chachamim* say, "He saw that there was no hope that any *tzadikim* would arise from him or his descendants until the end of all generations. Once Moshe saw that this was so he consulted the *malachim* (that constantly surrounded him) and he asked, 'Has this one incurred the death penalty?' They replied, 'Yes.'

- What difference would it have made if the Mitzri was to have any descendants who were *tzadikim*, if he was indeed *chayav misah* then apparently he should have been killed regardless of his descendants?

- Why did Moshe have to ask the *malachim* if the *Mitzri* was *chayav misah*?

Later in the sedrah, it says (3.10)

וְעַתָּה לְכָה וְאֶשְׁלָחֲךָ אֶל פַּרְעֹה וְהוֹצֵא אֶת עַמִּי בְנֵי יִשְׂרָאֵל מִמִּצְרָיִם

And now come and J will send you to Pharoh, and you shall free My people, the benei yisrael, from Egypt.

The Pirkei de'Rebbi Eliezer (40) comments

אמר לו לך ואשלחך אל פרעה אמר לפניו רבון כל העולמים שלח נא ביד תשלח רצה לומר אותו ביד האיש שאתה עתיד לשלוח אמר לו לא אמרתי לך ואשלחך אל ישראל אלא לך ואשלחך אל פרעה ולאותו האיש שאתה אומר אני שולח לעתיד לבא אל ישראל שנאמר הנה אנכי שולח לכם את אליהו הנביא וכו' והשיב לב אבות על בנים ולב בנים על אבותם

Moshe said to Hashem, "Master of the Universe, 'Send please in the hand of he whom you will send,'" meaning, in the hand of that man whom you will send at the end of days, Eliyahu *ha'navi*.

Hashem said to him, "Did I not tell you that I would send you to the *benei yisrael*. Rather go and I will send you to Pharoh, and concerning that man whom you refer to, I will send him in the future to the *benei yisrael*." As the *passuk* says, "Behold I will send you Eliyahu *ha'navi*, and he will return the hearts of the fathers to the sons and the hearts of the sons to the fathers."

- Why was Moshe's appointment to bring the *benei yisrael* out of Mitzrayim, a portend for Eliyahu *ha'navi* being sent to herald *mashiach*?

It would seem that we can explain as follows:

The gemara says in Shabbos (30b)

דיתיב רבן גמליאל וקא דריש עתידה אשה שתלד בכל יום שנאמר (ירמיהו ל"א, ח') הרה ויולדת יחדיו ליגלג עליו אותו תלמיד אמר אין כל חדש תחת השמש א"ל בא ואראך דוגמתן בעוה"ז נפק אחוי ליה תרנגולת ותו יתיב רבן גמליאל וקא דריש עתידים אילנות שמוציאין פירות בכל יום שנאמר (יחזקאל י"ז, כ"ג) ונשא ענף ועשה פרי מה ענף בכל יום אף פרי בכל יום ליגלג עליו אותו תלמיד אמר והכתיב אין כל חדש תחת השמש א"ל בא ואראך דוגמתם בעולם הזה נפק אחוי ליה צלף ותו יתיב רבן גמליאל וקא דריש עתידה ארץ ישראל שתוציא גלוסקאות וכלי מילת שנאמר (תהלים ע"ב, ט"ז) יהי פסת בר בארץ ליגלג עליו אותו תלמיד ואמר אין כל חדש תחת השמש אמר ליה בא ואראך דוגמתן בעולם הזה נפק אחוי ליה כמיהין ופטריות ואכלי מילת נברא בר קורא

Rabban Gamliel was sitting and he expounded a *passuk*: In the future, in the World-to-Come, a woman will give birth every day... A certain student scoffed at him and said: That cannot be, as it has already been stated: "There is nothing new under the sun" (Koheles 1:9). Rabban Gamliel said to him: Come and I will show you an example of this in this world. He took him outside and showed him a chicken that lays eggs every day.

And furthermore: Rabban Gamliel sat and he expounded a *passuk*: In the future, in the World-to-Come, trees will produce fruits every day... A certain student scoffed at him and said: Isn't it written: There is nothing new under the sun? He said to him: Come and I will show you an example of this in this world. He went outside and showed him a caper bush, part of which is edible during each season of the year.

And furthermore: Rabban Gamliel sat and he expounded a passuk: In the future, the World-to-Come, Eretz Yisrael will produce cakes and fine wool garments that will grow in the ground... A certain student scoffed at him and said: There is nothing new under the sun. He said to him: Come and I will show you an example in this world. He went outside and showed him truffles and mushrooms, which emerge from the earth over the course of a single night and are shaped like a loaf of bread. And with regard to wool garments, he showed him the covering of a heart of palm, a young palm branch, which is wrapped in a thin net-like covering.

We see from the gemara that the key to all future *geulah* must already exist in *olam ha'zeh*, because of the principle that אין כל חדש תחת השמש. We also know that the *geulah* from *Mitzrayim* was a portend for all future *geulah*, which is why, for example, the gemara says (Rosh Hashanah 11b)

ר' יהושע אומר בניסן נגאלו בניסן עתידין ליגאל מנלן אמר קרא (שמות י"ב, מ"ב) ליל שמורים ליל המשומר ובא מששת ימי בראשית

Rabbi Yehoshua says: In Nissan our forefathers were redeemed from Egypt and in Nissan the Jewish people will be redeemed. From where do we derive that the final *geulah* will be in Nissan? The *passuk* says: "It is a night of watching for Hashem for bringing them out from the land of Egypt; this is Hashem's night of watching, for all the *benei yisrael* throughout their generations" (Shemos 12:42). This teaches that the night of Pesach is a night that has been set aside for the purpose of geulah, from the six days of creation.

If so, it must be that the kernel of all future *geulah* was brought into *olam ha'zeh* when the *benei yisrael* were redeemed from *Mitzrayim*. Since all future *geulah* was brought into *olam ha'zeh* through Moshe, it was incumbent on him to ensure that all of the events leading up to the *geulah* would be just, as perceived by all future generations.

Therefore, if the *Mitzri* would ever have had any descendants who were *tzadikim* it would not have been appropriate for Moshe to kill him, and in the end, only the *malachim* could determine if this was an entirely just decision from the perspective of all generations.

Just as all future *geulah* was included in the *geulah* from Mitzrayim, so too was the task of all future leaders of the *benei yisrael*, up to and including Eliyahu *ha'navi*, contained in the responsibility of Moshe to bring the *benei yisrael* out of Mitzrayim. Therefore, included in Moshe's appointment to bring the *benei yisrael* out of Mitzrayim, was Hashem's promise that Eliyahu *ha'navi* would herald the coming of *mashiach*.

Va'era

The power of Hashem

The passuk says at the beginning of this week's sedrah (6.2)

וַיְדַבֵּר אֱלֹקִים אֶל מֹשֶׁה וַיֹּאמֶר אֵלָיו אֲנִי ה'

And Hashem spoke to Moshe and he said to him, "I am Hashem."

Initially the passuk uses the name אֱלֹקִים, which denotes the *middas ha'din* (the attribute of strict judgement), subsequently the *passuk* uses the four-letter name of Hashem, which denotes the *middas ha'rachamim* (the attribute of mercy).

Rashi explains as follows

וידבר אלקים אל משה: דיבר איתו משפט, על שהקשה לדבר ולומר למה הרעותה לעם הזה

And *Elokim* spoke to Moshe: He spoke with judgement to him, because he spoke harshly and said, "Why have you done ill to this people."

ויאמר אליו אני ה': נאמן לשלם שכר טוב למתהלכים לפני, ולא לחינם שלחתיך, כי אם לקיים דברי שדיברתי לאבות הראשונים.

And He said to him, "I am Hashem.": Trustworthy to pay goodly reward for those that walk before Me. And it is not for naught that I have sent you, but it is rather to fulfill My word that I spoke to the forefathers.

- How was the combination of the name of *Elokim* and the name of Hashem, an answer to Moshe's questioning of Hashem's ways?

It would seem that we can explain as follows:

The Shulchan Aruch (Orach Chaim, 5.1) says

יכוין בברכות פירוש המלות. כשיזכיר השם, יכוין פירוש קריאתו באדנות שהוא אדון הכל, ויכוין בכתיבתו ביו"ד ה"א שהיה והוה ויהיה. ובהזכירו אלקים, יכוין שהוא תקיף, בעל היכולת ובעל הכחות כֻּלם.

When a person says a *beracha* he should be aware of the translation of the words. When he says the name of Hashem, he should have the intention, regarding the way that the name of Hashem is read, that He is the master of all. And he should have the intention, regarding the way that the name of Hashem is written, that He was, is and will be. And when he says *Elokim*, he should have intention that He is mighty, the owner of all wherewithal and the owner of all powers.

In other words, the name of *Elokim* is the name of Hashem that reveals that it is only Hashem who gives power to all things that claim to have their own power.

Thus, when Hashem sought to harden Pharoh's heart in order to be able to apply the attribute of strict justice to him (which is signified by the name *Elokim*), He did so in order to break Pharoh's claim to be autonomously powerful, and to reveal that all of Pharoh's powers were only granted to him by Hashem. Only when the illusory façade of Pharoh's divine monarchy was destroyed, would the *benei yisrael* be entirely freed of Pharoh's claim over them.

On the other hand, the four-letter name of Hashem signifies that Hashem was, is and will be. This means to say that the four-letter name of Hashem represents Hashem's unfolding plan for the world and for the *benei yisrael*.

This understanding allows us to translate the passuk as follows:

וַיְדַבֵּר אֱלֹקִים אֶל מֹשֶׁה וַיֹּאמֶר אֵלָיו אֲנִי ה'

Hashem said to Moshe, "In order for the *benei yisrael* to be entirely freed of the influence of Pharoh, it is not sufficient that they are merely allowed to leave *Mitzrayim*, for if this was to occur then they may leave with the impression that Pharoh is indeed a divine king. The reason that I will harden Pharoh's heart is so that the *benei yisrael* will come to recognise My name of *Elokim*, meaning that they will understand that Pharoh only ever had any power because this was granted to him by Me.

Once the *benei yisrael* achieve this understanding, they will be able to carry this understanding of the way My power is expressed in the world, throughout the unfolding of My plan for the world, so that they themselves will be able to wield the power that they saw wielded by Pharoh, but remain uncorrupted by the abilities granted to them."

Moshe thought that he had been sent simply to free the *benei yisrael* from the grasp of Pharoh, in which case as long as Pharoh agreed to let the *benei yisrael* go, he would have fulfilled his mission. Hashem told Moshe that actually the purpose of the *benei yisrael* going free from *Mitzrayim* was so that they would be able to simultaneously represent the name of *Elokim* and of Hashem. In other words, that they would be able to be the purveyors of Hashem's might in *olam hazeh*, but in a kind, compassionate and self-effacing manner, unlike Pharoh who took the power that had been granted to him for himself.

Such a redemption could only be affected by the hardening of Pharoh's heart and the subsequent miracles that would reveal Hashem's ownership of all power and that would teach the *benei yisrael* to use the power granted to them, to sanctify Hashem's name in the world.

The plague of pestilence

The *passuk* in this week's *sedrah* (9:5) says

וַיָּשֶׂם ה' מוֹעֵד לֵאמֹר מָחָר יַעֲשֶׂה ה' הַדָּבָר הַזֶּה בָּאָרֶץ

And Hashem set an appointed time saying, "Tomorrow Hashem will bring this pestilence to the land."

- Why does the Torah use the word מוֹעֵד (an appointed time) with regards to the time set for the plague of pestilence, but not with regards to any of the other plagues?

The Pachad Yitzchak explains as follows:

The Maharal (Gevuros Hashem 57) explains that each of the plagues corresponded to one of the *eser ma'amaros* of *brias ha'olam* (10 utterances of creation).

Plague	Utterance	Connection
Blood	וַיֹּאמֶר אֱלֹקִים הִנֵּה נָתַתִּי לָכֶם אֶת כָּל עֵשֶׂב זֹרֵעַ זֶרַע אֲשֶׁר עַל פְּנֵי כָל הָאָרֶץ וְאֶת כָּל הָעֵץ אֲשֶׁר בּוֹ פְרִי עֵץ זֹרֵעַ זָרַע לָכֶם יִהְיֶה לְאָכְלָה And Hashem said, "See, I give you every seed-bearing plant that is upon all the earth, and every tree that has seed-bearing fruit; they shall be yours for food."	When people eat, the food becomes part of their blood.
Frogs	וַיֹּאמֶר אֱלֹקִים יִשְׁרְצוּ הַמַּיִם שֶׁרֶץ נֶפֶשׁ חַיָּה And Hashem said, "Let the waters bring forth swarms of living creatures, and birds that fly above the earth across the expanse of the sky."	The water creatures became destructive.
Lice	וַיֹּאמֶר אֱלֹקִים יִקָּווּ הַמַּיִם מִתַּחַת הַשָּׁמַיִם אֶל מָקוֹם אֶחָד וְתֵרָאֶה הַיַּבָּשָׁה וַיְהִי כֵן And Hashem said, "Let the water below the sky be gathered into one area, that the dry land may appear." And it was so.	The earth was destroyed and turned into lice.

Plague	Utterance	Connection
Wild animals	וַיֹּאמֶר אֱלֹקִים תּוֹצֵא הָאָרֶץ נֶפֶשׁ חַיָּה לְמִינָהּ בְּהֵמָה וָרֶמֶשׂ וְחַיְתוֹ אֶרֶץ לְמִינָהּ וַיְהִי כֵן. And Hashem said, "Let the earth bring forth every kind of living creature: cattle, creeping things, and wild beasts of every kind." And it was so.	The animals became destructive.
Pestilence	וַיֹּאמֶר אֱלֹקִים יְהִי מְאֹרֹת בִּרְקִיעַ הַשָּׁמַיִם לְהַבְדִּיל בֵּין הַיּוֹם וּבֵין הַלָּיְלָה וְהָיוּ לְאֹתֹת וּלְמוֹעֲדִים וּלְיָמִים וְשָׁנִים And Hashem said, "Let there be lights in the expanse of the sky to separate day from night; they shall serve as signs for the set times, for the days and for the years.	The pestilence came through an influence of disease which was caused by a disordering of the heavenly bodies.

Plague	Utterance	Connection
Boils	וַיֹּאמֶר אֱלֹקִים נַעֲשֶׂה אָדָם בְּצַלְמֵנוּ כִּדְמוּתֵנוּ וְיִרְדּוּ בִדְגַת הַיָּם וּבְעוֹף הַשָּׁמַיִם וּבַבְּהֵמָה וּבְכָל הָאָרֶץ וּבְכָל הָרֶמֶשׂ הָרֹמֵשׂ עַל הָאָרֶץ And Hashem said, "Let us make man in our image, after our likeness. They shall rule the fish of the sea, the birds of the sky, the cattle, the whole earth, and all the creeping things that creep on earth."	The boils disfigured those who became infected.
Hail	וַיֹּאמֶר אֱלֹקִים יְהִי רָקִיעַ בְּתוֹךְ הַמָּיִם וִיהִי מַבְדִּיל בֵּין מַיִם לָמָיִם And Hashem said, "Let there be a firmament in the midst of the water, that it may separate water from water."	The hail came from the firmament.
Locusts	וַיֹּאמֶר אֱלֹקִים תַּדְשֵׁא הָאָרֶץ דֶּשֶׁא עֵשֶׂב מַזְרִיעַ זֶרַע עֵץ פְּרִי עֹשֶׂה פְּרִי לְמִינוֹ אֲשֶׁר זַרְעוֹ בוֹ עַל הָאָרֶץ וַיְהִי כֵן And Hashem said, "Let the earth sprout vegetation: seed-bearing plants, fruit trees of every kind on earth that bear fruit with the seed in it." And it was so.	The locusts ate the fruit.

Plague	Utterance	Connection
Darkness	וַיֹּאמֶר אֱלֹקִים יְהִי אוֹר וַיְהִי אוֹר And Hashem said, "Let there be light"; and there was light.	Light was removed.
Death of the firstborn	בְּרֵאשִׁית בָּרָא אֱלֹקִים אֵת הַשָּׁמַיִם וְאֵת הָאָרֶץ In the beginning of Hashem's creation of the heavens and the earth.	The firstborn were the beginning of their families.

According to this correlation, pestilence corresponds to the utterance of (Bereishis 1.14)

וַיֹּאמֶר אֱלֹקִים יְהִי מְאֹרֹת בִּרְקִיעַ הַשָּׁמַיִם לְהַבְדִּיל בֵּין הַיּוֹם וּבֵין הַלָּיְלָה וְהָיוּ לְאֹתֹת וּלְמוֹעֲדִים וּלְיָמִים וְשָׁנִים

Hashem said, "Let there be lights in the expanse of the sky to separate day from night; they shall serve as signs for the set times, for the days and for the years.

This means to say that pestilence came through a disordering of the heavenly bodies which are used to determine the passage of time.

This was a punishment for the misuse of the passage of the seasons and the times of the year by the Mitzrim (Egyptians) for their idolatrous and nefarious purposes. Therefore when the plague of pestilence was to come, Hashem created a set time for its arrival. In other words, the set time of the plague of pestilence served to disrupt the set times that the Mitzrim had created by employing the cycle of the heavenly bodies to their own ends.

This is why the Torah says (Shemos 9.5)

וַיָּשֶׂם ה' מוֹעֵד לֵאמֹר מָחָר יַעֲשֶׂה ה' הַדָּבָר הַזֶּה בָּאָרֶץ

And Hashem set an appointed time saying, "Tomorrow Hashem will bring this pestilence to the land."

Bo

The plague of locusts

The *passuk* says at the beginning of this week's sedrah (10.1-2)

וַיֹּאמֶר ה' אֶל מֹשֶׁה בֹּא אֶל פַּרְעֹה כִּי אֲנִי הִכְבַּדְתִּי אֶת לִבּוֹ וְאֶת לֵב עֲבָדָיו לְמַעַן שִׁתִי אֹתֹתַי אֵלֶּה בְּקִרְבּוֹ. וּלְמַעַן תְּסַפֵּר בְּאָזְנֵי בִנְךָ וּבֶן בִּנְךָ אֵת אֲשֶׁר הִתְעַלַּלְתִּי בְּמִצְרַיִם וְאֶת אֹתֹתַי אֲשֶׁר שַׂמְתִּי בָם וִידַעְתֶּם כִּי אֲנִי ה'.

And Hashem said to Moshe, "Go to Pharoh. For I have hardened his heart and the hearts of his servants, in order that I may display these My signs among them, and in order that you may recount in the hearing of your sons and of your sons' sons how I made a mockery of the Egyptians and how I displayed My signs among them – in order that you may know that I am Hashem.

- Why does the *passuk* say specifically regarding the plague of locusts that the purpose of the plague was that the *benei yisrael* should recount it to their children and to their children's children?

Also, the *passuk* does not specify that the next plague was the plague of locusts. The Ramban comments on this omission as follows.

ובאלה שמות רבה (י"ג ד') ראיתי ולמען תספר באזני בנך הודיעו הקדוש ברוך הוא למשה מה מכה יביא עליהם וכתב אותה משה ברמז,

ולמען תספר באזני בנך ובן בנך זו מכת הארבה כמה דתימר עליה לבניכם ספרו ובניכם לבניהם וגו' (יואל א' ג')

Hashem told Moshe which plague He was going to bring, and Moshe wrote it as a hint. Since the *passuk* says, "And in order that you should recount it in the hearing of your sons and your sons' sons," we understand that this is referring to the plague of locusts, as we see in the *passuk* in Yoel where the *passuk* says concerning a plague of locusts, "You will recount it to your sons and your sons to their sons."

- Why is the plague of locusts hinted to through that which the *benei yisrael* would retell it to the children?

Later, the *passuk* says (10.9)

וַיֹּאמֶר מֹשֶׁה בִּנְעָרֵינוּ וּבִזְקֵנֵינוּ נֵלֵךְ בְּבָנֵינוּ וּבִבְנוֹתֵנוּ בְּצֹאנֵנוּ וּבִבְקָרֵנוּ נֵלֵךְ כִּי חַג ה' לָנוּ

And Moshe replied, "We will go with our young and our old, we will go with our sons and daughters, our flocks and herds, for we must observe the festival of Hashem."

The medrash comments on this *passuk*

כי חג ה' לנו, זה חג הסוכות

For we must observe the festival of Hashem, this refers to the festival of Succos.

- Why does the *passuk* allude to Succos if this would only happen later?

It would seem that we can explain as follows[19]:

The Maharal says (דרשה לשבת הגדול ד"ה הנה המכה הראשונה)

כי לכך נקרא ארבה, כי יש להם רבוי ביותר וכו' כי הכתוב אומר (משלי ל') מלך אין לארבה, ונראה הפירוש כי שאר מינים יש להם כח קשור עד שכל המין נחשב אחד, אבל הארבה אין להם דבר זה רק יש להם הרבוי כמו שנקראו וכו' כי המלך מקשר ומאחד כל העם והם אחד על ידי המלך שהוא אחד, אבל הארבה אין לו דבר זה רק נקראו ארבה על שם הרבוי, שאין כח שהוא מקשר אותם, ולכך הם פרטיים, ואלו שאר מינים נחשבים כמו אחד

The reason that locusts are called ארבה (which means "many") is because the *passuk* says in Mishlei that locusts do not have a king (meaning that there is no specific locust which is in charge of the other locusts, instead they travel as a swarm). Therefore the locusts are not unified, and each travels on its own, which is not case with other animals which do have a king, so that the king unifies them into a group.

Through the plague of locusts, Hashem demonstrated to Pharoh, that his people only served him because they understood that they would be better off with this arrangement, thus in reality they were separate and not unified under him, like a swarm of locusts.

---

[19] עיין בספר דברי יואל

Pharoh had understood that the *benei yisrael* wanted to serve Hashem for the same reason as the Egyptians served him, in other words, that the *benei yisrael* wanted to serve Hashem because this would cause them to be better off in some way. That is why Pharoh reasoned that only the men would need to go to serve Hashem (10.10-11)

וַיֹּאמֶר אֲלֵהֶם יְהִי כֵן ה' עִמָּכֶם כַּאֲשֶׁר אֲשַׁלַּח אֶתְכֶם וְאֶת טַפְּכֶם רְאוּ כִּי רָעָה נֶגֶד פְּנֵיכֶם. לֹא כֵן לְכוּ נָא הַגְּבָרִים וְעִבְדוּ אֶת ה' כִּי אֹתָהּ אַתֶּם מְבַקְשִׁים וַיְגָרֶשׁ אֹתָם מֵאֵת פְּנֵי פַרְעֹה.

But he said to them, "May Hashem be with you the same as J mean to let your children go with you! [Clearly, you are bent on mischief.] Not so! Let the men go and serve Hashem, since that is what you want." And they were expelled from Pharaoh's presence.

This means to say, since Pharoh understood that the *benei yisrael* wanted to exchange himself for Hashem, therefore only the men would need to go, since in Egypt, only the men needed to see Pharoh, in order to best arrange their commercial and military affairs.

To exclude this type of sovereignty, the *passuk* alludes to Succos, on which we have the *mitzva* of *Hakhel* (Devarim 31.12)

הַקְהֵל אֶת הָעָם הָאֲנָשִׁים וְהַנָּשִׁים וְהַטַּף וְגֵרְךָ אֲשֶׁר בִּשְׁעָרֶיךָ לְמַעַן יִשְׁמְעוּ וּלְמַעַן יִלְמְדוּ וְיָרְאוּ אֶת ה' אֱלֹקֵיכֶם וְשָׁמְרוּ לַעֲשׂוֹת אֶת כָּל דִּבְרֵי הַתּוֹרָה הַזֹּאת

Gather the people, the men, the women and the children and the strangers in your communities, so that they may hear and learn to revere Hashem your G-d and to observe faithfully every word of this teaching.

We see from this *mitzva* that the service of Hashem is not one of convenience, but is rather one of awe and reverence, so that all parts of the *benei yisrael* are engaged in the *mitzva* of learning Torah in the *beis ha'mikdash*.

Since the plague of locusts accentuated the involvement of even the children in the service of Hashem, the *passuk* says specifically with regards to this plague that in the future the *benei yisrael* would include the children in celebrating Pesach, by recounting the miracles of Yetzias Mitzrayim.

Beshalach

Yosef and *krias yam suf*

The *passuk* says at the beginning of this week's sedrah (13.17-19)

וַיְהִי בְּשַׁלַּח פַּרְעֹה אֶת הָעָם וְלֹא נָחָם אֱלֹהִים דֶּרֶךְ אֶרֶץ פְּלִשְׁתִּים כִּי קָרוֹב הוּא כִּי אָמַר אֱלֹקִים פֶּן יִנָּחֵם הָעָם בִּרְאֹתָם מִלְחָמָה וְשָׁבוּ מִצְרָיְמָה. וַיַּסֵּב אֱלֹקִים אֶת הָעָם דֶּרֶךְ הַמִּדְבָּר יַם סוּף וַחֲמֻשִׁים עָלוּ בְּנֵי יִשְׂרָאֵל מֵאֶרֶץ מִצְרָיִם. וַיִּקַּח מֹשֶׁה אֶת עַצְמוֹת יוֹסֵף עִמּוֹ כִּי הַשְׁבֵּעַ הִשְׁבִּיעַ אֶת בְּנֵי יִשְׂרָאֵל לֵאמֹר פָּקֹד יִפְקֹד אֱלֹקִים אֶתְכֶם וְהַעֲלִיתֶם אֶת עַצְמֹתַי מִזֶּה אִתְּכֶם.

And it was when Pharoh sent the people and Hashem did not lead them by way of the land of the Pelishtim, although it was nearer, for Hashem said, "Lest the people have a change of heart when they see war, and return to Egypt." So Hashem led the people a roundabout way, by way of the desert at the Yam Suf. And the benei yisrael went up armed out of the land of Egypt.

And Moshe took with him the bones of Yoseph, who had exacted an oath from the *benei yisrael*, saying, "Hashem will be sure to remember you, and then you shall carry up my bones from here with you."

The gemara in Sotah (13a) comments

ת"ר בא וראה כמה חביבות מצות על משה רבינו שכל ישראל כולן נתעסקו בביזה והוא נתעסק במצות שנאמר (משלי י', ח') חכם לב יקח מצות וגו' ומנין היה יודע משה רבינו היכן יוסף קבור אמרו סרח בת אשר נשתיירה מאותו הדור הלך משה אצלה אמר לה כלום את יודעת היכן יוסף קבור אמרה לו ארון של מתכת עשו לו מצרים וקבעוהו בנילוס הנהר כדי שיתברכו מימיו הלך משה ועמד על שפת נילוס אמר לו יוסף יוסף הגיע העת שנשבע הקב"ה שאני גואל אתכם והגיעה השבועה שהשבעת את ישראל אם אתה מראה עצמך מוטב אם לאו הרי אנו מנוקין משבועתך מיד צף ארונו של יוסף

The *chachamim* taught, "Come and see how beloved *mitzvos* are to Moshe our teacher. As, at the time of *yetzias mitzrayim*, all of the *benei yisrael* were involved in taking the plunder from Egypt, and he was involved in the performance of *mitzvos*, as it is stated, 'The wise in heart will take *mitzvos*.'"

And from where did Moshe know where Yoseph was buried? The *chachamim* said, "Serach, the daughter of Asher, remained from the generation that initially descended to Egypt with Yaacov.

Moshe went and said to her, 'Do you know where Yoseph is buried?' She said to him, 'The Egyptians fashioned a metal casket for him and set it in the Nile River so that its water would be blessed.' Moshe went and stood on the bank of the Nile. He said, 'Yoseph, Yoseph, the time has arrived about which Hashem took an oath saying that I will redeem you. And the time for fulfillment of the oath that you administered to the Jewish people that they will bury you in Eretz Yisrael has arrived. If you show yourself, it is good, but if not, we are absolved from your oath.' Immediately, the casket of Yoseph floated to the top of the water."

- It would appear difficult to understand why the gemara asks where Yoseph was buried, and answers that Moshe asked Serach. Why is it not possible that Moshe knew where Yosef was buried through *nevuah* or *ruach ha'kodesh*?

It would seem that it is possible to explain as follows[20]:

Later in the sedrah (14.27), it says

וַיֵּט מֹשֶׁה אֶת יָדוֹ עַל הַיָּם וַיָּשָׁב הַיָּם לִפְנוֹת בֹּקֶר לְאֵיתָנוֹ וּמִצְרַיִם נָסִים לִקְרָאתוֹ וַיְנַעֵר ה' אֶת מִצְרַיִם בְּתוֹךְ הַיָּם.

And Moshe held out his arm over the sea, and at daybreak the sea returned to its normal state, and the Egyptians fled at its approach. But Hashem hurled the Egyptians into the sea.

The medrash (בראשית רבה, ה', ה') comments

אמר ר' יוחנן תנאין התנה הקב"ה עם הים שיהא נקרע לפני ישראל הדא הוא דכתיב (שמות י"ד) וישב הים לאיתנו לתנאו שהתנה עמו

Rabbi Yochanan said, "Hashem made a condition with the sea, when it was created, that it should allow itself to be split

---

[20] עיין בספר יקר מפז

before the *benei yisrael*. This is what the *passuk* means when it says וישב הים לאיתנו. That means to say, instead of understanding לאיתנו as "to its might", we understand לאיתנו as "to the condition that Hashem agreed with it initially when the sea was created".

According to the medrash, the word לְאֵיתָנוֹ means both "to its might" and also "according to the condition that was made with it." This is because, had *krias yam suf* not been a condition made with the sea when it was created, then that which the sea would have continued to act as normal after *krias yam suf*, would have been a new creation.

In other words, since the original way in which the sea acted would have been terminated with *krias yam suf*, returning the sea to its normal behaviour after *krias yam suf* would have required a new creation of the normal order of the sea, the same as occurred during *ma'aseh bereishis*.

Thus, it was only possible for the sea to continue with its original might after *krias yam suf* because *krias yam suf* had originally been a condition in creating the sea.

The Mechilta (בשלח ג') says that the sea split in the merit of Yosef

שמעון איש קטרון אומר, בזכות עצמות של יוסף אני קורע להם את הים, שנאמר ויעזוב בגדו אצלה וגו', וכתיב הים ראה וינוס

> Shimon from Katron said, "Hashem said, 'I will split the sea for them in the merit of the bones of Yosef.'" As it says, "And he left his garment with her and he fled," and it says, "The sea saw and it fled."

Just as *krias yam suf* did not diminish the might of the sea, despite the interruption to the normal way in which the sea behaves, so too did the merit and the might of Yosef cause the *galus* of the *benei yisrael* in Mitzrayim not to cause an interruption to the agreement that Hashem made with the avos.

As the medrash says (Vayikra Rabbah 32.5)

יוסף ירד למצרים וגדר עצמו מן הערוה ונגדרו ישראל בזכותו

> Yosef went down to Mitzrayim and he guarded himself from immorality, and all of the *benei yisrael* were able to guard themselves from immorality in his merit.

Since the merit of Yosef was the source of the uninterruptedness of the *benei yisrael*, it is not possible that Moshe divined his resting place through *nevuah*, because had Moshe done so, this would have indicated that Yosef was remembered as part of a new agreement with the *benei yisrael*.

That is why the gemara says that it must be that Moshe determined the resting place of Yosef through Serach, who represented the uninterrupted chain of the *mesorah* of the *benei yisrael*.

Krias yam suf

It says in this week's *sedrah* (14:15)

וַיֹּאמֶר ה' אֶל מֹשֶׁה מַה תִּצְעַק אֵלָי דַּבֵּר אֶל בְּנֵי יִשְׂרָאֵל וְיִסָּעוּ

And Hashem said to Moshe, "Why do you cry out to Me? Tell the *benei yisrael* to go forward."

The Mechilta comments on this *passuk*

> רבי אליעזר אומר אמר הקב"ה למשה משה בני נתונים בצרה הים סוגר ושונא רודף ואתה עומד ומרבה בתפלה... ר' יהודה בן בתירה אומר אמר לו הקב"ה כבר עשיתי הבטחה שהבטחתי אברהם אביכם שנאמר וישם את הים לחרבה, ובני ישראל הלכו ביבשה בתוך הים. רבי שמעון בן יוחאי אומר כבר חמה ולבנה מעידין בהם שקרעתי להם את הים שנאמר כי כה אמר ה' נותן שמש לאור יומם חוקות ירח וכוכבים לאור לילה רוגע הים ויהמו גליו ה' צבקות שמו (ירמיה ל"א).

Rabbi Eliezer says, "Hashem said to Moshe, my children are in distress, the sea is locking them in and the enemy is pursuing them and you are standing there and praying before Me?"
Rabbi Yehudah ben Beseira says, "Hashem said to him, I have already done the promise that I promised Avraham their

father, as the *passuk* says, 'And it turned the sea into dry land,' and it says, 'And the *benei yisrael* went on dry land in the midst of the sea.'"

Rabbi Shimon ben Yochai says, "[Hashem said,] 'The sun and the moon are already testifying that I split the sea for the *benei yisrael*.' As the *passuk* says, 'For thus says Hashem, Who established the sun for light by day, and the statutes of the moon and stars for light by night, Who stirs up the sea into roaring waves, His name is the Lord of Hosts.'"

- Why did the sun and the moon testify concerning *krias yam suf*?

- Why does the Mechilta say that the sun and the moon were already testifying to this effect, if the sea had not yet split?

The gemara says in Sanhedrin (91b)

תניא אמר רבי מאיר מניין לתחיית המתים מן התורה שנאמר (שמות ט"ו, א') אז ישיר משה ובני ישראל את השירה הזאת לה' שר לא נאמר אלא ישיר מכאן לתחיית המתים מן התורה

Rabbi Meir said: Where is the resurrection of the dead hinted in the Torah? It is derived from the *passuk* which says, "Then Moshe and the *benei yisrael* will sing this song to Hashem" (Shemos 15.1). It is not stated, "Sang." Rather, the term "they will sing" is stated, indicating that Moshe will come back to life and sing this song in the future. From here it is proved that resurrection of the dead is derived from the Torah.

- Why is techiyas ha'meisim hinted at krias yam suf?

It would appear that we can explain as follows:

The Zohar says (זוהר חלק א' דף לג ע"א)

> תא חזי, כתיב לבתר, יקוו המים מתחת השמים אל מקום אחד, מתחת השמים ממש, אל מקום אחד, לאתר דאקרי אחד, ואיהו ים תתאה, דהא איהו אשלים לאחד, ובלא איהו לא אקרי אחד, ומשמע דכתיב יקוו, דביה מתכנשין כלהו מיא, כמה דאת אמר (קהלת א' ז') כל הנחלים הולכים אל הים וגו'

It is written, "Let the waters that are under the heavens to one place." [According to the simple translation, why does the *passuk* need to specify that it is referring to the waters that are under the heavens, is this not obvious from the context?] Rather the *passuk* means to say as follows, "The waters should be gathered away from being under the heavens to one place, meaning to the place that is called One. And this is the nethermost sea, because it completes the Oneness, and without it there can be no Oneness.

Therefore the *passuk* writes correctly 'let there be gathered', for in this sea is gathered all waters, as it says, 'All streams flow into the sea, Yet the sea is never full.'"

Water has no form, therefore water is generally taken to represent formlessness. But water also refers to the Torah, as the gemara says in Taanis (7a)

אמר רבי חנינא בר אידי, למה נמשלו דברי תורה למים, דכתיב, הוי כל צמא לכו למים (ישעיהו נ"ה א')

Rabbi Chanina bar Idi said, "Where are the words of Torah compared to water, as it is written, 'Hoi all those who are thirsty, come and drink from the waters [of the Torah].'"

The world in which we live does not possess a sufficiently elevated form and structure to allow the full acknowledgment and recognition of *mitzvos* and Torah. Therefore, it often seems that such good deeds leave no impression, and go to waste, as if it were.

The Zohar comes to teach us that in reality, and that no good intention or deed is ever lost. Rather this water of Torah and *mitzvos*, flows into the repository of Oneness, that will be revealed on the day when (Zecharia 14.9)

וְהָיָה ה' לְמֶלֶךְ עַל כָּל הָאָרֶץ בַּיּוֹם הַהוּא יִהְיֶה ה' אֶחָד וּשְׁמוֹ אֶחָד

And Hashem will be the king over the entire world, on that day Hashem will be One and His name will be One.

Subsequently we can understand that when Hashem led the *benei yisrael*, on dry land, into the depths of the sea, Hashem created the portend for that day on which all lost impressions of Torah and *mitzvos*, which have been "swept into the sea" during the course of history, will be restored to the *benei yisrael*.

For example, the *benei yisrael* saw at Har Sinai that Hashem had never forgotten their slavery in Mitzraim, as it says in Mishpatim (Shemos 24.10):

וַיִּרְאוּ אֵת אֱלֹקֵי יִשְׂרָאֵל, וְתַחַת רַגְלָיו כְּמַעֲשֵׂה לִבְנַת הַסַּפִּיר, וּכְעֶצֶם הַשָּׁמַיִם לָטֹהַר

And they saw the G-d of the *benei yisrael*, and under His feet there was the likeness of a brick of sapphire, like the very sky for purity.

On which Rashi comments

כמעשה לבנת הספיר: היא היתה לפניו בשעת השעבוד, לזכור צרתן של ישראל, שהיו משועבדים במעשה לבנים

This brick of sapphire had been before Him during the period of slavery as a symbol of the sorrows of the *benei yisrael*, for they were enslaved to do brick-work.

At Har Sinai, the *benei yisrael* saw how the lowly slave labour that they had been forced to do was transformed by Hashem into the most elevating experience of Matan Torah.

Similarly, in the future, the *benei yisrael* will see that no effort they exerted to uphold the Torah was ever lost, whereupon they will shine with their own supernal light, as the gemara says (Bava Basra (8b))

(דניאל י"ב, ג,) והמשכילים יזהירו כזוהר הרקיע וגו' זה דיין שדן דין

אמת לאמתו (דניאל י"ב, ג,) ומצדיקי הרבים ככוכבים לעולם ועד אלו גבאי צדקה במתניתא תנא והמשכילים יזהירו כזוהר הרקיע זה דיין שדן דין אמת לאמתו וגבאי צדקה ומצדיקי הרבים ככוכבים לעולם ועד אלו מלמדי תינוקות

"And they who are wise shall shine like the brightness of the firmament; and they who turn many to righteousness like the stars for ever and ever" (Daniel 12:3). "And they who are wise shall shine like the brightness of the firmament"; this is a judge who judges an absolutely true judgment. "And they who turn many to righteousness like the stars for ever and ever"; these are the charity collectors, who facilitate the giving of charity.

It was taught in a *beraisa*: "And they who are wise shall shine like the brightness of the firmament"; this is a judge who judges an absolutely true judgment and also charity collectors. "And they who turn many to righteousness like the stars for ever and ever"; these are teachers of young children.

This restoration is the subject of *techiyas hameisim* (the resurrection of the dead), because *techiyas ha'meisim* does not only mean that those who have passed away will be brought back to life. Rather it also means that all deeds of truth, *tzedakah* and Torah will be restored and brought to give life to those who effected them.

Hence, at *krias yam suf*, the sun and the moon testified that this process of the restoration of seemingly lost Torah and *mitzvos* to the *benei yisrael*, that will cause them to shine with their own supernal light, had already begun.

Yisro

Yisro's blessing

The passuk says at the beginning of this week's sedrah (18.1-12)

וַיִּשְׁמַע יִתְרוֹ כֹהֵן מִדְיָן חֹתֵן מֹשֶׁה אֵת כָּל אֲשֶׁר עָשָׂה אֱלֹקִים לְמֹשֶׁה וּלְיִשְׂרָאֵל עַמּוֹ כִּי הוֹצִיא ה' אֶת יִשְׂרָאֵל מִמִּצְרָיִם. וַיִּקַּח יִתְרוֹ חֹתֵן מֹשֶׁה אֶת צִפֹּרָה אֵשֶׁת מֹשֶׁה אַחַר שִׁלּוּחֶיהָ. וְאֵת שְׁנֵי בָנֶיהָ אֲשֶׁר שֵׁם הָאֶחָד גֵּרְשֹׁם כִּי אָמַר גֵּר הָיִיתִי בְּאֶרֶץ נָכְרִיָּה. וְשֵׁם הָאֶחָד אֱלִיעֶזֶר כִּי אֱלֹקֵי אָבִי בְּעֶזְרִי וַיַּצִּלֵנִי מֵחֶרֶב פַּרְעֹה.

And Yisro the priest of Midian, Moshe's father-in-law, heard all that Hashem had done for Moshe and for the *benei yisrael*, that Hashem had brought the *benei yisrael* out of Mitzrayim. And Yisro, Moshe's father-in-law, took Tzipporah, Moshe's wife, after she had been sent home. And her two sons, of whom one was named Gershom, that is to say, "For J was a stranger in a foreign land," and the other was named Eliezer, meaning, "For the G-d of my father was my help, and He delivered me from the sword of Pharoh."

Rashi says

וַיִּשְׁמַע יִתְרוֹ: מה שמועה שמע ובא קריעת ים סוף ומלחמת עמלק

And Yisro heard: What news did he hear and come? The splitting of the Reed Sea and the war with Amalek.

לְמֹשֶׁה וּלְיִשְׂרָאֵל: שקול משה כנגד כל ישראל

For Moshe and for the *benei yisrael*: This teaches you that Moshe was as worthy as the rest of the *benei yisrael*.

כִּי הוֹצִיא ה' אֶת יִשְׂרָאֵל מִמִּצְרָיִם: זו גדולה על כולם

That Hashem had brought the *benei yisrael* out of Mitzrayim: This was greater than all of the other miracles.

- Why does the *passuk* mention that Moshe was as worthy as the rest of the *benei yisrael* regarding the miracles of the Splitting of the Reed Sea and the war with Amalek, and not regarding the miracle of *yetzias mitzrayim*?

- If that which Hashem brought the *benei yisrael* out of *Mitzrayim* was greater than all the other miracles, then why did Yisro not come because of this miracle?

The sedrah continues (18.11)

וַיִּחַדְּ יִתְרוֹ עַל כָּל הַטּוֹבָה אֲשֶׁר עָשָׂה ה' לְיִשְׂרָאֵל אֲשֶׁר הִצִּילוֹ מִיַּד מִצְרָיִם. וַיֹּאמֶר יִתְרוֹ בָּרוּךְ ה' אֲשֶׁר הִצִּיל אֶתְכֶם מִיַּד מִצְרַיִם וּמִיַּד פַּרְעֹה אֲשֶׁר הִצִּיל אֶת הָעָם מִתַּחַת יַד מִצְרָיִם. עַתָּה יָדַעְתִּי כִּי גָדוֹל ה' מִכָּל הָאֱלֹקִים כִּי בַדָּבָר אֲשֶׁר זָדוּ עֲלֵיהֶם.

And Yisro rejoiced over all the kindness that Hashem had shown the *benei yisrael* when He delivered them from the Egyptians. "Blessed be Hashem," Yisro said, "who delivered you from the Egyptians and from Pharaoh, and who delivered the people from under the hand of the Egyptians. Now I know that Hashem is greater than all other gods, for with the thing that they schemed against them were they punished."

The gemara in Sanhedrin (94a) says

> כיוצא בדבר אתה אומר (שמות י"ח, י') ויאמר יתרו ברוך ה' אשר הציל אתכם תנא משום רבי פפייס גנאי הוא למשה וששים ריבוא שלא אמרו ברוך עד שבא יתרו ואמר ברוך ה'

We have learnt in the name of Rabbi Papayas, "It was a bad reflection on Moshe and the 600,000 that they did not say ברוך ה' until Yisro came and said ברוך ה'."

- If the benei yisrael said shirah at the yam suf, why did it matter that they did not use the expression ברוך ה' till Yisro came?

It would seem that we can explain as follows:

The gemara in Avoda Zara (3a) relates how in the future, the nations of the world will ask Hashem to give them a *mitzva* to do, in order so that they too can receive the reward of keeping the Torah.

אמרו לפניו רבש"ע תנה לנו מראש ונעשנה. אמר להן הקב"ה שוטים שבעולם, מי שטרח בערב שבת יאכל בשבת, מי שלא טרח בערב שבת מהיכן יאכל בשבת. אלא, אף על פי כן מצוה קלה יש לי, וסוכה שמה. לכו ועשו אותה. ומי מצית אמרת הכי והא אמר רבי יהושע בן לוי מאי דכתיב (דברים ז', י"א) אשר אנכי מצוך היום, היום לעשותם ולא למחר לעשותם, היום לעשותם ולא היום ליטול שכר. אלא, שאין הקב"ה בא בטרוניא עם בריותיו. ואמאי קרי ליה מצוה קלה, משום דלית ביה חסרון כיס מיד כל אחד [ואחד] נוטל והולך ועושה סוכה בראש גגו והקדוש ברוך הוא מקדיר עליהם חמה בתקופת תמוז וכל אחד ואחד מבעט בסוכתו ויוצא שנאמר (תהלים ב', ג') ננתקה את מוסרותימו ונשליכה ממנו עבותימו

The nations of the world will say before Him, "Master of the Universe, give us the Torah afresh and we will perform its *mitzvos*." The Holy One, Blessed be He, will say to them in response, "Fools of the world! Do you think you can request this? One who prepares on Shabbos eve will eat on Shabbos, but one who did not prepare on Shabbos eve, from where will he eat on Shabbos? But even so, I have an easy *mitzva* to fulfill, and its name is *succah*, go and perform it…

Immediately, each and every gentile will take materials and go and construct a *succah* on top of his roof. And Hashem will set upon them the heat of the sun in the season of Tammuz and each and every one will kick his succah and leave, as it is stated: "Let us break their bands asunder, and cast away their cords from us." (Tehillim 2.3)

The nations of the world will perceive that they are capable as a whole, of keeping the Torah. However when each and every one is commanded to individually uphold the *mitzvos* against all eventualities, then each and every one will see that they are unable to individually uphold the Torah.

Conversely, when the *benei yisrael* accepted the Torah, not only did the entirety of the *benei yisrael* accept the Torah together, but they also accepted the Torah on condition that every individual would by themselves uphold the entire Torah, if needed. That is why the entire world was created in the merit of each and every *tzadik* (ילקוט שמעוני רמז ה')

אמר רבי אלעזר אפילו בשביל צדיק אחד העולם נברא, שנאמר וירא אלקים את האור כי טוב, ואין טוב אלא צדיק, שנאמר אמרו צדיק כי טוב (ישעיהו ג' י')

Rabbi Elazar said, "The world was created for even one *tzadik*, as the *passuk* says, 'And Hashem saw that the light was good,' and the word good refers to a *tzadik*, as it says in Yeshaya, 'Say about the *tzadik* that he is good.'"

Similarly[21], the difference between the *benei yisrael* saying *shirah* at *krias yam suf* and Yisro saying ברוך ה' is that when the *benei yisrael* said *shirah*, they acknowledged that Hashem had saved

---

[21] כך שמעתי מהגר"מ סלומון שליט"א

them all together and so they all said shirah together. However, when Yisro said 'ברוך ה this meant to say that he understood that all of the *nissim* that Hashem had done, could equally have been done for each and every one of the *benei yisrael*, so that each individually could say 'ברוך ה for the *nissim* that they had experienced.

The uniqueness of the *benei yisrael*, wherein each and every one of the *benei yisrael* accepts the whole Torah individually, was created through *yetzias mitzrayim*, when Hashem separated the *benei yisrael* from the multitudinous of *Mitzrayim* and the other nations of the world. Therefore, regarding *yetzias mitzrayim* itself, the *passuk* says כִּי הוֹצִיא ה' אֶת יִשְׂרָאֵל מִמִּצְרָיִם – That Hashem brought the *benei yisrael*, as a whole, out of Mitzrayim.

However, regarding the subsequent *nissim* of *krias yam suf* and the war with Amalek, the passuk says אֵת כָּל אֲשֶׁר עָשָׂה אֱלֹקִים לְמֹשֶׁה וּלְיִשְׂרָאֵל עַמּוֹ – "All that Hashem did for Moshe and for the *benei yisrael* His people," since now the *benei yisrael* were on a level at which every miracle could equally be performed even for every *tzadik*.

The reason that Yisro came to the *benei yisrael* is because he realised that the *benei yisrael* had now attained the level at which everyone would accept the whole Torah individually, and the level at which all *nissim* could be equally performed for every one of the *benei yisrael*.

Subsequently, even although on an absolute scale, *yetzias mitzrayim* was a greater *miracle* than the miracles of *krias yam suf* and the war with Amalek, nevertheless the miracles that represented the newfound stature of the *benei yisrael* were *krias yam suf* and the war with Amalek, so it was because of these miracles that Yisro came to join the *benei yisrael*.

Avodah zarah

It says in this week's *sedrah* (20:2)

אָנֹכִי ה' אֱלֹקֶיךָ אֲשֶׁר הוֹצֵאתִיךָ מֵאֶרֶץ מִצְרַיִם מִבֵּית עֲבָדִים. לֹא יִהְיֶה לְךָ אֱלֹהִים אֲחֵרִים עַל פָּנָי.

I Hashem your G-d who brought you out of the land of Egypt, from the house of slaves. You shall have no other gods in My presence.

The Mechilta comments on this *passuk*

"אֱלֹהִים אֲחֵרִים." וְכִי אֱלֹהוֹת הֵן? וַהֲלֹא כְּבָר נֶאֱמַר: (יְשַׁעְיָה ל"ז,י"ט) וְנָתְנוּ אֶת אֱלֹהֵיהֶם בָּאֵשׁ, כִּי לֹא אֱלֹהִים הֵמָּה"! וּמַה תַּלְמוּד לוֹמַר "אֱלֹהִים אֲחֵרִים?" אֶלָּא שֶׁאֲחֵרִים קוֹרְאִין אוֹתָם אֱלֹהוּת...

רַבִּי אֱלִיעֶזֶר אוֹמֵר: (שְׁמוֹת כ', ב') "אֱלֹהִים אֲחֵרִים", שֶׁהֵם מְחַדְּשִׁים לָהֶם אֱלֹהוּת בְּכָל יוֹם. הָא כֵּיצַד? הָיָה לוֹ שֶׁלַּזָּהָב וְנִצְרַךְ לוֹ, עֲשָׂאוֹ שֶׁלַּכֶּסֶף. הָיָה לוֹ שֶׁלַּכֶּסֶף וְנִצְרַךְ לוֹ, עֲשָׂאוֹ שֶׁלַּנְּחֹשֶׁת. הָיָה לוֹ שֶׁלַּנְּחֹשֶׁת וְנִצְרַךְ לוֹ, עֲשָׂאוֹ שֶׁלַּבַּרְזֶל, שֶׁלַּבְּדִיל אוֹ שֶׁלָּעוֹפָרֶת. וְכֵן הוּא אוֹמֵר: (דְּבָרִים ל"ב,י"ז) חֲדָשִׁים מִקָּרֹב בָּאוּ.

רַבִּי יִצְחָק אוֹמֵר: אִלּוּ נִפְרַט לָהֶם כָּל שֵׁם כָּל שֵׁם עֲבוֹדָה זָרָה, לֹא הָיָה מַסְפִּיק לָהֶם כָּל הָעוֹרוֹת שֶׁבָּעוֹלָם!

Other gods: And are they gods, but does the *passuk* not say, "And they shall place their gods in fire, for they are not gods"? Rather the *passuk* means to refer to those things which other people call gods.

Rabbi Eliezer said, "They are called 'other gods' because they invent new gods every day. How so? If he (the idol worshipper) had an idol made of gold and he needed the gold, then he would melt down the first idol and make a new one of silver. If he an idol made of silver and he needed the silver, then he would melt down the silver idol and make a new one of copper. If he had an idol of copper and he needed the copper, he would melt down the copper idol and make a new one of iron, tin or ore…"

Rabbi Yitzchak said, "Were the *passuk* to have specified the names of the different types of Avodah Zarah (instead of using the potentially misleading phrase אלהים אחרים), there would not be sufficient parchments in the world (to list all the names). (Therefore the *passuk* simply refers to אלהים אחרים, as a catch-all phrase.)

- Why, according to Rabbi Eliezer, does the *passuk* infer that the essence of *avodah zarah* is evidenced through that which those who serve עבודה זרה constantly create new cheaper forms of עבודה זרה?

Furthermore, it would seem that according to Rabbi Yitzchak there are potentially a limitless number of types of עבודה זרה. However this is contradicted by various מאמרי חז"ל which imply that the number of types of עבודה זרה is indeed limited. For example concerning Yisro, the *passuk* says (Shemos 18:11)

עַתָּה יָדַעְתִּי כִּי גָדוֹל ה' מִכָּל הָאֱלֹקִים כִּי בַדָּבָר אֲשֶׁר זָדוּ עֲלֵיהֶם

Now I know that Hashem is greater than all gods, for they were punished with the thing through which they schemed against them.

Rashi comments on this *passuk*

מכל האלהים: מלמד שהיה מכיר בכל ע"א שבעולם שלא הניח ע"א שלא עבדה (מכילתא)

Than all other gods: This teaches that he recognised every type of עבודה זרה in the world, because he did not leave any Avodah Zarah that he had not served (to try it out to see if it was true).

- Why then does Rabbi Yitzchak say that it would have been impossible for the Torah to list all of the different types of *avodah zarah*?

The Mechilta continues:

"עַל פָּנָי". לָמָה נֶאֱמַר? שֶׁלֹא לִתֵּן פִּתְחוֹן פֶּה לְיִשְׂרָאֵל לוֹמַר "לֹא נִצְטַוְּנָה עַל עֲבוֹדָה זָרָה, אֶלָּא מִי שֶׁיָּצָא מִמִּצְרָיִם". לְכָךְ נֶאֱמַר "עַל פָּנַי" לוֹמַר, מָה אֲנִי חַי וְקַיָּם לְעוֹלָם וּלְעוֹלְמֵי עוֹלָמִים, אַף אַתָּה וּבִנְךָ וּבֶן בִּנְךָ, לֹא

תַּעֲבֹד עֲבוֹדָה זָרָה עַד סוֹף כָּל הַדּוֹרוֹת.

Why does the *passuk* say that you may not serve Avodah Zarah "in my presence". So that the *benei yisrael* should not be able to claim that only those who came out of Mitzraim were commanded not to serve Avodah Zarah. Therefore the *passuk* says "in my presence" so as to say, just as I live and endure for all eternity, so too for you and your children and your grandchildren, you shall not serve Avodah Zarah until the end of all generations.

It would seem that the reason that the Torah has to warn that specifically the *issur* of Avodah Zarah applies for all generations, although the Torah is not concerned about this possible טענה concerning other *mitzvos*, is that the *benei yisrael* could say that new types of Avodah Zarah that did not exist at the time of Matan Torah are not covered in this *issur*, as the אור החיים says in Parshas Re'eh (Devarim 13:7) on the *passuk*:

כִּי יְסִיתְךָ אָחִיךָ בֶן אִמֶּךָ אוֹ בִנְךָ אוֹ בִתְּךָ אוֹ אֵשֶׁת חֵיקֶךָ אוֹ רֵעֲךָ אֲשֶׁר כְּנַפְשְׁךָ בַּסֵּתֶר לֵאמֹר נֵלְכָה וְנַעַבְדָה אֱלֹקִים אֲחֵרִים אֲשֶׁר לֹא יָדַעְתָּ אַתָּה וַאֲבֹתֶיךָ

If your brother, your own mother's son, or your son or daughter, or your wife, or your closest friend entices you in secret, saying, "Come let us worship other gods"— whom neither you nor your fathers have known...

On which the אור החיים comments:

ואומרו אשר לא ידעת, פירוש בא בטענה נגד מה שנתחייב האדם בקבלת התורה שלא לעבוד אלהים אחרים ואומר לו כי אין עליו החיוב אלא דוקא בעבודה זרה שידע וקבל שלא לעובדה אבל עבודה זרה של אלהים לא ידועה בעולם אין עליו טענת מה שקבל שלא לעבוד כי לא עלה זה על דעת אז כשקבל והוא אומרו אשר לא ידעת אתה ולא אתה לבד אלא ואבותיך גם הם כשקבלו עליהם איסור עבודה זרה לא ידעו זו

The מסית comes with an argument to counteract that which a person is obliged through קבלת התורה not to serve other gods. Namely, the מסית says to the person he is trying to persuade that this *issur* only applies to avodah zarah that existed in the world at the time of מתן תורה. Indeed, how could the *benei yisrael* have meant that they would not serve an עבודה זרה that did not exist at the time of מתן תורה, because at that time no-one thought to serve this עבודה זרה in the first place. Subsequently the מסית claims that it is not possible that the *issur* of avodah zarah applies to a new avodah zarah which no-one knew of previously.

- If this is indeed the argument which the *passuk* in the *aseres ha'dibros* is coming to refute, how does that which Hashem lives forever, widen the prohibition of לא יהיה לך to include new types of avodah zarah? If the *benei yisrael* only accepted not to serve those types of avodah zarah which existed at the time of Matan Torah, then even with the endurance of that prohibition forever, it would still not come to include new types of avodah zarah which the *benei yisrael* never accepted to not serve?

It would seem that we can explain as follows:

The *pessukim* in Daniel (perek 2:31 -33) describe how Nevuchadnezzar saw in a dream a great idol

אַנְתְּ מַלְכָּא חָזֵה הֲוַיְתָ וַאֲלוּ צְלֵם חַד שַׂגִּיא צַלְמָא דִּכֵּן רַב וְזִיוֵהּ יַתִּיר קָאֵם לְקָבְלָךְ וְרֵוֵהּ דְּחִיל. הוּא צַלְמָא רֵאשֵׁהּ דִּי דְהַב טָב חֲדוֹהִי וּדְרָעוֹהִי דִּי כְסַף מְעוֹהִי וְיַרְכָתֵהּ דִּי נְחָשׁ. שָׁקוֹהִי דִּי פַרְזֶל רַגְלוֹהִי מִנְּהֵין דִּי פַרְזֶל וּמִנְּהֵין דִּי חֲסַף.

O king, as you looked on, there appeared a great statue. This statue, which was huge and its brightness surpassing, stood before you, and its appearance was awesome. The head of that statue was of fine gold; its chest and arms were of silver; its stomach and thighs, of bronze; its legs were of iron, and its feet part iron and part clay.

The *pessukim* continue to explain that this idol represented the various kingdoms that would rule the world till the coming of *mashiach*. The head of gold was Nevuchadnezzar (Bavel), the chest of silver was the kingdom of Madai and Paras, the stomach of copper was the kingdom of Alexander the Great, and the fourth kingdom is the kingdom of Rome.

Even although the different parts of the idol represented different kingdoms which fought with each other, they are all formed part of that single idol that seeks to counteract the rule of Hashem in the world. In other words, even although the kingdoms after Nevuchadnezzar appeared to be totally different and to have their own display of might, they were merely different forms of the *avodah zarah* of Bavel, which was the first world empire that sought to rule independently of Hashem's rule.

With each subsequent change of form, the *avodah zarah* became more obviously cheaper and less worthy, until the whole world will see the bankruptcy of this usurpation of the sovereignty of Hashem, whereupon *mashiach* will come.

Rabbi Eliezer, in his explanation of the term אלהים אחרים, mentions the same series of materials (gold, silver, copper, iron, ore (clay)) as the *pessukim* in Daniel. This is because, just as with the great empires which will rule the world, each rules in a more decadent manner than the previous one, of which it is merely a different form, so too is it with every *avodah zarah*. The *avodah zarah* will appear initially golden and majestic to its worshipper, but in the end will appear as being worth nothing more than clay, although its worshipper will still continue to be enslaved to it in that state.

Similarly, Rabbi Yitzchak, says specifically that there are a limitless number of the names of *avodah zarah*. He does not say that there are a limitless number of types of *avodah zarah*, because these are indeed limited. Rather he says that the names of *avodah zarah* are limitless. This is because, just as the idolatry of Bavel dresses itself up in the different guises of the subsequent empires in order to appear as a new desirable idea, so too does all *avodah zarah* change its appearance, and so its name, to people, although this is always really the same *avodah zarah*, just in a different guise.

This is also why Hashem saying that He is eternal, precludes the *benei yisrael* in future generations from serving new forms of *avodah zarah*.

The new forms of *avodah zarah* are really just the old forms of *avodah zarah*, just in a beguiling new form. This is not obvious to people who live in the time when the *avodah zarah* is נתחדש, but it is obvious from the perspective of Matan Torah.

Therefore Hashem reminded the *benei yisrael* that if they view themselves, in each generation, as a link from the time of Matan Torah till the time of Mashiach, they will not be subject to this illusion of newness, and they will be saved from becoming enslaved to those old types of עבודה זרה which constantly reappear in a new guise.

The *mitzva* to believe in Hashem

It says in this week's *sedrah* (20:2)

אָנֹכִי ה' אֱלֹקֶיךָ אֲשֶׁר הוֹצֵאתִיךָ מֵאֶרֶץ מִצְרַיִם מִבֵּית עֲבָדִים

I am Hashem your G-d who brought you out of the land of Egypt, from the house of slavery.

The Rambam (ספר המצות, מצוה א') says that this *passuk* defines the first of the *taryag* (613) *mitzvos*:

היא הצווי אשר צונו בהאמנת האלקות והוא שנאמין שיש שם עלה וסבה הוא פועל לכל הנמצאים והוא אמרו אנכי ה' אלוקיך

The first *mitzva* is that which Hashem commanded us to believe in a G-d, that is, that we should believe that there is One who is the Source and the Cause. He creates all that exists, and this is what Hashem said [in the first of the *Aseres*

Hadibros] – I am Hashem your G-d.

The Ramban (השגות הרמב"ן על סה"מ, עשה א') however, quotes the Behag (the *Baal Halachos Gedolos*) who is of the opinion that believing in Hashem is a pre-requisite to the *taryag* mitzvos, but is not itself one of the *taryag mitzvos*:

ועם כל זה ראיתי לבעל ההלכות שלא ימנה אותה מצוה בכלל תרי"ג... אבל האמונה במציאותו יתעלה שהודיע אותה אלינו באותות ובמופתים ובגילוי השכינה לעינינו הוא העיקר והשורש שממנו נולדו המצות לא ימנה בחשבונן

All of that said, I saw that the Behag did not count this *mitzvah* as one of his 613... Rather, belief in His existence, which He informed us of via miracles and signs and the revelation of His presence before our eyes, is the foundation and root from which all *mitzvos* are born, but is not itself counted in the list of *mitzvos*.

According to the Behag, once we are aware of the presence of Hashem then we can accept His *mitzvos* but believing in Hashem cannot possibly be one of the *Taryag mitzvos*, because if someone does not believe in Hashem then there can be no *mitzvos*.

- What is basis of the *machlokess* between the Rambam and the Behag? Why does the Rambam say that belief in Hashem is one of the *taryag mitzvos* whereas the Behag argues and says that this is rather the pre-requisite to the *mitzvos*?

It is possible that this *machlokess* is based on a different *machlokess* between the Rambam and the Behag concerning the nature of the *taryag mitzvos*.

The *taryag mitzvos*

The Rambam in Moreh Nevuchim (3:31) explains that the reason that Hashem gave us the *taryag mitzvos* is as follows:

> אבל העניין כמו שזכרנו בלא ספק והוא שכל מצוה מאלו השש מאות ושלוש עשרה מצוות היא לנתינת דעת אמיתי או להסיר דעת רע או לנתינת סדר ישר או להסיר עול או להתלמד במדות טובות או להזהיר ממדות רעות. הכל נתלה בשלשה דברים בדעות ובמדות ובמעשי ההנהגה המדינית...

But the truth is undoubtedly as we have said, that every one of the six hundred and thirteen *mitzvos* serves to inculcate some correct understanding, to remove some erroneous understanding, to establish a proper order in society, to remove evil, to be trained in good character traits or to warn against bad character traits. Everything depends on three things: understanding, character traits, and social conduct...

According to the Rambam, the purpose of the *mitzvos* is to train and to refine the human personality. Through complete observance of the *mitzvos* one may come to correct beliefs and ideas, wholesome character traits and propensities, a correct approach to the underlying principles of life and constructive behavior patterns and thought processes.

The Behag seems to have a different understanding of the purpose of the *mitzvos*, however. The Behag writes in the introduction to his enumeration of the *taryag mitzvos* as follows:

> דרש רבי שמלאי שש מאות ושלש עשרה מצות נצטוו ישראל. אמר רב המנונא מאי קראה, תורה צוה לנו משה. תורה בגימטריא הכי הוי, שש מאות ואחת עשרה הואי? אנכי ולא יהיה מפי הגבורה שמעום, שלש מאות וששים וחמשה מצות לא תעשה ומאתים וארבעים ושמונה מצות עשה, כל המקיימם זוכה לעולם הבא וכל העובר עליהן נידון בשבעה עונשין – סקילה, שריפה, הרג וחנק, מיתה וכרת ומלקות.

Rabbi Simlai expounded, the *benei yisrael* were commanded to perform 613 *mitzvos*. Said Rav Hamnuna, we derive this from the *passuk* that says, "Moshe commanded us concerning the Torah (the *gematria* (numerical value) of the word Torah is 613).

The gemara asks, does the *gematria* of the word Torah come to 613, surely it is only 611? The gemara answers that we heard the first two of the *Aseres Hadibros* (Ten Commandments) directly from Hashem. So Hashem commanded us regarding two *mitzvos* and Moshe Rabbeinu commanded us concerning the other 611, altogether we have 613.

There are 365 *mitzvos lo sa'aseh* (injunctions) and 248 *mitzvos aseh* (positive commandments). Anyone who keeps them merits *olam habah* and anyone who transgresses them is judged with seven punishments – stoning, burning, beheading, strangulation, *misah min ha'shamayim* (death which is administered by the heavenly court), *kares* (spiritual excision) and *malkos* (flogging).

It seems that according to the Behag, we do not seek reasons for the *taryag mitzvos* in terms that are constructive in *olam ha'zeh*. Rather the *taryag mitzvos* are simply prohibitory and mandatory injunctions, the observance of which will cause us to be rewarded in *olam habah*, and the transgression of which will cause us to be punished by *beis din*, as emissaries of Hashem, or directly by the heavenly tribunal.

The punishments administered by *beis din*

This difference in understanding of the purpose of the *taryag mitzvos* gives rise to a *machlokess* between the Rambam and the Behag concerning whether the punishments administered by *beis din* are included in the *taryag mitzvos* (I.e., "Is there a *mitzva* which is incumbent upon *beis din* to apply corporal punishment?")

According to the Behag, as mentioned, the punishments administered by *beis din* are part of the ultimate reward and punishment that is destined for one who keeps or who transgresses the *taryag mitzvos*, however they themselves are not a part of the *taryag mitzvos*.

The Rambam however, in the Sefer Hamitzvos (ספר המצות, שורש י"ד) explains:

והנה קיום אלו הגדרים כלם מצות עשה כי אנחנו נצטווינו שנהרוג זה ושנלקה זה ושנסקול זה ושנקריב קרבן על מה שעברנו עליו

Upholding these safeguards are all a positive commandment because we are commanded that we should kill this one and that we should give *malkos* to this one and that we should stone this one and that we should bring a korban for that which we have transgressed.

Since the Rambam is of the opinion that the purpose of the *taryag mitzvos* is to prescribe an appropriate way to live in *olam ha'zeh*, therefore the Rambam explains that the purpose of the punishments that are administered by *beis din* is to preserve and to protect this wholesome pattern of living that is prescribed by the Torah. According to this understanding, the Rambam describes the punishments administered by *beis din* as safeguards not only because they safeguard the observance of the Torah, but also because they safeguard the healthy state which man is meant to achieve through observance of the Torah.

The first of the *Aseres Hadibros*

Similarly, it would seem that the *machlokess* between the Rambam and the Behag as to whether there is a *mitzvah* to believe in Hashem can be thus explained:

According to the Rambam, belief in Hashem is counted as one of the *taryag mitzvos* because believing in Hashem is part of the wholesome way of life that is prescribed by the Torah. Hashem revealed Himself to the *benei yisrael* at Har Sinai and said, "This is the appropriate way for you to live:

- Continue to remember that I exist.

- Do not serve idols.

- Do not swear falsely in Hashem's name."

And so on.

According to the Behag, however, the meaningfulness of the *mitzvos* is that they are instructions from Hashem which must be fulfilled simply because Hashem has so commanded. Therefore the presumption inherent in the acknowledgment of each *mitzvah* is that Hashem is currently commanding us concerning that *mitzvah*, and that He is telling us that if we perform that *mitzvah* then we will merit *olam habah*.

Since, according to the Behag, the entire framework of the *mitzvos* is that Hashem is prompting us to keep His commandments in *olam ha'zeh* in order that we should merit *olam habah*, belief in Hashem is understood to be the basis of the *taryag mitzvos*, but is not itself included in their enumeration.

Havdalah

It says in this week's *sedrah* (20:7)

זָכוֹר אֶת יוֹם הַשַּׁבָּת לְקַדְּשׁוֹ

Remember the day of the Shabbos to sanctify it.

The Rambam explains (ספר המצוות, מצות עשה קנ"ה) that this *passuk* refers to the obligation to recite *Kiddush* and also the obligation to recite *Havdalah*:

והמצוה הקנ"ה היא שצוונו לקדש את השבת ולאמר דברים בכניסתו וביציאתו, נזכור בם גודל היום הזה ומעלתו והבדלו משאר הימים הקודמים ממנו והבאים אחריו. והוא אמרו יתעלה זכור את יום השבת לקדשו. כלומר זכרהו זכר קדושה והגדלה. וזו היא מצות קדוש. ולשון מכילתא זכור את יום השבת לקדשו קדשהו בברכה. ובביאור אמרו (פסחים ק"ו א') זכרהו על היין. ואמרו גם כן קדשהו בכניסתו וקדשהו ביציאתו. כלומר ההבדלה שהיא גם כן חלק מזכירת שבת מתוקנת ומצווה.

The 155th *mitzva* is that He commanded us to sanctify Shabbos and to say appropriate words when Shabbos comes in and when Shabbos goes out. We should remember in these words the greatness of this day, its excellence and its separateness from the mundane days which precede it and which come after it.

And this is what Hashem said, "Remember the day of the Shabbos to sanctify it". Which means to say, "Remember it as a day of holiness and greatness." And this is the *mitzva* of *Kiddush*. And the way that the *mechilta* expresses this *mitzva* is, "Remember the day of the Shabbos to sanctify it; sanctify it with a *beracha*." And in explanation they said, "Remember it over wine." And they said also, "Sanctify it when it comes in and sanctify it when it goes out." As if to say, announcing the departure of Shabbos is the completion of our remembrance of Shabbos.

The Rambam specifies the formula of *Kiddush* and of *Havdalah* as follows (Hilchos Shabbos, 29:2-3) as follows:

וזה הוא נוסח קידוש היום. ברוך אתה ה' אלוקינו מלך העולם, אשר קידשנו במצוותיו ורצה בנו, ושבת קודשו באהבה וברצון הנחילנו,זיכרון למעשה בראשית, תחילה למקראי קודש, זכר ליציאת מצריים. כי בנו בחרת ואותנו קידשת מכל העמים, ושבת קודשך באהבה וברצון הנחלתנו. ברוך אתה ה', מקדש השבת.

This is formula for *Kiddush*, "Blessed are you Hashem, our G-d, King of the universe, who sanctified us with his *mitzvos* and who was pleased with us, and his holy *shabbos* with love and with good will he bequeathed to us, as a remembrance of creation, the first of the holy convocations, a remembrance to *yetzias mitzrayim*. Because in us You chose and us You sanctified from all the peoples, and your holy *shabbos* with love and good will you bequeathed to us. Blessed are you Hashem, who sanctifies the *shabbos*.

וזה הוא נוסח ההבדלה. ברוך אתה ה' אלוקינו מלך העולם, המבדיל בין קודש לחול, ובין אור לחושך, ובין ישראל לגויים, ובין יום השביעי לששת ימי המעשה. ברוך אתה ה', המבדיל בין קודש לחול.

And this is the formula for *Havdalah*, "Blessed are You Hashem, our G-d, King of the universe, who separates between the holy and the mundane, between light and darkness, between the *benei yisrael* and the nations of the world and between the seventh day and the six days of activity. Blessed are You Hashem, who separates between the holy and the mundane.

- Why is it that the formula for *Kiddush* only mentions the chosenness of the *benei yisrael* and the holiness of the Shabbos, however the formula for *Havdalah* mentions general ideas of separation, such as the separation between the light and darkness?

The Duvno Maggid (the preacher of Duvno, Rabbi Yaakov Krantz z"l) explains with the following *mashal* (parable):

> The king was very proud of his royal painter, who was able to create paintings that were almost lifelike in their perfection, so the King called all his ministers to admire his works of art.
>
> On the first day, the painter showed the ministers a painting of the countryside, which looked so lifelike you could almost step into it.
>
> "But," objected one of the ministers, "In the real countryside, the trees blow in the breeze, and in this picture the trees are stationary?"
>
> So the king told the painter to make a better painting for the next day.
>
> The next day the painter showed the ministers a painting of a city scene, which looked so lifelike you could almost hear the horses' hooves clattering over the cobble stones.
>
> "But," objected the same minister, "In the real city, the carriages are pulled along the streets by the horses, and in this picture the carriages don't move?"

So the king told the painter to make an even better painting for the next day.

The next day the painter showed the ministers a painting of the queen sitting on her throne. The painting was so lifelike that the diamonds in the queen's crown appeared to sparkle in the light.

"But," objected the same minister, "The real queen has wrinkles in her forehead, and in this picture the queen's forehead is perfectly smooth?"

At this, the king motioned to his guards, who removed the minister and cast him into gaol.

The Duvno Maggid explains that we find ourselves in the same position as the king's ministers.

Hashem has placed us in His world and has given us powers of discernment and understanding. We can use these powers for our personal gain, to think about how we can advance our personal agenda. Or we can use our powers of discernment to perceive the holiness that Hashem has placed in creation in order to strengthen our service of Hashem.

When we observe Shabbos we demonstrate that we have chosen to identify *olam ha'zeh* as a place in which we can serve Hashem and observe His Torah. Therefore at the close of Shabbos, not only do we thank Hashem for the elevation of Shabbos that we have now experienced, but we also thank Hashem that we have merited to use our powers of differentiation in order to discern that which is holy and elevated.

Hence not only does the *berachah* of *Havdalah* refer to the separateness between Shabbos and weekdays, but it also refers to various other types of discernment. For we thank Hashem that we have merited to perceive that which He deems to be beautiful and wholesome in His creation.

Mishpatim

Foundation through justice

The *passuk* says at the beginning of this week's *sedrah* (21.1)

וְאֵלֶּה הַמִּשְׁפָּטִים אֲשֶׁר תָּשִׂים לִפְנֵיהֶם

And these are the laws that you should place before them.

The medrash comments on this *passuk*

דבר אחר וְאֵלֶּה הַמִּשְׁפָּטִים הדא היא דכתיב (תהלים קמ"ז, י"ט) [מַגִּיד דְּבָרָיו לְיַעֲקֹב חֻקָּיו וּמִשְׁפָּטָיו לְיִשְׂרָאֵל. לֹא עָשָׂה כֵן לְכָל גּוֹי וּמִשְׁפָּטִים בַּל יְדָעוּם הַלְלוּ קָהּ.] מגיד דבריו ליעקב אלו הדברות. חוקיו ומשפטיו לישראל אלו המשפטים. לפי שאין מדותיו של הקב"ה כמדת בשר ודם מדת בשר ודם מורה לאחרים לעשות והוא אינו עושה כלום הקב"ה אינו כן אלא מה שהוא עושה הוא אומר לישראל לעשות ולשמור

The *passuk* says, "And these are the laws."

This is as it is written in Tehillim, "He told His commandments to Yaakov, His statutes and laws to the *benei yisrael*. He did not do so for any other nation, and He did not tell them these laws. *Hallelukah*."

"He tells His word to Yaakov," this refers to the *Aseres Ha'dibros*.

"His statutes and His laws to the *benei yisrael*," this refers to the civil laws.

Because the way of Hashem is not as the way of man. Men tell other people what to do, but they do not keep their own laws. Hashem does not do so, however. Rather, He only tells the *benei yisrael* to do and guard what He Himself does.

(This means to say that, according to the medrash, when the *passuk* says in Tehillim, "He tells His word to Yaakov, His statutes and His laws to the *benei yisrael*," the *passuk* means that Hashem tells the *benei yisrael* to keep those laws that Hashem applies to Himself.)

- What is the connection between Hashem only giving the Torah to the *benei yisrael* and between Hashem keeping the laws of the Torah?

It would seem that we can explain as follows:

The Zohar says[22]

תשובה הוא אחד מתרי"ג מצות ושבת עד ה' אלוקיך וגומר ואינו מועיל אלא דווקא לישראל ולא לגוי וא"ת ננוה שהיה מועיל להם תשובה שנאמר וירא ה' כי שבו מדרכיהם הרעה וגומר וינחם ה' על הרעה וגומר והם היו גוים ולמה היה מועיל להם תשובה. חדא לפי שהעמידו דיניהם על דין תורה שאפילו גזל מריש ובנאו בבירה היה מקעקע את כל הבירה והחזיר הגזילה לבעליו ולפי שדנו כדין ישראל לפיכך היה מועיל בהם תשובה

Teshuvah is one of the 613 *mitzvos* as the *passuk* says, "And you will return to Hashem your G-d," and *teshuvah* only helps for the *benei yisrael* and not for a non-Jew. And if you will ask that Hashem accepted the *teshuvah* of the people of Ninveh, yet they were not Jews? There are three reasons for this. The first reason is because they accepted to judge by Torah law, so that even if one stole a beam and he built it into a mansion, he would destroy the entire mansion in order to be able to return the beam to its owner.

It is evident from the Zohar that the difference between the laws of the Torah and the laws of the *umos ha'olam* is that according to the Torah, it may be necessary to destroy an entire mansion in order to return a beam, whereas according to the laws of the *umos ha'olam*, this would never be required.

This is because, according to the laws of the Torah, every building is imbued with the *kedushah* that allows it to be used for its role in ensuring the continuity of the *benei yisrael*. Therefore if

---

[22] מובא בספר דברי שמואל

one of the beams was stolen, the building is no longer fit for this purpose and the whole building must be dismantled in order that the beam can be returned to its rightful owner. On the other hand, according to the understanding of the *umos ha'olam*, a house has no intrinsic *kedushah* so it does not matter how it was built, and therefore there is no reason for the owner of the building to not merely return the value of the beam to its owner.

The reason that the medrash makes a connection between Hashem only giving the Torah to the *benei yisrael* and between Hashem keeping the Torah, is that since Hashem keeps the *halachos* of the Torah, as if it were, regarding the way in which He runs the world, therefore the everyday items we earn by keeping the monetary *halachos*, become elevated to the level at which they too become part of Hashem's plan for the world and for the *benei yisrael*.

The medrash continues

> דבר אחר וְאֵלֶּה הַמִּשְׁפָּטִים הדא היא דכתיב (תהלים צ"ט) ועוז מלך משפט אהב... ואם עשיתם את הדינין עתיד הקב"ה להחזיר לכם בתי דיניין שלכם שנאמר (ישעיה, א') ואשיבה שופטיך כבראשונה. מה כתיב אחריו ציון במשפט תפדה

> The *passuk* says in Tehillim, "Strength is to the King who loves justice..." But if you did keep the monetary laws, Hashem will rebuild your courts of law, as the *passuk* says, 'And I will restore your judges as of old,' and the *passuk* continues, 'Tzion shall be redeemed through justice.'"

Since observing the Torah monetary laws elevates everything we have to the level that it is part of Hashem's plan for the future of the *benei yisrael*, the reward for this *mitzva* is the promised continuation of the *benei yisrael* until we merit to see the restoration of the *beis din* in Yerushalayim.

Terumah

Donating to the *mishkan*

The *passuk* says at the beginning of this week's *sedrah* (25.2)

דַּבֵּר אֶל בְּנֵי יִשְׂרָאֵל וְיִקְחוּ לִי תְּרוּמָה מֵאֵת כָּל אִישׁ אֲשֶׁר יִדְּבֶנּוּ לִבּוֹ תִּקְחוּ אֶת תְּרוּמָתִי

Speak to the *benei yisrael* and tell them that they should take for me a tithe, from every person whose heart so moves him you should accept my tithe.

Rashi comments

ויקחו לי תרומה: לי לשמי

And they should take for me a tithe: This means they should take it *lishmah* (for My name).

- Why does the Torah mention specifically with regards to donating to the *mishkan* that this *mitzvah* should be done *lishmah*?

The Medrash Tanchuma comments

ויקחו לי תרומה, זה שאמר הכתוב כי לקח טוב נתתי לכם (משלי ד' ב') אמר רבי שמעון בן לקיש, שני פרקממטוטין עומדין זה עם זה, אחד בידו מטכסא ואחד בידו פלפלין. אמרו זה לזה בוא ונחליף ביני ובינך. נטל זה את הפלפלין, וזה המטכסא. מה שביד זה אין ביד זה, ומה שביד זה אין ביד זה. אבל התורה אינה כן, זה שונה סדר זרעים וזה שונה סדר מועד, השנו זה לזה, נמצא ביד זה שנים וביד זה שנים, יש פרקמטיא יפה מזו, הוי כי לקח טוב נתתי לכם.

And they should take for me a tithe. This is what the *passuk* refers to when it says, "For a goodly instruction have I given to you." Rabbi Shimon ben Lakish said, "Two traders stand next to each other, one has silk and the other has peppers. They said to each other, 'Let us make an exchange between us.' This one took the peppers and the other took the silk. So it comes out, that each one loses what the other gains.

But with the Torah it is not so, for example, one learns Zeraim and the other learns Moed, then each teaches the other. So it comes out that each one has in his hand two *sedarim*. Is there any merchandise better than this?"

- What is the connection between the donation to the *mishkan* and the fact that two people can share their Torah and neither lose in the process?

The Medrash Rabbah says

> ד"א וְיִקְחוּ לִי תְּרוּמָה הה"ד (משלי כ"ב, א') נבחר שם מֵעֹשֶׁר רב [מכסף ומזהב חן טוב] נבחר שמו של משה, שנאמר (תהלים ק"ו, כ"ג) לולי משה בחירו, וכן הוא אומר (שמות ל"ג, י"ז) ואדעך בשם, מעשרו של קרח, שנאמר (במדבר ט"ז, י"ז) חמשים ומאתים מַחְתֹּת... ד"א נבחר שמו של פנחס מן עשרו של זמרי... ד"א נבחר שמו של מרדכי מעשרו של המן...

And they should take for me a tithe. This refers to that which it says, "A good name is better than much wealth." Moshe's name was better than the wealth of Korach. Pinchos's name was better than the wealth of Zimri. Mordechai's name was better than the wealth of Haman.

- What is the connection between that which a good name is better than wealth, and the *passuk* of וְיִקְחוּ לִי תְּרוּמָה?

It would seem that we can explain as follows[23]:

The Yalkut Shimoni says

> ויקחו לי תרומה. מי שנאמר בו לה' הארץ ומלואה, אשר לו הים והוא עשהו ואומר הן לה' אלקיך השמים הוא צריך לבשר ודם. אלא שחומד לישראל לשרות שכינתו בהם, כאב שמחמד לבניו, לכך נאמר ויקחו לי.

And they should take a tithe for me. He about whom it says, "To Hashem is the world and its fullness," "To whom is the sea and He created it," "Behold Hashem possesses the

---

[23] עיין בספר דברי יואל

heavens," does He need the gifts of flesh and blood?

Rather He desires the *benei yisrael* so that He can rest His *shechinah* among them, like a father who desires his sons, therefore it says, "And they should take for me."

Apparently the Yalkut Shimoni should have said אלא שחומד לשרות שכינתו בישראל - "rather he desires to make His *shechinah* dwell among the *benei yisrael*", and not אלא שחומד לישראל לשרות שכינתו בהם - "rather he desires the *benei yisrael*, to make His *shechinah* dwell among them"?

It would appear from the Yalkut Shimoni that the *mishkan* itself was representative of the *benei yisrael*, so that Hashem desired that there should be a representation of the *benei yisrael* before Him, on which he would rest His *shechinah*. This means to say that the *benei yisrael* did not simply donate the materials with which the *mishkan* was made, rather the materials that they donated were donated as a keepsake of themselves whereby they would be remembered before Hashem.[24]

---

[24] See also Medrash Rabbah, Tetzaveh, 36.1

וְאַתָּה תְּצַוֶּה [אֶת בְּנֵי יִשְׂרָאֵל וְיִקְחוּ אֵלֶיךָ שֶׁמֶן זַיִת זָךְ כָּתִית לַמָּאוֹר]. הדא הוא דכתיב (ירמיהו י"א, ט"ז) זַיִת רַעֲנָן יְפֵה פְרִי תֹאַר קָרָא ה' שְׁמֵךְ. וכי לא נקראו ישראל אלא כזית הזה בלבד, והלא בכל מיני אילנות נאים ומשובחים נקראו ישראל

And you shall command the *benei yisrael* to bring you clear oil of beaten olives for lighting. About this is written, Hashem named you "Verdant olive tree, fair, with choice fruit."

And are the *benei yisrael* only likened to an olive tree? But are the *benei yisrael* not compared to all sorts of pleasant and praiseworthy trees?

That is why the Yalkut Shimoni says שחומד לישראל לשרות שכינתו בהם – "That he desires the *benei yisrael* so that He can rest His *shechinah* among them," for Hashem did not need the materials of which the *mishkan* was made, as He owns the heavens and the earth. Instead He desired donations that would be representative of the *benei yisrael*, so that when Hashem rested His *shechinah* in the *mishkan*, He thereby also rested His *shechinah* amidst the *benei yisrael*.

Subsequently we can understand that the reason that the Medrash Rabbah quotes the *passuk* that says, "A good name is better than much wealth," is because each donation to the *mishkan* represented the name, i.e. the essence of the *neshama*, of the person who gave that donation.

Furthermore, we can understand the intention of the Medrash Tanchuma is that just as when two people share their Torah knowledge with each other, each one gains the insights of the other, without the other incurring any loss, so too when the *benei yisrael* gave their donations to the *mishkan*, they thereby shared the *madregah* that had accomplished with each other, so that each of the *benei yisrael* was able to perceive the *madregah* of the entire *benei yisrael*, when they entered the *mishkan*.

At first sight the medrash would seem difficult to understand, because the *passuk* at the beginning of Tetzaveh does not compare the *benei yisrael* to olive oil, rather it commands them to donate olive oil for the lighting of the menorah.

It would seem therefore that the medrash understands that the *benei yisrael* were not simply commanded to donate olive oil to the *mishkan*, rather they were commanded to donate the תכונת הנפש (attribute of the soul) that is likened to olive oil.

Since each person's donation to the *mishkan* represented their unique perception of Hashem, this means that each person gave the aspect that they understood in the name of Hashem, to the building of the *mishkan*.

This is why Rashi says

ויקחו לי תרומה: לי לשמי

> **And they should take for me a tithe**: This means they should take it *lishmah* (for My name).

In other words, each person donated their own unique understanding of the name of Hashem to the *mishkan*, so that in the entire *mishkan* would be represented the entire meaning of the name of Hashem.

Tetzaveh

The Western Lamp of the menorah

It says at the beginning of this week's *sedrah* (27:20)

וְאַתָּה תְּצַוֶּה אֶת בְּנֵי יִשְׂרָאֵל וְיִקְחוּ אֵלֶיךָ שֶׁמֶן זַיִת זָךְ כָּתִית לַמָּאוֹר לְהַעֲלֹת נֵר תָּמִיד

And you should command the *benei yisrael* and they should bring to you clear olive oil, crushed, for lighting, to burn a constant light.

Rashi comments on this *passuk*:

תמיד: כל לילה ולילה קרוי תמיד

[Even although the *menorah* did not burn during the day, nevertheless the *passuk* says that the *menorah* burnt constantly, meaning to say that] since the *menorah* was lit every night this is called this it burnt constantly.

The Ramban, however, says:

ומדרש רבותינו אינו כך אלא כך שנו בספרי (ריש בהעלותך) יאירו שבעת הנרות (במדבר ח' ב')... תמיד (שם) שיהא נר מערבי דולק תדיר שממנו מדליקין את המנורה בין הערבים

Rashi's explanation does not seem to go according to the Sifri, which explains that the reason that the *passuk* says that the *menorah* burnt constantly is because the Western Lamp of the *menorah* burnt the whole day till the time came to light the *menorah* the next evening, when the Western Lamp was used to re-light the *menorah*.

- Why does the *passuk* refer specifically to the Western Lamp?

The Baal Haturim says at the beginning of this week's *sedrah*

לא הזכיר משה בזה הסדר משא"כ בכל החומש שמשעה שנולד משה אין סדר שלא הוזכר בה (חוץ ממשנה תורה) והטעם משום שאמר מחני נא מספרך אשר כתבת וקללת חכם אפי' על תנאי באה ונתקיים בזה

The Torah does not mention Moshe's name in this week's *sedrah* as opposed to the rest of the Chumash. Because from the time Moshe was born there is no *sedrah* where Moshe's name is not mentioned (except in Sefer Devarim which is because Moshe himself was speaking).

The reason is because Moshe said after the *chet ha'egel* (the sin of the Golden Calf) - וְאִם אַיִן מְחֵנִי נָא מִסִּפְרְךָ אֲשֶׁר כָּתָבְתָּ – "And if you will not forgive the *benei yisrael*, then wipe me out from Your book which You have written."

And we have a general rule that if a *chacham* makes a curse then it takes effect even if the curse was made conditionally and the condition was not fulfilled. Therefore Moshe's curse on himself was fulfilled through that which his name is not mentioned in this *sedrah*.

- Why was Tetzaveh chosen to be that *sedrah* from which Moshe's name was omitted?

Rabbeinu Bachya (on Pirkei Avos) explains that the understanding of the Torah which is attainable through our efforts is divided up into six categories:

- חכמה: Wisdom
- בינה: Insight
- עצה: Council
- גבורה: Strength
- דעת: Intelligence
- יראת ה': Fear of Hashem

These six categories of understanding are listed in the *passuk* in Yeshaya (11:2) which says

וְנָחָה עָלָיו רוּחַ ה' רוּחַ חָכְמָה וּבִינָה רוּחַ עֵצָה וּגְבוּרָה רוּחַ דַּעַת וְיִרְאַת ה'

And a spirit of Hashem will rest on him, a spirit of wisdom and insight, a spirit of council and strength, a spirit of intelligence and fear of Hashem.

There is a seventh level of understanding, however, which is greater than all of these and which is given as a gift from Hashem as a reward for one's efforts to understand the Torah. This is the level of רוח ה' – the spirit of Hashem.

(According to Rabbeinu Bachya, all of these seven levels of understanding are represented in the menorah. The central stem of the menorah represents the level of רוח ה', and the other branches represent the six categories of understanding which can be attained through our toil in Torah.)

- It would seem difficult to understand why the *passuk* in Yeshaya lists רוח ה' first. If this is the greatest level of understanding, and is granted as a gift by Hashem once someone achieves the other six levels of understanding, then this level should be listed last?

It would seem that we can explain as follows:

The six categories of understanding of the Torah which can be attained through toil in the Torah are those levels of understanding which can be understood by joining the letters of the אלף בית (the Hebrew alphabet) into words and thoughts. The level of רוח ה' however, relates to the light of the Torah which is hidden in each letter of the אלף בית, before it has been joined into words.

When a person is granted the level of understanding of רוח ה', then he perceives the light of the Torah which is hidden in the letters of the אלף בית. Once a person achieves this level of understanding, the light of the Torah which is revealed to him in the אלף בית before it has been joined into words, spreads out to fill those other six levels of understanding of the Torah, which he understood previously.

Since those six levels of understanding are comprised of the letters of the אלף בית in combination, therefore when the light of the אלף בית itself is revealed to a person, this light also fills his prior understanding which was, in the end, also based on combining the letters of the אלף בית. Therefore, the reason that the *passuk* in Yeshaya mentions the level of רוח ה' first, is because the level of רוח ה' spreads into the other levels of understanding as well.

Moshe wanted his name to be blotted out, in order to save the *benei yisrael*. As a reward for this self-sacrifice, Hashem gave Moshe the gift of understanding that can only be understood before the letters of the אלף בית are joined into words. Since Moshe did not want the letters of his name to joined into the word Moshe, Hashem gave him the understanding of the Torah that exists before the letters of the Torah are joined into words.

This level of understanding of the Torah is represented by the Western Lamp[25], which burnt till the next evening through a miracle, represents the level of Torah understanding which is given as a gift. The other six lamps of the menorah which only burnt according to the amount of oil that was placed in them,

---

[25] This assumes that the Western Lamp is the central lamp of the menorah, which goes according to the opinion of the Rambam (הלכות בית הבחירה, ג', ח').

ששת הנרות הקבועים בששת הקנים היוצאים מן המנורה כולן פניהם לנר האמצעי שעל קני המנורה וזה הנר האמצעי פניו כנגד קדש הקדשים והוא הנקרא נר מערבי

> The six lamps that are fixed in the six branches that come out of the central column of the menorah all turn towards the central lamp, and the central lamp is turned towards the *kodesh ha'kedashim* and is called the Western Lamp.

represent the levels of Torah understanding that can be understood through toil.

That is why in the first *passuk* in Tetzaveh, Moshe's name is hidden, and the Torah commands that we should light the central lamp of the menorah.

The greatness of Aharon

The *passuk* says in this week's sedrah (29.1)

וְזֶה הַדָּבָר אֲשֶׁר תַּעֲשֶׂה לָהֶם לְקַדֵּשׁ אֹתָם לְכַהֵן לִי לְקַח פַּר אֶחָד בֶּן בָּקָר וְאֵילִם שְׁנַיִם תְּמִימִם

And this is what you shall do to them to consecrate them to serve me as *cohanim*. Take a young bull of the herd and two rams without blemish.

The medrash comments on this *passuk*

וְזֶה הַדָּבָר אֲשֶׁר תַּעֲשֶׂה לָהֶם. הה"ד (תהלים קי"ט, פ"ט) לְעוֹלָם ה' דְּבָרְךָ נִצָּב בַּשָּׁמָיִם. אמר דוד כשם שאתה אמת שנאמר (ירמיה י', י') וה' אלקים אמת, כך דברך אמת שנאמר לְעוֹלָם ה' דְּבָרְךָ נִצָּב בַּשָּׁמַיִם, אל תאמר בַּשָּׁמָיִם אלא כַּשָּׁמָיִם. כשם שמתחלה גזר ונעשו שמים אף דבר שדברת לקדש את אהרן ואת בניו קיים לעולם שנאמר (במדבר כ"ה, י"ג) והיתה לו ולזרעו אחריו ברית כְּהֻנַּת עולם. למה כך (ישעיה נ"ה,

י"א) כן יהיה דברי אשר יצא מפי. לכך נאמר וְזֶה הַדָּבָר.

And this is what you shall do to them to consecrate them. This is what is stated in Tehillim, "Forever Hashem, Your word stands in the heavens." Dovid said, "Just as You are true, as the *passuk* says, 'And Hashem is true,' so too is your word true, as the *passuk* says, 'Forever Hashem, Your word stands in the heavens.'

Do not read בשמים – in the heavens, rather read כשמים – like the heavens. Just as in the beginning Hashem commanded and the heavens were made, so too the word that You spoke to sanctify Aharon and his sons stands forever, as the *passuk* says, 'And it will be to him and his descendants after him as an eternal covenant of *kehunah*.' Why is this so? Because the *passuk* says, 'So too will be My word that comes out of my mouth,' that is why it says, 'And this is the matter.'

- Why does the medrash finds it necessary to explain that the word of Hashem to appoint the *kohanim* endures forever, more so than any other part of the Torah?

- What is the connection between Hashem creating the heavens and Aharon being appointed as a *cohen*?

The *passuk* says in Korach (Bamidbar 16.5)

וַיְדַבֵּר אֶל קֹרַח וְאֶל כָּל עֲדָתוֹ לֵאמֹר בֹּקֶר וְיֹדַע ה' אֶת אֲשֶׁר לוֹ וְאֶת הַקָּדוֹשׁ וְהִקְרִיב אֵלָיו וְאֵת אֲשֶׁר יִבְחַר בּוֹ יַקְרִיב אֵלָיו

And he spoke to Korach and all his company, saying, "In the morning Hashem will make known who is His and who is holy, and He will draw him close to himself. He will draw close to Himself the one whom He has chosen.

Rashi comments

> ומדרשו בקר א"ל משה גבולות חלק הקב"ה בעולמו יכולים אתם להפוך בקר לערב כן תוכלו לבטל את זו שנאמר (בראשית א') ויהי ערב ויהי בוקר ויבדל כך (דברי הימים א' כ"ג) ויבדל אהרן להקדישו וגו'

Moshe said to Korach, 'Hashem has placed boundaries in His world. Can you then turn morning into evening? Similarly you will not be able to annul this decree, as it says, 'And it was evening and it was morning… and Hashem separated between the light and the darkness,' so too, 'And Hashem separated Aharon to sanctify him.''

- It would seem difficult to understand what Moshe was conveying to Korach. If Korach believed that Hashem had appointed Aharon then he did not need the analogy of the difference between morning and evening. And if Korach did not believe that Hashem had appointed Aharon then he would not find the analogy to morning and evening any more compelling than Moshe's original selection of Aharon?

It would seem that we can explain as follows[26].

The Shlah says (תורה שבכתב, תצוה, תורה אור)

> כבר בארתי בארוכה בפרשת תרומה כי המשכן הוא כבריאת שמים וארץ וצבאיהם מעלה ומטה. והמשכן הוא תיקון. ואהרן הוא תיקון לאדם הראשון שנתרחק, אבל באהרן כתיב (שמות כ"ח, א') ואתה הקרב אליך את אהרן וגו'. וזהו סוד (ויקרא ט"ז, י"ז) וכל אדם לא יהיה באהל, רומז על אדם קדמאה. והעולם נברא בחסד כמו שנאמר (תהלים פ"ט, ג') עולם חסד יבנה, והבנין של מעלה סוד ז' ימי בראשית הפנימיים הוא מתחיל מחסד, וכן באהרן כתיב (דברים ל"ג, ח') תומיך ואוריך לאיש חסידך, וכן היא מדתו בסוד כהן לוי ישראל הוא חסד גבורה תפארת

The building of the *mishkan* mirrored the creation of the heavens, the earth and all their hosts, so that building the *mishkan* rectified the heavens and the earth. Similarly, Aharon rectified the fall of Adam when he was distanced from Hashem. We know that the world was created through *chesed*, as the *passuk* says in Tehillim, "The world was founded through *chesed*," hence the creation of the inner meaning of the world during the seven days of Bereishis, began with the *middah* of *chesed*. Thus, the *middah* of Aharon is *chesed*, as the *passuk* says, "And of Levi he said, 'Let Your Urim ve'Tumim be to Your man of *chesed*.'"

Korach reasoned that since Aharon was chosen due to the *madregah* that he had acquired, then if he would also reach that *madregah* he should also be chosen as a *cohen*.

---

[26] עיין בספר יקר מפז

Moshe refuted Korach's argument by explaining that Aharon, through his personal *avodah*, had traversed the entire process whereby Hashem had created the inner meaning of the world during *ma'aseh bereishis* (creation). This means to say that Aharon had recreated the world of *chesed* in which the *benei yisrael* would always be able to achieve a *kapparah* (atonement) through the *avodah* in the *beis ha'mikdash*.

Therefore, just as Korach would be unable to imagine changing the physical way in which the world operates, so too would it be unimaginable for him to traverse the personal *avodah* of Aharon, whereby was recreated the pristine *chesed* that existed at the time of creation.

Similarly, the medrash says that Aharon's appointment as *cohen* is eternal just as the creation of the heavens is eternal. Since Aharon recreated a pristine world of *chesed* and forgiveness, such as had not existed since the creation of Adam *ha'rishon*, therefore his appointment as the *cohen gadol* was also as immutable as *ma'aseh bereishis*.

Moshe's loan to the *benei yisrael*

The passuk says at the beginning of this week's sedrah (30.12)

כִּי תִשָּׂא אֶת רֹאשׁ בְּנֵי יִשְׂרָאֵל לִפְקֻדֵיהֶם וְנָתְנוּ אִישׁ כֹּפֶר נַפְשׁוֹ לַה' בִּפְקֹד אֹתָם וְלֹא יִהְיֶה בָהֶם נֶגֶף בִּפְקֹד אֹתָם

When you count the *benei yisrael* according to their enrollment, then each man shall give a ransom for his soul to Hashem, so that no plague may come upon them through their being enrolled.

The Medrash Tanchuma (3) comments on this *passuk* as follows.

כי תשא את ראש בני ישראל. כך פתח רבי תנחומא בר אבא, מתוקה שנת העובד אם מעט אם הרבה יאכל, והשבע לעשיר איננו מניח לו לישון (קהלת ה' י"א). אמרו לו לשלמה... והרי אמרת והשבע לעשיר איננו מניח לו לישון, מה הוא. ודאי מניח לו לישון. שכל מי שהוא שבע, המאכל מביאהו לידי שינה. אמר להם, בעשירי תורה אני מדבר ולא בעשירי ממון. כיצד. היה אדם גדול ועשיר בתורה למד תלמידים הרבה ורבץ תורה ברבים ושבע מן התורה, אף על פי שהוא מת, אין התלמידים שהעמיד מניחין לו לישון, אלא יושבין ועוסקין תלמידיו בתורה ובתלמוד ובהלכה ואגדות, ואומרים תלמידיו הלכות ושמועות משמו ומזכירין שמו בכל שעה, ואין מניחין אותו לישון בקבר...

וכן משה למד תורה לישראל והדריכן למצות, ונתן להם סדרי תורה ופרשיות שקוראים בהם בכל שבת ובכל חדש ובכל מועד, והם מזכירים אותו בכל פרשה ופרשה. ובפרשת שקלים אמר משה לפני

הקדוש ברוך הוא, רבונו של עולם, משאני מת אין אני נזכר. אמר לו הקדוש ברוך הוא, חייך, כשם שאתה עומד עכשיו ונותן להם פרשת שקלים ואתה זוקף את ראשן, כך בכל שנה ושנה שקוראין אותה לפני, כאלו את עומד שם באותה שעה וזוקף את ראשן. מנין. ממה שקראו בענין וידבר ה' אל משה לאמר, כי תשא את ראש. שא את ראש לא נאמר, אלא כי תשא.

Rabbi Tanchuma said, "The *passuk* says in Koheles, 'The sleep of the labourer is sweet if he has eaten little or much, but the wealth of the rich man allows him no sleep.'

The *chachamim* said to Shlomo, 'How can you say that the wealth of the rich man allows him no sleep? Certainly it allows him to sleep, because anyone who has eaten to his fill will sleep well.'

Shlomo replied, 'I am talking about people who are wealthy in Torah, and not about people who are wealthy in money. Because when such a person dies, the *talmidim* say over *halachos* and explanations in his name, and they do not allow him to sleep in the grave.'"

So too you find that Moshe taught Torah to the *benei yisrael* and he showed them how to do *mitzvos*, and he gave them *sedros* which they read on Shabbos and on Yom Tov. And they mention Moshe in every *parsha* that they read.

Concerning פרשת שקלים Moshe said to Hashem, "Master of the Universe, after I die no-one will remember me." Hashem replied to him, "By your life, just as you are standing now and you are giving them פרשת שקלים and by doing so you make them stand proudly, so too every year when they read this *parshah* before

Me it will be as if you are standing there and making them stand proudly."

This is why the *passuk* says כי תשא, meaning, "When you will raise (in the future)."

- If every *talmid chacham* whose talmidim learn his Torah is not forgotten, then why did Moshe feel that he would be forgotten, to the extent that Hashem had to give him a special promise that he would be remembered through פרשת שקלים?

The Medrash Rabbah says at the beginning of this week's *sedrah* (39, 1)

א"ל הקב"ה משה חייבין לי ישראל מה שלוו הימני שנאמר "כִּי תִשָּׂא" כמה דתימא (דברים כד, י): "כי תשה ברעך" אמור להם שיפרעו מה שהם חייבים לי הוי "כִּי תִשָּׂא" ואשלמה להם שנאמר (הושע ב, א): "והיה מספר בני ישראל כחול הים"

Hashem said to Moshe, "The *benei yisrael* owe me that which they borrowed from Me (the medrash explains that the word תשא can refer to a loan), tell them that they should pay Me what they owe Me, but in the end I will repay them as the *passuk* says, 'And the number of the *benei yisrael* shall be like the sand by the sea.'"

- What did the *benei yisrael* borrow from Hashem?

Later in the *sedrah*, the *passuk* says (31:18)

וַיִּתֵּן אֶל מֹשֶׁה כְּכַלֹּתוֹ לְדַבֵּר אִתּוֹ בְּהַר סִינַי שְׁנֵי לֻחֹת הָעֵדֻת לֻחֹת אֶבֶן כְּתֻבִים בְּאֶצְבַּע אֱלֹקִים

And Hashem gave to Moshe when He had finished speaking with Him on Har Sinai, the two לוחות of stone, inscribed by the finger of Hashem.

The Medrash Tanchuma (15) comments on this *passuk*

ויתן אל משה ככלתו. זה שאמר הכתוב, מתן אדם ירחיב לו ולפני גדולים ינחנו (משלי י"ח ט"ז), מתנה שאדם נותן משלו, ירחיב לו, כמעשה באבון רמאה שהיה בבצרה, והלכו רבותינו לשם לבקש פרנסה, ולא בקש לפסוק עד שפסקו כל בני בית הכנסת, ופסק הוא כנגד כולן, לפיכך קורין אותו אבון רמאה. מה עשו רבותינו. הושיבוהו אצלן, לקיים מה שנאמר, מתן אדם ירחיב לו וגו'

This is what the *passuk* says in Mishlei, "The gift that a man gives will provide him with ample space and will place him before great people." Like that which happened with Abun the Cheat who lived in Batzrah. The *chachamim* went there to collect for the yeshiva, and Abun did not want to say how much he would give until the entire shul had said how much they were going to donate.

After they had all said how much they would donate, Abun donated an equivalent amount to the rest of the shul. That is why they called him Abun the Cheat (because he cheated the rest of the shul by single-handedly matching their *mitzvah*). What did the *chachamim* do? They made him sit together with them, to fulfill that which the *passuk* says, "The gift that a man gives will provide him with ample space."

- What does the story about Abun have to do with the *passuk* of ויתן אל משה ככלותו?

It would seem that we can explain as follows[27]:

Rashi (30:15) explains that three donations are alluded to in this *parsha*:

לכפר על נפשתיכם: ...לפי שרמז להם כאן ג' תרומות שנכתב כאן תרומת ה' ג' פעמים אחת תרומת אדנים שמנאן כשהתחילו בנדבת המשכן ונתנו כל אחד ואחד מחצית השקל ועלה למאת הככר שנאמר (שמות ל"ח) וכסף פקודי העדה מאת ככר ומהם נעשו האדנים שנאמר ויהי מאת ככר הכסף וגו'

והשנית אף היא ע"י מנין שמנאן משהוקם המשכן הוא המנין האמור בתחלת חומש הפקודים (במדבר א') בא' לחדש השני בשנה השנית ונתנו כל אחד מחצית השקל והן לקנות מהן קרבנות צבור של כל שנה ושנה והושוו בהם עניים ועשירים ועל אותה תרומה נאמר לכפר על נפשותיכם שהקרבנות לכפרה הם באים והשלישית היא תרומת המשכן כמו שנא' (שמות ל"ה) כל מרים תרומת כסף ונחשת ולא היתה יד כולם שוה בה אלא איש איש מה שנדבו לבו

The *passuk* alludes to three different תרומות, since it uses the expression תרומת ה' three times. One mention is an allusion to the תרומה that was used for making the sockets of the *mishkan*, for Moshe counted them when they began to contribute towards the building of the *mishkan*, when each

---

[27] עיין בספר דברי יואל

person gave half a *shekel*, the total amounting to a hundred talents… and of these the sockets were made… The second תרומה was also levied to count them, for Moshe counted them again after the *mishkan* was erected; that is the counting referred to in the beginning of the Bamidbar and then too, everyone gave half a *shekel*.

These *shekalim* were used to buy the קרבנות ציבור each year. Rich and poor were made alike in regard to these half *shekalim*; and it is with reference to this תרומה that the *passuk* uses the expression לכפר על נפשתיכם, for the קרבנות were brought in order to achieve a כפרה for the *benei yisrael*.

The third תרומה was that offered for the building of the *mishkan*, as it is said, (Shemos 35:24) "Every one that offered an offering of silver and brass…". In this תרומה however, they did not all participate equally, but each one brought whatever his heart prompted him to give.

It comes out from Rashi that all three תרומות revolved around the *mishkan*. One תרומה was used to cast the sockets of the *mishkan*, one תרומה was used to buy the קרבנות that were brought in the *mishkan* and one תרומה was used to count the *benei yisrael* after the completion of the *mishkan*.

We can understand that the significance of this association as follows:

The high *madregah* which the *benei yisrael* were granted when they came out of Mitzrayim was given to them as a gift (אתערותא דלעילא). Through this gift the benei yisrael experienced נבואה both at קריעת ים סוף and also at הר סיני. However, when the *benei yisrael* built the *mishkan*, this marked the start of the time when they were expected to reach this *madregah* by their own efforts, through their עבודה in the *mishkan* (אתערותא דלתתא).

The loan that Hashem gave to the *benei yisrael* was the ability to experience high מדרגות even when they had not earned these מדרגות through their own efforts. The repayment which the *benei yisrael* made was that they committed to earning these מדרגות through their עבודה in the *mishkan*. This mode of עבודת ה' was represented by the donation of the שקלים, because people generally gain money through their interactions with the practical, earthy aspects of עולם הזה. Therefore, by donating their money to the *mishkan* it was as if the *benei yisrael* were saying that they would elevate the most earthy aspects of their existence through their עבודת ה'.

However, just as Hashem loaned the מדרגות given through אתערותא דלעילא to the *benei yisrael*, so too Moshe loaned of his own *madregah* to the *benei yisrael* at the time that they made the עגל הזהב, as the Medrash Rabbah (Shemos 43, 1) says

ויאמר להשמידם (תהלים ק"ו כ"ג), מיד התחיל חוגר בתפלה. הוי, ויחל משה את פני ה' אלקיו, שעמד בקלות ראש לפני הקב"ה, לבקש צרכן של ישראל. הוי, ויחל משה.

Hashem said to destroy the *benei yisrael*, immediately Moshe began to gird himself with *tefillah*. Therefore the *passuk* says ויחל משה, since he stood in silliness (as if it were) before Hashem to ask for the needs of the *benei yisrael* (i.e. it was foolish for Moshe to stand before Hashem's wrath). That is why the *passuk* says ויחל משה, which can mean that Moshe began, but can also mean that Moshe made himself חולין.

Moshe knew that since he had not been part of the *aveirah* of the עגל הזהב that if his מדרגה would be sthared out among the *benei yisrael*, this would provide them with the ability to survive the מדת הדין that was poised against them in the aftermath of the עגל הזהב. In this way, Moshe caused the *benei yisrael* to be able to stand up straight again, after the חטא העגל.

The entire Torah that Moshe transmitted to the *benei yisrael* may not have been enough for Moshe personally to be revived by the Torah learning of the *benei yisrael*, because Moshe was merely the in-between to hand over the Torah from Hashem to the *benei yisrael*.

However since after the עגל Moshe gave the *benei yisrael* the ability to carry on and start making the *mishkan* by sacrificing of his own *madregah* which he had rightfully earned, this part of the Torah would personally always be accredited to Moshe, and thus revive him forever when the *benei yisrael* would learn the פרשת שקלים.

Just like Abun who gave more than his fair share, Hashem knew that Moshe had the ability to give away that which could not rightfully be expected of him, and therefore He gave Moshe the entire Torah as a gift, as Rashi explains (31, 18):

> **ככלתו:** ככלתו כתיב חסר שנמסרה לו תורה במתנה ככלה לחתן

> Moshe was unable to learn the entire Torah in such a short time, so the Torah was handed to him as a *kallah* is handed to the *chasan*.

Perpetuating *kedushah*

The *passuk* says at the beginning of this week's sedrah (35.1)

וַיַּקְהֵל מֹשֶׁה אֶת כָּל עֲדַת בְּנֵי יִשְׂרָאֵל וַיֹּאמֶר אֲלֵהֶם אֵלֶּה הַדְּבָרִים אֲשֶׁר צִוָּה ה' לַעֲשֹׂת אֹתָם

And Moshe assembled all of the congregation of the benei yisrael and he said to them, "These are the matters that Hashem has commanded to do."

The Ramban explains.

ויקהל משה את כל עדת בני ישראל: ...והנה משה אחר שצוה לאהרן והנשיאים וכל בני ישראל האנשים כל אשר דבר ה' אתו בהר סיני אחרי שבור הלוחות (לעיל ל"ד ל"ב) ונתן על פניו המסוה (שם פסוק ל"ג) חזר וצוה והקהילו אליו כל העדה אנשים ונשים ויתכן שהיה זה ביום מחרת רדתו ואמר לכולם ענין המשכן אשר נצטוה בו מתחלה קודם שבור הלוחות כי כיון שנתרצה להם הקב"ה ונתן לו הלוחות שניות וכרת עמו ברית חדשה שילך השם בקרבם הנה חזרו לקדמותם ולאהבת כלולותם ובידוע שתהיה שכינתו בתוכם כענין שצוהו תחלה כמו שאמר (לעיל כ"ה ח') ועשו לי מקדש ושכנתי בתוכם ולכן צוה אותם משה עתה בכל מה שנצטוה מתחלה

Moshe told the *benei yisrael* everything that Hashem said after he had broken the *luchos* and placed the veil over his face. He then assembled all the *benei yisrael* and instructed them concerning the *mishkan* about which he had been commanded before the breaking of the *luchos*.

This is because once Hashem became agreeable to the *benei yisrael* and gave Moshe the second *luchos* and made with them a new covenant, they returned to their original greatness when Hashem's love of the *benei yisrael* was as the love of a bridegroom to a bride. It then became obvious that His *shechinah* would be amongst them as Hashem had originally commanded Moshe, as it says, "And they should make for me a sanctuary, and I will dwell amongst them."

Therefore Moshe now commanded them everything that he had been commanded originally concerning the *mishkan*.

According to the Ramban, the words אלה הדברים refer to making the *mishkan*.

However, the gemara says in Shabbos (97b)

והתניא רבי אומר, דברים הדברים אלה הדברים אלו ל"ט מלאכות שנאמרו למשה בסיני

Rabbi Yehuda HaNasi said: Shabbos is mentioned in the *passuk*, "These are the things [*eleh ha'devarim*] that Hashem has commanded to perform them." (Shemos 35:1)

Apparently, the Torah could simply have stated, "This is the matter [*davar*]." When it states matters [*devarim*] in the plural, we see that the Torah is referring to two points. The addition of the definite article (the *heh* in the word *ha'devarim*) adds a third point. Furthermore, the gematria of the word *eleh* is thirty-six. Thus the phrase, "These are the things," alludes to three plus thirty-six, namely the thirty-nine prohibited *melachos* that were said to Moshe on Har Sinai.

- It is evident from this gemara that the *passuk* at the beginning of Vayakhel is referring to the 39 *melachos*. Why then does the Ramban say that the *passuk* is referring to making the *mishkan*?

The Yalkut Shimoni comments on this *passuk* as follows.

רבותינו בעלי אגדה אומרים מתחלת התורה ועד סופה אין בה פרשה שנאמר בראשה ויקהל אלא זאת בלבד. אמר הקב"ה, עשה לך קהילות גדולת ודרוש לפניהם ברבים הלכות שבת, כדי שילמדו ממך דורות הבאים להקהיל קהילות בכל שבת ושבת ולכנוס בבתי מדרשות ללמד ולהורות לישראל דברי תורה איסור והיתר כדי שיהא שמי הגדול מתקלס בין בני. מכאן אמרו, משה תקן להם לישראל שיהיו דורשין בעניינו של יום, הלכות פסח בפסח, הלכות עצרת בעצרת, הלכות החג בחג. אמר משה לישראל, אם אתם עושים כסדר הזה הקב"ה מעלה עליכם כאילו המלכתם אותו בעולמו, שנאמר, ואתם עדי נאם ה' ואני קל. וכן דוד הוא אומר, בשרתי צדק בקהל רב. וכי מה בשורה היו ישראל צריכין בימי דוד והלא כל ימיו של דוד מעין דוגמא של משיח היה. אלא פותח ודורש לפניהם דברי תורה שלא שמעתן אזן מעולם.

Our masters the experts in agaddah said: From the beginning of the Torah till the end of the Torah there is no *parshah* which begins with "And he assembled" except for this. Hashem said, "Make for yourself great assemblies and expound the *halachos* of Shabbos, so that the coming generations should learn from you to gather assemblies every Shabbos and to enter the *beis ha'medrash* to teach and instruct the *benei yisrael* in *divrei Torah* concerning what is forbidden and what is permitted, so that My great Name should be praised amongst My children."

From here they said, "Moshe enacted for the *benei yisrael* that they should expound on the subject of the day, the *halachos* of Pesach on Pesach, the *halachos* of Shavuos on Shavuos and the *halachos* of Succos on Succos."

Moshe said to the *benei yisrael*, "If you follow this set order, Hashem will consider for you as if you have made him the King in His world, as it says, 'You are My witnesses says Hashem, and I am G-d.'"

And so too Dovid said, "I announced righteousness in a great assembly." And what announcement (of salvation) did the *benei yisrael* need in the days of Dovid? Were not all the days of Dovid like the days of *mashiach*? Rather he got up and expounded before them *divrei Torah* that no-one had ever heard before.

- Why do we learn the obligation to learn the *halachos* of Shabbos on Shabbos from the mention of Shabbos that comes to teach that making the *mishkan* does not override Shabbos?

The *passuk* says in Ki Sisa (31.13)

וְאַתָּה דַּבֵּר אֶל בְּנֵי יִשְׂרָאֵל לֵאמֹר אַךְ אֶת שַׁבְּתֹתַי תִּשְׁמֹרוּ כִּי אוֹת הִוא בֵּינִי וּבֵינֵיכֶם לְדֹרֹתֵיכֶם לָדַעַת כִּי אֲנִי ה' מְקַדִּשְׁכֶם

Speak to the *benei yisrael* and say, "Nevertheless, you must keep My Shabbos (and not make the *mishkan* on Shabbos), for this is a sign between Me and you for all generations, that you may know that I Hashem have made you holy."

The gemara in Shabbos (10b) comments as follows.

ואמר רבא בר מחסיא אמר רב חמא בר גוריא אמר רב הנותן מתנה לחבירו צריך להודיעו שנאמר (שמות ל"א, י"ג) לדעת כי אני ה' מקדשכם תניא נמי הכי לדעת כי אני ה' מקדשכם אמר לו הקב"ה למשה מתנה טובה יש לי בבית גנזי ושבת שמה ואני מבקש ליתנה לישראל לך והודיעם

Rava bar Machsia said that Rav Chama bar Gurya said that Rav said: One who gives a gift to another must inform him that he is giving it to him. As it is stated: "Only keep My Shabbos for it is a sign between Me and you for your generations to know that I am Hashem Who sanctifies you" (Shemos 31:13). When Hashem gave Shabbos to the *benei yisrael*, He told Moshe to inform them about it. That was also taught in a *beraisa*: The *passuk* says: "For I am Hashem Who sanctifies you," meaning that Hashem said to Moshe: I have a goodly gift in My treasure house and Shabbos is its name, and I seek to give it to the *benei yisrael*, go and inform them about it...

The *benei yisrael* were commanded concerning Shabbos before *matan Torah*, as Rashi says (Shemos 15.25)

> במרה נתן להם מקצת פרשיות של תורה שיתעסקו בהם שבת ופרה אדומה ודינין

In Marah, He gave them some of the sections of the Torah so that they should engage in them; Shabbos, Parah Adumah and monetary laws.

- If so, why were the *benei yisrael* only told that Shabbos was a goodly gift later when they were told that making the *mishkan* does not override Shabbos?

It would seem that we can explain as follows:

The gemara in Shabbos says:

> אמר לו הקב"ה למשה מתנה טובה יש לי בבית גנזי ושבת שמה

Hashem said to Moshe: I have a goodly gift in My treasure house and Shabbos is its name.

Since Shabbos comes from the treasure house of Hashem, if one keeps Shabbos, this provides the ability to deposit other treasures in the treasure house of Hashem. Subsequently, when the *benei yisrael* were instructed to stop making the *mishkan* because of Shabbos, this did not mean there was to be a cessation of their acquisition of the *kedushah* of the *mishkan*. Rather it meant that the *benei yisrael* would be able to deposit and preserve the *kedushah* of the *mishkan* in the treasure house of Hashem, for all generations, even when they would no longer have the *mishkan* or the *beis ha'mikdash*.

Subsequently, we can understand that when the *passuk* in Ki Sisa says

וְאַתָּה דַּבֵּר אֶל בְּנֵי יִשְׂרָאֵל לֵאמֹר אַךְ אֶת שַׁבְּתֹתַי תִּשְׁמֹרוּ כִּי אוֹת הִוא בֵּינִי וּבֵינֵיכֶם לְדֹרֹתֵיכֶם לָדַעַת כִּי אֲנִי ה' מְקַדִּשְׁכֶם

Speak to the *benei yisrael* and say, "Nevertheless, you must keep My Shabbos (and not make the *mishkan* on Shabbos), for this is a sign between Me and you for all generations, that you may know that I Hashem have made you holy."

The *passuk* means to say that even though the *beis ha'mikdash* may be destroyed, through Shabbos there will be perpetuated for all generations, the *kedushah* that the *benei yisrael* attained through building the *mishkan* and the *beis ha'mikdash*.

Because the quality of Shabbos to perpetuate *kedushah* in the treasure house of Hashem became evident when the *benei yisrael* were commanded to stop making the *mishkan* on Shabbos, Hashem told Moshe "I have a goodly gift in my treasure house and Shabbos is its name" in Ki Sisa and not when the *benei yisrael* were commanded concerning Shabbos in Marah.

Similarly, when the *passuk* at the beginning of the *sedrah* says:

אֵלֶּה הַדְּבָרִים אֲשֶׁר צִוָּה ה' לַעֲשֹׂת אֹתָם

These are the matters that Hashem has commanded to do.

The *passuk* can be understood to be referring to both making the *mishkan* and also to the 39 *melachos*. Since the *kedushah* of the *melachos* involved in making the *mishkan* was perpetuated by not doing the 39 *melachos* on Shabbos, the *passuk* can be understood as follows.

אֵלֶּה הַדְּבָרִים אֲשֶׁר צִוָּה ה' לַעֲשֹׂת אֹתָם

By refraining from doing the 39 *melachos* on Shabbos, the *kedushah* of the *mishkan* that Hashem has commanded you to make, will acquire the permanence of the word of Hashem.

For this reason, the *halacha* that one should learn the *halachos* of Shabbos on Shabbos, is derived from the mention of Shabbos that teaches that making the *mishkan* does not override Shabbos.

Since learning the *halachos* of Shabbos on Shabbos provides access to the level of the universal and timeless *kedushah* of the great Name of Hashem, as the medrash says, "so that My great Name should be praised amongst My children," we learn this *halacha* from that mention of Shabbos which illustrates that through keeping Shabbos we merit to perpetuate the inviolable *kedushah* of our efforts in the treasure house of Hashem.

Pekudei

Avoiding the *ayin ha'ra*

It says in this week's *sedrah* (38:21)

אֵלֶּה פְקוּדֵי הַמִּשְׁכָּן מִשְׁכַּן הָעֵדֻת אֲשֶׁר פֻּקַּד עַל פִּי מֹשֶׁה עֲבֹדַת הַלְוִיִּם בְּיַד אִיתָמָר בֶּן אַהֲרֹן הַכֹּהֵן

These are the records of the *mishkan*, the *mishkan* of the testimony, which were listed according to Moshe's instructions — the work of the Leviim was under the direction of Itamar the son of Aharon the *cohen*.

Rashi explains

המשכן משכן, שני פעמים, רמז למקדש שנתמשכן בשני חורבנין על עונותיהן של ישראל

The *passuk* repeats the word משכן to hint at the *beis ha'mikdash* which was taken as a *mashkon* (a pledged asset for a loan) when it was twice destroyed because of the *aveiros* of the *benei yisrael*.

- Why does the *passuk* allude to the *beis ha'mikdash* being taken as a pledge specifically in the *sedrah* of Pekudei and not in any of the previous *sedros* that discuss the building of the *mishkan*?

The Gur Aryeh explains as follows:

ואם תאמר, ומאי ענינו לכאן לכתוב זה כאן, ולמה לא כתב זה בכל הפרשה שקדמה, אמנם דבר זה הוא מופלא בחכמה, וזה ידוע ממה שנשתברו הלוחות מפני שניתנו בפומבי ושלט בהם עין הרע, ומפני שכאן כתיב "אלה פקודי המשכן" שנמנו כל המשכן, ומפני כך שלט בהם עין הרע, שכל דבר שבמנין עין הרע שולט בו, ומפני שהיה מנין לכל דבר שבמשכן, שלט עין הרע בזה. וכן בית המקדש, כל דבר שהיה במקדש היה בו מנין כאשר נכתב בפירוש, וכל מקום שיש מנין עין הרע שולט בו.

The first *luchos* were broken because they were given with great publicity, and so an עין הרע overpowered them. Similarly here, because all the parts of the *mishkan* were enumerated, and because the items in the *beis ha'mikdash* were also enumerated (מלאכים א', פרק ו' – ז', עזרא פרק ח'), therefore the *beis ha'mikdash* was affected by an עין הרע, which led to its destruction.

- If counting leads to an עין הרע, why then were the items in the *beis ha'mikdash* counted?

It would seem that we can explain as follows:

The *passuk* says in Yechezkel (46:9)

וּבְבוֹא עַם הָאָרֶץ לִפְנֵי ה' בַּמּוֹעֲדִים הַבָּא דֶּרֶךְ שַׁעַר צָפוֹן לְהִשְׁתַּחֲוֹת יֵצֵא דֶּרֶךְ שַׁעַר נֶגֶב וְהַבָּא דֶּרֶךְ שַׁעַר נֶגֶב יֵצֵא דֶּרֶךְ שַׁעַר צָפוֹנָה לֹא יָשׁוּב דֶּרֶךְ הַשַּׁעַר אֲשֶׁר בָּא בוֹ כִּי נִכְחוֹ יֵצֵא

And when the people come before Hashem on the festivals, one who comes in through the northern gate to bow, should exit through the southern gate, and one who comes through the southern gate should exit through the northern gate. He should not exit through the gate whereby he entered, rather he should take the opposite exit.

Rabbi Yaakov Emden explains the reason for this *halacha* (פרקי אבות, פרק א', משנה ד')

כי הקפיד השי"ת שלא יראה השער ב' פעמים, פן ישוה בעיניו לשער ביתו וקירות הבית לקירותיו וכו', וזה היה עון העגל שהיה האהל בתוכם עד שמאסו בו ואמרו עשה לנו אלהים, ומשה רבינו ע"ה הרגיש בזה ונטה את האהל מחוץ למחנה הרחק מן המחנה.

Hashem was particular that an individual should not see the same gate twice, lest that person draw a similarity between the gates in the *beis ha'mikdash* and the gates in his house, and between the beams in the *beis ha'mikdash* and the beams in his house. And this caused the sin of the *egel ha'zahav*, because the *ohel mo'ed* became overly familiar to them until they rejected it, and so they said, "Make us a god." For this reason, Moshe moved his tent to outside of the camp.

Similarly, we can understand that the reason for the enumeration of the items in the *mishkan* was in order to impress on everyone the importance and the prestigiousness of every part of the *mishkan*. Only by recognising the specialness of the mishkan could the *benei yisrael* retain the required respect and reverence for the *mishkan*.

However, it is exactly this detailed impressiveness that can lead to an עין הרע. As the Zera Kodesh (Parshas Vayetze) says:

כי עין הרע בא מזה כאשר אדם רואה איזו דבר נאה או איזה גדולה בממון או בבנים או בגבורה או בכל מעלה והוא מתמיה מאוד על מעלתו של זה, אע״פ שמתמיה באהבה זה לזה אעפ״כ גורם רעה בזה שמתמיה, שהוא מפריד הדבר משורשו, כי אלו היה הרואה חכם ודבוק בהש״י לא היה מתמיה כלל, כי מה שייך לתמוה על מדת תפארתו של הקב״ה כביכול, כי זה שהוא רואה הוא לתפארת ה׳

An עין הרע comes when a person sees something beautiful or some greatness, whether this be of money or children or strength or any virtue, and he becomes very astonished at the greatness of this virtue. Even if his astonishment is well meant, nevertheless he causes evil, because through his astonishment he separates the thing from its source.

For if the person who saw the great virtue was a *chacham* and close to Hashem, he would never be astonished, because he realises that what he sees is simply a reflection of the glory of Hashem.

Preventing the *egel ha'zahav* from occurring again required that the *benei yisrael* should be impressed through the enumeration of the items in the *mishkan*, but it was exactly the creation of this great impression that led to the עין הרע that destroyed the *mishkan* and the *beis ha'mikdash*. Not until *klal yisrael* achieve complete atonement for the *egel ha'zahav* will it be possible for the third *beis ha'mikdash*, which will not attract an עין הרע despite its impressive stature, to be built and to last forever.

Vayikra

Calling Moshe

It says at the beginning of this week's *sedrah* (1:1)

וַיִּקְרָא אֶל מֹשֶׁה וַיְדַבֵּר ה' אֵלָיו מֵאֹהֶל מוֹעֵד לֵאמֹר

And He called to Moshe, and Hashem spoke to him from the Ohel Moed saying.

Rashi explains:

ויקרא אל משה: לכל דברות ולכל אמירות ולכל צוויים קדמה קריאה לשון חבה לשון שמלאכי השרת משתמשים בו שנאמר (ישעיה ו', ב') וקרא זה אל זה

Whenever Hashem spoke to Moshe, whether this was introduced by the words דבור or צווי or אמירה, this was preceded by a call (to prepare him for the forthcoming address). It is a way of expressing affection, the way the *malachim* address each other, as it says (Yeshaya 6:3) "And one called to another [and said, Holy, holy, holy is the Lord of Hosts]".

In other words, "And He called to Moshe," refers to the preparation for *nevuah*, whereas "And Hashem spoke to Him," refers to the actual *nevuah* that Moshe received from Hashem.

The Medrash Rabbah comments on this *passuk* as follows:

וַיִּקְרָא אֶל מֹשֶׁה, ולאדם לא קרא והלא כבר נאמר (בראשית ג', ט') ויקרא ה' אלקים אל האדם, אלא אין גנאי למלך לדבר עם אריסו, וַיְדַבֵּר ה' אֵלָיו ועם נח לא דבר והלא כבר נאמר (שם ח', ט"ו) וידבר אלקים אל נח אלא אין גנאי למלך לדבר עם נקדודו, וַיִּקְרָא אֶל מֹשֶׁה ולאברהם לא קרא (שם כ"ב, ט"ו) ויקרא מלאך ה' אל אברהם, אלא אין גנאי למלך לדבר עם פונדקי שלו.

וַיִּקְרָא אֶל מֹשֶׁה, ולֹא כאברהם, באברהם כתיב ויקרא מלאך ה' אל אברהם המלאך קורא והדבור מדבר ברם הכא אמר ר' אבין אמר הקב"ה אני הוא הקורא ואני המדבר שנאמר (ישעיה מ"ח, ט"ו) אֲנִי אֲנִי דִבַּרְתִּי אַף קְרָאתִיו הֲבִיאֹתִיו וְהִצְלִיחַ דַּרְכּוֹ

"And He called to Moshe."

But did he not also call to Adam? Does the *passuk* not say, "And Hashem called to the man"? Rather this is because it is not beneath the dignity of a king to talk with his tenant-farmer. (Adam is referred to as a tenant-farmer because he was placed in Gen Eden "to work it, and to guard it" (Bereishis 2.15).)

"And Hashem spoke to him."

But did not Hashem speak with Noach? Does the *passuk* not say "And Hashem spoke to Noach"? Rather this is because it is not beneath the dignity of the king to talk to with his herder. (Noach is referred to as a herder because he had to take care of the animals in the *tevah*.)

"And He called to Moshe."

But did He also not call to Avraham? Does the *passuk* not say,

"And the angel of Hashem called to Avraham"? Rather this is because it is not beneath the dignity of the king to talk with his inn-keeper (Avraham is referred to as an inn-keeper because the *passuk* says, "And he set up in inn" (Bereishis 21.33).)

"And He called to Moshe." This is not like the way that Hashem spoke to Avraham. With Avraham it says, "And the *malach* of Hashem called to Avraham," the *malach* called and the speech was spoken. However here, Rabbi Avin said, "Hashem said, 'I am the One who calls and I am the One who speaks.'" As the *passuk* says, "I, I spoke and I called him. I have brought him and he shall succeed in his mission."

The medrash appears to contradict itself. First the medrash says that the *passuk*, "And the angel of Hashem called to Avraham," denotes that Hashem spoke to Avraham. However, this is not construed to be exceptional because, "It is not beneath the dignity of the king to talk with his inn-keeper."

But then the medrash concludes that Moshe was greater than Avraham because concerning Avraham the *passuk* only says that a *malach* spoke to him, but concerning Moshe, Hashem Himself spoke to him.

- Why does the medrash begin by implying that Hashem spoke to Avraham directly but then conclude that Hashem only spoke to Avraham through the medium of a *malach*?

The *passuk* that relates how the *malach* spoke to Avraham says (Bereishis 22.11)

וַיִּקְרָ֨א אֵלָ֜יו מַלְאַ֤ךְ ה' מִן־הַשָּׁמַ֔יִם וַיֹּ֖אמֶר אַבְרָהָ֣ם | אַבְרָהָ֑ם וַיֹּ֖אמֶר הִנֵּֽנִי

And the *malach* of Hashem called to him from the *shamayim* and he said, "Avraham, Avraham." And he said, "Here I am."

- Why does the *passuk* use two words ("he called to him," and "he said") to describe how the *malach* spoke to Avraham?

- Why is there a *pesik* (a break signified by a vertical line in the trope) between the two names Avraham?

It seems that we can explain as follows[28]:

The Zohar says (פרשת נח, נ"ט ע"ב, תוספתא)

> למה נח נח תרי זמני, אלא כל צדיק וצדיק די בעלמא אית ליה תרין רוחין, רוחא חד בעלמא דין ורוחא חד בעלמא דאתי, והכי תשכח בכלהו צדיקי, משה משה, יעקב יעקב, אברהם אברהם, שמואל שמואל, שם שם

Why does the *passuk* (Bereishis 6.9) say Noach's name twice? This is because every tzadik has two spirits, one spirit in this world and one spirit in the world to come. This is why you will find that all *tzadikim* have their names repeated: "Moshe, Moshe" (Shemos 3.4), "Yaakov, Yaakov" (Bereishis

---

[28] עיין בספר בן הא-הא, פרשת נח, ד"ה אמנם

46.2), "Avraham, Avraham" (Bereishis 22.11), "Shmuel, Shmuel" (Shmuel 1, 1.3), "Shem, Shem" (Bereishis 11.10)

In other words, every person has two parts to their *neshama*. One part of the *neshama* comes down to *olam hazeh*, and is clothed in their body, the other part of their *neshama* remains in *olam habah*, even during their lifetime. *Tzadikim* are aware of the higher part of their *neshama*, even during their lifetime.

When the *passuk* says אַבְרָהָם ׀ אַבְרָהָם, the first Avraham refers to the higher *neshama* of Avraham, and the second Avraham refers to the portion of Avraham's *neshama* on *olam hazeh*. If so, it transpires that the initial approach of the *malach* was addressed to the higher *neshama* of Avraham, in *olam habah*. The message of the *malach* was then communicated to the part of Avraham's *neshama* in *olam hazeh*, through the awareness that Avraham had (even while alive) of his higher *neshama*.

Regarding Moshe, however, the Zohar says (זהר חלק ג', קלח ע"א)

בכלהו אתר דשמא אדכר תרי זמני פסיק טעמא בגווייהו. כגון אברהם אברהם, יעקב יעקב, שמואל שמואל, כלהו פסיק טעמא בגווייהו. חוץ ממשה משה דלא פסיק טעמא בגווייהו.

Wherever a name is mentioned twice, there is a *pesik* that splits the two names. For example, אַבְרָהָם ׀ אַבְרָהָם, יַעֲקֹב ׀ יַעֲקֹב, שְׁמוּאֵל ׀ שְׁמוּאֵל. The exception is Moshe, where the *passuk* says מֹשֶׁה מֹשֶׁה without a *pesik* between the two names.

Rabbi Chaim Volozhin explains (רוח חיים, פרקי אבות, א', א')

וזה כוונתם 'אברהם אברהם פסיק טעמיה בגוייה', ר"ל בין אברהם דלעילא שהוא הנפש בשרשה בעולם העליון, ובין אברהם השני כשהיא מלובשת בגוף בקצה האחרון שלה, יש הפסק בגוייה, שהגוף הוא מפסיק, שלא נזדכך חומרו כל כך באופן שלא יהיה חוצץ ומפסיק בין הארת הנשמה בעולם העליון לכשהיא מלובשת בגוף. אבל 'משה משה' לא פסיק טעמיה בגוייה, שנזדכך אצלו הגוף כל כך עד שלא היה חוצץ ומפסיק כלל בין הארת הנשמה כשהיא בעולם העליון לכשהיא בגוף

Between the two names Avraham there is a *pesik*, this is because although Avraham, even while alive, was aware of his higher *neshama* in *olam habah*, nevertheless there was still a division between the two parts of his *neshama*, since his body was not entirely purified. However between the two names Moshe there is no *pesik*. This is because there was no division at all between the two parts of his *neshama*, since his body was entirely purified [and spiritual].

Rabbi Chaim Volozhin continues to explain (ibid.) that because Moshe personally, through his purity, unified *olam hazeh* and *olam habah*, he was able to be the intermediary to receive the Torah from *olam habah*, and bring it into *olam hazeh*.

Based on this understanding, we can explain the medrash as follows:

Initially the medrash says that Hashem called directly to Avraham

> But did He also not call to Avraham? Does the *passuk* not say, "And the angel of Hashem called to Avraham"? Rather this is because it is not beneath the dignity of the king to talk with

his inn-keeper (Avraham is referred to as an inn-keeper because the *passuk* says, "And he set up in inn" (Bereishis 21.33).)

Here, the medrash means to say that Hashem spoke to the part of Avraham's *neshama* that was in *shamayim*.

Subsequently the medrash says that Hashem only spoke directly to Moshe, but indirectly to Avraham

> "And He called to Moshe." This is not like the way that Hashem spoke to Avraham. With Avraham it says, "And the *malach* of Hashem called to Avraham," the *malach* called and the speech was spoken. However here, Rabbi Avin said, "Hashem said, 'I am the One who calls and I am the One who speaks.'" As the *passuk* says, "I, I spoke and I called him. I have brought him and he shall succeed in his mission."

Here, the medrash means to say that Hashem spoke that part of Moshe's *neshama* which was in *olam hazeh*, directly, and in this way Moshe was greater than Avraham.

Therefore, when the *passuk* says, concerning Avraham

וַיִּקְרָא אֵלָיו מַלְאַךְ ה' מִן הַשָּׁמַיִם

And the *malach* of Hashem called to him from the *shamayim*

It means that Hashem called the higher part of Avraham's *neshama* that was in *shamayim*.

However, when the passuk says, concerning Moshe

וַיִּקְרָא אֶל מֹשֶׁה

And He called to Moshe

It means that Hashem called to the entirety of Moshe's *neshama*, both to the higher part of his *neshama* that was in *shamayim* and also to the lower part of his *neshama* that was in *olam hazeh*.

Therefore, regarding Avraham, the *passuk* continues

וַיֹּאמֶר אַבְרָהָם ׀ אַבְרָהָם

And he said, Avraham, Avraham

The speech was only directly addressed to the higher part of Avraham's *neshama*, signified by the first occurrence of his name.

However, regarding Moshe, the *passuk* continues

וַיְדַבֵּר ה' אֵלָיו

And Hashem spoke to him

Because Hashem spoke directly to all parts of Moshe's *neshama*, even that part which was in *olam hazeh*, the *passuk* simply uses the word אֵלָיו, "to him," to refer to Moshe, since even his most mundane aspect was able to directly hear the word of Hashem.

Spiritual ascendancy

It says at the beginning of this week's *sedrah*

צַו אֶת אַהֲרֹן וְאֶת בָּנָיו לֵאמֹר זֹאת תּוֹרַת הָעֹלָה הִוא הָעֹלָה עַל מוֹקְדָה עַל הַמִּזְבֵּחַ כָּל הַלַּיְלָה עַד הַבֹּקֶר וְאֵשׁ הַמִּזְבֵּחַ תּוּקַד בּוֹ

Command Aharon and his sons saying, "This is the *halacha* for a *korban olah*. The *korban olah* shall remain where it is burned on the *mizbeach* all night till the morning, while the fire on the *mizbeach* is kept going on it."

Rashi comments on this *passuk*

צו את אהרן: אין צו אלא לשון זרוז מיד ולדורות. אמר רבי שמעון, ביותר צריך הכתוב לזרז במקום שיש בו חסרון כיס

The word צו means to warn the *cohanim* to do this *mitzva* with alacrity, immediately and for all generations. Rabbi Shimon said, "The *passuk* has specifically to warn you to do *mitzvos* with alacrity where the performance of the *mitzva* involves monetary loss."

- Why does the Torah not use the word צו in all *mitzvos* which require expenditure of money, such as the *mitzva* to give תרומות and מעשרות?

It seems that we can explain as follows:

The Medrash Tanchuma (פרשת צו, סימן א') says

וידבר ה', צו את אהרן ואת בניו... אם בקשת להקריב קרבן, לא תגזול לאדם כלום. למה, כי אני ה' אוהב משפט שונא גזל בעולה. ואימתי אתה מעלה עולה ואני מקבלה, כשתנקה כפיך מן גזל. מה הוא הגזל, דוד אמר, מי יעלה בהר ה' ומי יקום במקום קדשו, נקי כפים ובר לבב (תהלים כ"ד, ג'-ד') זאת תורת העולה, מי שהוא נקי כפים מן הגזל, הוא יעלה בהר ה'

If you want to bring a *korban*, then do not steal anything from anybody. Why? Because the *passuk* says, "For I am Hashem Who loves justice and Who hates theft in a *korban olah*."

And when can you bring a *korban olah* and I will accept it? When you cleanse your palms of theft. What is theft? Dovid said, "Who will rise up on the mountain of Hashem and who will stand in His holy place? He who has clean palms and is pure of heart."

Therefore the *passuk* says, "This is the *halacha* of a *korban olah*." One whose palms are clean from theft, he will rise on the mountain of Hashem.

It appears from the medrash[29] that there are two levels of honesty. One level is attained by refraining from outright dishonesty, such as theft. A higher level is attained by ensuring that one does not take advantage of situations by subconsciously tipping business dealings in his own favour.

---

[29] עיין מסילת ישרים, פרק י'

The medrash means that Hashem only accepts *korbanos* when the *korban* is brought in a monetarily pure manner wherein the person bringing the *korban* has entirely cleansed himself of any type of dishonesty and deception. Through this, it is possible to "rise on the mountain of Hashem".

Why does purity from dishonesty lead to ascending the mountain of Hashem?

The gemara in Bava Basra (75b) says

> ואמר רבה א"ר יוחנן עתיד הקב"ה להגביה את ירושלים ג' פרסאות למעלה... ושמא תאמר יש צער לעלות ת"ל (ישעיהו ס', ח') מי אלה כעב תעופינה וכיונים אל ארובתיהם אמר רב פפא ש"מ האי עיבא תלתא פרסי מידלי

And Rabbah said in the name of Rabbi Yochanan, "Hashem will raise Yerushalayim three *parsaos* upwards... And lest you say that there will be pain in ascending to Yerushalayim when it will be raised so high, the *passuk* says, "Who are these that fly as a cloud, and as doves to their dove-cotes."

The Maharal (Chiddushei Agados) comments on this gemara as follows:

> ואמר שמא יש צער לעלות ר"ל שמא לישראל הדרים בה מפני כבידת החומר שהוא מבדיל בינם ובין הקדושה יהיה להם צער וקשה לעלות וכו' ועל זה אמר וכיונים אל ארובתיהם ידוע שהעוף לכך פורח באויר מפני קלות החומר שיש לו ואינו מונע לעוף לעלות לאויר וכן ישראל יהיו דומים לעוף שיהיה חומר שלהם זך וטוב עד שלא יהיה מעכב ומונע מן כבידות החומר לעלות ולקנות במדרגה הקדושה

And concerning this, the gemara says, "And if you will say that the *benei yisrael* will experience pain in rising to this [perfect level of *kedushah*]," meaning to say, "And if you say that because of their earthiness it will be difficult and painful for the *benei yisrael* to rise to this level," therefore the *passuk* they will rise as a dove flies to the dove-cote.

This means that just as a bird flies naturally and lightly, so too will the *benei yisrael* rise up to the perfect *kedushah* of Yerushalayim due to their purified and spiritual lightness.

In order to achieve a level of natural spiritual ascendancy, it is necessary to be separated from any entanglement with earthy mundane matters, that can be caused by deceit and dishonesty[30].

Hence we can understand that when Rashi says, concerning the *korban olah*, ביותר צריך הכתוב לזרז במקום שיש בו חסרון כיס – "The *passuk* has specifically to warn you to do *mitzvos* with alacrity where the performance of the *mitzva* involves monetary loss," he is not simply referring to relinquishing the cost of the *korban olah* with a whole heart.

Rather he means to say that in order bring an *olah*, it is necessary to totally relinquish the attitude of desiring money altogether. By doing this, it is possible to acquire the natural spiritual ascendancy that is attained by bringing a *korban* to Hashem.

---

[30] See also page 28, Meriting rescue

The atonement of the *benei yisrael*

It says at the beginning of this week's *sedrah* (Vayikra 9.1)

וַיְהִי בַּיּוֹם הַשְּׁמִינִי קָרָא מֹשֶׁה לְאַהֲרֹן וּלְבָנָיו וּלְזִקְנֵי יִשְׂרָאֵל. וַיֹּאמֶר אֶל אַהֲרֹן קַח לְךָ עֵגֶל בֶּן בָּקָר לְחַטָּאת וְאַיִל לְעֹלָה תְּמִימִם וְהַקְרֵב לִפְנֵי ה'. וְאֶל בְּנֵי יִשְׂרָאֵל תְּדַבֵּר לֵאמֹר קְחוּ שְׂעִיר עִזִּים לְחַטָּאת וְעֵגֶל וָכֶבֶשׂ בְּנֵי שָׁנָה תְּמִימִם לְעֹלָה. וְשׁוֹר וָאַיִל לִשְׁלָמִים לִזְבֹּחַ לִפְנֵי ה' וּמִנְחָה בְּלוּלָה בַשָּׁמֶן כִּי הַיּוֹם ה' נִרְאָה אֲלֵיכֶם.

And it was on the eighth day that Moshe called Aharon and his sons, and the elders of the *benei yisrael*. And he said to Aharon, "Take a calf for a *chatas* and a perfect ram for an *olah* and bring them before Hashem.

And speak to the *benei yisrael* saying, 'Take a he-goat for a chatas and a calf and a lamb, perfect yearlings, for an *olah*. And an ox and a ram for a *shelamim* to bring before Hashem, and a *minchah* with oil mixed in. For today Hashem will appear to you.'"

The Sifra (ספרא על ויקרא ט' ג') comments on these *pessukim*

ויאמר אל אהרן קח לך עגל בן בקר לחטאת. מלמד שאמר לו משה לאהרן, אהרן אחי, אף על פי שנתרצה המקום לכפר על עונותיך, צריך אתה ליתן לתוך פיו של שטן. שלח דורון לפניך עד שלא תכנס למקדש

שמא ישנאך בביאתך למקדש.

ושמא תאמר אין צריך כפרה אלא אני, והלא אף ישראל צריכים כפרה שנאמר ואל בני ישראל תדבר לאמר קחו שעיר עזים לחטאת.

וכי מה ראו ישראל להביא יותר מאהרן. אלא אמר להם, אתם יש בידכם בתחלה ויש בידכם בסוף. יש בידכם תחלה, וישחטו שעיר עזים (בראשית ל"ז, ל"א) ויש בידכם בסוף, עשו להם עגל מסכה (שמות ל"ב, ח'). יבא שעיר עזים ויכפר על מעשה עזים, יבא עגל ויכפר על מעשה עגל.

"Take a calf for a *chatas* and a perfect ram for an *olah* and bring them before Hashem." This teaches you that Moshe said to Aharon, "Aharon my brother, even though Hashem was agreeable and forgave you for your son (of making the *egel ha'zahav*) you still need to place something in the mouth of the *satan*. Send a gift before you, before you enter the sanctuary in case he will hate you when you enter the sanctuary.

And if you will say, 'Only I need an atonement.' But do not the *benei yisrael* also need an atonement, as the *passuk* says, And speak to the *benei yisrael* saying, 'Take a he-goat for a *chatas*.'"

And why were the *benei yisrael* obliged to bring more *korbanos* [for atonement] than Aharon (Aharon brought a calf and ram, whereas the *benei yisrael* brought a he-goat, a calf and a lamb)? Rather he said to them, "You have in your hands from the beginning and at the end."

"You have in your hands from the beginning," as the *passuk* says, "And they [the brothers] slaughtered a he-goat." "And you have in your hands at the end," as the *passuk* says, "They have made for themselves a cast calf."

Let the he-goat come and atone for the deed done with the goat, and let the calf come and atone for the deed done with the calf.

- In what way was the sale of Yosef the start of that which ended with the sin of the *egel ha'zahav*?

It would appear that we can explain as follows[31]:

The *sedrah* continues (9.6)

וַיֹּאמֶר מֹשֶׁה זֶה הַדָּבָר אֲשֶׁר צִוָּה ה' תַּעֲשׂוּ וְיֵרָא אֲלֵיכֶם כְּבוֹד ה'

And Moshe said, "This is the matter that Hashem has commanded you should do, so that the *shechinah* will appear to you."

Moshe did not appear to add any additional instructions for the *benei yisrael* in this *passuk*. The Yalkut Shimoni explains that Moshe said to the *benei yisrael*

אמר להן משה לישראל אותו יצר הרע העבירו מלבבכם ותהיו כלכם ביראה אחת ובעצה אחת לשרת לפני המקום, כשם שהוא יחידי בעולם

---

[31] עיין בספר אמרי שפר

כך תהא עבודתכם מיוחדת לפניו שנאמר ומלתם את ערלת לבבכם וגו'. מפני מה, כי ה' אלקיכם הוא אלקי האלקים וגו'. עשיתם כן וירא אליכם כבוד ה'.

Moshe said to the *benei yisrael*, "Remove that *yetzer hara* from your hearts and be all in one fear and in one council to serve before Hashem. Just as he is One in the world so too your *avodah* should be unified before Him, as the *passuk* says, ומלתם את ערלת לבבכם – 'And you should remove the dullness of your hearts.' Why? Because Hashem your G-d is the G-d of all G-ds... If you do so, then the *shechinah* will appear to you."

In other words, Moshe exhorted the *benei yisrael* that in order for the *shechinah* to rest on the work of their hands, they had to overcome that *yetzer ha'ra* that caused them to be divided in their approach to *avodas Hashem*.

From Moshe's previous reference to the sale of Yosef, it seems that Moshe was referring to the *yetzer ha'ra* that had caused the dispute between Yosef and the brothers. This dispute can be understood as follows.

Yosef was a proponent of embracing even the most material aspects of worldly existence in *avodas Hashem*.

Thus

- Yosef is described (Bereishis 39.6) as, "Now Yoseph was well built and handsome."

- In Rashi (Bereishis 49.22), "His gracefulness attacks the eye that looks at him." "The daughters of Egypt used to climb up to gaze at his beauty… many daughters climbed, each of them to any place from which she could best obtain a glimpse of him."

- Yosef is described (Devarim 33.17) as, "His firstborn ox, glory is his."

The brothers saw Yosef's embracing of the earthy aspect of human existence as dangerous, and they felt that it is not possible to harness all man's passions in the service of Hashem. Instead, such passions should be subdued and quelled[32].

---

[32] After the brothers sold Yosef as a slave, they dipped his coat into the blood of a goat (Bereishis 37.31):

וַיִּקְחוּ אֶת כְּתֹנֶת יוֹסֵף וַיִּשְׁחֲטוּ שְׂעִיר עִזִּים וַיִּטְבְּלוּ אֶת הַכֻּתֹּנֶת בַּדָּם

Then they took Yoseph's tunic, slaughtered a kid goat, and dipped the tunic in the blood.

Rashi explains

שעיר עזים: דמו דומה לשל אדם

They took a kid goat because its blood is similar to the blood of a man.

The Imrei Yosher explains that in addition to the obvious reason for needing blood that was similar to that of a man, the brothers also spilt blood which was similar to that of a man, to indicate that they had slaughtered the *yetzer hara*.

שלכך שחטו שעיר עזים ולא כבש או פר לרמוז ששחטו וכבשו את יצרם בשחיטת השעיר

The reason that they slaughtered a kid goat and not a sheep or a cow was to allude to the fact that they conquered and slaughtered the *yetzer hara*.

By disposing of Yosef they thought that they had disposed of that *yetzer hara* which Yosef sought to embrace in his service of Hashem.

However, this rejection of Yosef's unique contribution led to the *benei yisrael* later serving the *egel ha'zahav*, which was created through the misappropriated power of Yosef, as the Medrash Tanchuma (Ki Sisa, 19) says

ויש אומרים, שמיכה היה שנתממכך בבנין, מה שהציל משה מן הלבנים. נטל הלוח שכתב עליו משה, עלה שור, כשהעלה ארונו של יוסף. השליכו לתוך הכור בין הנזמים, ויצא העגל

Michah took the tablet upon which was written עלה שור – "Arise oh ox," which Moshe had used to raise the coffin of Yosef from the Nile. He threw the tablet into the molten gold and the *egel ha'zahav* emerged.

Since the *benei yisrael* rejected the possibility of the power of Yosef being used for the good, this rebounded on them so that, in the end, they used the power of Yosef for *avodah zarah*. That is why the Sifra calls the *egel ha'zahav* the culmination of the sin of the sale of Yosef.

Therefore Moshe told the *benei yisrael* that in order to be forgiven for the חטא of the *egel ha'zahav*, they must first remove the disputatiousness between the brothers and Yosef concerning the correct way in עבודת ה', and that they must unite to serve Hashem with a common purpose, combining their disparate strengths and approaches, so as to serve Hashem as one people with one heart.

Tazria

Rising above *tzara'as*

It says in this week's *sedrah* (13.2)

אָדָם כִּי יִהְיֶה בְעוֹר בְּשָׂרוֹ שְׂאֵת אוֹ סַפַּחַת אוֹ בַהֶרֶת וְהָיָה בְעוֹר בְּשָׂרוֹ לְנֶגַע צָרָעַת וְהוּבָא אֶל אַהֲרֹן הַכֹּהֵן אוֹ אֶל אַחַד מִבָּנָיו הַכֹּהֲנִים

When a person has on the skin of his body a swelling, a rash, or a discoloration, and it develops into leprosy on the skin of his body, and it shall be brought to Aharon the *cohen* or to one of his sons, the *cohanim*.

The medrash (15.4) comments on this *passuk*

ד"א אָדָם כִּי יִהְיֶה בְעוֹר בְּשָׂרוֹ הה"ד (משלי י"ט, כ"ט) נָכוֹנוּ לַלֵּצִים שְׁפָטִים [וּמַהֲלֻמוֹת לְגֵו כְּסִילִים...] משל למטרונה שנכנסה לתוך פלטין של מלך כיון דחמית מגלביא תלן דחלת אמר לה המלך אל תתייראי אלו לעבדים ולשפחות אבל את לאכול ולשתות ולשמוח כך כיון ששמעו ישראל פרשת נגעים נתייראו א"ל משה אל תתייראו אלו לאו"ה אבל אתם לאכול ולשתות ולשמוח שנאמר (תהלים ל"ב, י') רבים מכאובים לרשע והבוטח בה' חסד יסובבנו

[With regards to the *korbanos*, the *passuk* says (Vayikra 1.2), "When one of you brings a *korban* to Hashem." However here, the *passuk* just says, "When one has in the skin of his flesh," and does not say "of you." The medrash explains that this is because *tzara'as* is more likely to affect the אומות העולם and not the *benei yisrael*, hence *tzara'as* is not destined for "you."]

As the *passuk* says in Mishlei, "Punishments are prepared for scoffers. And blows for the backs of fools." [The medrash understands that the word ומהלמות (blows) is an acronym – מה אלו לאומות.] It is analogous to a noblewoman who entered the king's palace. When she saw the straps hanging on the wall, she became afraid. The king said to her, "Do not be afraid. These are for the slaves and the maidservants, but there is nothing for you to do but to eat and drink and rejoice."

Similarly, when the *benei yisrael* heard the parsha of *tzara'as* they became afraid, Moshe said to them, "Do not be afraid, these are for the אומות העולם but for you there is nothing to do but to eat and drink and rejoice." As the *passuk* says, "There are many pains for the *rasha*, but for one who trusts in Hashem, kindness shall surround him."

- What is the connection between trusting in Hashem and not receiving *tzara'as*?

It would seem that we can explain as follows:

The Zohar says (רעיא מהימנא, פרשת עקב, דף רע"ג ע"א)

תליתאה למיכל שלשה סעודתין בשבת כמה דאוקמוה רבנן דמתניתין דאמר חד מינייהו יהא חלקי עם גומרי שלש סעודות בשבת דאינון שלימו דשבע ברכאן דצלותא לאשלמא בהון לעשר ורזא דענג ונהר יוצא מעדן להשקות את הגן. ומאן דלא מקיים לון ואית ליה רשו לקיימן אתהפך ליה לנגע צרעת. ובגין דלא ייתי להאי אמר קב"ה לוו עלי ואני

פורע אז תתענג על ה'

The third obligation is to eat three meals on שבת as the gemara says (שבת קי"ח ע"ב)

אמר ר' יוסי יהא חלקי מאוכלי שלש סעודות בשבת

Rabbi Yossi said, "May my portion be with those who eat three meals on שבת."

This is the secret of ענג (delight) on שבת, [which is referred to in the *passuk* (Yeshaya 58.13)

אִם תָּשִׁיב מִשַּׁבָּת רַגְלֶךָ עֲשׂוֹת חֲפָצֶיךָ בְּיוֹם קָדְשִׁי וְקָרָאתָ לַשַּׁבָּת עֹנֶג לִקְדוֹשׁ ה' מְכֻבָּד וְכִבַּדְתּוֹ מֵעֲשׂוֹת דְּרָכֶיךָ מִמְּצוֹא חֶפְצְךָ וְדַבֵּר דָּבָר. אָז תִּתְעַנַּג עַל ה' ...

If you refrain from trampling the שבת, from pursuing your affairs on My holy day; If you call the שבת a delight, the day of Hashem "honoured"; And if you honour it and do not go on your ways or look to your affairs or strike bargains, then you will rejoice in Hashem...]

But if someone does not fulfill the obligation to have three meals on Shabbos, and he has the wherewithal to do so, then the ענג (delight) of Shabbos is turned for him to נגע (*tzara'as*). (I.e. the letters of ענג are rearranged to spell נגע.) And in order that he should not come to this, Hashem said, "Borrow on my account." Then you will rejoice in Hashem.

The phrase לוו עלי ואני פורע – "Borrow on My account and I will repay," also occurs in the gemara in Beitza (15b)

מאי כי חדות ה' היא מעוזכם אמר רבי יוחנן משום רבי אליעזר בר' שמעון אמר להם הקדוש ברוך הוא לישראל בני לוו עלי וקדשו קדושת היום והאמינו בי ואני פורע

What is the meaning of the *passuk* that says, "For the joy of Hashem is your strength"? Rabbi Yochanan said in the name of Rabbi Eliezer, the son of Rabbi Shimon, "Hashem said to the *benei yisrael*, 'My children, borrow on My account, and sanctify the sanctity of Shabbos and Yom Tov with wine, and trust in Me, and I will repay the debt.'"

Rashi explains

חדות ה': שמחה שאתם עושים בשביל הקב"ה הרי היא מעוזכם היא תעזור אתכם לשלם הקפותיכם ומלוותיכם שתלוו בשבילה

The joy of Hashem: The rejoicing that you do for the sake of Hashem is your strength. That joy will help you to pay your store loans and your monetary loans that you will borrow for it.

Rashi's explanation does not appear to be in line with the simple meaning of the gemara. The gemara says that Hashem said, 'My children, borrow on My account, and sanctify the sanctity of Shabbos and Yom Tov with wine, and trust in Me, and I will repay the debt.'" This implies that Hashem Himself will cause events to occur whereby the *benei yisrael* will be able to pay their debts.

However Rashi says, "That joy will help you to pay your store loans and your monetary loans that you will borrow for it." This implies that the benei yisrael will gather the strength and fortitude to work and pay their debts, through their rejoicing.

In order to answer this apparent contradiction, it seems that we must say that if one rejoices in the service of Hashem, then automatically he will find that his *parnassah* becomes available to him, as the gemara says in Kiddushin (82b)

תניא ר"ש בן אלעזר אומר מימי לא ראיתי צבי קייץ וארי סבל ושועל חנווני והם מתפרנסים שלא בצער והם לא נבראו אלא לשמשני ואני נבראתי לשמש את קוני מה אלו שלא נבראו אלא לשמשני מתפרנסים שלא בצער ואני שנבראתי לשמש את קוני אינו דין שאתפרנס שלא בצער אלא שהרעותי את מעשי וקיפחתי את פרנסתי

Rabbi Shimon ben Elazar said, "In all my days, I never saw a deer that had to work as a fruit watchman, or a lion that had to work as a porter, or a fox that had to work as a storekeeper. They receive their livelihood without any difficulty and they are only created to serve me. But I am created to serve Hashem, so all the more so I should receive my livelihood without any difficulty. Rather this is because I have made my deeds deficient and thereby I have cut off my livelihood.

We see from the gemara that if a person fulfills their function in *avodas Hashem* as naturally and joyously as a deer is a deer, a lion is a lion and a fox is a fox, then automatically all their needs will be provided for.

Thus, if one comes to Yom Tov or Shabbos and is unable to afford the needs of Yom Tov or Shabbos, this means that they were unable to reach that level of joy in *avodas Hashem* that would have caused these needs to be provided for.

In this case, Hashem says - לוו עלי ואני פורע, "Borrow on My account and I will repay." This means, "Even although you have not been able to elevate yourselves to the required level of joy in *avodas Hashem*, which is indicated by that which you cannot afford the needs of Yom Tov and Shabbos, nevertheless borrow and be joyous on my account. Buy whatever you need to put yourself into a joyous frame of mind, and rejoice on Shabbos and Yom Tov in a holy rejoicing that you have borrowed from My treasure-house of rejoicing and sustenance. If you take this loan of joy from Me, then I will pay back the physical loan that you took out in order to feel *simcha* on Shabbos and Yom Tov."

Therefore that which the gemara says, "Borrow on My account and I will repay," and that which Rashi says, "That joy will help you to pay your loans," is the same. Because the person "borrowed joy" from Hashem, therefore automatically their *parnassah* will fall into place, since they are now able to serve Hashem naturally and joyously.

Based on this explanation, we can understand that when the Zohar says - ובגין דלא ייתי להאי אמר קב"ה לוו עלי ואני פורע, "And in order that he should not come to this, Hashem said, 'Borrow on my account,'" the Zohar means to say that in order that a person should always merit *simchah* in *avodas Hashem*, and thus escape the punishment of *tzara'as*, a person should borrow the rejoicing itself from Hashem. So that although one may feel that according to what they have accomplished to date they are not worthy to rejoice in Hashem, nevertheless they should trust in Hashem to gird themselves with rejoicing.

This is why the Zohar says that one who trusts in Hashem is saved from *tzara'as*. *Tzara'as* is indicative of a contradiction between the internal spiritual state and the external spiritual state of a person. Through rejoicing in Hashem, one is able to achieve the same inner level of spirituality that is represented by their outer demeanour. However, it is not always possible to come through their own efforts to such rejoicing.

Therefore Hashem says, "Borrow the rejoicing itself from Me, even although you may not feel you have merited such elevated joy, and I will repay both the spiritual loan and also the associated physical loan, that you have taken from Me."

The order of *tzara'as*

This week's *sedrah* discusses the *halachos* of *tzara'as* that affects people, clothing and houses, in that order.

Concerning people, the *passuk* says (Vayikra 13.2)

אָדָם כִּי יִהְיֶה בְעוֹר בְּשָׂרוֹ שְׂאֵת אוֹ סַפַּחַת אוֹ בַהֶרֶת

When a person has in the skin of his body a swelling, a rash, or a discoloration

Then concerning clothes, the *passuk* says (Vayikra, 13.47)

וְהַבֶּגֶד כִּי יִהְיֶה בוֹ נֶגַע צָרָעַת

When *tzara'as* occurs in a garment…

And finally, concerning houses, the *passuk* says (14:34)

כִּי תָבֹאוּ אֶל אֶרֶץ כְּנַעַן אֲשֶׁר אֲנִי נֹתֵן לָכֶם לַאֲחֻזָּה וְנָתַתִּי נֶגַע צָרַעַת בְּבֵית אֶרֶץ אֲחֻזַּתְכֶם

When you come to the land of Kana'an which I give to you as an inheritance, and I will place *tzara'as* in a house of the land which you will have acquired.

The medrash comments (Vayikra Rabbah 17:4)

רב הונא בשם רבי יהושע בר אבין ורבי זכריה חתניה דרבי לוי בשם רבי לוי אין בעל הרחמים נוגע בנפשות תחלה... ואף נגעים הבאים על האדם תחלה הן באים בביתו חזר בו טעון חליצה ואי לאו טעון נתיצה הרי הן באים על בגדיו חזר בו טעון כביסה ואי לאו טעון שריפה הרי הם באים על גופו חזר בו יטהר ואי לאו, בדד ישב

Rabbi Huna said, "Hashem does not initially punish people directly. If a person has sinned, *tzara'as* will affect his house. If he does *teshuvah*, it will be a light *tzara'as* that can be peeled off the wall, if not then the *tzara'as* will remain and his house will have to be destroyed.

Subsequently, the *tzara'as* will affect his clothes. If he does *teshuva* then the *tzara'as* will go away and the clothes will need *tevilah*, if not then the clothes will need to be burned.

Subsequently, the *tzara'as* will come on to his body. If he does *teshuvah* then he will become *tahor*, if not then he will have to sit alone outside the camp.

According to the medrash, it would seem that first the Torah should have discussed *tzara'as* of houses, then *tzara'as* of clothes and finally *tzara'as* of people. However, as mentioned above, the Torah explains the *halachos* of *tzara'as* in reverse order, first addressing people, then clothes and finally houses.

- Why does the Torah explain the *halachos* of *tzara'as* in the reverse of the order in which *tzara'as* happens?

The medrash continues

בְּבֵית אֶרֶץ אֲחֻזַּתְכֶם, זֶה בֵּית הַמִּקְדָּשׁ, שֶׁנֶּאֱמַר (יחזקאל כ"ד, כ"א) הִנְנִי מְחַלֵּל אֶת מִקְדָּשִׁי גְּאוֹן עֻזְּכֶם. (ויקרא י"ד, ל"ה) וּבָא אֲשֶׁר לוֹ הַבַּיִת, זֶה הַקָּדוֹשׁ בָּרוּךְ הוּא, שֶׁנֶּאֱמַר (חגי א', ט') יַעַן בֵּיתִי אֲשֶׁר הוּא חָרֵב. (ויקרא י"ד, ל"ה) וְהִגִּיד לַכֹּהֵן, זֶה יִרְמְיָה, שֶׁנֶּאֱמַר (ירמיה א', א') מִן הַכֹּהֲנִים אֲשֶׁר בַּעֲנָתוֹת. (ויקרא י"ד, ל"ה) כְּנֶגַע נִרְאָה לִי בַּבָּיִת, זוֹ טִינֹפֶת עֲבוֹדָה זָרָה, וְיֵשׁ אוֹמְרִים זֶה צַלְמוֹ שֶׁל מְנַשֶּׁה... (ויקרא י"ד, ל"ו) וְצִוָּה הַכֹּהֵן וּפִנּוּ אֶת הַבַּיִת (מלכים א' י"ד, כ"ו) וַיִּקַּח אֶת אוֹצְרוֹת בֵּית ה'. (ויקרא י"ד, מ"ה) וְנָתַץ אֶת הַבַּיִת, (עזרא ה', י"ב) וּבַיְתָא דְנָה סַתְרֵהּ. (ויקרא י"ד, מ"ה) וְהוֹצִיא אֶל מִחוּץ לָעִיר, (עזרא ה', י"ב) וְעַמָּה הַגְלִי לְבָבֶל.

יָכוֹל לְעוֹלָם, תַּלְמוּד לוֹמַר (ויקרא י"ד, מ"ב) וְלָקְחוּ אֲבָנִים אֲחֵרוֹת, שֶׁנֶּאֱמַר (ישעיה כ"ח, מ"ב) לָכֵן כֹּה אָמַר ה' אֱלֹקִים הִנְנִי יִסַּד בְּצִיּוֹן אָבֶן אֶבֶן בֹּחַן פִּנַּת יִקְרַת מוּסָד מוּסָּד הַמַּאֲמִין לֹא יָחִישׁ.

"In the land of your inheritance," this refers to the *beis ha'mikdash*. "Then the house owner should come," this refers to Hashem. And he should tell the *cohen*, this refers to Yirmiyah (who was a *cohen*). "A blemish has appeared in the house," this refers to *avodah zarah*. "And the *cohen* shall command and they shall empty the house," this refers to the king of Mitzrayim plundering the treasures of the *beis ha'mikdash*. "And he shall destroy the house," this refers to Nevuchadnezzar destroying the *beis ha'mikdash*. "And he shall take them out of the city," this refers to Nevuchadnezzar exiling the *benei yisrael* to Bavel.

You may think this will be forever. Therefore the *passuk* says, "And they should take other stones." This refers to the rebuilding of the *beis ha'mikdash*.

- Why does the medrash compare the destruction of the *beis ha'mikdash* to the destruction of a house that is infected with *tzara'as*?

The analogy of the destruction of the *beis ha'mikdash* corresponds to a person who found *tzara'as* affecting their house except for one detail. The medrash compares taking the infected stones to outside of the city with the *benei yisrael* going into *galus*. However, according to the previous analogy, the equivalent of the infected stones being removed would have been the removal of the stones of the *beis ha'mikdash*.

- Why does the medrash compare taking the infected stones outside the city to the *benei yisrael* going into *galus*?

It seems that we can explain as follows[33]:

Tzara'as shows that the person affected is spiritually removed from the item that has *tzara'as*.

- *Tzara'as* of a house indicates that the owner uses his house for his own purposes and not for the service of Hashem.

- *Tzara'as* on clothes indicates that the owner uses his clothing for his own purposes and not for the service of Hashem.

---

[33] עיין בספר שערי צדק

- *Tzara'as* on the body indicates that the *metzora* uses his body for his own purposes and not for the service of Hashem.

In giving us Eretz Yisrael, our clothes and our bodies, Hashem also allowed us their natural *kedushah*, which influences us to use these items for purposes of holiness.

If we nevertheless only use our bodies, clothes and houses for mundane purposes, we repel this natural inclination to *kedushah* first from our bodies, then from our clothes and finally from our houses. The Torah arranges the different types of *tzara'as* in the order that the removal of this natural *kedushah* will occur, and thus discusses first *tzara'as* of the body, then *tzara'as* of clothes and finally *tzara'as* of houses.

However, in His kindness, Hashem brings *tzara'as* on a person in the reverse order of what is happening spiritually. First Hashem shows a person (via *tzara'as*) that his house is not being used for *avodas Hashem*, then He shows a person that his clothes are not being used for *avodas Hashem* and finally He indicates that his body is not being used for *avodas Hashem*.

Regarding the analogy of *tzara'as* to the *beis ha'mikdash*, we can understand that the greatest manifestation of the natural inclination to serve Hashem is present in the *beis ha'mikdash*. Through the purification of the *korbanos*, we are drawn to serve Hashem in purity and holiness. When the *beis ha'mikdash* was destroyed, and we no longer have the order of the *korbanos*, the greatest natural inclination to *kedushah* with which we are left is the *kedushah* that is inherent in the very bodies of the *benei yisrael*.

In this way, when the *kedushah* that was previously present in the of the stones of the *beis ha'mikdash* was removed from us with the destruction of the *beis ha'mikdash*, the only vestige of this *kedushah* remained in the bodies of the *benei yisrael*, who then went into *galus*.

That is why the medrash says:

> "And he shall destroy the house," this refers to Nevuchadnezzar destroying the *beis ha'mikdash*. "And he shall take them out of the city," this refers to Nevuchadnezzar exiling the *benei yisrael* to Bavel.

The remnant of the *kedushah* of the stones of the *beis ha'mikdash*, went into *galus* in the form of the bodies of the *benei yisrael*.

However, when *mashiach* comes, this *kedushah* will manifest itself once more in the stones of the third *beis ha'mikdash*.

> You may think this will be forever. Therefore the *passuk* says, "And they should take other stones." This refers to the rebuilding of the *beis ha'mikdash*.

Acharei mos

The timelessness of Yom Kippur

It says at the beginning of this week's *sedrah* (16.1-3)

וַיְדַבֵּר ה' אֶל מֹשֶׁה אַחֲרֵי מוֹת שְׁנֵי בְּנֵי אַהֲרֹן בְּקָרְבָתָם לִפְנֵי ה' וַיָּמֻתוּ. וַיֹּאמֶר ה' אֶל מֹשֶׁה דַּבֵּר אֶל אַהֲרֹן אָחִיךָ וְאַל יָבֹא בְכָל עֵת אֶל הַקֹּדֶשׁ מִבֵּית לַפָּרֹכֶת אֶל פְּנֵי הַכַּפֹּרֶת אֲשֶׁר עַל הָאָרֹן וְלֹא יָמוּת כִּי בֶּעָנָן אֵרָאֶה עַל הַכַּפֹּרֶת. בְּזֹאת יָבֹא אַהֲרֹן אֶל הַקֹּדֶשׁ בְּפַר בֶּן בָּקָר לְחַטָּאת וְאַיִל לְעֹלָה.

And Hashem spoke to Moshe after the death of the two sons of Aharon who died when they drew too close to the presence of Hashem. And Hashem said to Moshe, "Speak to Aharon your brother [and tell him that] he is not to come at any time into the *kodesh ha'kedashim* behind the curtain, in front of the cover that is upon the *aron ha'kodesh*, so that he should not die; for J appear in a cloud over the cover. With this shall Aharon enter the *kodesh ha'kedashim*, with a bull for a sin offering and a ram for a burnt offering.

Rashi comments

בזאת: גימטריא שלו ד' מאות ועשר רמז לבית ראשון

> The numerical value of בזאת is 410, this alludes to the first *beis ha'mikdash* which stood for 410 years.

- According to the literal translation of the *passuk*, the word בזאת, "with this," refers to the *korbanos* that the *cohen gadol* brings on Yom Kippur, so the word בזאת refers to a thing and not to a time.

How then does the allusion (in the word בזאת) to the time for which the first *beis ha'mikdash* stood, fit into the meaning of the *passuk*, "With 'this' Aharon shall enter the *kodesh ha'kedashim*"?

The medrash comments on this *passuk*

בזאת יבא אהרן, הדא היא דכתיב (תהלים כ"ז, א') לְדָוִד ה' אוֹרִי וְיִשְׁעִי מִמִּי אִירָא. רבי אלעזר פתר קריא בים. אורי, בים שנאמר (שמות י"ד, כ') ויאר את הלילה. וישעי, התיצבו וראו את ישועת ה'. ממי אירא, ויאמר משה אל תיראו. ה' מעוז חיי, (שם ט"ו, ב') עזי וזמרת קה. ממי אפחד (שם, ט"ז) תפול עליהם אימתה ופחד. בקרוב עלי מרעים, (שם י"ד, י') ופרעה הקריב. לאכול את בשרי, (שם ט"ו, ט') אמר אויב ארדוף אשיג וגו'... צָרַי וְאֹיְבַי לִי (תהלים קל"ו, ט"ו) ונער פרעה וחילו.

"With this Aharon shall come into the *kodesh ha'kedashim*." This is a reference to that which it is written in Tehillim, "To David, 'Hashem is my light and my salvation, from whom should I fear? [Hashem is the stronghold of my life, whom should I dread? When evil men assail me to devour my flesh, it is they, my foes and my enemies, who stumble and fall. Should an army besiege me, my heart would have no fear. Should war beset me, still would I be confident.]'"

Rabbi Elazar interpreted these *pessukim* in reference to *krias yam suf*.

"My light," this was at the sea, as it says, "And it lit up the night."

"And my salvation," as it says, "Stand firm and see the salvation of Hashem."

"From whom should I fear?" As it says, "And Moshe said, 'Do not fear.'"

"Hashem is the stronghold of my life," as it says, "My strength and cutting-down [power] is Hashem."

"From whom should I tremble?" As it says, "May fear and dread fall on them."

"When evil people draw close to me," as it says, "And Pharoh drew close."

"To devour my flesh," as it says, "The enemy said, 'I will pursue them, catch them up etc.'"

- How did the fact that Moshe said "Do not fear," cause *David ha'melech* to not fear?

- Corresponding to the *passuk* in Tehillim, "And my salvation," the medrash quotes the *passuk* that says, "Stand firm and see the salvation of Hashem." Apparently the medrash could better have quoted the *passuk* that says (Shemos 14.30), "And Hashem saved the *benei yisrael* on that day from the hand of *Mitzrayim*"?

(I.e. the *passuk* of, "Stand firm and see the salvation of Hashem," refers to Moshe exhorting the *benei yisrael* to trust in Hashem. But the *passuk* of "And Hashem saved the *benei yisrael* on that day from hand of Mitzrayim," refers to what actually occurred. Apparently the medrash should have quoted the second *passuk*, as this would have been a greater source of solace for *David ha'melech*.)

It would seem that we can explain as follows:

The Zohar says (58b)

רבי שמעון אמר, הא אוקימנא מלה בעתו, והכי הוא ודאי, והכא אתא קודשא בריך הוא לאזהרא לאהרן, דלא יטעי בההוא חובא דטעו בנוי, דהא האי עת ידיעא, בגין כך לא יטעי לחבר עת אחרא לגבי מלכא, הדא הוא דכתיב, ואל יבא בכל עת אל הקדש, כלומר אף על גב דיחמי עידן דאתמסר בידא אחרא לאתנהגא עלמא, ויתמסר בידוי לייחד ביה לקרבא ליה לקודשא, דהא אנא ושמי חד הוא, ובגיני כך ואל יבא בכל עת אל הקדש, ואי בעי למנדע במה ייעול, בזאת, בזאת יבא אהרן אל הקדש, דהאי זאת היא עת דאחידת בשמי, בהאי י' דרשימא בשמי ייעול אל הקדש, (אבל) ואל יבא בכל עת

Rabbi Shimon said, "...Hashem came here to warn Aharon that he should not sin in the same way that his sons sinned.

For this time [that is appropriate for the service of the *cohen gadol* in the *kodesh ha'kedashim*] is known, and therefore Aharon should not seek to cleave [through another] time to the King. This is what the *passuk* says, "And he should not come at any time to the *kodesh ha'kedashim*." This means to say, even if Aharon sees that the way in which the world is conducted, centres around another time, and that time is handed into the hands of Aharon so that is able to unify the name of Hashem by uplifting that time to holiness, nevertheless, since I am one with My name, therefore, "He should not come at any time to the *kodesh ha'kedashim*."

And if he wants to know with what he should enter, he should enter בזאת, "With this." "With this Aharon should come to the *kodesh he'kedashim*." Because this זאת ("this") is the time which adheres to My name. With the letter *yud* which is manifest in My name he should come to the *kodesh ha'kedashim*…

The *yud* in the name of Hashem represents *olam habah*, as the gemara says in Menachos (29b)

מאי דכתיב (ישעיהו כ"ו, ד') בטחו בה' עדי עד כי בקה ה' צור עולמים... כדדרש ר' יהודה בר ר' אילעאי אלו שני עולמות שברא הקב"ה אחד בה"י ואחד ביו"ד ואיני יודע אם העולם הבא ביו"ד והעולם הזה בה"י אם העולם הזה ביו"ד והעולם הבא בה"י כשהוא אומר (בראשית ב', ד') אלה תולדות השמים והארץ בהבראם אל תקרי בהבראם אלא בה"י בראם [הוי אומר העולם הזה בה"י והעולם הבא ביו"ד]

The letters *yud* and *heh* that constitute the name of Hashem refer to the two worlds that Hashem created, one with the letter *heh* and one with the letter *yud*. And I do not know whether the World-to-Come was created with the letter *yud* and this world was created with the letter *heh*, or whether this world was created with the letter *yud* and the World-to-Come was created with the letter *heh*.

However, the *passuk* states in Bereishis (2.4), "These are the generations of the heaven and of the earth when they were created [*behibare'am*]." Do not read it as *behibare'am*, meaning, "When they were created," rather read it as *be'heh bera'am*, meaning, "He created them with the letter *heh*." This *passuk* demonstrates that the heaven and the earth (i.e. this world) were created with the letter *heh*, and therefore the World-to-Come must have been created with the letter *yud*.

Olam ha'bah is represented by the letter *yud* because[34] the letter *yud* is written as a point. This signifies that from the perspective of *olam ha'bah*, things exist as their essential unity, prior to being expressed in their forms of *olam ha'zeh*. *Olam ha'zeh*, on the other hand, is represented by the letter *heh* which has four sides, because in *olam ha'zeh* things assume a spatial and temporal form, which is represented by the four directions.

---

[34] עיין בספר אור תורה להגרי"א חבר ז"ל

The Zohar says that the word בזאת refers to "the time that cleaves to the letter *yud* in the name of Hashem." Time is specific to *olam hazeh*, and the letter *yud* refers to *olam habah*. Therefore it must be that the Zohar means to refer to the time of Yom Kippur which tends towards and joins the timelessness of *olam habah*.

In the course of our annual efforts in *olam hazeh*, which is the world of doing and becoming, we can lose touch with the pure direction that is true to our quintessential selves. On Yom Kippur, we do *teshuvah* and return to our true essence as indicated by the perspective of *olam habah*, the world of being and unity.

Because Yom Kippur is the time which draws us close to the timeless perspective of *olam habah*, Yom Kippur is also the time that ties together the experiences of all the generations, who are otherwise separated by the passage of time in *olam hazeh*.

Hence, through the *madregah* of Yom Kippur, *David ha'melech* was able to draw vigour and strength by connecting to the events of *krias yam suf*, as they were unfolding. This is why the medrash quotes the *pessukim* which describe the events of *krias yam suf* as they happened, and not the *pessukim* which refer to *krias yam suf* after the event.

This is also why Rashi says

בזאת: גימטריא שלו ד' מאות ועשר רמז לבית ראשון

> The numerical value of בזאת is 410, this alludes to the first *beis ha'mikdash* which stood for 410 years.

Through the *avodah* of Yom Kippur, the *cohen gadol* was able to grasp in his hand, as if it were, all of the holiness of every Yom Kippur ever celebrated in the *beis ha'mikdash*, and with this timeless holiness he would enter into the *kodesh ha'kedashim*.

Kedoshim

The gift of holiness

It says at the beginning of this week's *sedrah* (19.2)

דַּבֵּר אֶל כָּל עֲדַת בְּנֵי יִשְׂרָאֵל וְאָמַרְתָּ אֲלֵהֶם קְדֹשִׁים תִּהְיוּ כִּי קָדוֹשׁ אֲנִי ה' אֱלֹקֵיכֶם

Speak to all of the congregation of the *benei yisrael* and say to them, "You should be holy because I, Hashem your G-d, am holy."

Rashi comments on this *passuk* as follows

דבר אל כל עדת בני ישראל: מלמד שנאמרה פרשה זו בהקהל מפני שרוב גופי תורה תלוין בה

This (the addition of the words כל עדת) teaches us this section was proclaimed in a complete assembly, because most of the fundamental teachings of the Torah are dependent on it.

The Gur Aryeh explains

> אַף עַל גַב שֶׁגַם שְׁאָר הַפָּרָשִׁיוֹת נֶאֶמְרוּ לְכָל יִשְׂרָאֵל (עירובין נד ע"ב), כְּמוֹ שֶׁכָּתַב גַם כֵּן רָשִׁ"י בְּסוֹף פָּרָשַׁת כִּי תִשָּׂא (שמות ל"ד, ל"ב) כֵּיצַד סֵדֶר מִשְׁנָה כו' נִכְנְסוּ כָּל הָעָם כו', מוּכָח מִזֶּה שֶׁכָּל הַתּוֹרָה נֶאֶמְרָה לְכָל יִשְׂרָאֵל, שֶׁאֲנִי הָתָם, שֶׁלֹא הָיָה מְחוּיָיבִים שֶׁיָּבוֹאוּ כָּל יִשְׂרָאֵל, שֶׁאִם לֹא הָיָה לָהֶם פְּנַאי לֹא הָיוּ בָּאִים, שֶׁלֹא קָאָמַר הָתָם אֶלָּא כֵּיצַד סֵדֶר מִשְׁנָה, אֲבָל בְּפָרָשָׁה הַזֹּאת הָיָה מַקְהִיל כָּל יִשְׂרָאֵל, וְהָיוּ צְרִיכִין לָבוֹא.

Even although the other sections were also stated to all of the *benei yisrael*... [this section is different because] there attendance was optional, and if someone did not have time he would not come, whereas here attendance was obligatory.

- What is the importance of the *mitzva* of קדושים תהיו, "You shall be holy," that made it obligatory for the whole of *klal yisrael* to hear this *mitzva* together?

The medrash (ויקרא רבה, כ"ד, ג') comments on this *passuk*

> קדשים תהיו, הה"ד (תהלים כ', ג') ישלח עזרך מקדש

The *passuk* says, קדושים תהיו, "You shall be holy." This is an application of that which is stated in Tehillim, ישלח עזרך מקודש, "He will send your aid from (the place of) holiness."

- What is particular about this aid of Hashem to the *benei yisrael*, that it should come from a place of holiness?

Regarding the *mitzvah* to be holy, the medrash (Shemos Rabbah 38.2) says

דבר אחר, וְזֶה הַדָּבָר, הא הוא דכתיב (חבקוק א', י"ב) הֲלֹא אַתָּה מִקֶּדֶם ה' אֱלֹקַי קְדֹשִׁי וְלֹא נָמוּת...

עד שלא עמד אדם הראשון ואכל את האילן כך היית אומר שלא יאכל מן האילן ולא ימות שנאמר הֲלֹא אַתָּה מִקֶּדֶם ה' אֱלֹקַי קְדֹשִׁי וְלֹא נָמוּת. אלא מפני שביטל צוויך, הבאת עליו מיתה להכות את הבריות שנאמר ה' לְמִשְׁפָּט שַׂמְתּוֹ. אתה גוזר ואומר קדושים תהיו לאלקיכם, וכן זֶה הַדָּבָר אֲשֶׁר תַּעֲשֶׂה לָהֶם לְקַדֵּשׁ אֹתָם. רבון העולם אתה מבקש שנהא קדושים, הסר ממנו המות. שנאמר הֲלֹא אַתָּה ה' אֱלֹקַי קְדֹשִׁי וְלֹא נָמוּת

The *passuk* says (Shemos 29.1), "And this is the matter that you should do to them to sanctify them to be כהנים to me. Take a young bull of the herd and two perfect rams."

This relates to that which it is written (Chabakuk 1.12), "Are you not from days of yore Hashem my G-d, my Holy One, and we will not die."

Before Adam got up and ate from the Tree of Knowledge, I thought that he should not eat from the Tree of Knowledge and he should not die, as the *passuk* says, "Are you not from days of yore Hashem my G-d, my Holy One, and we will not die." But because he annulled your commandment you brought death on him with which to smite people, as the *passuk* says (ibid.), "Hashem, you have set him for judgement."

But you decree and you say, "You should be holy to your G-d" and "This is the matter that you should do to them to sanctify them." Master of the Universe, you request that we should be holy, then remove death from us! As the *passuk* says, "Are you not from days of yore Hashem my G-d, my Holy One, and we will not die."

- Why does the medrash say that if Hashem commanded us to be holy then we must perforce be granted the immortality that was enjoyed by Adam before he ate from the Tree of Knowledge?

It would seem that we can explain as follows[35].

Normally we understand that following Adam having eaten from the Tree of Knowledge, we have free will so that we are presented with the choice of good and bad in every action that we take. It seems, however, that there is one area in which free will is limited and the balance is swayed in our favour.

The gemara says in Bava Basra (דף ט"ז ע"א)

(איוב י', ז') על דעתך כי לא ארשע ואין מידך מציל. אמר רבא בקש איוב לפטור את כל העולם כולו מן הדין אמר לפניו רבונו של עולם בראת שור פרסותיו סדוקות בראת חמור פרסותיו קלוטות בראת גן עדן בראת גיהנם בראת צדיקים בראת רשעים מי מעכב על ידך ומאי אהדרו ליה חבריה דאיוב (איוב ט"ו, ד') אף אתה תפר יראה ותגרע שיחה לפני אל ברא הקדוש ברוך הוא יצר הרע ברא לו תורה תבלין

---

[35] עיין בספר פחד יצחק, סוכות, מאמר י"ט, ה'

The Gemara continues to discuss the statements of Iyov: "Although You know that I am not wicked, and there is none that can deliver out of Your hand" (Iyov 10:7). Rava says: Iyov sought to exempt the whole world from judgment, (by claiming that all of a person's actions are directed by Hashem, and therefore one cannot be held culpable for his misdeeds.)

Iyov said before Hashem: Master of the Universe, You created the ox with split hooves, making it kosher, and You created the donkey with closed hooves, making it forbidden; You created the Garden of Eden, and You created Gehinnom; (and similarly,) You created righteous people and You created wicked people; who can restrain You? (Seeing that You created people as either righteous or wicked, You cannot later complain about their actions.)

And how did Iyov's friends answer him? "You do away with fear, and impair devotion before Hashem" (Iyov 15:4). True, Hashem created the *yetzer ha'ra* (evil inclination), but He also created the Torah as an antidote to counter its effects and prevent it from gaining control of a person.

It would appear difficult to understand the rebuttal of Iyov's friends. Since the *yetzer ha'ra* knows that were a person to learn Torah then he would beat the *yetzer ha'ra*, the first thing that the *yetzer ha'ra* will do is to persuade the person to not learn Torah.

It is evident from this gemara[36] that since a person knows that

---

[36] עיין בספר מכתב מאליהו, חלק ג', עמוד 47

the only way to overpower the *yetzer ha'ra* that seeks to destroy him is by learning Torah, the *yetzer ha'ra* does not have the ability to stop a person learning Torah, should he choose to do so.

The mandate of the *yetzer ha'ra* to make a person doubt themselves when they choose to learn Torah is restricted, and the decision to learn Torah breaks through any impediment that could be placed in a person's way to stop them achieving their objective.

This means to say that, with respect to the holiness that is granted to us through the study and observance of the Torah, the normal rules of free will do not apply. Rather, this holiness brings us back, to a certain degree, to that level of pure vitality that was enjoyed by Adam before he ate from the Tree of Knowledge, that granted him free will.

In this way, the *mitzva* of קדושה is given as an aid to the *benei yisrael*, so that they should not inevitably be faced with equal choice between good and bad, however hard they try to come closer to Hashem. Instead, by aggregating the cumulative holiness that we gain from learning Torah and doing *mitzvos*, we are able to build a platform of *kedushah* that is impervious to any attempt of the *yetzer ha'ra* to undo our accomplishments.

By this token, the *mitzva* of קדושים תהיו is given as an aid to the *benei yisrael*, that frees them from the diminution in stature and life-force that Adam experienced when he ate from the Tree of Knowledge. Breaking the limitations of our corporeal existence, in this way, was something that could only be accomplished by all of the congregation of the *benei yisrael*, standing together.

Emor

The balance of the *kohanim*

It says at the beginning of this week's *sedrah* (21.1)

וַיֹּאמֶר ה' אֶל מֹשֶׁה אֱמֹר אֶל הַכֹּהֲנִים בְּנֵי אַהֲרֹן וְאָמַרְתָּ אֲלֵהֶם לְנֶפֶשׁ לֹא יִטַּמָּא בְּעַמָּיו. כִּי אִם לִשְׁאֵרוֹ הַקָּרֹב אֵלָיו לְאִמּוֹ וּלְאָבִיו וְלִבְנוֹ וּלְבִתּוֹ וּלְאָחִיו. וְלַאֲחֹתוֹ הַבְּתוּלָה הַקְּרוֹבָה אֵלָיו אֲשֶׁר לֹא הָיְתָה לְאִישׁ לָהּ יִטַּמָּא.

Hashem said to Moshe, "Speak to the *cohanim*, the sons of Aharon, and say to them, 'None shall make himself impure for any [dead] person among his kin. Except for the relatives that are closest to him: his mother, his father, his son, his daughter, and his brother. Also for an unmarried sister, who is close to him because she has not married, for her he may defile himself.'"

The medrash comments on this *passuk* as follows

> וַיֹּאמֶר ה' אֶל מֹשֶׁה אֱמֹר אֶל הַכֹּהֲנִים, זֶה שֶׁאָמַר הַכָּתוּב (תהלים י"ט, ג') יוֹם לְיוֹם יַבִּיעַ אֹמֶר, תַּנְיָא בְּאֶחָד בִּתְקוּפַת נִיסָן וּבְאֶחָד בִּתְקוּפַת תִּשְׁרֵי הַיּוֹם וְהַלַּיְלָה שָׁוִין, מִכָּאן וָאֵילָךְ הַיּוֹם לוֹוֶה מִן הַלַּיְלָה וְהַלַּיְלָה מִן הַיּוֹם וּפוֹרְעִין זֶה לָזֶה בְּפִיּוּסִין, הַכֹּל בְּלִי שְׁטָר וּבְלִי גְזַר דִּין, הֱוֵי יוֹם לְיוֹם וְגוֹ', אֲבָל לְמַטָּה כַּמָּה שְׁטָרוֹת וְכַמָּה גְּזַר דִּין.

The *passuk* says, וַיֹּאמֶר ה' אֶל מֹשֶׁה אֱמֹר אֶל הַכֹּהֲנִים, "Hashem said to Moshe, "Speak to the cohanim, the sons of Aharon."

This is what the *passuk* in Tehillim refers to when it says יוֹם לְיוֹם יַבִּיעַ אֹמֶר, "One day talks to the other." We have learnt, on the first day of the season of Nissan and on the first day of the season of Tishrei, the day and the night are of equal length.

From then on, the day borrows from the night (i.e. the day is longer than the night) and the night is longer than the day (i.e. the night is longer than the day) and they console and repay each other (i.e. the degree to which the day is longer than the night, is made up when the night, commensurately, is longer than the day). All is done without a document and without a legal ruling. This is what the *passuk* means when it says יוֹם לְיוֹם יַבִּיעַ אֹמֶר, "One day talks to the other."

But below, on earth, when people do business and lend each other money, there are many documents and many legal rulings involved.

- What is the connection between the balance between night and day, and the *passuk* of אמור אל הכהנים?

It would seem that we can explain as follows:

The gemara says in Succah (53b)

אמר ליה הואיל ואדכרתן הכי אתמר. בשעה שכרה דוד שיתין קפא תהומא ובעא למשטפא עלמא. אמר דוד מי איכא דידע אי שרי למכתב שם אחספא ונשדיה בתהומא ומנח.
ליכא דקאמר ליה מידי. אמר דוד כל דידע למימר ואינו אומר יחנק בגרונו. נשא אחיתופל ק"ו בעצמו ומה לעשות שלום בין איש לאשתו

אמרה תורה שמי שנכתב בקדושה ימחה על המים לעשות שלום לכל העולם כולו על אחת כמה וכמה. אמר ליה שרי. כתב שם אחספא ושדי לתהומא ונחית תהומא שיתסר אלפי גרמידי. כי חזי דנחית טובא אמר כמה דמידלי טפי מירטב עלמא אמר חמש עשרה מעלות ואסקיה חמיסר אלפי גרמידי ואוקמיה באלפי גרמידי.

Rav Chisda continued and said to him, "Since you reminded me of this matter, this is what was originally stated. 'At the time that Dovid dug the channels (beneath the place where the *beis ha'mikdash* was to be built), the waters of the depths rose and sought to inundate the world. David said, "Is there anyone who knows whether it is permitted to write the name of Hashem on an earthenware shard? If it is permitted, we will write it and throw it into the depths, and they will subside."

There was no one who said anything to him. David said, "Anyone who knows what to say and does not say it, may he be strangled in his throat." Then Achithophel made a קל וחומר and said, "Just as in order to make peace between a man and his wife in the case of a *sota*, the Torah said, 'My Name will be erased in the water,' to establish peace for the whole world, all the more so it is permitted." He said to David, "It is permitted."

He wrote the name of Hashem on an earthenware shard and cast it into the depths, and the waters in the depths subsided sixteen thousand *amos*. When he saw that they subsided excessively, he said, "The higher the waters are in the aquifers, the more fertile is the soil of the world." He recited the fifteen שיר המעלות and elevated them fifteen thousand *amos*, and established them at a depth of one thousand *amos*.'"

In explanation of the allegory of the water of the depths, the medrash says (בראשית רבה, ב, ' ד')

על פני תהום, זה גלות ממלכת הרשעה, שאין להם חקר כמו התהום. מה התהום הזה אין לו חקר, אף הרשעים כן

> The *passuk* says, "And the earth was unformed and void, with darkness over the surface of the deep." When the *passuk* says "the deep," it refers to our exile amongst the evil empire, whose wickedness has no limit, like the depths. Just as it is impossible to plumb the depths of the deep parts of the ocean, so too is it impossible to plumb the depths of the depravity of the *reshaim*.

According to this allegory, if David wanted to dig channels into the waters of the depths when he came to lay the foundation of the *beis ha'mikdash*, this means that David wanted the spiritual influence of the *beis ha'mikdash* to be able to descend into and influence the deepest depths of the deeds of the *reshaim*.

However, by piercing through to and seeking to influence this level of human nature, David put himself in danger that he would be overwhelmed by the untrammeled wildness such depravity can unleash.
In order to regain his balance, David was permitted to use the Name of Hashem that miraculously preserves the *kedushah* of the *benei yisrael* when it seems that this will be overwhelmed by the intractability of human nature.

In the end, David was able to create a balance wherein the service in the *beis ha'mikdash* would be able to influence the limitless depths of human nature, although these depths would be kept at a safe distance so that they should not overwhelm the *cohanim* whose *avodah* brought the presence of Hashem into the *beis ha'mikdash*.

In this way, the *cohanim*, through their *avodah* in the *beis ha'mikdash*, become the nexus of the moral struggle of man. The *cohanim* seek to grasp the highest levels of spirituality that they can attain, and simultaneously they seek to influence the lowest levels that the human being can fall to.

When these two endeavours are evenly balanced, "the day is equal to the night." When there is a preponderance of elevation, "the day exceeds the night." And when the cohanim must turn the majority of their efforts to uplifting those who have fallen, "the night exceeds the day."

When this happens, the *cohanim* must bend down to "defile" themselves by involving themselves with those who require their spiritual assistance, before stepping back into the unadulterated purity of the *beis ha'mikdash*.

Hence the back and forth nature of the *cohanim* in the *beis ha'mikdash* is reflected in the back and forth of the balance of day and night, which balance will only be perfected with the coming of *mashiach*.

As the medrash says (ibid.)

וְרוּחַ אֱלֹקִים מְרַחֶפֶת, זֶה רוּחוֹ שֶׁל מֶלֶךְ הַמָּשִׁיחַ

"And the spirit of Hashem was hovering over the face of the water." This is the spirit of the king who is *mashiach*.

Behar

The holiness of *she'mitah*

The *passuk* at the beginning of this week's *sedrah* (25.1-2) introduces the *mitzva* of *she'mitah* as follows:

וַיְדַבֵּר ה' אֶל מֹשֶׁה בְּהַר סִינַי לֵאמֹר

Hashem spoke to Moshe on Har Sinai. Speak to the *benei yisrael* and say to them, "When you enter the land that I am giving to you, the land shall have a year of rest dedicated to Hashem."

Rashi comments:

בהר סיני: מה ענין שמיטה אצל הר סיני והלא כל המצוות נאמרו מסיני אלא מה שמיטה נאמרו כללותיה ודקדוקיה מסיני אף כולן נאמרו כללותיהן ודקדוקיהן מסיני כך שנויה בת"כ ונ"ל שכך פירושה לפי שלא מצינו שמיטת קרקעות שנשנית בערבות מואב במשנה תורה למדנו שכללותיה ופרטותיה כולן נאמרו מסיני ובא הכתוב ולמד כאן

> על כל דבור שנדבר למשה מסיני היו כולם כללותיהן ודקדוקיהן וחזרו ונשנו בערבות מואב

Why does the Torah mention that the *mitzva* of *she'mitah* specifically was given on Har Sinai? Were not all the *mitzvos* given on Har Sinai? Rather this comes to teach that just as the general rules and minute details of *she'mitah* were commanded on Har Sinai, so too were all the *mitzvos* with all their general rules and their minute details commanded on Har Sinai. Thus it is in taught in Toras Cohanim (Sifra, Behar, 1.1).

And it seems to me that the explanation is as follows: Since we do not find in Devarim that the laws concerning *she'mitah* were repeated in the plains of Moav, we may infer that all its general rules and specific prescriptions must have been commanded on Har Sinai. Therefore the mention of בהר סיני here is unnecessary, but the Torah by mentioning it intends to teach regarding every *mitzva* that was spoken to Moshe that they, their general rules and minute details, were commanded on Har Sinai and were only repeated again in the plains of Moav.

- Why was the *mitzva* of *she'mitah* chosen to teach us that all of the other *mitzvos* were stated in their entirety on Har Sinai?

The *sedrah* continues (25.2-4)

דַּבֵּר אֶל בְּנֵי יִשְׂרָאֵל וְאָמַרְתָּ אֲלֵהֶם כִּי תָבֹאוּ אֶל הָאָרֶץ אֲשֶׁר אֲנִי נֹתֵן לָכֶם וְשָׁבְתָה הָאָרֶץ שַׁבָּת לַה'. שֵׁשׁ שָׁנִים תִּזְרַע שָׂדֶךָ וְשֵׁשׁ שָׁנִים תִּזְמֹר כַּרְמֶךָ וְאָסַפְתָּ אֶת תְּבוּאָתָהּ. וּבַשָּׁנָה הַשְּׁבִיעִת שַׁבַּת שַׁבָּתוֹן יִהְיֶה לָאָרֶץ שַׁבָּת לַה' שָׂדְךָ לֹא תִזְרָע וְכַרְמְךָ לֹא תִזְמֹר.

Speak to the *benei yisrael* and say to them, "When you enter the land that I give to you, the land shall observe a year of rest to Hashem. Six years you may sow your field and six years you may prune your vineyard and gather in its produce. But in the seventh year the land shall have a year of complete rest, a שבת of Hashem. You shall not sow your field or prune your vineyard.

- It would appear that the *passuk* that says initially, "When you enter the land that I give to you, the land shall observe a year of rest to Hashem," is superfluous.

  Since The *sedrah* continues to say, "Six years you may sow your field... but in the seventh year the land shall have a year of complete rest, a שבת of Hashem," why is it necessary for the *passuk* to say initially "the land shall observe a year of rest to Hashem"?

- Additionally, why in the first *passuk* does it just say, "And the land shall rest [a year of rest] to Hashem." But in the latter *passuk* it says more emphatically , "It will be a year of rest to the land, a year of rest to Hashem"?

It would seem that we can explain as follows:

It says in פסוק ב'

וְשָׁבְתָה הָאָרֶץ שַׁבָּת לַה'

The land shall observe a year of rest to Hashem.

On which Rashi comments:

שבת לה': לשם ה' כשם שנאמר בשבת בראשית

> **A year of rest to Hashem**: This means a rest in honour of Hashem (not a rest for Hashem) in the same sense as these words are used in the case of the weekly שבת (Shemos 20.10) where שבת לה' cannot mean "a day for Hashem to rest."

Since the Torah uses the same terminology both for *she'mitah* and also for שבת, it is evident that there is a similarity between these two types of rest.

This similarity may be understood based on the following idea from the Mesillas Yesharim (פרק א')

ואם תעמיק עוד בעניין תראה כי העולם נברא לשימוש האדם, אמנם הנה הוא עומד בשקול גדול, כי אם האדם נמשך אחר העולם ומתרחק מבוראו, הנה הוא מתקלקל ומקלקל העולם עמו; ואם הוא שולט בעצמו ונדבק בבוראו ומשתמש מן העולם רק להיות לו לסיוע לעבודת בוראו, הוא מתעלה והעולם עצמו מתעלה עמו. כי הנה עילוי גדול הוא לבריות כולם, בהיותם משמשי האדם השלם המקודש בקדושתו יתברך...

והנה על העיקר הזה העירונו ז"ל במדרש קהלת, שאמרו ז"ל (קהלת רבה פ"ז), ראה את מעשי האלוקים וגו', בשעה שברא הקדוש ברוך

The holiness of she'mitah

הוא את אדם הראשון נטלו והחזירו על כל אילני גן עדן ואמר לו, ראה מעשי כמה נאים ומשובחים הן, וכל מה שבראתי בשבילך בראתי, תן דעתך שלא תקלקל ותחריב את עולמי.

If you look deeper into the matter, you will see that this world was created for man's use. But, behold the world stands in a great balance. For if man is drawn after the world and distances himself from his Creator, behold, he corrupts himself and corrupts the world with him. But if he rules over himself and clings to his Creator, and uses the world only as an aid to serve his Creator - then he elevates himself and elevates the world with him. For all creations are greatly elevated when they serve the wholesome man, who is sanctified with the holiness of Hashem.

Our sages alerted us to this fundamental principle in the medrash on Koheles which says as follows:

The *passuk* says (Koheles 7:13) "See the works of G-d." [This refers to the following event.] When Hashem created Adam, He took him and led him past all the trees of *Gan Eden* and said to him, "See how beautiful and excellent are my works. All that I have created, I have created for your sake. Be careful that you do not become corrupt and destroy My world."

During the days of the week, it is our responsibility to lift up the world, through our actions, so that both we and the world draw closer to Hashem. On Shabbos however, the world rests to Hashem. This means to say, that whereas during the week we have to struggle to draw the world closer to Hashem, on Shabbos the world displays its natural propensity to draw close to

Hashem of its own accord. In this state, the world becomes similar to the World to Come, when all things will naturally draw close to Hashem. This is why we say that שבת is מעין עולם הבא, "Similar to the World to Come."

Hence Shabbos is a day of rest from our labour to draw the world to Hashem, and on Shabbos we are invigorated by the *kedushah* that wells out from the world itself, and that gives us the strength to carry on with our labours the following week.

The same idea applies to the cycle of six years work in the fields and the seventh year of a rest to Hashem. Hence we can understand that the *pessukim* that describe the *mitzva* of *she'mitah* (25.2-4) mean to say as follows:

> Speak to the *benei yisrael* and say to them, "When you come to the land that I am giving to them[, and you toil in the land and you observe the מצות התלויות בארץ, those *mitzvos* that can only be kept in Eretz Yisrael and that relate to your agricultural labours, where the purpose of these *mitzvos* is to draw both yourselves and also Eretz Yisrael closer to Hashem,] then [, after six years of toil,] the land shall observe a Shabbos to Hashem [, which, in a similar way to Shabbos which we observe each week, will demonstrate the natural propensity of the world to draw close to Hashem.]
>
> For six years you shall sow your fields and for six years you shall prune your vines and you shall gather its produce. [And then, by observing the מצות התלויות בארץ, you will elevate both yourselves and the land, together with you.]

[However,] in the seventh year it will be a year of rest to the land, a Shabbos to Hashem, you shall not sow your field and you shall not prune your vine. [And this is because, since in *she'mitah* the land will demonstrate its natural holiness to come closer to Hashem, therefore now the roles are reversed, and the land shall, specifically in its unworked natural state, bring you closer to Hashem together with itself.]

In this way, we can understand that the first time the *passuk* mentions that the land shall rest to Hashem, the *passuk* means to reveal the natural holy state of Eretz Yisrael in which it is not necessary for you to elevate the land. And the second time the *passuk* mentions that the land will rest to Hashem, it means to say that not only will the land rise up by itself towards Hashem, but you too will be elevated together with it, by refraining from your efforts to elevate the world during the six years of labour.

Based on this explanation, we can explain that the reason that specifically *she'mitah* is chosen to be that *mitzvah* which illustrated that all of the *mitzvos* were given in their entirety on Har Sinai is because shemitah represents the final purified state of natural self-elevation that we will attain when *mashiach* comes.

So the Torah comes to teach us, that not only does shemitah include this grain of the holiness of the world to come, but all *mitzvos* are equally holy, and all *mitzvos* lead us to a state where we will not need to toil to bring ourselves and the world closer to Hashem, but rather (Yeshaya 11.9)

כִּי מָלְאָה הָאָרֶץ דֵּעָה אֶת ה' כַּמַּיִם לַיָּם מְכַסִּים

The whole world will become filled with the knowledge of Hashem, [as naturally] as the water covers the sea.

Bechukosai

Complete blessing

It says at the beginning of this week's *sedrah* (26.3-5)

אִם בְּחֻקֹּתַי תֵּלֵכוּ וְאֶת מִצְוֺתַי תִּשְׁמְרוּ וַעֲשִׂיתֶם אֹתָם. וְנָתַתִּי גִשְׁמֵיכֶם בְּעִתָּם וְנָתְנָה הָאָרֶץ יְבוּלָהּ וְעֵץ הַשָּׂדֶה יִתֵּן פִּרְיוֹ. וְהִשִּׂיג לָכֶם דַּיִשׁ אֶת בָּצִיר וּבָצִיר יַשִּׂיג אֶת זָרַע וַאֲכַלְתֶּם לַחְמְכֶם לָשֹׂבַע וִישַׁבְתֶּם לָבֶטַח בְּאַרְצְכֶם.

If you follow My laws and faithfully observe My commandments, I will grant your rains in their season, so that the earth shall yield its produce and the trees of the field their fruit. Your threshing shall overtake the vintage, and your vintage shall overtake the sowing; you shall eat your fill of bread and dwell securely in your land.

- The *passuk* says ונתתי גשמיכם בעתם – "And I will grant your rains in their season." Apparently the *passuk* should rather have said ונתתי גשמים בעתם – "And I will grant rains in their seasons," not "your rains"?

The medrash comments

אם בחקותי תלכו, הה"ד (תהלים קי"ט, נ"ט) חשבתי דרכי ואשיבה רגלי אל עדותיך. אמר דוד רבש"ע בכל יום ויום הייתי מחשב ואומר למקום פלוני ולבית דירה פלונית אני הולך והיו רגלי מביאות אותי לבתי כנסיות ולבתי מדרשות הה"ד ואשיבה רגלי אל עדותיך

"If you will go [in the way of] My commandments." This is a reference to that which is written in Tehillim (119.59), "I have considered my ways, and have turned back my legs to Your decrees." Dovid said, "Master of the Universe, every day I would think and say that I should go to a particular place or to a particular house and nevertheless my legs would take me to synagogues and halls of Torah study." Hence the *passuk* says "and have turned back my legs to Your decrees," because it was my legs that turned me back.

According to the medrash, when the *passuk* says "If you will go [in the way of] My commandments," it means, "If you go unwittingly in the way of My commandments." So that even when you thought to attend to business affairs and other matters, your feet led you to the synagogues and the halls of Torah study.

- Why are the blessings dependant specifically on the unwitting observance of the Torah?

The medrash continues (35.4)

אִם בְּחֻקֹּתַי תֵּלֵכוּ, חקים שבהם חקקתי את השמים והארץ שנאמר (ירמיה ל"ג, כ"ה) אם לא בריתי יומם ולילה חקות שמים וארץ לא שמתי. חקים שבהם חקקתי את השמש ואת הירח שנאמר (שם ל"א, ל"ד) כה אמר ה' נותן שמש לאור יומם חקת ירח וכוכבים לאור לילה. חקות שבהם חקקתי את הים שנאמר (משלי ח', כ"ט) בשומו לים חקו. חוקות שבהם חקקתי את החול שנאמר (ירמיה ה', כ"ב) אשר שמתי חול גבול לים. חוקים שבהם חקקתי את התהום שנאמר (משלי ח', כ"ז) בחוקו חוג על פני תהום, חוק וחוג לגזירה שוה.

When the *passuk* says אם בחקותי תלכו – "If you go in the way of my statutes," it refers to the statutes with which I carved out the heaven and the earth. It also refers to the statutes with which I carved out the sun and the moon. It also refers to the statutes with which I carved out the sea. It also refers to the statutes with which I carved out the sand. And it also refers to the statues with which I carved out the abyss.

- In what way do the *benei yisrael* observe the statutes with which Hashem carved out the heaven and the earth?

It seems that we can explain as follows:

The medrash continues further (35.5)

ר' לוי בשם ר' חמא ברבי חנינא אמר חוקים שהם חקוקים על יצה"ר הה"ד (ישעיה י', א') הוי החוקקים חקקי און. אמר ר' לוי משל למקום אדרימון שהוא משובש בגייסות מה עשה המלך הושיב בו קוסטרינוס בשביל לשמרו כך אמר הקב"ה תורה קרויה אבן ויצר הרע קרוי אבן, תורה קרויה אבן שנאמר (שמות כ"ד, י"ב) את לוחות האבן והתורה והמצוה. יצה"ר קרוי אבן דכתיב (יחזקאל ל"ו, כ"ו) והסירותי את לב האבן מבשרכם. תורה אבן, יצר הרע אבן, האבן תשמור את האבן.

Rabbi Levi said in the name of Rabbi Chama the son of Rabbi Chanina said: The words of the Torah are called חוקים because they are engraved on the יצר הרע. That is what the *passuk* refers to when it says (Yeshaya, 10.1)

הוֹי הַחֹקְקִים חִקְקֵי אָוֶן וּמְכַתְּבִים עָמָל כִּתֵּבוּ. לְהַטּוֹת מִדִּין דַּלִּים וְלִגְזֹל מִשְׁפַּט עֲנִיֵּי עַמִּי לִהְיוֹת אַלְמָנוֹת שְׁלָלָם וְאֶת יְתוֹמִים יָבֹזּוּ.

Ho. Those who write out evil laws and compose iniquitous documents. To subvert the cause of the poor, to rob of their just rights the needy of My people, that widows may be their spoil and fatherless children their booty.

(The literal meaning of the *passuk* refers to those who write out evil statutes in order to pervert the course of justice. However the medrash seems to translate the *passuk* as follows, הַחֹקְקִים חִקְקֵי אָוֶן – "Hashem writes out statutes on sin itself (referring to the *yetzer ha'ra*)".)

Rabbi Levi said: It is analogous to a wilderness that was full of bandits. What did the king do? He settled an executioner in the wilderness in order to guard it. (The medrash compares the *yetzer ha'ra* to a wilderness that is overrun with robbers, and the Torah to the king's executioner who is placed in the wilderness in order to make it habitable. Analogously, the *yetzer ha'ra* is tamed and made safe, by the Torah.)

Similarly Hashem said: The Torah is called a stone, and the יצר הרע is called a stone. The stone should guard the stone.

The medrash comes to teach is that through the Torah, it is possible to transform the power of the *yetzer ha'ra* to good. This was the level achieved by the *avos* (forefathers), as the Yerushalmi (ברכות פרק ט', הלכה ה') says

אברהם אבינו עשה יצר הרע טוב דכתיב (נחמיה ט', ח') ומצאת את לבבו נאמן לפניך. אמר רבי אחא והפשיר עמו וכרות עמו הברית והחסד וגומר. אבל דוד לא היה יכול לעמוד בו והרגו בלבבו. מאי טעמא (תהלים, ק"ט) ולבי חלל בקרבי.

Avraham transformed the *yetzer ha'ra* into good, as the *passuk* says, "And you found his hearts (the *yetzer ha'tov* and the *yetzer ha'ra*) trustworthy before you..."

Once a person has reached the level at which they have sublimated the *yetzer ha'ra* to the service of Hashem, the whole world will automatically fall into place for them, in order so that they continue in their service of Hashem. As the *sefer* Beis Elokim says (שער התשובה פרק י"ח סוף שער השני)

כי הגאולה היא תשועת שעבוד הגוף, והתשובה היא תשועת שעבוד הנפש, כי אין שעבוד מלכיות גדול משעבוד המלך הזקן וכסיל והוא היצר הרע, וכמו שהגאולה היא היפך השעבוד כן התשובה היא היפך העוונות, ובעוד שהנפש היא משועבדת ליצר הרע, ראוי גם כן שהגוף יהיה משועבד למלכיות, אבל כשהנפש שחררה עצמה משעבוד היצר במה ששבה בתשובה גמורה ראוי ג"כ שיהיה הגוף משוחרר משעבוד המלכיות

For redemption is salvation from servitude of the body, and repentance is salvation from servitude of the soul, for there is no greater servitude of the soul than being enslaved to the *yetzer ha'ra*. As long as the soul is enslaved to the *yetzer ha'ra*, it is fitting that the body should be enslaved to the monarchies, but when the soul frees itself from being enslaved to the *yetzer ha'ra* through that which one does complete repentance, it is then fitting that the body should be redeemed from being enslaved to the monarchies.

Once a person reaches the level at which all the forces that they find within themselves are sublimated to the service of Hashem, all the forces of creation too will be sublimated towards aiding that person in the service of Hashem, and the opposing forces of godless rule will lose their right to be supported.

At this level, at which the very statues with which Hashem carved out the heavens and the earth, the sun and the moon, the sea, the sand and the abyss, resonate with the service of Hashem, all earthly considerations fall away.

Dovid did not consider himself to be on such a level, so he intended to take care of his pressing mundane affairs. But his very legs knew otherwise, and led him to the synagogue and to the study hall of Torah, where his prayer and Torah study drew all creation into alignment with his mundane needs.

It is to this level of wholeness of the service of Hashem that the *passuk* alludes at the start of this week's sedrah. That is why the medrash explains that the *passuk* means to say that such blessings will come when one serves Hashem even unwittingly, as Dovid did.

This is also why the *passuk* uses the word גשמיכם - "your rains," as opposed to just saying גשמים - "rains". The word גשם can also mean earthiness. Hence we can understand that the *passuk* means to say that if even the farthest reaches of earthiness become yours, and are sublimated to your service of Hashem, then Hashem will commensurately make all of nature and the rains, turn in your favour.

Bamidbar

Declaring the oneness of Hashem

The *passuk* says at the beginning of this week's sedrah (1.1-2):

> וַיְדַבֵּר ה' אֶל מֹשֶׁה בְּמִדְבַּר סִינַי בְּאֹהֶל מוֹעֵד בְּאֶחָד לַחֹדֶשׁ הַשֵּׁנִי בַּשָּׁנָה הַשֵּׁנִית לְצֵאתָם מֵאֶרֶץ מִצְרַיִם לֵאמֹר. שְׂאוּ אֶת רֹאשׁ כָּל עֲדַת בְּנֵי יִשְׂרָאֵל לְמִשְׁפְּחֹתָם לְבֵית אֲבֹתָם בְּמִסְפַּר שֵׁמוֹת כָּל זָכָר לְגֻלְגְּלֹתָם.

And Hashem spoke to Moshe in the *midbar* of Sinai in the *Ohel Moed* on the first day of the second month, in the second year following the exodus from the *Mitzrayim* saying. "Take a census of all the *benei yisrael* by the families of its fathers' houses, listing the names of every male, head by head."

The medrash[37] comments:

> מה הקב"ה יחיד ואין לו תמורה שנאמר אֵין קָדוֹשׁ כַּה' כִּי אֵין בִּלְתֶּךָ (שמואל א', ב', ב') כך לא ימיר ישראל באומה אחרת וזה הוא שאמר דּוֹדִי לִי וַאֲנִי לוֹ (שה"ש ב', ט"ז) אל תמירוני כשם שאיני ממיר אתכם, [שהרי] אתם קרויים צאן [ו]כשם שאין ממירין בהמה בבהמה כך איני ממיר אתכם.

[Why did the Torah juxtapose the *mitzva* to count the *benei yisrael* to the *halachos* of *temurah* (the prohibition to swap a

---

[37] מובא בספר תולדות יצחק וברבנו בחיי

korban for a different animal) that are explained at the end of *Sefer Vayikra*? This is to teach you that] just as Hashem is One and has no replacement, as the *passuk* says, "There is none as holy as Hashem for there is none besides You," so too Hashem will not exchange the *benei yisrael* for a different nation. This is what the *passuk* means when it says, "My Beloved is to me and I am to Him."

[Hashem says,] "Do not exchange Me [for other gods], just as I do not exchange you [for a different nation.] For you are called sheep, [as the *passuk* says, "The *benei yisrael* are as a scattered flock," (Yirmiyah 50, 17) and just as it is forbidden to swap a sheep that is a *korban* for a different sheep (even if the second sheep is better than the first), so too I will not exchange you.

It would appear difficult to understand the comparison between the *benei yisrael* not exchanging Hashem for idols, and Hashem not exchanging the *benei yisrael* for another people. For regarding Hashem the medrash says, "Hashem is One and has no replacement," but regarding the *benei yisrael* the medrash says, "Hashem will not exchange the *benei yisrael* with a different nation."

- How is the impossibility of Hashem being exchanged, comparable to Hashem choosing by His own volition not to exchange the *benei yisrael*?

It would seem that we can explain as follows.

The Zohar[38] says that when a person performs a mitzva, the mitzva goes before him and announces

פלנייא עבד יתי ומפלנייא אנא

So-and-so performed me and from so-and-so I am.

The initial statement of the mitzva, "So-and-so performed me," is a simple announcement that the mitzva was performed by a particular person and therefore they should receive the appropriate reward. Additionally, the mitzva continues, "And from so-and-so I am." This means to say that the person gave of themselves to the performance of the mitzva, so now the very essence and kedushah of that person is encapsulated and embedded within that mitzva.

Similarly[39] when a person is makdish (sanctifies) a korban, the owner of the korban gives of their own personal kedushah in order to sanctify the korban. Subsequently, the korban may not be swapped for a different animal, even if the second animal is superior to the first, because this would dissolve the bond between the owner of the korban and the kedushah they imbued into their korban.

Based on this introduction, we can understand the comparison the medrash makes between the impossibility of exchanging Hashem and Hashem's choosing not to exchange the benei yisrael.

---

[38] מובא בספר זבח השלמים

[39] עיין בזה בספר מעשה רוקח, ריש מסכת תמורה

The *benei yisrael* are ready to sacrifice their lives in order to fulfill the *mitzva* of declaring the unity of Hashem. Subsequently, the *kedushah* of the *benei yisrael* is imbued into the world's understanding of Hashem's unity. In reward for the *benei yisrael* dedicating their very existence to make the world know the oneness of Hashem, Hashem in turn bequeaths the gift of oneness to the *benei yisrael*, so that He will never exchange them for another people.

In other words, Hashem chooses not to swap the *benei yisrael* for any other people because the quality of uniqueness and irreplaceability is invested in the *benei yisrael*, as a reward for their dedication in representing the oneness of Hashem. Hence, the medrash compares the impossibility of swapping Hashem for any other god, to that which Hashem chooses not to exchange the *benei yisrael* for another people.

This is analogous to the *issur* of *temurah* because a *korban* may not be swapped for another, better animal since that would compromise the personal *kedushah* invested in the *korban* by its owner. So too Hashem will never swap the *benei yisrael* for another nation due to the dedication and self-sacrifice the *benei yisrael* have made in order to make it known to the world that Hashem is One.

Naso

Eretz Yisrael and *galus*

It says in this week's *sedrah* (5.1-4)

וַיְדַבֵּר ה' אֶל מֹשֶׁה לֵּאמֹר. צַו אֶת בְּנֵי יִשְׂרָאֵל וִישַׁלְּחוּ מִן הַמַּחֲנֶה כָּל צָרוּעַ וְכָל זָב וְכֹל טָמֵא לָנָפֶשׁ. מִזָּכָר עַד נְקֵבָה תְּשַׁלֵּחוּ אֶל מִחוּץ לַמַּחֲנֶה תְּשַׁלְּחוּם וְלֹא יְטַמְּאוּ אֶת מַחֲנֵיהֶם אֲשֶׁר אֲנִי שֹׁכֵן בְּתוֹכָם. וַיַּעֲשׂוּ כֵן בְּנֵי יִשְׂרָאֵל וַיְשַׁלְּחוּ אוֹתָם אֶל מִחוּץ לַמַּחֲנֶה כַּאֲשֶׁר דִּבֶּר ה' אֶל מֹשֶׁה כֵּן עָשׂוּ בְּנֵי יִשְׂרָאֵל.

Hashem spoke to Moshe saying, "Command the *benei yisrael* to send out from the camp anyone who is a מצורע or a זב and anyone who is a טמא מת (people who have contracted various types of spiritual impurity). They should send out both men and women and put them outside the camp so that they do not defile their camp, in which I dwell among them."

The *benei yisrael* did so, and they sent them outside of the camp. Just as Hashem spoke to Moshe, so the *benei yisrael* did.

The Medrash Rabbah (7.10) comments on these *pessukim*

דָּבָר אַחֵר, צַו אֶת בְּנֵי יִשְׂרָאֵל, רַבָּנָן פָּתְרִין קְרָיָה בַּגָּלוּת, צַו אֶת בְּנֵי יִשְׂרָאֵל, עַל שֶׁעָבְרוּ יִשְׂרָאֵל עַל הַמִּצְווֹת נִתְחַיְּבוּ שִׁלּוּחַ, זֶה גָּלוּת, הֲדָא

הוּא דִּכְתִיב וִישַׁלְּחוּ מִן הַמַּחֲנֶה, אֵין וִישַׁלְּחוּ אֶלָּא לְשׁוֹן גָּלוּת, כְּמָה דְתֵימָא (ירמיה ט"ו, א') שַׁלַּח מֵעַל פָּנַי וְיֵצֵאוּ. מִן הַמַּחֲנֶה, זוֹ אֶרֶץ יִשְׂרָאֵל, שֶׁשָּׁם הַשְּׁכִינָה חוֹנָה... (במדבר ה', ג') אֲשֶׁר אֲנִי שֹׁכֵן בְּתוֹכָם, רָמַז לָהֶם שֶׁבְּכָל מָקוֹם שֶׁגָּלוּ שְׁכִינָה עִמָּהֶם... וַיַּעֲשׂוּ כֵן בְּנֵי יִשְׂרָאֵל וַיְשַׁלְּחוּ אוֹתָם אֶל מִחוּץ לַמַּחֲנֶה, כֵּיוָן שֶׁחָטְאוּ, גָּלוּ. (במדבר ה', ד') כַּאֲשֶׁר דִּבֶּר ה' אֶל מֹשֶׁה כֵּן עָשׂוּ בְּנֵי יִשְׂרָאֵל, מַה דִּבֶּר הַקָּדוֹשׁ בָּרוּךְ הוּא לְמֹשֶׁה, שֶׁאִם יַעֲשׂוּ תְּשׁוּבָה בַּמַּלְכִיּוֹת שֶׁיִּהְיוּ שָׁם, הַקָּדוֹשׁ בָּרוּךְ הוּא מְקַבְּצָם, שֶׁנֶּאֱמַר (דברים ל', א'-ו'): וְהָיָה כִּי יָבֹאוּ עָלֶיךָ כָּל הַדְּבָרִים הָאֵלֶּה הַבְּרָכָה וְהַקְּלָלָה וגו' וֶהֱבִיאֲךָ ה' אֱלֹהֶיךָ וגו' וּמָל ה' אֱלֹהֶיךָ וגו'. כֵּן עָשׂוּ בְּנֵי יִשְׂרָאֵל, שֶׁעֲתִידִין יִשְׂרָאֵל שֶׁיַּעֲשׂוּ תְּשׁוּבָה בְּאַחֲרִית הַיָּמִים וְהֵם נִגְאָלִים, שֶׁנֶּאֱמַר (ישעיה ל', ט"ו) בְּשׁוּבָה וָנַחַת תִּוָּשֵׁעוּן.

The *chachamim* interpreted these *pessukim* as an allusion to *galus*.

- **Command the *benei yisrael* and they shall send out**: Because the *benei yisrael* transgressed the *mitzvos* they had to be sent out.

- **From the camp**: This refers to Eretz Yisrael, where the *shechinah* dwells.

- **In which I dwell among them**: The *passuk* hints that everywhere the *benei yisrael* are sent in *galus*, the *shechinah* will go with them.

- **And the *benei yisrael* did so and they send them outside of the camp**: Once they sinned they were sent into *galus*.

- **Just as Hashem spoke to Moshe**: Hashem told Moshe

that if the *benei yisrael* would do *teshuvah*, then He would gather them back to Eretz Yisrael.

- **So the *benei yisrael* did**: Because the *benei yisrael* will do *teshuvah*, Hashem will return them to Eretz Yisrael at the end of this *galus*.

It would appear difficult to understand how the *mashal* of the *medrash* fits into the literal translation of the *pessukim*.

- In the *pessukim*, the *benei yisrael* remained in the camp and only sent out those people who were *tameh* (ritually unclean). However, when the *benei yisrael* were sent into *galus*, the entirety of the *benei yisrael* went out of Eretz Yisrael and no-one remained behind?

It seems that we can explain as follows.

The Alshich (Bereishis 12.1) says:

> עוד ידענו מחכמי האמת כי אין דבר רוחני קדוש הולך ממקום שיעתק. ויעקר לגמרי ממקום שהיה בו. כ"א ששם ישאר עיקר שורשו. וממציאותו מתפשט והולך אל מקום החפץ. א"כ איפה נפשות עם בני ישראל. אשר הן הנה חלק אלוק ממעל. הלא בבואנה אל העוה"ז. ישאירו שורשיהן למעלה תחת כנפי השכינה. היא ארץ העליונה אשר היא לעומת ארץ הקדושה. כי על כן שתיהן ארצות החיים יקראו. באופן כי אין נפש קדושה באה למטה לארץ. שלא ישאר שורשה במקומה העליון. עם ה' אלקים...

> וממוצא דבר יצא כי העבד ישראל השוכן בא"י אשר היא לעומת ארץ העליונה דבק בשורשו. כי אויר א"י קדוש הוא. וימשך בו דרך ישרה

> איכות שורש נפשו. אל נפשו אשר בקרבו. נמצא כי שלם יקרא בלי פירוד מניה וביה ממנו לשורשו. משא"כ בהיותו בח"ל. כי איזה הדרך ימשך איכות שורש נפשו אשר בארץ העליונה אשר לעומת התחתונה. דרך עקלתון אל טומאת אויר ארץ אל נפש קרב איש השוכן אתה בתוך טומאתה.

A spiritual thing is never uprooted entirely from its place. Rather, its main root will always remain in its place, although its existence spreads out to the place to which it is called. Therefore, when the souls of the *benei yisrael* come to *olam hazeh*, they leave their root in Eretz Yisrael above which is parallel to Eretz Yisrael below. And that is why both of these lands are called the land of life.

It therefore transpires that if one lives in Eretz Yisrael he is immediately connected to his root in Eretz Yisrael above, and therefore he is considered to be whole. On the other hand, if one lives outside Eretz Yisrael, his root remains in the Eretz Yisrael above, but he is only tangentially connected to his root, by means of that which Hashem always dwells with the *benei yisrael*, despite their being in *galus*.

We see from the Alshich that the root of the *benei yisrael* always remains in Eretz Yisrael, even when we are sent into *galus*.

Subsequently we can understand that the medrash means to say that even when the *benei yisrael* went into *galus*, nevertheless the spiritual root of the *benei yisrael* remained in Eretz Yisrael. Therefore, it was as if the *benei yisrael* sent out their own physical manifestation to *galus*, whilst in spirit they were never exiled from their land.

Beha'alosechah

The light of the menorah

It says at the beginning of this week's *sedrah* (8.1-3)

וַיְדַבֵּר ה' אֶל מֹשֶׁה לֵּאמֹר. דַּבֵּר אֶל אַהֲרֹן וְאָמַרְתָּ אֵלָיו בְּהַעֲלֹתְךָ אֶת הַנֵּרֹת אֶל מוּל פְּנֵי הַמְּנוֹרָה יָאִירוּ שִׁבְעַת הַנֵּרוֹת. וַיַּעַשׂ כֵּן אַהֲרֹן אֶל מוּל פְּנֵי הַמְּנוֹרָה הֶעֱלָה נֵרֹתֶיהָ כַּאֲשֶׁר צִוָּה ה' אֶת מֹשֶׁה.

And Hashem spoke to Moshe saying, "Speak to Aharon and say to him, 'When you light the lamps [of the *menorah*], towards the centre of the *menorah* the seven lamps should shine.'"

And Aharon did so, towards the centre of the *menorah* he lit its lamps, as Hashem had commanded Moshe.

Rashi comments as follows.

בהעלתך: למה נסמכה פרשת המנורה לפרשת הנשיאים? לפי שכשראה אהרן חנוכת הנשיאים, חלשה דעתו, שלא היה עמהם בחנוכה, לא הוא ולא שבטו. אמר לו הקב"ה, חייך, שלך גדולה משלהם, שאתה מדליק ומטיב את הנרות.

Why is the section that treats with the *menorah* juxtaposed with the section that deals with the *korbanos* of the *nesi'im* (princes)?

Because when Aharon saw the *korbanos* of dedication

brought by the *nesi'im* he felt distressed because neither he or his tribe were included with them in the dedication.

Whereupon Hashem said to him, "By your life! Your part is of greater importance than theirs, for you will kindle and set in order the lamps [of the *menorah*]."

The Ramban asks

ולא נתברר לי, למה ניחמו בהדלקת הנרות, ולא ניחמו בקטורת בקר וערב, ששיבחו בו הכתוב (דברים ל"ג י') ישימו קטורה באפך, ובכל הקרבנות, ובמנחת חביתין, ובעבודת יום הכפורים שאינה כשרה אלא בו, ונכנס לפני ולפנים, ושהוא קדוש ה' עומד בהיכלו לשרתו ולברך בשמו, ושבטו כלו משרתי אלקינו. ועוד מה טעם לחלישות הדעת הזו, והלא קרבנו גדול משל נשיאים, שהקריב בימים ההם קרבנות הרבה כל ימי המלואים וכו'.

It is unclear to me why he comforted Aharon with the lighting of the *menorah* and he didn't comfort him with the daily incense and with all of the *korbanos* (that could only be brought by the *cohanim*) and with the daily meal offering and the special *korbanos* of Yom Kippur (which could only be brought by the *cohen gadol*) when he entered into the *kodesh he'kedashim*...

Additionally, why would Aharon be upset? Did he not also bring many *korbanos*, more than the *nesi'im*, during the dedication of the *mishkan*?

Because of this question, the Ramban explains that the medrash quoted in Rashi refers to Chanukah.

אבל ענין ההגדה הזו, לדרוש רמז מן הפרשה על חנוכה של נרות שהיתה בבית שני על ידי אהרן ובניו, רצוני לומר חשמונאי כהן גדול ובניו.

ובלשון הזה מצאתיה במגלת סתרים לרבינו נסים, שהזכיר האגדה הזו ואמר, ראיתי במדרש, כיון שהקריבו שנים עשר שבטים ולא הקריב שבט לוי וכו', אמר לו הקב"ה למשה דבר אל אהרן ואמרת אליו, יש חנכה אחרת שיש בה הדלקת הנרות ואני עושה בה לישראל על ידי בניך נסים ותשועה וחנכה שקרויה על שמם, והיא חנכת בני חשמונאי, ולפיכך הסמיך פרשה זו לפרשת חנכת המזבח, עד כאן לשונו.

Rather this teaching comes to hint at the rededication of the second *Beis Ha'mikdash* which took place through the *cohen gadol* and his sons at the time of Chanukah...

And so I found in the teachings of Rav Nissim Gaon, "When each of the twelve tribes brought dedication-offerings and the tribe of Levi did not, Hashem said to Moshe, 'Speak to Aharon and say to him, "when you light the lamps..." There is another Chanukah [dedication] wherein there will be lighting of lamps. I will perform miracles and salvation for the *benei yisrael* through your children. And it will be a dedication known by their name...'"

Rashi, however, does not refer to Chanukah. Therefore it would appear that, according to Rashi, there is a direct correlation between the *korbanos* brought by the *nesi'im* and the *menorah*, which is why it was specifically the *menorah* that appeased Aharon for not being included in the inaugural *korbanos* of the *nesi'im*.

- According to Rashi, what is the connection between the *korbanos* of the *nesi'im* and lighting the *menorah*?

It would appear that we can explain as follows.

The *mishkan*

The *passuk* says in Naso (7.84)

זֹאת חֲנֻכַּת הַמִּזְבֵּחַ בְּיוֹם הִמָּשַׁח אֹתוֹ מֵאֵת נְשִׂיאֵי יִשְׂרָאֵל קַעֲרֹת כֶּסֶף שְׁתֵּים עֶשְׂרֵה מִזְרְקֵי כֶסֶף שְׁנֵים עָשָׂר כַּפּוֹת זָהָב שְׁתֵּים עֶשְׂרֵה

This was the inaugural *korban* from the princes of the *benei yisrael* on the day of its being anointed. 12 silver bowls, 12 silver basins and 12 gold ladles.

The Yalkut Shimoni (717) comments

רבי ישמעאל אומר, מה תלמוד לומר מאת נשיאי ישראל. אלא מלמד שנדבו מעצמן כולן שוה ולא הקריב אחד מהן יותר על חברו, שאלו הקריב אחד מהן יותר על חברו, לא היה אחד מהן דוחה את השבת. אמר להם המקום אתם חלקתם כבוד אחד לחברו, ואני חולק לכם כבוד. ויאמר ה' אל משה נשיא אחד ליום.

Rabbi Yishmael said, "What does the *passuk* come to teach you when it says 'from the princes of the *benei yisrael*'? [Surely this is obvious.] Rather it teaches you that they contributed on their own initiative, and that the *korban* of each was the same, and that one did not offer more than his fellow, for had one offered more than his fellow, none of the offerings would have pushed aside Shabbos [since the shechinah would not have rested in the mishkan]."

Hashem said to them, "You showed honour one to the other, and I will show honour to you." As it is stated, "And Hashem said to Moshe, 'They shall offer their korban, each prince on his day.'"

Each tribe had their own nuances in their avodas Hashem (the way in which they served Hashem). Therefore, each nasi, as representative of his tribe, had his own unique intentions when bringing his inaugural korban. Nevertheless, each nasi independently came to the conclusion that they should bring exactly the same korban as every other nasi. Despite the difference in their inner feelings of dedication, each nasi sublimated the external form of their avodah (service) to that which was common to all of the benei yisrael.

It was this humility that was expressed in the inaugural korbanos that caused the shechinah to rest in the mishkan. In other words, the shechinah rested in the mishkan because it embodied the self-effacing combination of the individual ways of serving Hashem, of all the benei yisrael.

The menorah

Concerning the menorah, the Shlah (סוף פרשת תרומה, ד"ה המנורה) writes:

> המנורה כתבתי למעלה היא צורת אדם וצריכה להיות מקשה חיבור אחד דהיינו לב לשמים גם רומז שיהיה בלב אחד עם כל ישראל מגדול ועד קטן מקשה עד יריכה עד פרחה דהיינו מגדולו ועד קטן

> The menorah represents the totality of the form of man (i.e.

the way in which all parts of man combine in a wholesome manner). Therefore it must be beaten out of one block of gold to signify that a person must be unified in his dedication to the service of Hashem, despite the disparate tendencies he may find in his heart. This also signifies that a person should be unified in their heart with the rest of the *benei yisrael*, from great to small.

Just as the *mishkan* represents the unification of the different individual ways of serving Hashem of all the *benei yisrael*, so too the *menorah* represents the unification of all the different thoughts and ideas that man finds within himself, concerning the correct way to serve Hashem.

Given these introductions, we can understand Rashi as follows.

לפי שכשראה אהרן חנוכת הנשיאים חלשה דעתו, שלא היה עמהם בחנוכה, לא הוא ולא שבטו. אמר לו הקב"ה, חייך שלך גדולה משלהם, שאתה מדליק ומטיב את הנרות.

When Aharon saw that he and his tribe were not included in the merging of the different ways of serving Hashem of all of the *benei yisrael*, that caused the *shechinah* to rest in the *mishkan*, he felt feint, since he perceived that the purity of his intentions was not sufficient for he and his tribe to be included in this self-abnegating ascendancy.

Thereupon Hashem comforted him and He said, "By your life, yours is greater than theirs, because you light and prepare the lamps of the *menorah*. And whereas the *korbanos* brought by the *nesi'im* represent the convergence of the different ways of service of Hashem of all the *benei yisrael*, the lighting of the *menorah* represents the daily convergence of all the ways of service of Hashem that an individual finds within their own heart."

The unity of purpose embodied in the *menorah* allowed each individual to serve Hashem with one heart. This personal concordance allowed the subsequent unity of the *shevatim* when they came to serve Hashem in the inauguration of the *mishkan*, as one man with one heart.

Shelach lechah

The trees of Eretz Yisrael

It says in this week's *sedrah* (13.20)

וּמָה הָאָרֶץ הַשְּׁמֵנָה הִוא אִם רָזָה הֲיֵשׁ בָּהּ עֵץ אִם אַיִן וְהִתְחַזַּקְתֶּם וּלְקַחְתֶּם מִפְּרִי הָאָרֶץ וְהַיָּמִים יְמֵי בִּכּוּרֵי עֲנָבִים

[Moshe told the *meraglim*,] "And what is the land, is the soil fertile or poor? Does it contain trees or not? And you should strengthen yourselves and take from the fruit of the land." And it was the season of the first ripe grapes.

Rashi comments on this *passuk*:

הֲיֵשׁ בָּהּ עֵץ: אִם יֵשׁ בָּהֶם אָדָם כָּשֵׁר שֶׁיָּגֵין עֲלֵיהֶם בִּזְכוּתוֹ

Does it have a tree: Is there among them a *tzadik* who will protect them with his merits?

- Why did Moshe choose the analogy of a tree to describe the *tzadik* whose merit would protect the inhabitants of the land?

The Sifsei Chachamim explains that the reason Rashi says that a tree refers to a *tzadik*, is because if the soil was fertile that would automatically imply there were trees. Alternatively, since Moshe commanded them to take from the fruit of the land, it is evident that Moshe already knew the land had trees.

Nevertheless, the simple meaning of the *passuk* remains that Moshe told them to see if there were indeed trees in Eretz Yisrael.

- Why did Moshe ask the *meraglim* to see if Eretz Yisrael contained trees, if he already knew that is what they would find?

The Targum Yonasan ben Uziel translates this *passuk* as follows.

וּמָה שְׁבַח אַרְעָא הַשְׁמִינִין אִינוּן פֵּרְיַהּ אִין פַּתְרָנִין הָאִית בָּהּ אִילָנִין דְּמֵיכָל אִין לָא.

And what is the praise of the land. Are the fruits luscious or poor, does it contain fruit trees or not?

- Apparently, the Targum Yonasan ben Uziel should have said - האית בה אילנין טעונין פירות דמיכל - "Does it contain fruit-bearing trees," and not - הָאִית בָּהּ אִילָנִין דְּמֵיכַל – which literally means, "Does it contain edible trees"?

It would seem that we can explain as follows.

The *passuk* says in Bereishis (1.11):

וַיֹּאמֶר אֱלֹקִים תַּדְשֵׁא הָאָרֶץ דֶּשֶׁא עֵשֶׂב מַזְרִיעַ זֶרַע עֵץ פְּרִי עֹשֶׂה פְּרִי לְמִינוֹ אֲשֶׁר זַרְעוֹ בוֹ עַל הָאָרֶץ וַיְהִי כֵן

And Hashem said, "Let the earth sprout vegetation: seed-bearing plants, fruit trees of every kind on earth that bear fruit with the seed in it." And it was so.

Rashi comments on this *passuk*

עֵץ פְּרִי: שיהא טעם העץ כטעם הפרי, והיא לא עשתה כן אלא ותוצא הארץ וגו' ועץ עושה פרי ולא העץ פרי, לפיכך כשנתקלל אדם על עונו נפקדה גם היא על עונה

Fruit trees: [So that the trees themselves would be like the fruit, meaning] that the taste of the trees should be the same as the fruit. The earth did not however do this, but instead "the earth brought forth a tree yielding fruit," and the tree itself was woody and tasteless. Therefore, when Adam was cursed for his sin, the earth was also punished.

The Michtav Me'Eliyahu (vol. 4, pg. 115) explains that man is compared to a tree. The fruit, which are the purpose of the tree, represent the *mitzvos*, which are the purpose of man. The wood, which is the wherewithal through which the tree produces fruit, represents the capabilities and possessions that are given to man, to enable him to perform *mitzvos*.

Had the taste of the fruit permeated the entire tree, it would be impossible for man to divert his wherewithal away from the performance of the *mitzvos*. Since the taste of the tree was not the same as the taste of the fruit, man is able to use those vessels that have been given to him for *mitzva* performance, for his own ends.

According to this explanation, we can understand that when the Targum Yonasan ben Uziel says הַאִית בַּהּ אִילָנִין דְמֵיכַל – which literally means "does it contain edible trees", the Targum means to allude the level at which the taste of the trees is indeed the same as the taste of the fruit. This represents the level at which man perceives no other purpose in the good things with which he is provided, other than to serve Hashem.[40]

If the *meraglim* could perceive this level of *kedushah* in the richness of Eretz Yisrael, then they would merit to conquer the land from its present inhabitants and to turn the fullness of Eretz Yisrael to the service of Hashem.

---

[40] Moshe asked the *meraglim*, "Does it have a tree," meaning is there among them a *tzadik* who will protect them with his *zechus*, because had there been a *tzaddik* in Eretz Yisrael who served Hashem on this level, he would have protected its inhabitants by providing them with a connection to this level.

In other words, Moshe did not merely ask the *meraglim* to see if there were trees in Eretz Yisrael. Rather he asked them to reach that level of commitment and sacrifice at which the wealth and fullness of Eretz Yisrael would only ever represent opportunity to further serve Hashem.

Korach

Unity in service of Hashem

Moshe told Korach and his followers (16.6 - 7)

זֹאת עֲשׂוּ קְחוּ לָכֶם מַחְתּוֹת קֹרַח וְכָל עֲדָתוֹ. וּתְנוּ בָהֵן אֵשׁ וְשִׂימוּ עֲלֵיהֶן קְטֹרֶת לִפְנֵי ה' מָחָר וְהָיָה הָאִישׁ אֲשֶׁר יִבְחַר ה' הוּא הַקָּדוֹשׁ רַב לָכֶם בְּנֵי לֵוִי.

This you should do, "You, Korach and all your gathering, take fire pans, and tomorrow put fire in them and place *ketores* on them before Hashem. Then the man whom Hashem chooses, he shall be the holy one. It is enough for you, O sons of Levi!"

Rashi explains:

זאת עשו קחו לכם מחתות: מה ראה לומר להם כך אמר להם בדרכי

העכו"ם יש נימוסים הרבה וכומרים הרבה וכולם (ס"א ואין כולם) מתקבצים בבית אחד

אנו אין לנו אלא ה' אחד ארון אחד ותורה אחת ומזבח אחד וכהן גדול אחד ואתם ר"ן איש מבקשים כהונה גדולה אף אני רוצה בכך הא לכם תשמיש חביב מכל היא הקטרת החביבה מכל הקרבנות וסם המות נתון בתוכו שבו נשרפו נדב ואביהוא

לפיכך התרה בהם והיה האיש אשר יבחר ה' הוא הקדוש כבר הוא בקדושתו וכי אין אנו יודעים שמי שיבחר הוא הקדוש אלא אמר להם משה הריני אומר לכם שלא תתחייבו מי שיבחר בו יצא חי וכולכם אובדים (במדבר רבה)

Moshe said to them, "According to the custom of the idolaters there are numerous forms of worship, and numerous priests, and they do not assemble in one temple. We, however, have one G-d, one *aron ha'kodesh*, one Torah, one *mizbeach* and one *cohen gadol*. Yet you, 250 men, all demand to be the *cohen gadol*?

I would also like this for myself. Here you have a service which is more dear than any other, it is the offering of the *ketores*, which is dearer to Hashem than all the *korbanos*. But a deadly poison is contained in it, for through it Nadav and Avihu were burnt."

...Moshe said to them, "I am telling you this in order that you should not imperil your lives, for only he whom Hashem will choose will live, but all of you will perish."

Apparently Moshe was making two separate points, either of which comprises a valid argument. The first point is that there can be only one *cohen gadol*, not 250. The second point is that bringing the *ketores* incorrectly is dangerous.

- What is the connection between the argument that there can only be one *cohen gadol* and the fact that the *ketores* may cause harm?

- Why does danger lie in incorrectly bringing *ketores*, more so than any other *avodah*?

- Apparently, whichever *avodah* specific to the *cohen gadol* would have been chosen for the test, only Aharon would have survived?

It would seem that we can explain as follows.

The Malbim explains (שמות ל', א'):

> ומזבח הקטורת מציין את הריח והרוחניות שעולה מלמטה למעלה וקושר כל העולמות ע"י מעשה העבודה

> The *mizbeach* of the *ketores* represents the fragrance and the spirituality that rises from this world to the higher worlds and which ties together (since the word קטור can also mean to tie) all the worlds through the *avodah* in the *beis ha'mikdash*.

It is through the *ketores* that all the other services in the *beis ha'mikdash* are elevated and are connected to the highest *madregah* they can reach. Therefore, whereas it is possible for there to be variance from the correct intention with regard to the other services, and that service will still be accepted with Divine favour, such is not the case for the *ketores*.

Since the *ketores* unifies and elevates all the other services in the *beis ha'mikdash*, the intention of the one who performs the service of the *ketores* must be entirely *le'shem shamayim* (for the sake of Heaven). If the intention of the person who performs the service of the *ketores* is not entirely *le'shem shamayim* so that they have ancillary intentions, then such a bringing of *ketores* cannot serve to unify and elevate all the other services in the *beis ha'mikdash*, because the *ketores* itself was not an entirely altruistic act.

Subsequently, the reason danger lies in the performance of the *ketores* is because if this service is not performed with the purest of intentions, then the intended elevation of all the other services remains incomplete, so that those services will not be elevated throughout all the higher worlds. Since one who brings *ketores* incorrectly causes a hindrance to the elevation of all the other previously performed services, they may be killed due to the spiritual tension which they thereby create.

Similarly, it is the obligation of the *cohen gadol* to unify and elevate all of the services that are performed in the *mishkan* or in the *beis ha'mikdash*. If the purity of intention of the *cohen gadol* is lacking, there will be a shortfall in all the services performed in the *beis ha'mikdash*, and not only in his own personal *avodah*.

Therefore Moshe's argument that there is only one, unifying *cohen gadol*, and his argument that there lies danger in performing the service of the *ketores* incorrectly, are in fact one and the same argument.

Chukas

The purity of the *parah adumah*

The *passuk* says at the beginning of this week's sedrah (19,1-3).

וַיְדַבֵּר ה' אֶל מֹשֶׁה וְאֶל אַהֲרֹן לֵאמֹר. זֹאת חֻקַּת הַתּוֹרָה אֲשֶׁר צִוָּה ה' לֵאמֹר, דַּבֵּר אֶל בְּנֵי יִשְׂרָאֵל וְיִקְחוּ אֵלֶיךָ פָרָה אֲדֻמָּה תְּמִימָה אֲשֶׁר אֵין בָּהּ מוּם אֲשֶׁר לֹא עָלָה עָלֶיהָ עֹל. וּנְתַתֶּם אֹתָהּ אֶל אֶלְעָזָר הַכֹּהֵן וְהוֹצִיא אֹתָהּ אֶל מִחוּץ לַמַּחֲנֶה וְשָׁחַט אֹתָהּ לְפָנָיו.

And Hashem spoke to Moshe and Aharon, saying: This is the statute of the Torah that Hashem has commanded, "Speak to the *benei yisrael* and they should bring you a red cow without blemish, in which there is no defect and on which no yoke has been placed. And you shall give it to Elazar the *cohen*. It shall be taken outside of the camp and slaughtered in his presence."

Rashi comments:

זאת חקת התורה: לפי שהשטן ואומות העולם מונין את ישראל לומר מה המצוה הזאת ומה טעם יש בה, לפיכך כתב בה חקה, גזירה היא מלפני ואין לך רשות להרהר אחריה

Because the *satan* and the nations of the world tease the *benei yisrael* saying, "What is this (odd) *mitzva* and what is its reason?" Therefore the *passuk* uses the word חוקה, meaning a statute. Hashem said, "It is a decree from before Me and you have no permission to ponder its reason."

It would appear difficult to understand this Rashi. If the *benei yisrael* are indeed concerned about the criticism of the nations of the world, and turn to Hashem to ask the reason for the *mitzva* of *parah adumah*, then it would seem they would be told, "It is not possible for you to understand the reason for this *mitzva* because it is too deep for you to understand."

- Why did Hashem tell the *benei yisrael* that they do not have permission to ponder the reason for the *mitzva* of *parah adumah*?

- Furthermore, why does the Torah address the teasing of the nations of the world regarding the *mitzva* of *parah adumah* more so than with other *chukim* (statutes) such as *sha'atnez* (the prohibition of wearing wool mixed with linen) and *kilayim* (the prohibition to grow two different crops in close proximity)?

Rashi continues:

> **ויקחו אליך**: לעולם היא נקראת על שמך פרה שעשה משה במדבר

It will always be called by your name, "The *parah* (red cow) that Moshe made in the *midbar*."

- Why is it specifically *parah adumah* that reminds us of the way that the *mitzvos* were performed in the *midbar*?

It would seem that we can explain as follows.

The Yalkut Shimoni says:

> פרה, זו מצרים שנאמר עגלה יפהפיה מצרים. אדומה, זו בבל שנאמר אנת הוא רישא דדהבא. תמימא זו מדי וכו'. אשר אין בה מום זה יון וכו'. אשר לא עלה עליה עול זה זו מלכות רביעיתא שלא קבלו עליהן עול של הקב"ה וכו'. ונתתם אותה אל אלעזר הכהן וכו' ושחט אותה לפניו שנאמר כי זבח לה' בבצרה וגו'.

"A cow," this refers to Mitzrayim which is compared to a beautiful calf. "Red," this refers to Bavel which is compared to red gold. "Perfect," this refers to Madai whose kings conduct themselves well. "That has no blemish," this refers to Yavan. "On which no yoke has been placed," this refers to Edom which does not accept the yoke of Hashem. "And you shall give it to Elazar the *cohen*... and he should slaughter it before him," this refers to the downfall of the nations amongst whom the *benei yisrael* were exiled, as it says, "There will be a slaughter to Hashem in Batzrah."

דבר אחר פרה אלו ישראל שנאמר כי כפרה סוררה סרר ישראל. אדומה אלו ישראל שנאמר אדמו עצם מפנינים. תמימה אלו ישראל שנאמר יונתי תמתי, אשר אין בה מום אלו ישראל שנאמר כלך יפה רעיתי ומום אין בך. אשר לא עלה עליה עול זה דורו של ירמיה שלא קבלו עליהם עולו של הקב"ה וכו'. והוציא אותה אל מחוץ למחנה ועמה הגלי לבבל וכו'. ואסף זה הקב"ה וכו' את אפר הפרה אלו גליותיהם של ישראל. והניח אל מחוץ למחנה במקום טהור זה ירושלים שהיא טהורה.

Another explanation. "A cow," this refers to the *benei yisrael* who are compared to wayward cow. "Red," this refers to the *benei yisrael* who are compared to red jewels. "Perfect," this refers to the *benei yisrael* who are called a perfect dove. "That has no blemish," this refers to the *benei yisrael* who have no blemish. "On which no yoke has been placed," this refers to the generation of Yirmiyah who did not accept the yoke of Hashem... "And he shall take it outside of the camp," this refers to the exile of the *benei yisrael* to Bavel. "And he shall gather the ashes," this refers to Hashem who will gather the exiles of the *benei yisrael*. "And he shall place it outside the camp in a pure place," this refers to Yerushalayim which is pure.

According to the Yalkut Shimoni, exactly the same words in the Torah hint to both the nations amongst which the *benei yisrael* are exiled, and also to the *benei yisrael* in exile. This leads us to understand that according to the Yalkut Shimoni, the *mitzva* of *parah adumah* alludes to the interaction between the *benei yisrael* and the nations of the world, that will ultimately result in the coming of *mashiach*.

In other words, the *parah adumah* is an exceptional *korban* that is brought outside the camp of the *benei yisrael* in the *midbar*, or outside of Yerushalayim. Thus it alludes to the *avodas Hashem* (service of Hashem) of the *benei yisrael* in *galus*, after they are exiled from their land.

Galus

The *benei yisrael* were sent into *galus* because they did not keep the Torah in Eretz Yisrael, when it was easy for them to do so, as the *passuk* says (דברים כ"ח מ"ז):

תַּחַת אֲשֶׁר לֹא עָבַדְתָּ אֶת ה' אֱלֹקֶיךָ בְּשִׂמְחָה וּבְטוּב לֵבָב מֵרֹב כֹּל

[You will be sent into *galus*] because you did not serve Hashem joyously and with a good heart when you had an abundance of all things.

As a repentance, the *benei yisrael* are challenged to keep the Torah in *galus*, despite the difficulties presented to them and the self-sacrifice that this requires, as the *passuk* says (דברים ד', כ"ט):

וּבִקַּשְׁתֶּם מִשָּׁם אֶת ה' אֱלֹקֶיךָ וּמָצָאתָ כִּי תִדְרְשֶׁנּוּ בְּכָל לְבָבְךָ וּבְכָל נַפְשֶׁךָ

And you will seek Hashem from there (in galus) and you shall find Him when you seek Him with all your heart and with all your soul (i.e. even if this involves you sacrificing your life in order to observe the Torah).

Nevertheless, living in *galus* presents its own dangers, since the *benei yisrael* may be influenced by the nations among whom they live, as it says in Tehillim (106.35)

וַיִּתְעָרְבוּ בַגּוֹיִם וַיִּלְמְדוּ מַעֲשֵׂיהֶם

And they mingled with the nations and they learned from their deeds.

If we are to understand that the *parah adumah* is the *mitzva* that contains the secret of how the *benei yisrael* can both flourish in *galus* and also not be influenced by the nations of the world, then it must be that this *mitzva* at once provides the allowable interface between the *benei yisrael* and the nations of the world and at the same time provides the correct degree of insulation between the *benei yisrael* and the nations of the world.

Thus, the nations of the world tease the *benei yisrael* concerning the reason for the *mitzva* of *parah adumah*, because they know that were they able to understand the reason for this *mitzva*, then they would be able to overcome the purity and insulation of the *benei yisrael*, and assimilate them entirely. Therefore Hashem prohibits the *benei yisrael* from seeking to understand the *mitzva* of *parah adumah*, for were they to begin to understand this *mitzva*, that itself would be the cause of their undoing.

However, in order to strengthen their resolve not to become reconciled with the nations of the world, the *benei yisrael* seek a source of strength by remembering the time that they were protected by and sustained by Hashem in the *midbar*.

That is why specifically within the *mitzva* of *parah adumah*, that teaches the *benei yisrael* how to utilise the opportunity to serve Hashem when they are "outside of the camp" and far from Yerushalayim, there remains a constant reminder of the way things should really be, and of how Moshe kept the *mitzvos* of Hashem, with humility and purity, when the *benei yisrael* were alone with Hashem, in the *midbar*.

Balak

Balak's *korbanos*

It says in this week's *sedrah* (23.1)

וַיֹּאמֶר בִּלְעָם אֶל בָּלָק בְּנֵה לִי בָזֶה שִׁבְעָה מִזְבְּחֹת וְהָכֵן לִי בָּזֶה שִׁבְעָה פָרִים וְשִׁבְעָה אֵילִים

And Bilam said to Balak, "Build me seven altars here and prepare seven bulls and seven rams here for me."

The gemara in Horiyos (10b) comments

אמר רב יהודה אמר רב לעולם יעסוק אדם בתורה ובמצוות אפילו שלא לשמה שמתוך שלא לשמה בא לשמה שבשכר מ"ב קרבנות שהקריב בלק הרשע זכה ויצתה ממנו רות דאמר רבי יוסי ברבי חנינא רות בת

בנו של עגלון בן בנו של בלק מלך מואב

Rav Yehuda says that Rav said, "A person should always engage in Torah study and the performance of *mitzvos*, even if he does so not for its own sake, as through the performance of *mitzvos* not for its own sake, one comes to perform them for its own sake. For in reward for the forty-two offerings that Balak sacrificed to Hashem, he merited and Ruth was descended from him, as Rabbi Yosi, the son of Rabbi Chanina, said, 'Ruth was the daughter of the son of Eglon, the grandson of Balak, king of Moav.'"

Similarly, the gemara says in Pesachim (50b)

רבא רמי כתיב (תהלים נ"ז, י"א) כי גדול עד שמים חסדך וכתיב (תהלים ק"ח, ה') כי גדול מעל שמים חסדך הא כיצד כאן בעושין לשמה וכאן בעושין שלא לשמה וכדרב יהודה דאמר רב יהודה אמר רב לעולם יעסוק אדם בתורה ומצות אף על פי שלא לשמה שמתוך שלא לשמה בא לשמה

Rava asked, "It is written, 'For Your mercy is great unto the heavens, and Your truth reaches the skies' (Tehillim 57.11). And it is also written, 'For Your mercy is great above the heavens, and Your truth reaches the skies' (Psalms 108:5). [How can these *pessukim* be reconciled?]"

The Gemara answers:

Where the *passuk* says that Hashem's mercy is above the heavens, it is referring to a case where one performs a *mitzva* for its own sake, and where the *passuk* says that Hashem's mercy reaches the heavens, it is referring to a case where one performs a mitzva not for its own sake.

This is according to the statement of Rav Yehuda in the name of Rav, "A person should always engage in Torah study and performance of *mitzvos*, even not for their own sake, as through the performance of *mitzvos* not for their own sake, one comes to perform them for their own sake."

However, the gemara says in Berachos (17a)

וכל העושה שלא לשמה נוח לו שלא נברא

[Rava said,] one who does them *mitzvos* for their own sake, it would have been preferable for him had he not been created.

This appears to contradict the gemara in Berachos and Horiyos which says that a person should learn Torah and do *mitzvos* שלא לשמה.

Rashi explains

העושה שלא לשמה נוח לו שלא נברא: פירוש שאינו לומד כדי לקיים אלא לקנטר דבפרק מקום שנהגו (דף נ:) אמרינן רבא רמי כתיב עד שמים חסדך וכתיב מעל השמים כאן בעוסק שלא לשמה כו' והתם איירי במקיים כדי שיכבדוהו וכן משמע בירושלמי דפירקין

When do we say that if someone learns Torah not for its own sake, then it would have been better for him had he not been created, that is when he does not learn Torah in order to keep the Torah, but rather he learns the Torah in order to argue and to prove himself right.

For in Pesachim Rava says that a person should always learn Torah not for its own sake. Rather, that "not for its own sake" of Rava is referring to someone who learns Torah in order that people should honour him, which is permissible. The "not for its own sake" of our gemara is referring to one who learns Torah in order to put down other people.

- It would appear difficult to understand Rashi. Since we learn the rule of לעולם יעסוק אדם בתורה ובמצות אפילו שלא לשמה שמתוך שלא לשמה בא לשמה from Balak, who brought *korbanos* in order to be able to destroy the *benei yisrael*, it would appear that even when the שלא לשמה includes damaging intentions towards others, we should still apply this principle?

It would seem that we can explain as follows:

The medrash says (Eichah Rabbah, *pesichah* 2)

אמר רבי אבא בר כהנא: לא עמדו פילוסופין לאומות העולם, כבלעם בן בעור וכאבנימוס הגרדי. אמרו להם: יכולין אנו להזדווג לאומה זו? אמרו להם: לכו וחזרו על בתי כנסיות שלהם, אם התינוקות מצפצפין בקולן אי אתם יכולין להם, ואם לאו אתם יכולין להם. שכן הבטיחם אביהם ואמר להם: (בראשית כ"ז כ"ב): "הקול קול יעקב והידים ידי עשו:" כל זמן שקולו של יעקב בבתי כנסיות ובתי מדרשות, אין הידים ידי עשו. וכל זמן שאין קולו מצפצף בבתי כנסיות ובתי מדרשות, הידים ידי עשו.

Rabbi Abba bar Kahana said, "...the nations of the world asked Bilam, 'Are we able to attack the *benei yisrael*?'

He said to them, 'Go round their בתי כנסיות, if the children are learning Torah then you cannot defeat them, and if not, then you can. For so Yitzchak promised them, that as long as the voice would be the voice of Yaakov, then the hands would not be the hands of Esav.'"

The *derasha* would seem difficult to understand, as the *passuk* says that the voice is the voice of Yaakov and the hands are the hands of Esav, which implies that even when the voice is the voice of Yaakov, at the same time the hands will still be the hands of Esav. Rather we must understand that the *derasha* means that when the voice is the voice of Yaakov then it is immaterial that the hands are the hands of Esav, because Esav will become an adjunct to Yaakov and Esav's hands will work for Yaakov's benefit, even to the detriment of Esav's own intentions.

Similarly, when the *benei yisrael* learn Torah, even the power of the *tefillos* of the nations of the world, which ask for victory against the *benei yisrael*, will be turned in favour of the *benei yisrael*. Hence, Dovid, who defeated the nations of the world, was born in the merit of the *tefillos* of Balak, who brought *korbanos* in order that the nations of the world should defeat the *benei yisrael*.

However, all this only applies if the voice is the voice of Yaakov, which means to say that one learns Torah as a part of the Torah learning of the entire nation of the benei yisrael. But if one takes Torah for one's-self, in order to wield the Torah against someone else, then this is no longer the Torah of Yaakov, because this Torah is no longer the domain of all of the *benei yisrael*.

That is why there is a difference between the damaging intention of Balak, in bringing his *korbanos*, and the damaging intentions of one who learns Torah על מנת לקנטר. In the case of Balak, the Torah of the *benei yisrael* swayed the efficacy of his *tefillos* to the cause of the *benei yisrael*.

However, if one learns Torah על מנת לקנטר, such that that Torah is no longer the voice of Yaakov, then it is not possible for that intention to be rectified, because the Torah itself, the power of which normally rectifies incorrect intentions, has been diverted to only be of benefit to that person.

Pinchas

Kehunah and vengeance

It says in this week's *sedrah*

פִּינְחָס בֶּן אֶלְעָזָר בֶּן אַהֲרֹן הַכֹּהֵן הֵשִׁיב אֶת חֲמָתִי מֵעַל בְּנֵי יִשְׂרָאֵל בְּקַנְאוֹ אֶת קִנְאָתִי בְּתוֹכָם וְלֹא כִלִּיתִי אֶת בְּנֵי יִשְׂרָאֵל בְּקִנְאָתִי. לָכֵן אֱמֹר הִנְנִי נֹתֵן לוֹ אֶת בְּרִיתִי שָׁלוֹם.

Pinchas the son of Elazar the son of Aharon the cohen, has turned back My wrath from the benei yisrael by taking My revenge for Me, so that I did not destroy the benei yisrael in My anger.

Say, therefore, "Behold I grant him My pact of peace."

The Zohar comments on this *passuk*

ת"ח כל כהן דקטיל נפש פסיל ליה כהונתיה לעלמין דהא ודאי פסיל ההוא דרגא דיליה לגביה ופנחס מן דינא פסיל לכהנא הוה ובגין דקנא ליה לקב"ה אצטריך לחסא ליה כהונת עלמין ליה ולבנוי אבתריה לדרי דרין

If a *cohen* kills someone, then his *kehunah* becomes *passul* forever. Therefore, according to the strict *halachah*, Pinchos was *passul* from becoming a *cohen*. However because he was jealous for Hashem, the *passuk* has mercy on him to give him eternal *kehunah*, to him and to his children after him for all generations.

The *halacha* that a *cohen* who killed someone is *passul* to do *birchas cohanim* and to perform the *avodah*, is brought in Berachos (32b)

אמר רבי יוחנן כל כהן שהרג את הנפש לא ישא את כפיו שנאמר (ישעיהו א', ט"ו) ידיכם דמים מלאו

Rabbi Yochanan said, "A *cohen* who killed someone may not do *birchas cohanim*, as the *passuk* says, 'Your hands are full of blood.'"

This *halacha* is quoted in Orach Chaim (128.35)

כהן שהרג את הנפש אפילו בשוגג לא ישא את כפיו

If a *cohen* kills someone, even accidentally, then he may not do *birchas cohanim*.

The Mishna Berurah comments (אות קכ"ח)

ואם אנסוהו להרוג נושא את כפיו ואע"ג דברציחה קי"ל דיהרג ואל יעבור מ"מ אם עבר ולא נהרג לא מיפסל לנשיאת כפים בשביל זה

If they forced him to kill, then he may do *birchas cohanim*. Even although he should have been מוסר נפש not to kill the other person, nevertheless if he killed, so that he himself should not be killed, he does not become *passul* to do *birchas cohanim*.

It would seem from the Mishna Berurah that all the more so if a *cohen* killed lawfully, such as in the case of Pinchos who killed Zimri, then he can still do *birchas cohanim*.

- Why then does the Zohar say that Pinchos should have become *passul* to do the *avodah* because he killed Zimri?

Similarly, the Chizkuni says on this *passuk*

ד"א בריתי שלום דואג היה פן יפסיד כהונתו דאמרי' כהן שהרג את הנפש לא ישא את כפיו עד שהבטיחו הקב"ה הואיל והרציחה לשם שמים היתה כמו שמפרש והולך

Pinchos was afraid he would lose the *kehunah* because the gemara says that if a *cohen* kills someone then he may not do *birchas cohanim*. That is why it was necessary for Hashem to promise him that since the murder had been לשם שמים, that he could still become a *cohen*.

- Since Pinchas knew about himself that his motivation had been לשם שמים, why did he need Hashem's promise that he could still become a *cohen*?

The Targum Yonasan ben Uziel translates the above *passuk* as follows

בִּשְׁבוּעָא אֵימַר לֵיהּ מִן שְׁמִי הָאֲנָא גְזַר לֵיהּ יַת קְיָמִי שְׁלָם וְאַעְבְּדִינֵיהּ מַלְאָךְ קַיָּים וְיֵיחֵי לְעַלְמָא לִמְבַשְׂרָא גְאוּלְתָּא בְּסוֹף יוֹמַיָא

Swear to him in My name, Behold I make with him My pact of peace, and I will make him an immortal *malach*, and he will live forever to herald the redemption at the end of days.

- In what merit did Pinchas become a *malach*?

It would seem that we can explain as follows:

The gemara says in Sanhedrin (82a)

א"ר חסדא הבא לימלך אין מורין לו איתמר נמי אמר רבה בר בר חנה א"ר יוחנן הבא לימלך אין מורין לו ולא עוד אלא שאם... נהפך זמרי והרגו לפנחס אין נהרג עליו שהרי רודף הוא

Rav Chisda said, "Had Pinchas asked the *beis din* if he should kill Zimri, then *beis din* would not have instructed him to do so." Rabbi Yochanan said further, "Had Zimri killed Pinchas this would have been justified because Pinchas was pursuing Zimri to kill him, without the instruction of *beis din*.

Pinchas was only allowed to kill Zimri according to his own personal feelings of avenging the *chilul Hashem* of Zimri, but not according to the decision of *beis din*. In other words, this is not a *halachah* which is decided intellectually and with reasoning, but is rather a *halachah* which applies when someone has a reaction of vengeance for the *chilul Hashem* that has taken place.

Therefore, from the perspective of *beis din*, Pinchas killed Zimri in an act of passion, and not as a rational deed. Subsequently, even although Pinchas was justified in killing Zimri, it would still be possible to disqualify him from the *kehunah*, because his murder of Zimri had been passionate, and not impartial. That is why the Zohar and the Chizkuni say that Hashem Himself had to promise Pinchas that he would still be able to become a *cohen*.

Since Pinchas elevated even his body to such a level that it would be able to react passionately and autonomously in order to make a *kiddush Hashem*, therefore his body achieved the same level of kedushah as his נשמה שכלית, the intelligence of the נשמה. And so just as the *neshama* lives forever, so too did his body.

Matos

The *passuk* says in this week's sedrah (30.6)

וְאִם הֵנִיא אָבִיהָ אֹתָהּ בְּיוֹם שָׁמְעוֹ כָּל נְדָרֶיהָ וֶאֱסָרֶיהָ אֲשֶׁר אָסְרָה עַל נַפְשָׁהּ לֹא יָקוּם וַה' יִסְלַח לָהּ כִּי הֵנִיא אָבִיהָ אֹתָהּ

But if her father annulled her promise on the day he finds out, none of her vows or self-imposed prohibitions shall stand, and Hashem will forgive her, since her father annulled her promise.

Rashi quotes the Sifri which explains this *passuk* as follows.

> **וה' יסלח לה**: במה הכתוב מדבר באשה שנדרה בנזיר ושמע בעלה והפר לה והיא לא ידעה ועוברת על נדרה ושותה יין ומטמאה למתים זו היא שצריכה סליחה ואע"פ שהוא מופר ואם המופרים צריכים סליחה

ק"ו לשאינן מופרים

Which case is the passuk referring to? It is speaking of a woman who vowed that she would become a nazir, and whose husband heard it and annulled it for her, but she knew it not, and transgressed her *neder* and drank wine or made herself unclean by means of a dead person.

It is such a woman who requires forgiveness even though her *neder* has been annulled. And if those whose vows have been annulled require forgiveness in such a case (because they thought they were transgressing their *nedarim*), how much more is this so for those whose *nedarim* have not been annulled and who have transgressed them.

The gemara in Kiddushin (81b) gives a similar explanation.

דתניא (במדבר ל', י"ג) אישה הפרם וה' יסלח לה במה הכתוב מדבר באשה שנדרה בנזיר ושמע בעלה והפר לה והיא לא ידעה שהפר לה בעלה והיתה שותה יין ומטמאה למתים רבי עקיבא כי הוה מטי להאי פסוקא הוה בכי אמר ומה מי שנתכוין לאכול בשר חזיר ועלה בידו בשר טלה אמרה תורה צריכה כפרה וסליחה מי שנתכוין לאכול בשר חזיר ועלה בידו בשר חזיר על אחת כמה וכמה

It is taught in a *beraisa* concerning a husband who nullified the vow of his wife. "Her husband has made them null and Hashem will forgive her" (Bamidbar 30:13). With regard to what case is the *passuk* speaking? (Why would the woman require forgiveness if her husband has nullified her vow?) It is referring to a woman who vowed to be a *nazir*, and her husband heard and nullified her vow. And she did not know that her husband had nullified her neder, and she drank wine and contracted impurity from a dead person, violating her presumed vow.

When Rabbi Akiva came to this *passuk* he would cry. He said, "And if with regard to one who intended to eat pork, and kosher lamb came up in his hand, like this woman who intended to violate her vow but in fact did not, the Torah nevertheless says, 'She requires atonement and forgiveness,' all the more so does one who intended to eat pork and pork came up in his hand require atonement and forgiveness."

It would appear to be difficult to understand the terminology of the gemara. We can understand that in a case where one intended to eat pork and took lamb instead, that it is appropriate to say, "And kosher lamb came up in his hand." The gemara uses the term "came up" in this case, because what happened was accidental and unintended.

However, in a case where the person intended to eat pork and did indeed succeed in doing so, then it would seem that the expression "pork came up in his hand" is not appropriate. Rather it would seem that the gemara should have said, "All the more so does one who intended to eat pork and did so, require forgiveness and atonement."

- Since what happened was intended, then that which he picked up the pork to eat it, was a direct straightforward action, and not something that happened by coincidence?

It would seem that we can explain as follows.

The gemara says in Chullin (7a-b)

> דרבי פנחס בן יאיר הוה קאזיל לפדיון שבויין... אקלע לההוא אושפיזא רמו ליה שערי לחמריה לא אכל חבטינהו לא אכל נקרינהו לא אכל אמר להו דלמא לא מעשרן עשרינהו ואכל אמר ענייה זו הולכת לעשות רצון קונה ואתם מאכילין אותה טבלים ומי מיחייבא והתנן הלוקח לזרע ולבהמה וקמח לעורות ושמן לנר ושמן לסוך בו את הכלים פטור מהדמאי התם הא אתמר עלה אמר רבי יוחנן לא שנו אלא שלקחן מתחלה לבהמה אבל לקחן מתחלה לאדם ונמלך עליהם לבהמה חייב לעשר

Rabbi Pinchas ben Ya'ir was going to engage in the redemption of captives… After crossing the River Ginai, Rabbi Pinchas ben Ya'ir came to a certain inn. His hosts cast barley before his donkey for him to eat. The donkey did not eat it. The hosts sifted the barley with a utensil, but the donkey did not eat it. They separated the chaff from the barley by hand, but the donkey did not eat it. They wondered why the donkey would not eat the barley.

Rabbi Pinchas ben Ya'ir said to his hosts, "Perhaps you did not take ma'aser from the barley?" They took *ma'aser* and the donkey ate it. Rabbi Pinchas ben Ya'ir said, "This poor animal is going to perform the will of its Maker, and you are feeding it untithed produce?"

The Gemara asks: And is one who purchases grain that is demai in order to feed his animal obliged to take *ma'aser*? But didn't we learn in a mishna (Demai 1:3), "One who purchases grain in the market for sowing or for feeding an animal, or flour to process animal hides, or oil to kindle a lamp, or oil to smear on vessels is exempt from the obligation of taking *demai*?"

The Gemara answers: There, it was stated with regard to that mishna that Rabbi Yochanan says, "They taught this only in a case where one purchased those items initially for the animal or for the other purposes enumerated in the mishna, but if he purchased them initially for a person and reconsidered and decided to use them for an animal, then he is obliged to tithe the *demai*."

It would seem difficult to understand this gemara, in light of the Rambam in his introduction to Pirkei Avos (Shemoneh Perakim, *perek* 6).

שֶׁהָרָעוֹת אֲשֶׁר הֵן אֵצֶל הַפִּילוֹסוֹפִים רָעוֹת, אֲשֶׁר אָמְרוּ שֶׁמִּי שֶׁלֹּא יִתְאַוֶּה אֲלֵיהֶן יוֹתֵר חָשׁוּב מִן הַמִּתְאַוֶּה אֲלֵיהֶן וְיִכְבֹּשׁ אֶת יִצְרוֹ מֵהֶן, הֵם הָעִנְיָנִים הַמְפֻרְסָמִים אֵצֶל כָּל בְּנֵי אָדָם שֶׁהֵם רָעוֹת, כִּשְׁפִיכוּת דָּמִים, וּגְנֵבָה, וּגְזֵלָה, וְאוֹנָאָה, וּלְהַזִּיק לְמִי שֶׁלֹּא הֵרַע לוֹ, וְלִגְמֹל רַע לְמֵיטִיב לוֹ, וְלִבְזוֹת אָב וָאֵם וְכַיּוֹצֵא בָּאֵלּוּ. וְהֵן הַמִּצְווֹת שֶׁאָמְרוּ עֲלֵיהֶן הַחֲכָמִים, זִכְרוֹנָם לִבְרָכָה שֶׁאִלּוּ לֹא נִכְתְּבוּ רְאוּיוֹת הֵן לְכָתֵב. וְיִקְרְאוּ אוֹתָן קְצָת מֵחֲכָמֵינוּ הָאַחֲרוֹנִים אֲשֶׁר חָלוּ חֳלִי הַמְדַבְּרִים מִצְווֹת הַשִּׂכְלִיּוֹת. וְאֵין סָפֵק שֶׁהַנֶּפֶשׁ אֲשֶׁר תִּכְסֹף לְדָבָר מֵהֶם וְתִשְׁתּוֹקֵק אֵלָיו שֶׁהִיא חֲסֵרָה וְשֶׁהַנֶּפֶשׁ הַחֲשׁוּבָה לֹא תִתְאַוֶּה לְאֶחָד מֵאֵלּוּ הָרָעוֹת כְּלָל, וְלֹא תִצְטַעֵר בְּהִמָּנְעָהּ מֵהֶם.

אֲבָל הַדְּבָרִים שֶׁאָמְרוּ עֲלֵיהֶם הַחֲכָמִים, שֶׁהַכּוֹבֵשׁ אֶת יִצְרוֹ מֵהֶם הוּא יוֹתֵר חָשׁוּב וּגְמוּלוֹ יוֹתֵר גָּדוֹל הֵם הַתּוֹרוֹת הַשִּׁמְעִיּוֹת, וְזֶה אֱמֶת שֶׁאִלְמָלֵא הַתּוֹרָה לֹא הָיוּ רָעוֹת כְּלָל. וּמִפְּנֵי זֶה אָמְרוּ שֶׁצָּרִיךְ הָאָדָם שֶׁיַּנִּיחַ נַפְשׁוֹ אוֹהֶבֶת אוֹתָן וְלֹא יִהְיֶה לוֹ מוֹנֵעַ מֵהֶן רַק הַתּוֹרָה. וּבְחַן חָכְמָתָם, עֲלֵיהֶם

הַשָּׁלוֹם, וּבַמָּה שֶׁהִמְשִׁילוּ. שֶׁהֵם לֹא אָמְרוּ אַל יֹאמַר אָדָם אִי אֶפְשִׁי לַהֲרֹג הַנֶּפֶשׁ, אִי אֶפְשִׁי לִגְנֹב, אִי אֶפְשִׁי לְכַזֵּב, אֶלָּא אֶפְשִׁי, וּמָה אֶעֱשֶׂה, אָבִי שֶׁבַּשָּׁמַיִם גָּזַר עָלַי. אֲבָל הֵבִיאוּ דְבָרִים שֶׁשׁוֹמְעִים כֻּלָּם, בָּשָׂר בְּחָלָב, וּלְבִישַׁת שַׁעַטְנֵז, וַעֲרָיוֹת. וְאֵלוּ הַמִּצְווֹת וְכַיּוֹצֵא בָהֶן, הֵן אֲשֶׁר קְרָאָן הַשֵּׁם יִתְבָּרֵךְ חֻקּוֹת.

There are two types of *mitzvos*. On the one hand, we have *mitzvos* that we would have understood by ourselves even had they not been written in the Torah, such as murder, robbery and cheating. On the other hand, we have *mitzvos* that we only know because the Torah told us about them, such as not eating meat and milk together and not wearing *sha'atnez*.

Concerning the *mitzvos* that we would have understood by ourselves, it is preferable for a person not to want to do them at all. Concerning the *mitzvos* that we would not have understood if not for the Torah writing them, it is preferable for a person to adopt the attitude that they would like to do them, but nevertheless refrain because Hashem told them not to do them.

Considering the *mitzva* of not eating grain from which *ma'aser* has not been separated, this is a *mitzva* that we only know of because it is written in the Torah. If so, it would have been appropriate for Rabbi Pinchas ben Yair to have the attitude that he would have liked to eat untithed produce, but nevertheless refrained from doing so because the Torah prohibits this.

Since his donkey could only be attuned to Rabbi Pinchas ben Yair's feelings, and not his intellect, as a donkey only has feelings but no intellect, the donkey should have been willing to eat the demai, since Rabbi Pinchas ben Yair's basic sentiments would have been that he would be willing to eat such produce.

Rabbi Mordechai Miller z"l explained that from the fact that Rabbi Pinchas ben Yair's donkey did not want to eat the *demai*, we see that there is a higher level than that which the Rambam addresses. At the level attained by Rabbi Pinchas ben Yair, his body became attuned to the saturation of Torah knowledge which he had accomplished, so that his body instinctively would not eat *demai*. Subsequently, his donkey also became attuned to this higher intuition.

A similar idea is evident in the Mesillas Yesharim (Perek 1), which says as follows.

ואם תעמיק עוד בעניין תראה כי העולם נברא לשימוש האדם, אמנם הנה הוא עומד בשקול גדול, כי אם האדם נמשך אחר העולם ומתרחק מבוראו, הנה הוא מתקלקל ומקלקל העולם עמו. ואם הוא שולט בעצמו ונדבק בבוראו ומשתמש מן העולם רק להיות לו לסיוע לעבודת בוראו, הוא מתעלה והעולם עצמו מתעלה עמו. כי הנה עילוי גדול הוא לבריות כולם, בהיותם משמשי האדם השלם המקודש בקדושתו יתברך.

And if you look deeper into this matter you will see that the world is created in order to serve man, however it stands in a great balance. For if a man is dragged after the world and is distanced from his creator, then he is corrupted and the world becomes corrupted together with him.

However if he rules over himself and cleaves to his creator and uses the world only to assist him in his service of Hashem, then he rises and the world rises together with him.

For it is a great uplifting for the entire creation to serve the perfected man who is sanctified with Hashem's holiness.

Since the Mesillas Yesharim does not differentiate between *mitzvos* which we would have understood by ourselves and *mitzvos* which we only know because they are written in the Torah, it is evident that even the latter type of *mitzvos* contain an intrinsic *kedushah* vis-à-vis the things regarding which they are commanded. In the case of Rabbi Pinchas ben Yair, even his body became attuned to the *kedushah* of not eating *demai*, and therefore his donkey also refrained from doing so.

With this introduction, we can understand why the gemara in Kiddushin says "One who intended to eat pork and pork came up in his hand require atonement and forgiveness." This is because even if one intends to eat pork, which is a negative *mitzva* we would not have known had it not been written in the Torah, the *kedushah* of this *mitzva* should influence the world in such a way that it should conspire to prevent this from occurring. Subsequently, we can only ever say that the non-kosher food "came up in his hand," because naturally speaking, this should never have occurred.

Masei

The travels of the *benei yisrael*

The *passuk* says at the start of this week's *sedrah* (33.1 - 2)

אֵלֶּה מַסְעֵי בְנֵי יִשְׂרָאֵל אֲשֶׁר יָצְאוּ מֵאֶרֶץ מִצְרַיִם לְצִבְאֹתָם בְּיַד מֹשֶׁה וְאַהֲרֹן. וַיִּכְתֹּב מֹשֶׁה אֶת מוֹצָאֵיהֶם לְמַסְעֵיהֶם עַל פִּי ה' וְאֵלֶּה מַסְעֵיהֶם לְמוֹצָאֵיהֶם.

These are the journeys of the *benei yisrael* who came out of Mitzraim according to their hosts, in the charge of Moshe and Aharon. Moses wrote down the places that they left to go on their journeys as directed by Hashem. And these were their journeys, by the places they left..."

The medrash comments on this *passuk*:

> ...אמר להם הקדוש ברוך הוא וכאלו כל גדולי עולם יראו וברחו מן שונאיהם כל אותן מ' שנה שעשיתם במדבר לא הנחתי אתכם לברוח אלא הייתי מפיל שונאיכם לפניכם במה שהייתי עמכם ולא עוד אלא כמה נחשים וכמה שרפים וכמה עקרבים היו שם שנאמר (דברים ח', ט"ו) נחש שרף ועקרב, ולא הנחתי אותם להזיק אתכם לכך אמר הקב"ה למשה כתוב את המסעות שנסעו ישראל במדבר כדי שיהיו יודעים מה נסים שעשיתי להם מנין ממה שקרינו בענין אלה מסעי

> Hashem said to the *benei yisrael*, the greatest people of the world (Yaakov, Moshe and Dovid) feared and fled from their enemies, but all of those 40 years when you were in the *midbar* I did not leave you to flee, but rather I made your

enemies fall before you through that which I was with you. And not only that, but there were many snakes, serpents and scorpions there, and I did not allow them to hurt you. That is why Hashem said to Moshe, "Write down the journeys that the *benei yisrael* made in the *midbar*, so that they should know what *nissim* I did for them."

- If the journeys of the *benei yisrael* were made according to the directions of Hashem, why would you think that Hashem would have caused the *benei yisrael* to have to flee, while they were going on the route in which He had commanded them?

The medrash comments further on this *passuk*

זה שאמר הכתוב (תהלים ע"ז, כ"א) נָחִיתָ כַצֹּאן עַמֶּךָ בְּיַד מֹשֶׁה וְאַהֲרֹן. מה נחית, נוטריקון הוא, נחית, רבי אליעזר אומר נסים עשית עמהם חיים נתת להם ים קרעת להם תורה נתת להם, ועל ידי מי, על ידי משה ואהרן.

This is what the *passuk* in Tehillim is referring to when it says, "You led (נָחִיתָ) Your people like a flock, in the care of Moses and Aaron." What does the word נָחִיתָ mean? It is an acronym:

- *Nun* stands for the *nissim* which you performed for them.

- *Ches* stands for the life (*chayim*) that you gave them.

- *Yud* stands for the *Yam Suf* which you split for them.

- *Tof* stands for the Torah that you gave to them.

And through whom? Through Moshe and Aharon.

It would seem difficult to understand what the medrash is adding. We know from the *pessukim* in the Torah that Hashem split the *yam suf* for the *benei yisrael*, saved their lives in the *midbar*, gave them the Torah and performed other *nissim* for them.

- What more do we learn by saying that these things form the acronym נחית?

Later on the medrash says:

ד"א אֵלֶּה מַסְעֵי, למה זכו ליכתב בתורה כל המסעות האלו, על שקבלו את ישראל. ועתיד הקדוש ברוך הוא ליתן שכרן, דכתיב (ישעיהו ל"ה, א') יְשֻׂשׂוּם מִדְבָּר וְצִיָּה וְתָגֵל עֲרָבָה וְתִפְרַח כַּחֲבַצָּלֶת. פָּרֹחַ תִּפְרַח וְתָגֵל [אַף גִּילַת וְרַנֵּן כְּבוֹד הַלְּבָנוֹן נִתַּן לָהּ הֲדַר הַכַּרְמֶל וְהַשָּׁרוֹן הֵמָּה יִרְאוּ כְבוֹד ה' הֲדַר אֱלֹקֵינוּ]. ומה מדבר על שקבל ישראל כך, המקבל תלמידי חכמים לתוך ביתו עאכ"ו.

Why did all these encampments merit to be written in the Torah? Because they received the *benei yisrael*. And in the future Hashem will pay their reward, as the *passuk* says, "The arid desert shall be glad, the wilderness shall rejoice and shall blossom like a rose. It shall blossom abundantly, [it shall also exult and be happy.

The honour of Lebanon will be given to it, the splendour of Carmel and the Sharon. They shall behold the honour of Hashem, the splendour of our G-d.]" And if the desert which accepted the *benei yisrael* received such a reward, then all the more so will be the reward for one who accepts a *talmid chacham* into his house.

- Why do the places in the *midbar* in which the *benei yisrael* camped, have to wait for the coming of *mashiach* in order to receive their reward?

It would seem that we can explain as follows:

The gemara says in Sotah (22a)

דההיא אלמנה דהואי בי כנישתא בשיבבותה כל יומא הות אתיא ומצלה בי מדרשיה דר' יוחנן אמר לה בתי לא בית הכנסת בשיבבותך אמרה ליה רבי ולא שכר פסיעות יש לי

There was a certain widow in whose neighbourhood there was a *shul*, and despite this every day she went and prayed in the *yeshiva* of Rabbi Yochanan. Rabbi Yochanan said to her, "My daughter, is there not a *shul* in your neighbourhood?" She said to him, "My master, don't I attain a reward for all the steps I take while walking to pray in the *yeshiva*?[41]"

The gemara mentions the idea of שכר פסיעות – the reward for walking to a *mitzva*, specifically with regard to *tefillah*. Since

---

[41] See (ס' צ', ס"ק ל"ז) משנה ברורה who is of the opinion that it is a *mitzva* to daven in the furthest *shul* in one's town in order that one be rewarded for the *mitzva* of walking there.

tefillah represents a journey to new spiritual vistas, the physical journey that one takes to *shul* also becomes part of this spiritual travelling and ascendancy.

Similarly, each journey that the *benei yisrael* took in the *midbar* represented one further rung in the spiritual ladder that the *benei yisrael* had to climb in order to enter Eretz Yisrael in a spiritual, as well as a physical manner.

However, the spiritual journey that the *benei yisrael* undertook in their travels, was not always synonymous with their physical movement. For example, the *passuk* says (Bamidbar 10.33)

וַיִּסְעוּ מֵהַר ה' דֶּרֶךְ שְׁלֹשֶׁת יָמִים וַאֲרוֹן בְּרִית ה' נֹסֵעַ לִפְנֵיהֶם דֶּרֶךְ שְׁלֹשֶׁת יָמִים לָתוּר לָהֶם מְנוּחָה

And they travelled from the mountain of Hashem a distance of three days journey. The *aron* of the covenant of Hashem travelled in front of them on that three days' journey to seek out a resting place for them.

The Ramban explains (Bamidbar 10.35)

אבל ענין המדרש הזה מצאו אותו באגדה שנסעו מהר סיני בשמחה כתינוק הבורח מבית הספר. אמרו שמא ירבה ויתן לנו מצות. וזהו ויסעו מהר ה', שהיה מחשבתם להסיע עצמם משם מפני שהוא הר ה'.

The *passuk* says that they travelled from the mountain of Hashem, meaning to say that they travelled away from Har Sinai exactly because it was the mountain of Hashem, like a child running away from school. They thought, "Maybe Hashem will give us even more *mitzvos*."

Subsequently, to the extent that the *benei yisrael* were not prepared to undergo the transformation that was represented by their physical journey, they remained spiritually in the place from which they had travelled.

The journey that the *benei yisrael* made in the *midbar* will only be entirely complete when *mashiach* comes, at which time the *benei yisrael* will indeed have progressed from each encampment to the next, and acquired the level which that journey represents. That is why the places in which the *benei yisrael* encamped will only bloom when *mashiach* comes, because only then will the journey of the *benei yisrael* through those places be completed and achieve its fruition.

Since the *benei yisrael* did not completely acquire the spiritual level of each place through which they passed, you may have thought that their journey would become disjointed and unfulfilling.

Therefore the *passuk* in Tehillim comes to teach you that Hashem still led the *benei yisrael* gently (נחית), so that Hashem joined together all of the spiritual acquisitions which the *benei yisrael* were to make (*nissim, chayim, yam suf, torah*) into one continuous path of elevation on which the *benei yisrael* would be able to continue to progress, even after they left the *midbar*.

And you may also have thought, that since the *benei yisrael* did not entirely acquire the *madregah* represented by each place through which they passed, that they would have been driven back by the nations who could now claim that the *benei yisrael* had not proven themselves worthy to be the conquerors of Eretz Yisrael and the pathways to it. That is why the *passuk* comes to tell you that despite all this, Hashem never caused the *benei yisrael* to have to flee from their enemies or suffer any harm.

Devarim

The healing power of the Torah

It says at the beginning of this week's *sedrah*

אֵלֶּה הַדְּבָרִים אֲשֶׁר דִּבֶּר מֹשֶׁה אֶל כָּל יִשְׂרָאֵל בְּעֵבֶר הַיַּרְדֵּן בַּמִּדְבָּר בָּעֲרָבָה מוֹל סוּף בֵּין פָּארָן וּבֵין תֹּפֶל וְלָבָן וַחֲצֵרֹת וְדִי זָהָב

These are the words that Moshe addressed to all of the *benei yisrael* on the other side of the Yarden. Through the *midbar*, in the Aravah near Suph, between Paran and Tophel, Lavan, Chatzeros, and Di Zahav.

The medrash comments on this *passuk* as follows:

אמר הקב"ה ראה לשונה של תורה מה חביבה שמרפא את הלשון מנין שכן כתיב (משלי ט"ו, ד') מרפא לשון עץ חיים, ואין עץ חיים אלא

תורה שנאמר (שם ג', י"ח) עץ חיים היא למחזיקים בה. ולשונה של תורה מתיר את הלשון תדע לך לע"ל הקב"ה מעלה מג"ע אילנות משובחים. ומה הוא שבחן שהן מרפאין את הלשון שנאמר (יחזקאל מ"ז, י"ב) וְעַל הַנַּחַל יַעֲלֶה עַל שְׂפָתוֹ מִזֶּה וּמִזֶּה [כָּל עֵץ מַאֲכָל לֹא יִבּוֹל עָלֵהוּ וְלֹא יִתֹּם פִּרְיוֹ לָחֳדָשָׁיו יְבַכֵּר כִּי מֵימָיו מִן הַמִּקְדָּשׁ הֵמָּה יוֹצְאִים וְהָיָה פִרְיוֹ לְמַאֲכָל וְעָלֵהוּ לִתְרוּפָה].

מנין שהיא רפואה של לשון שנאמר, והיה פריו למאכל ועליהו לתרופה. רבי יוחנן ורבי יהושע בן לוי, חד אמר לתרפיון וחד אמר כל שהוא אלם ולועט הימנו לשונו מתרפא ומצהצחה מיד בדברי תורה, שכך כתיב מזה ומזה ואין מזה ומזה אלא תורה שנאמר (שמות ל"ב, ט"ו) מזה ומזה הם כתובים.

ר"ל אמר מה לנו ללמוד ממקום אחר נלמוד ממקומו הרי משה עד שלא זכה לתורה כתיב בו (שם ד', י') לֹא אִישׁ דְּבָרִים אָנֹכִי. כיון שזכה לתורה נתרפא לשונו והתחיל לדבר דברים מנין ממה שקרינו בענין אֵלֶּה הַדְּבָרִים אֲשֶׁר דִּבֶּר מֹשֶׁה.

Hashem said, "See the language of the Torah, how dear it is, for it even heals the tongue." From where do we know this? For the *passuk* says, "The Tree of Life heals the tongue," and the Tree of Life refers to the Torah, as the *passuk* says, "It is a Tree of Life for those who hold onto it."

And the language of the Torah frees the tongue. You may know that this is so for in the future Hashem will grow in Gan Eden admirable trees, and what is their praise? That they will heal the tongue, as the *passuk* says, "All kinds of trees for food will grow up on both banks of the stream. Their leaves will not wither nor their fruit fail; they will yield new fruit every month, because the water for them flows from the Beis Hamikdash. Their fruit will serve for food and their leaves for healing..."

Rabbi Yochanan and Rabbi Yehoshua ben Levi argued concerning this matter. One said that the leaves will be medicine, and one said, anyone who is mute and eats from it his tongue will be healed and he will be immediately able to talk in *divrei torah*. For the *passuk* says מזה ומזה (on either bank), and the words מזה ומזה are a reference to the Torah, as we find concerning the *luchos* the *passuk* says מזה ומזה הם כתובים (they were written on either side).

Reish Lakish said, "Why do you need to learn from somewhere else? You may learn this from its own place. For before Moshe learnt Torah he said, 'I am not a man of words.' But once he learnt Torah his tongue was healed and he started speaking many words. How do we know this? For the *passuk* says, 'These are the words that Moshe spoke.'"

- Why is the Torah here alluded to with the words מזה ומזה?

It would seem that we can explain as follows[42]:

The Tosefta (Sotah 7.7) says

שמא יאמר אדם בדעתו הואיל ובית שמאי מטמאין ובית הלל מטהרין איש פלוני אוסר איש פלוני מתיר [למה] אני למד תורה מעתה [תלמוד לומר] דברים אלה הדברים כל הדברים נתנו מרועה אחד כלם קל אחד בראן פרנס אחד נתנן רבון כל המעשים ברוך הוא אמרן אף אתה עשה לבך חדרי חדרים והכניס בו דברי בית שמאי ודברי בית הלל

---

[42] עיין בספר יקר מפז

דברי המטמאין ודברי המטהרין

Lest a person think, "Since Beis Shammai say it is *tameh* and Beis Hillel say it is *tahor*, so-and-so says it is *assur* and so-and-so says it is *mutar*, why then should I learn Torah? Therefore the Torah comes to teach you as follows:

- In Va'eschanan the *passuk* says וַיְדַבֵּר ה' אֲלֵיכֶם מִתּוֹךְ הָאֵשׁ קוֹל דְּבָרִים אַתֶּם שֹׁמְעִים וּתְמוּנָה אֵינְכֶם רֹאִים זוּלָתִי קוֹל. Here the Torah uses the word דברים.

- Also in Va'eschanan, the *passuk* says אֶת הַדְּבָרִים הָאֵלֶּה דִּבֶּר ה' אֶל כָּל קְהַלְכֶם בָּהָר מִתּוֹךְ הָאֵשׁ הֶעָנָן וְהָעֲרָפֶל קוֹל גָּדוֹל וְלֹא יָסָף וַיִּכְתְּבֵם עַל שְׁנֵי לֻחֹת אֲבָנִים וַיִּתְּנֵם אֵלָי. Here the Torah uses the term הדברים.

- At the beginning of Devarim, the *passuk* says אֵלֶּה הַדְּבָרִים אֲשֶׁר דִּבֶּר מֹשֶׁה אֶל כָּל יִשְׂרָאֵל בְּעֵבֶר הַיַּרְדֵּן בַּמִּדְבָּר בָּעֲרָבָה מוֹל סוּף בֵּין פָּארָן וּבֵין תֹּפֶל וְלָבָן וַחֲצֵרֹת וְדִי זָהָב. Here the Torah uses the phrase אלה הדברים.

- Prior to the *aseres ha'dibros*, the *passuk* says, (Shemos 20.1), וַיְדַבֵּר אֱלֹקִים אֵת כָּל־הַדְּבָרִים הָאֵלֶּה לֵאמֹר. Here the Torah uses the phrase כל הדברים.

Each expression of "words" mentioned in the Torah (going from "words", to "the words", to "these are the words" and to "all the words") implies a greater and greater number of words. The fact that the Torah uses all these different ways to describe the words of the Torah teaches you that all opinions in the Torah are given by Hashem. So too you should make your heart into rooms and compartments and bring into the different rooms the words of Beis Shammai and the words of Beis Hillel, the words of the those who say the matter is *assur* and the words of those who say the matter is *mutar*.

The *sedrah* begins with the words אלה הדברים to allude that the Torah is comprised of many contradictory points of view. The reason that the Torah is comprised of contradictory points of view is because the source of the Torah is in a higher world than the one in which we live. Each point of view is one facet of the Torah, as perceived from one perspective. This is why the *luchos* could be read from either side, since all ways of perceiving the *aseres ha'dibros* are valid and complementary.

Moshe was not limited to understanding only one perspective of the Torah, rather he was able to understand all perspectives of the Torah, since he was able to perceive the source of the Torah in *shamayim*. However, such a level of truth was not accepted in Mitzrayim, and therefore there he was impeded in his speech. But once the Torah was given, Moshe was able to present the Torah to each of the *benei yisrael* in the way that was most meaningful to them and that related to the source of their existence in the higher world from which the Torah emanates.

This is why concerning Moshe's ability to address the *benei yisrael*, the medrash uses the allusion of מזה ומזה to refer to *divrei torah*. Because just as the *luchos* could be read מזה ומזה, so too were the *benei yisrael* able to relate to the words of Torah of Moshe, each one in his own way, מזה ומזה.

Because the Torah that Moshe taught the *benei yisrael* was connected to the source of each *neshama*, it brought healing to the *benei yisrael*[43]. And that is why the same *passuk* that refers to the healing capacity of the Torah refers to the Torah as מזה ומזה.

Va'eschanan

The cities of refuge

It says in this week's *sedrah* (4.41 - 42)

אָז יַבְדִּיל מֹשֶׁה שָׁלֹשׁ עָרִים בְּעֵבֶר הַיַּרְדֵּן מִזְרְחָה שָׁמֶשׁ. לָנֻס שָׁמָּה רוֹצֵחַ אֲשֶׁר יִרְצַח אֶת רֵעֵהוּ בִּבְלִי דַעַת וְהוּא לֹא שֹׂנֵא לוֹ מִתְּמוֹל שִׁלְשׁוֹם וְנָס אֶל אַחַת מִן הֶעָרִים הָאֵל וָחָי.

Then Moshe set aside three cities on the east side of the Yarden, to which a murderer could escape, one who unwittingly slew a fellow man without having been hostile to him in the past; he could flee to one of these cities and live.

---

[43] Similarly, the word בריא – healthy, is related to the word ברא – to create, because when one is connected to the original way in which they were created by Hashem, they automatically become healthy.

The Medrash Rabbah comments (Vayikra 22.2)

ורבנן אמרי (קהלת ה', ח') ויתרון ארץ, אפילו דברים שאתם רואים בעולם מיותרין כגון זבובין פרעושים ויתושים אף הן בכלל ברייתו של עולם דכתיב (בראשית ב', א') ויכולו השמים והארץ וכל צבאם.

מלך לשדה נעבד, זה הקדוש ברוך הוא דכתיב ביה (תהלים צ"ג, א') ה' מלך גאות לבש. לשדה נעבד, זו ציון דכתיב (מיכה ג', י"ב) ציון שדה תחרש.

לפיכך, אוהב כסף לא ישבע כסף, אוהב מצות לא ישבע מצות, ואוהב בהמון וגו', שכל מי שהומה ומהמה אחר המצות ומצוה קבועה לדורות אין לו מה הנאה יש לו תדע לך שהוא כן שהרי משה כמה מצות וצדקות עשה וכמה מעשים טובים היה בידו ויש לו מצוה קבועה לדורות הדא היא דכתיב (דברים ד', מ"א) אז יבדיל משה

The *passuk* says in Koheles (5.9)

אֹהֵב כֶּסֶף לֹא יִשְׂבַּע כֶּסֶף וּמִי אֹהֵב בֶּהָמוֹן לֹא תְבוּאָה גַּם זֶה הָבֶל

The medrash explains this *passuk* as follows:

One who loves money never has his fill of money, nor a lover of wealth his fill of harvest: Because anyone who roars after *mitzvos*, but nevertheless he does not leave behind him any *mitzva* that is founded for all generations, what benefit does he have from all his work? You may know that this is so, because Moshe did many *mitzvos* and charitable acts, and he had many good deeds in his hand, but he had only one *mitzva* which was founded for all generations, as the *passuk* says, "Then Moshe set aside three cities…"

- Why does the medrash only consider Moshe's separating the three cities as his heritage for all generations, and not the entire Torah which Moshe brought to the *benei yisrael*?

It would seem that we can explain as follows:

The *passuk* says in Ha'azinu (Devarim 32.40)

כִּי אֶשָּׂא אֶל שָׁמַיִם יָדִי וְאָמַרְתִּי חַי אָנֹכִי לְעֹלָם

For I raise My hand to heaven and I swear, "As I live forever"

The Ramban explains:

בעבור כי בעת הגלות השליך משמים ארץ תפארת ישראל יאמר שישאנה עתה בעת רצון אל השמים העליונים והיא היד הגדולה הנלחמת לישראל וזה טעם ואמרתי חי אנכי לעולם כי אני מחיה ידי החזקה בהיותי משנן ברק חרבי וסומך אותם לאחוז במשפטן של ישראל ולהשיב נקם לצרי כי אז יהיה השם שלם והכסא שלם

Because at the time of *galus*, Hashem would cast from the heavens to the earth, all the glory of the *benei* yisrael. Therefore the *passuk* says that now, at the time of the good will of Hashem, that Hashem would carry it to the uppermost heavens, and this is the mighty hand that always fights for the *benei yisrael* (even during *galus*).

Thus Hashem says that He will cause His mighty hand to live forever by sharpening His flashing blade and supporting His hand to seek justice for the *benei yisrael* and to take revenge from those that harass the *benei yisrael*. For only then will Hashem's Name will be whole and Hashem's throne be whole.

All of the כבוד שמים that happened in the *midbar*, and the resting of the *shechinah* on the *benei yisrael* that happened in the *midbar*, is a continuously alive experience, that anyone in any generation of the *benei yisrael* can directly draw strength and inspiration from, as if the events in the *midbar* immediately preceded them.

For example, it says in the Haggadah

בְּכָל דּוֹר וָדוֹר חַיָּב אָדָם לִרְאוֹת אֶת עַצְמוֹ כְּאִלּוּ הוּא יָצָא מִמִּצְרַיִם, שֶׁנֶּאֱמַר וְהִגַּדְתָּ לְבִנְךָ בַּיּוֹם הַהוּא לֵאמֹר, בַּעֲבוּר זֶה עָשָׂה ה' לִי בְּצֵאתִי מִמִּצְרָיִם (שמות י"ג ח')

In every generation a person is obliged to see himself as if he came out of *Mitzraim*. As the *passuk* says, "And you should tell your son on that day saying, 'Because of this Hashem wrought for me when I came out of *Mitzraim*.'"

Since the living glory of יציאת מצרים is maintained forever in *shamayim*, we are therefore able to immediately experience יציאת מצרים, as if we ourselves were there. And just as the experience of יציאת מצרים is maintained forever, so too are all of the revelations of the *shechinah* that the *benei yisrael* perceived in the *midbar*, such as מתן תורה and קריעת ים סוף, maintained forever.

On the other hand, once the *benei yisrael* entered Eretz Yisrael, the chain of the successive generations of the *benei yisrael* began. This chain forms a series of events in the history of the *benei yisrael*, which we experience sequentially from the time that they happened until the present day (and not as an immediate experience).

Almost all of Moshe's *mitzvos*, acts of charity and good deeds related to the time of the *benei yisrael* in the *midbar*. These good deeds are not transmitted to us through the lens of the generations, but are rather immediately available to us, because the חיות with which these events were imbued, persists till today. The only thing that Moshe did which we perceive through the lens of the passage of the generations, was his separating the three ערי מקלט, as this comprised the beginning of the settling of the *benei yisrael* in Eretz Yisrael.

Because of Moshe's love of the *mitzvos*, he was able to overcome the *gezera* that he would not enter into Eretz Yisrael, by starting off the chain of the practical observance of the מצות התלויות בארץ, which continues until today.

Miracles through water

It says in this week's *sedrah* (9.1)

שְׁמַע יִשְׂרָאֵל אַתָּה עֹבֵר הַיּוֹם אֶת הַיַּרְדֵּן לָבֹא לָרֶשֶׁת גּוֹיִם גְּדֹלִים וַעֲצֻמִים מִמֶּךָּ עָרִים גְּדֹלֹת וּבְצֻרֹת בַּשָּׁמָיִם. עַם גָּדוֹל וָרָם בְּנֵי עֲנָקִים אֲשֶׁר אַתָּה יָדַעְתָּ וְאַתָּה שָׁמַעְתָּ מִי יִתְיַצֵּב לִפְנֵי בְּנֵי עֲנָק.

Hear, O *benei yisrael*. You are about to cross the Yarden to go in and dispossess nations greater and more populous than you, great cities fortified to the sky. A people great and tall, sons of giants, of whom you know and you have heard it said, "Who can stand up to the children of the giants?"

The medrash (3.8) comments on this *passuk*

> שְׁמַע יִשְׂרָאֵל אַתָּה עֹבֵר הַיּוֹם אֶת הַיַּרְדֵּן, הלכה אדם מישראל ששותה מים לצמאו אומר ברוך שהכל נהיה בדברו רבי טרפון אמר בורא נפשות רבות וחסרונם.
>
> רבנן אמרי בא וראה כל הנסים שעשה הקב"ה לישראל לא עשאן אלא על המים כיצד עד שהן במצרים עשה להם נסים ביאור. אמר רבי יצחק היו המצריים וישראל הולכין לשתות מים מן הנהר המצרי שותה דם וישראל שותה מים וכשיצאו ישראל ממצרים לא עשה להם נסים אלא על המים מנין שנאמר (תהלים קי"ד, ג') הַיָּם רָאָה וַיָּנֹס.

מה ראה רבי נהוראי אמר שם המפורש ראה חקוק על המטה ונקרע, רבי נחמיה אמר כביכול ידו של הקב"ה ראה ונקרע שנאמר (שם ע"ז, י"ז) ראוך מים יחילו. באו למרה כשעלו מן הים והיו המים מרים עשה שם להם נסים מנין שנאמר (שמות ט"ו, כ"ה) ויורהו ה' עץ וגו'. בסלע עשה להם נסים במים מנין שנאמר (במדבר כ', ח') ודברתם אל הסלע וגו'. בבאר עשה להם ניסים ואמרו שירה שנאמר (שם כ"א, י"ז) אז ישיר ישראל. אמר להם משה הוו יודעין כל נסים שעשה לכם הקב"ה לא עשה אלא על המים ואף בשעה שתעברו את הירדן לירש את הארץ עתיד הוא לעשות לכם נסים במי הירדן

The *halachah* is that if one drinks water because they are thirsty, then they say the *berachah* of שהכל נהיה בדברו. Rabbi Tarfon says that they must say the *berachah* of בורא נפשות (for the *beracha* prior to drinking water. The ר"ן explains that Rabbi Tarfon's reasoning is that water was created before the ten utterances with which the world was created, therefore it is not possible to say that water came into being בדברו - through an utterance of Hashem.)

The *chachamim* said, "Come and see. All the *nissim* that Hashem performed for the *benei yisrael*, He only performed on the water... (The medrash lists the following *nissim* that were done with water; קריעת ים סוף, דם, making the water sweet in מרה, bringing water out from the rock, the Well of Miriam.)

Moshe said to them, 'You should know that all of the *nissim* that Hashem performed for you, He only did on water. So too when you cross the Yarden to inherit Eretz Yisrael, He will do *nissim* for you with the waters of the Yarden.'"

- What is the connection between saying the *berachah* of שהכל on water and Hashem performing *nissim* for the *benei yisrael* through water?

- Why did the *nes* that allowed the *benei yisrael* to enter Eretz Yisrael occur specifically through water?

- Why did the *benei yisrael* entering Eretz Yisrael through a *nes* that occurred through water allow them to dispossess nations mightier than them?

It would seem that we can explain as follows[44]:

The *passuk* says later in the sedrah (11.10-11)

כִּי הָאָרֶץ אֲשֶׁר אַתָּה בָא שָׁמָּה לְרִשְׁתָּהּ לֹא כְאֶרֶץ מִצְרַיִם הִוא אֲשֶׁר יְצָאתֶם מִשָּׁם אֲשֶׁר תִּזְרַע אֶת זַרְעֲךָ וְהִשְׁקִיתָ בְרַגְלְךָ כְּגַן הַיָּרָק. וְהָאָרֶץ אֲשֶׁר אַתֶּם עֹבְרִים שָׁמָּה לְרִשְׁתָּהּ אֶרֶץ הָרִים וּבְקָעֹת לִמְטַר הַשָּׁמַיִם תִּשְׁתֶּה מָּיִם.

For the land that you are about to enter and possess is not like the land of Mitzrayim from which you have come. There the grain you sowed had to be watered by your own labours, like a vegetable garden, but the land you are about to cross into and possess, a land of hills and valleys, that soaks up its water from the rains of the heavens.

---

[44] עיין מאמרי פחד יצחק, פסח, מאמר פ"ט

Rashi comments

לא כארץ מצרים היא: הא למדת שחברון יפה מצוען ומצרים משובחת מכל הארצות שנאמר (בראשית י"ג) כגן ה' כארץ מצרים וצוען שבח מצרים היא שהיתה מקום מלכות שכן הוא אומר (ישעיהו ל') כי היו בצוען שריו וחברון פסולתה של ארץ ישראל לכך הקצוה לקבורת מתים ואע"פ כן היא יפה מצוען

It is not like the land of *Mitzraim*: Thus you may learn that Chevron was a finer city than Tzoan. Now *Mitzraim* is superior to all other lands, for it is stated of it, (Bereishis 13:10) "Like the garden of Hashem, like the land of *Mitzraim*", and Tzoan was the best city in *Mitzrayim*, because it was the seat of royalty, as it says, (Yeshaya 30:4) "For in Tzoan were its princes." Chevron was the worst city in Canaan, and for this reason they set it apart for a place of burial, and yet it was finer than Tzoan.

It would seem difficult to understand how Eretz Yisrael was agriculturally superior to Mitzrayim, if Mitzrayim was better than all other lands. If so, it would seem that Eretz Yisrael was qualitatively superior to *Mitzraim*, rather than being superior in the quantity of its abundance.

Since the water of Eretz Yisrael comes directly from Hashem, through rain and dew, and is not provided by man's labour, the blessing that resides in Eretz Yisrael is an expression of the inherent *kedushah* with which Eretz Yisrael was created. Thus the fruits of Eretz Yisrael carry with them the pristine *berachah* of purity amongst abundance.

However, the nations that had waxed mighty in Canaan did not grow because of their connection to this *beracha* of *kedushah*, rather they brutishly served *avodah zarah* and the strength of their own hands. But it was exactly because of their strange and malformed growth that the *benei yisrael*, who did cleave to the natural *kedushah* of Eretz Yisrael as represented by its water, were able to replace them.

This is why the prelude to the *benei yisrael* displacing nations mightier than them, was their crossing through the waters of the Yarden in a miraculous manner.

When Hashem performed nissim for the *benei yisrael* through water, this indicated that the success of the *benei yisrael* would come through the fresh pristine *kedushah* inherent in the world that belongs to Hashem. And so too when we say a *berachah* on water, we continue the influence of these *nissim* of *berachah* that accompanied the creation of the nation of Hashem.

The protection of the Torah

It says at the beginning of this week's *sedrah* (11.26)

רְאֵה אָנֹכִי נֹתֵן לִפְנֵיכֶם הַיּוֹם בְּרָכָה וּקְלָלָה

See, this day I set before you blessing and curse.

The Da'as Zekeinim Mi'baalei Tosafos explains why the *passuk* uses the word "today" (היום), as follows:

בעולם הזה הם ברכה וקללה אבל לימות המשיח כלם ברכה

In *olam hazeh* they are a blessing and a curse, but when *mashiach* comes they will be entirely a blessing.

This explanation implies that the קללות (curses) will be turned into ברכות (blessings) when *mashiach* comes. However, since the *benei yisrael* will keep the Torah when *mashiach* comes, it would seem obvious that they will then receive only ברכות (blessings).

- What is the advantage of the curses becoming blessings, more so than simply receiving blessings?

It would seem we can understand as follows:

The gemara says in Yoma (54b):

אמר ריש לקיש בשעה שנכנסו נכרים להיכל ראו כרובים המעורין זה

בזה הוציאון לשוק ואמרו ישראל הללו שברכתן ברכה וקללתן קללה
יעסקו בדברים הללו מיד הזילום שנאמר (איכה א', ח') כל מכבדיה
הזילוה כי ראו ערותה

Reish Lakish said: When gentiles came to destroy the Beis *Ha'mikdash* and entered the *heichal*, they saw the *keruvim* embracing each other.

They brought them out to the marketplace and they said, "These people, whose blessing is a blessing and whose curse is a curse, should they be involved in such matters?"

Immediately they denigrated them, as the *passuk* says in Eichah (1.8), "All those who honoured her denigrated her, for they saw her nakedness."

The Maharsha asks a question on this gemara, based on the gemara in Bava Basra (99a):

רבי יוחנן ור' אלעזר חד אמר פניהם איש אל אחיו וחד אמר פניהם
לבית ולמ"ד פניהם איש אל אחיו הא כתיב (דברי הימים ב' ג', י"ג)
ופניהם לבית לא קשיא כאן בזמן שישראל עושין רצונו של מקום כאן
בזמן שאין ישראל עושין רצונו של מקום

The gemara asks: How were the *keruvim* standing? Rabbi Yochanan and Rabbi Elazar disagree about this. One says, "Their faces were turned one toward the other." And one says, "Their faces were turned toward the *heichal*."

The gemara asks: But according to the one who says that their faces were turned one toward the other, isn't it written:

"And their faces were toward the *heichal*" (Divrei Ha'yamim II 3:13)? How does he explain the meaning of this *passuk*?

The gemara answers: This is not difficult, as their faces miraculously changed directions in reflection of the people's relationship to Hashem. Here, when it states that the *keruvim* faced each other, it was when the people did the will of Hashem. There, the *passuk* that describes that the *keruvim* faced the *heichal* and not toward each other, was when the people did not do the will of Hashem.

If the *keruvim* faced away from each other when the people did not do the will of Hashem, then at the time of the destruction of the *beis ha'mikdash*, when the people did not do the will of Hashem, it would appear the *keruvim* should have faced away from each other.

It would appear from this gemara that at the time of the destruction of the *beis ha'mikdash*, the *keruvim* embraced each other because Hashem was preparing the *benei yisrael* for *galus*, in which Hashem's love for the *benei yisrael* would express itself in a different manner than the way it was expressed in the time of the *beis ha'mikdash*. So that whereas during the time of the *beis ha'mikdash* the love of Hashem for the *benei yisrael* was evident in the physical structure of the *beis ha'mikdash*, afterwards this love was hidden within the words of the Torah.

The *aron ha'kodesh* represents the Torah, because the *luchos* were placed in the *aron ha'kodesh*, as the *passuk* says (Shemos 25.21):

וְנָתַתָּ אֶת הַכַּפֹּרֶת עַל הָאָרֹן מִלְמָעְלָה וְאֶל הָאָרֹן תִּתֵּן אֶת הָעֵדֻת אֲשֶׁר אֶתֵּן אֵלֶיךָ

Place the cover on top of the *aron*, and in the aron you should place the *luchos* of the covenant that ƒ will give you.

And it was within the words of the Torah that the closeness between Hashem and the *benei yisrael* was hidden after the destruction of the *beis ha'mikdash*, as the gemara says in Berachos (8a)

מיום שחרב בית המקדש אין לו להקב"ה בעולמו אלא ארבע אמות של הלכה בלבד

> From the day that the *beis ha'mikdash* was destroyed, Hashem has nothing else in His world other than the four *amos* of *halacha*.

Thus the *keruvim* embraced each other to show that although the physical structure that housed them was being destroyed, the love of Hashem for the *benei yisrael* that they represented, would endure within the Torah.

Since the closeness of Hashem to the *benei yisrael* was now contained within the words of the Torah, it would be impossible for any words to cause harm to the *benei yisrael*, so long as they cleaved to the Torah.

This means to say, because the *benei yisrael* would seek to understand what was happening to them in the light of the Torah and according to the understanding bequeathed to them by the

Torah, any words that would now be directed against the *benei yisrael* would be deflected by the love of Hashem that lies within the Torah and transformed into a deeper understanding of the Torah itself.

Furthermore, just as the love of Hashem represented in the physical structure of the *beis ha'mikdash* was transmuted into words of Torah when the *beis ha'mikdash* was destroyed, so too will the love of Hashem represented in the words of the Torah be transmuted into physical blessings in Eretz Yisrael with the arrival of *mashiach*.

And since the Torah will have served as the vehicle that absorbed the curses served to the *benei yisrael* in *galus* and will have transformed these curses into a deeper understanding of the Torah, all the words of those curses will be reassembled into new blessing, in Eretz Yisrael.

Shoftim

Judging truthfully

It says at the beginning of this week's *sedrah* (16.18)

> שֹׁפְטִים וְשֹׁטְרִים תִּתֶּן לְךָ בְּכָל שְׁעָרֶיךָ אֲשֶׁר ה' אֱלֹקֶיךָ נֹתֵן לְךָ לִשְׁבָטֶיךָ וְשָׁפְטוּ אֶת הָעָם מִשְׁפַּט צֶדֶק

You shall appoint judges and officers in all your cities that Hashem gives you for your *shevatim*, and they shall judge the people with righteous justice.

The medrash comments on this *passuk*

> הלכה, קרובו של אדם מהו שיהא מותר לו לישב בדינו? כך שנו חכמים, אלו הן הקרובים, אביו ואחיו ואחי אביו ואחי אמו וכו'. למה כן? אלא כשם שהקרוב פסול להעיד כן הוא פסול לדון. ומה ראית לומר כן? אמר רבי שמעון בן יוחאי כתיב (דברים כ"א) ונגשו הכהנים בני לוי כי בם בחר ה' אלקיך לשרתו ולברך בשם ה' ועל פיהם יהיה כל ריב וכל נגע. בא וראה, הקיש נגעים לריבים וריבים לנגעים. מה נגעים ביום אף דינים ביום, ומה ריבים פרט לקרוב אף נגעים פרט לקרוב.

Is it permissible for someone's relative to preside as a judge over his court-case? The *chachamim* have taught, "These are considered close relatives: His father, his brother, his paternal uncle, his maternal uncle etc." To what effect? [This comes to tell you that] just as a relative may not testify, so too he may not judge."

And what caused you to make this statement?

Rabbi Shimon bar Yochai said, "The *passuk* says (Devarim 21.5)

וְנִגְּשׁוּ הַכֹּהֲנִים בְּנֵי לֵוִי כִּי בָם בָּחַר ה' אֱלֹקֶיךָ לְשָׁרְתוֹ וּלְבָרֵךְ בְּשֵׁם ה' וְעַל פִּיהֶם יִהְיֶה כָּל רִיב וְכָל נָגַע

The *cohanim*, the sons of Levi, shall draw close, for Hashem has chosen them to serve Him and to bless in the name of Hashem, and every lawsuit and case of *tzara'as* is subject to their ruling.

> You see that the *passuk* compares lawsuits to *tzara'as* and *tzara'as* to lawsuits. [From this we may learn that] just as *tzara'as* can only be examined by daylight, so too may lawsuits only be judged by day. And just as lawsuits may not be judged by a relative so too cases of *tzara'as* may not be examined by a relative.

- Why does the medrash discuss relatives being *passul* to judge, on this *passuk*?

- Why does the medrash bring the *halachah* of a relative not inspecting *tzara'as*, if it was only trying to prove that a relative may not judge?

The source that relatives cannot judge appears in the Yerushalmi (Sanhedrin 3.9) which says

[לֹא יוּמְתוּ אָבוֹת עַל בָּנִים וּבָנִים לֹא יוּמְתוּ עַל אָבוֹת אִישׁ בְּחֶטְאוֹ יוּמָתוּ.] לֹא יומתו אבות על בנים למה לי? והלא כבר נאמר איש בחטאו יומתו? אלא שלא יהיו העדים קרובים לבעלי הדין. ומנין אף הדיינים? שנאמר ובנים לא יומתו על אבות.

[The *passuk* says (Devarim 24.16), "Parents shall not be put to death for children, nor children be put to death for parents: a person shall be put to death only for his own crime."]

Why does the *passuk* have to say, "Fathers should not die through their sons"? Does it not already state, "Each man should die through his own sin?" Rather this comes to teach you that the witnesses should not be close relatives to the litigants. And how do we know that the same applies for the *dayanim*? Because the *passuk* says, "And sons should not die through their fathers."

- It is evident from the Yerushalmi that the reason that a relative may not judge is because the *passuk* compares judging to *edus*. If so, why does the medrash not bring this *hekesh*?

It would seem we can explain as follows[45]:

The *passuk* says at Matan Torah (Shemos 20.14)

---

45 עיין בספר כסף נבחר

וְכָל הָעָם רֹאִים אֶת הַקּוֹלֹת וְאֶת הַלַּפִּידִם וְאֵת קוֹל הַשֹּׁפָר וְאֶת הָהָר עָשֵׁן וַיַּרְא הָעָם וַיָּנֻעוּ וַיַּעַמְדוּ מֵרָחֹק

And all the people saw the thunder and the lightning, the sound of the shofar and the mountain smoking. And when the people saw this, they fell back and stood at a distance.

Rashi comments on this *passuk*

רואים את הקולות: רואין את הנשמע שאי אפשר לראות במקום אחר

They saw that which is normally heard (the thunder), which is normally impossible.

What does Rashi mean that they saw that which is normally heard?

The mishna says in Negaim (3.1)

הַכֹּל כְּשֵׁרִים לִרְאוֹת אֶת הַנְּגָעִים, אֶלָּא שֶׁהַטֻּמְאָה וְהַטָּהֳרָה בִּידֵי כֹהֵן. אוֹמְרִים לוֹ אֱמֹר טָמֵא, וְהוּא אוֹמֵר טָמֵא. אֱמֹר טָהוֹר, וְהוּא אוֹמֵר טָהוֹר.

All are qualified to inspect *negaim*, but only a *cohen* may declare them unclean or clean. [A cohen who is an *am ha'aretz* is told by a *talmid chacham*, "Say, 'Unclean,'" and he repeats "Unclean." Or [he is told] "Say, 'Clean,'" and he repeats "Clean."

Since the *passuk* says (Vayikra 13.12) לְכָל מַרְאֵה עֵינֵי הַכֹּהֵן, "according to the sight of the *cohen*," only a *cohen* who has sighted the *tzara'as*, may pronounce the *tzara'as* as *tahor* or *tameh*. If the *cohen* does not know the *halacha*, then a *talmid chacham* tells him whether to say טמא or טהור. The statement of the *talmid chacham* has no effect, however.

It is evident from this mishna, that the *halachos* of דיני ממונות and the *halachos* of determining *tzara'as* as *tameh* or *tahor*, are fundamentally different. Deciding דיני ממונות depends on the חכמה of the דיין who must work out the *halachah*. However deciding the status of *tzara'as* depends on how the *cohen* sees the *tzara'as*. If it appears to him to be *tameh* then he pronounces it *tameh* and it becomes *tameh*. If it appears to him to be *tahor* then he pronounces it *tahor* and it becomes *tahor*.

If so, it is noteworthy that Rabbi Shimon bar Yochai learns the *halachos* of determining דיני ממונות and determining *tzara'as* from each other. For example, Rabbi Shimon bar Yochai says, "Just as *tzara'as* can only be examined by daylight, so too may lawsuits only be judged by day." This is apparently no comparison. *Tzara'as* can only be examined by day because the status of the *tzara'as* depends on the way that the *cohen* sees it, and the *cohen* will see the *tzara'as* differently by day than by night. However the *pesak* in דיני ממונות depends on the determination of the דיין in the application of the *halacha*, which apparently is not affected by day or night.

Subsequently, it would seem that we must understand the statement of Rabbi Shimon bar Yochai as follows:

Just as regarding *tzara'as* the *halacha* depends on the inspection of the *cohen*, so too with דיני ממונות, even though this is primarily decided according to the חכמה of the דיין, nevertheless there is an aspect of deciding דיני ממונות which is similar to deciding cases of *tzara'as*, and which therefore depends on the sighting of the דיין. Therefore דיני ממונות must be decided by day, when things look clearer, and when the דיין is able to perceive everything that is happening by the light of day, in order to gain a general comprehension of what is going on between the litigants.

In this way, the דיין sees that which is normally heard.

Similarly, Rabbi Shimon bar Yochai says, "And just as lawsuits may not be judged by a relative so too cases of *tzara'as* may not be examined by a relative." It is obvious why a lawsuit may not be judged by a relative, because his thinking will be warped in favour of his relation.

But it is not so obvious why *tzara'as* may not be inspected by a *cohen* who is a relative. Surely it is not possible for the *cohen* to persuade himself that the *tzara'as* looks different to that which it actually does, just because the person who has the *tzara'as* is related to him?

We see from this statement of Rabbi Shimon bar Yochai that even regarding *tzara'as* which is visually inspected, it is possible for the *cohen* to think differently concerning that which he sees, because of his subjectiveness.

Therefore the Torah warns the *cohen* to be honest concerning what he sees, and to pronounce the status of the *tzara'as* correctly. We derive this *halachah* from דיני ממונות. Therefore it is evident that that which a relative is *passul* to judge דיני ממונות is not because he will necessarily think incorrectly, but rather it is because he will see the whole situation incorrectly.

The Torah warns the דיין to be understanding and see the overall situation correctly, before he comes to examine the minute details of the case. In this way the דיין hears (in order to gain understanding), that which is normally seen (the general situation).

When the medrash learns that a relative is *passul* to be a judge, the medrash means that this is because, as a judge, the relative may be able to think straightly and correctly, but they will not be able to be רואין את הנשמע ושומעין את הנראה, "See that which is heard, and hear that which is seen."

By making the comparison to the *halachos* of inspecting *tzara'as*, the medrash teaches us that the reason for the *halachah* (derived in the Yerushalmi) that relatives may not judge, is because a דיין must be able to reach the clarity of thought and vision that the *benei yisrael* reached at Har Sinai, which will not be possible for him to do if he relies solely on his ability to work out the *halacha*.

And that is why the medrash quotes this *halacha* on the *passuk* that instructs the *benei yisrael* to appoint דיינים.

One *mitzva* leads to another *mitzva*

It says in this week's *sedrah* (22.6-7)

כִּי יִקָּרֵא קַן צִפּוֹר לְפָנֶיךָ בַּדֶּרֶךְ בְּכָל עֵץ אוֹ עַל הָאָרֶץ אֶפְרֹחִים אוֹ בֵיצִים וְהָאֵם רֹבֶצֶת עַל הָאֶפְרֹחִים אוֹ עַל הַבֵּיצִים לֹא תִקַּח הָאֵם עַל הַבָּנִים. שַׁלֵּחַ תְּשַׁלַּח אֶת הָאֵם וְאֶת הַבָּנִים תִּקַּח לָךְ לְמַעַן יִיטַב לָךְ וְהַאֲרַכְתָּ יָמִים.

If, along the road, you chance upon a bird's nest, in any tree or on the ground, with fledglings or eggs and the mother sitting over the fledglings or on the eggs, do not take the mother together with her young. Let the mother go, and take only the young, in order that it will be good for you and you will have long life.

The Medrash Tanchuma comments as follows

שנו רבותינו, מצוה גוררת מצוה ועבירה גוררת עבירה.

וראית בשביה וגו' מה כתיב בתריה? כי תהיין לאיש שתי נשים וגו'. שתים בבית – מריבה בבית, ולא עוד, אחת אהובה ואחת שנואה, או שתיהן שנואות. מה כתיב אחריו? כי יהיה לאיש בן סורר ומורה. כל מאן דנסיב יפת תאר – נפיק מינייהו בן סורר ומורה...

ומצוה גוררת מצוה, מנין? דכתיב כי יקרא קן צפור לפניך שלח תשלח

וגו' למען ייטב לך והארכת ימים. אחריו מה כתיב? כי תבנה בית חדש, תזכה לבנות בית חדש ולעשות מעקה. מה כתיב אחריו? לא תזרע כרמך כלאים, תזכה לכרם ולזרוע שדה. מה כתיב אחריו? לא תחרוש בשור ובחמור, תזכה לשווריםוחמורים. מה כתיב אחריו? לא תלבש שעטנז, תזכה לבגדים נאים מן צמר ולבגדים נאים מפשתים. מה כתיב אחריו? גדילים תעשה לך, תזכה למצות ציצית. מה כתיב אחריו? כי יקח איש אשה, תזכה לאשה ולבנים. הרי למדנו שמצוה גוררת מצוה ועבירה גוררת עבירה, לפיכך נסמכו פרשיות אלו זו לזו.

We have learnt, "One *mitzva* draws another *mitzva* in its wake, and one *aveirah* draws another *aveirah* in its wake."

"And you see in the captives etc.," what does it say after that? When there will be to a man two wives. When there are two in the house there is argument in the house, and not only that but, "One who is loved and one who is hated," or maybe both will be hated. What does it say after that? When there will be to a man a wayward and rebellious son. Anyone who marries a יפת תואר will have a son who is a בן סורר ומורה.

How do we know that one *mitzva* draws another *mitzva* after it? Because it says, "When you find a bird's nest you shall send away the mother etc. in order that it should be good for you and you should have a long life." What does it say next? "When you build a new house, you will merit to build a new house and make a parapet." What does it say after that? "You shall not sow your vineyard with כלאים, you will merit a vineyard and to sow a field." What does it say after that? "You should not plough with an ox and a donkey." You will merit oxen and donkeys. What does it say after that, "You should not wear שעטנז." You will merit nice clothes of wool and nice clothes of flax. What does it say after that? "You should make threads." You will merit the mitzva of ציצית. What does it say after that? "When a man takes a wife, you will merit a wife and children.

So we learn from here that one *mitzva* draws after it another *mitzva*, and one *aveirah* draws after it another *aveirah*. Therefore these two *parshiyos* are juxtaposed."

- What is the connection between the *mitzva* of שילוח הקן specifically and the *mitzvos* that are drawn after it?

It would seem that we can explain as follows:

The Medrash Rabbah says

מהו שלח תשלח את האם? אם קיימת מצווה זו, את ממהר לבוא מלך המשיח שכתוב בו: שילוח. מנין? שנאמר (ישעיה ל"ב) משלחי רגל השור והחמור. דבר אחר, אמר ר' תנחומא, אם קיימת המצווה הזאת, אתה ממהר את אליהו הנביא זכור לטוב שיבוא, שכתוב בו שילוח, שנאמר (מלאכי ג') הנה אנכי שולח לכם את אליהו הנביא והוא יבא וינחם אתכם. מנין? שנאמר (שם) והשיב לב אבות על בנים.

Why does the *passuk* use the double expression of שלח תשלח? If you observed this *mitzva*, you speed the arrival of *mashiach* concerning whom the *passuk* uses the term שילוח... Another explanation... if you observed this *mitzva*, you speed the arrival of Eliyahu ha'navi, concerning whom the *passuk* uses the term שילוח, as it says, "Behold I will send to you Eliyahu ha'navi," and he will come and comfort you...

As a reward for a person sending the mother bird out of his grasp, Hashem will send to the *benei yisrael* those things (*mashiach* and Eliyahu ha'navi) which are currently outside of their grasp.

Similarly, if a person performs the mitzva of שילוח הקן and thereby develops the ability to not own the things in his possession in a grasping manner, then Hashem will bestow bounty on him, because despite his pecuniary gains, he will not create his own realm, devoid of Hashem, but will rather consider himself the caretaker of that which he has been granted by Hashem.

The first thing which a person tends to make into his own domain, is his own house. Therefore, as a reward for performing the *mitzva* of שילוח הקן, the first thing that a person is granted is a house, which he will not consider his own domain, but will instead consider a place in which he may serve Hashem.

The second thing a person tends to consider as comprising his own domain is his fields, therefore this is the next thing Hashem will give him, wherein he can perform the מצות התלויות בארץ. Additionally Hashem will give him the wherewithal to plough these fields. The next thing a person acquires which makes him feel that he is master of his own domain is nice, honourable clothes. So this is the next thing that Hashem will give to a person who is able to own the possessions and influence granted to him by Hashem, in a selfless manner.

Finally Hashem will grant such a person a wife and a family, because even that he will not consider his own domain, but simply as a vehicle in which to further his *avodas Hashem*.

In this way, we can understand that the progression that starts with the *mitzva* of שילוח הקן is the opposite of that which occurs when a person marries a אשת יפת תואר. When someone marries an אשת יפת תואר, he does so for himself, and therefore the house that he thereby builds will ultimately exclude anyone but himself. Therefore the corollary will be: "One who is loved and one who is hated," "Or maybe both will be hated," and, "A wayward and rebellious son."

When an *aveirah* draws in its wake another *aveirah*, the person's domain becomes more and more exclusive. However, when a *mitzvah* draws in its wake another *mitzvah*, the person's domain becomes more and more elevated and inclusive, and hastens the coming of *mashiach* and Eliyahu *ha'navi*.

The holiness of *bikkurim*

It says at the beginning of this week's *sedrah* (26.1-2)

וְהָיָה כִּי תָבוֹא אֶל הָאָרֶץ אֲשֶׁר ה' אֱלֹקֶיךָ נֹתֵן לְךָ נַחֲלָה וִירִשְׁתָּהּ וְיָשַׁבְתָּ בָּהּ. וְלָקַחְתָּ מֵרֵאשִׁית כָּל פְּרִי הָאֲדָמָה אֲשֶׁר תָּבִיא מֵאַרְצְךָ אֲשֶׁר ה' אֱלֹקֶיךָ נֹתֵן לָךְ וְשַׂמְתָּ בַטֶּנֶא וְהָלַכְתָּ אֶל הַמָּקוֹם אֲשֶׁר יִבְחַר ה' אֱלֹקֶיךָ לְשַׁכֵּן שְׁמוֹ שָׁם.

When you enter the land that Hashem is giving you as an inheritance, and you possess it and settle in it. You shall take some of every first fruit of the soil, which you harvest from the land that Hashem is giving you, put it in a basket and go to the place where Hashem will choose to rest His name.

- Since *bikkurim* is only brought from the *shivas ha'minim*, and since most of the *shivas ha'minim* are fruit, why does the *passuk* only refer to פְּרִי הָאֲדָמָה and not also to פְּרִי הָעֵץ?

Rashi comments on this *passuk* as follows

והיה כי תבוא וגו' וירשתה וישבת בה: מגיד שלא נתחייבו בבכורים עד שכבשו את הארץ וחלקוה

When you enter the land etc.... and you possess it and you

settle in it. This teaches you that they were not obliged to bring *bikkurim* until they conquered and divided the land.

However, the Sifri says

> והיה כי תבוא אל הארץ. עשה מצוה האמורה בענין, שבשכרה תכנס לארץ.

> Do the *mitzva* that is stated in the section because in its merit you will enter the land.

- If the *benei yisrael* were only obliged to bring *bikkurim* after they had conquered and divided Eretz Yisrael, how could they enter the land in the merit of this *mitzva*?

The *sedrah* continues (26.11)

> וְשָׂמַחְתָּ בְכָל הַטּוֹב אֲשֶׁר נָתַן לְךָ ה' אֱלֹקֶיךָ וּלְבֵיתֶךָ אַתָּה וְהַלֵּוִי וְהַגֵּר אֲשֶׁר בְּקִרְבֶּךָ

And you shall rejoice in all the good that Hashem has given to you and to your household, together with the Levi and the *ger* who is in your midst.

Based on this *passuk*, the mishna says in Bikkurim (1.6)

> מֵעֲצֶרֶת וְעַד הֶחָג, מֵבִיא וְקוֹרֵא. מִן הֶחָג וְעַד חֲנֻכָּה, מֵבִיא וְאֵינוֹ קוֹרֵא

From Shavuos till Succos, one may both bring *bikkurim* and read the *parshah* of *bikkurim*. From Succos till Chanukah, one may bring *bikkurim* but not read the *parshah* of *bikkurim*.

The Bartenura explains

> דכתיב בפרשת ביכורים (דברים כ"ו) ושמחת בכל הטוב, אין קריאה אלא בזמן שמחה, מעצרת ועד החג, שאדם מלקט תבואתו ופירותיו ושמח בהם.

Since it says in the *passuk*, "And you shall rejoice in all the good," you see that you may only read the *parshah* of Bikkurim at the time of rejoicing when one harvests his grain and fruit and rejoices in them.

However the Medrash Tanchuma (Re'eh 11) comments on this *passuk*

> רבי יהושע דסכנין בשם רבי לוי אמר בזכות שני דברים ישראל מתחטאין לפני המקום בזכות שבת ובזכות מעשרות... דכתיב ושמחת בכל הטוב אשר נתן לך ה' אלהיך (דברים כ"ו י"א) ואין טוב אלא תורה, שנאמר כי לקח טוב נתתי לכם וגו' (משלי ד' ב')

Rabbi Yehoshua from Sichnin said in the name of Rabbi Levi, "In the merit of two things the *benei yisrael* are purified before Hashem. In the merit of Shabbos... and in the merit of *ma'aser* as it says, "And you shall rejoice in all the good that Hashem has given you." And there is no good save Torah, as the *passuk* says, "For a goodly portion I have given to you."

- It would appear difficult to understand the basis for the medrash. Since the ordinary *peshat* is that the *passuk* comes to say that you can only read the *parshah* of *bikkurim* between Shavuos and Succos, why does the medrash say that the *passuk* refers to rejoicing in the good of the Torah?

It would seem that we can explain as follows[46]:

The *passuk* says in Melachim (מלכים א', ז' נ"א), regarding the completion of the *beis ha'mikdash*

וַתִּשְׁלַם כָּל הַמְּלָאכָה אֲשֶׁר עָשָׂה הַמֶּלֶךְ שְׁלֹמֹה בֵּית ה' וַיָּבֵא שְׁלֹמֹה אֶת קָדְשֵׁי דָּוִד אָבִיו אֶת הַכֶּסֶף וְאֶת הַזָּהָב וְאֶת הַכֵּלִים נָתַן בְּאֹצְרוֹת בֵּית ה'

When all the work that King Shlomo had done in the House of Hashem was completed, Shlomo brought in the holy donations of his father David, the silver, the gold, and the vessels, and he deposited them in the treasury of the House of Hashem.

The Pesikta comments (ו', ו')

ד"א (מלכים א' ז') וַתִּשְׁלַם כָּל הַמְּלָאכָה [אֲשֶׁר עָשָׂה הַמֶּלֶךְ שְׁלֹמֹה בֵּית ה'] המלאכה אין כתיב כאן אלא כל המלאכה. מלאכת ששת ימי בראשית (בראשית ב') [וַיְבָרֶךְ אֱלֹקִים אֶת יוֹם הַשְּׁבִיעִי וַיְקַדֵּשׁ אֹתוֹ כִּי בוֹ שָׁבַת] מִכָּל מְלַאכְתּוֹ אֲשֶׁר בָּרָא אֱלֹקִים לַעֲשׂוֹת, ועשה אין כתיב כאן אלא לעשות, עדיין יש מלאכה אחרת. כיון שבא שלמה ובנה בית המקדש אמר הקב"ה עכשיו שלמה מלאכת השמים וארץ, ותשלם כל המלאכה. לכך נקרא שלמה שהשלים הקב"ה מלאכת ששת ימי בראשית לתוך מעשי ידיו.

The *passuk* says "And all of the work was completed." The *passuk* does not just say "the work", rather it says "all of the

---

[46] עיין בספר כסף נבחר

work". This refers to the work of Hashem in creating the world. We find an allusion to this idea in Bereishis, where the *passuk* says, "And Hashem blessed the seventh day and He sanctified it, for on it He rested from all His work that Hashem created and made." The *passuk* does not actually say "and made" (ועשה), rather it says "to make" (לעשות), there was still more work to be done. Once Shlomo came and built the *beis ha'mikdash*, Hashem said, "Now the work of heaven and earth is completed."

Thus the *passuk* says, "And all of the work was completed." That is why he is called Shlomo, because Hashem completed (שלם) the work of creation through his hands.

It is evident from the Pesikta, that Eretz Yisrael was not fully imbued with the *kedushah* that is given to it by Hashem, until the completion of the *beis ha'mikdash*. If so, it would not have been possible to fully realise the complete meaning of the *passuk* אֲשֶׁר תָּבִיא מֵאַרְצְךָ אֲשֶׁר ה' אֱלֹקֶיךָ נֹתֵן לָךְ, "That you will bring from your [holy] land which Hashem gives to you," until the completion of the *beis ha'mikdash*. Seemingly, the joy of bringing *bikkurim* should also have been incomplete till then.

In order to answer this conundrum, the medrash explains that the words וְשָׂמַחְתָּ בְכָל הַטּוֹב, also refer to the Torah. By rejoicing in the Torah, the *benei yisrael* were able to elevate themselves above the current limitations of קדושת הארץ, and attach themselves to that קדושת הארץ which Eretz Yisrael was going to have when the *beis ha'mikdash* would be built. In this way they were able to experience the complete שמחה of bringing ביכורים immediately upon entering Eretz Yisrael.

Through keeping the *mitzva* of bringing *bikkurim* in this elevated manner, and by connecting themselves to the *kedushah* that is inherent in the soil of Eretz Yisrael, the *benei yisrael* were promised that they would eventually merit to complete their entry into the holiness of Eretz Yisrael, with the building of the *beis ha'mikdash* in the days of Shlomo Ha'melech.

Nitzavim

The covenant of Hashem

It says at the beginning of this week's sedrah (29.9-13)

אַתֶּם נִצָּבִים הַיּוֹם כֻּלְּכֶם לִפְנֵי ה' אֱלֹקֵיכֶם רָאשֵׁיכֶם שִׁבְטֵיכֶם זִקְנֵיכֶם וְשֹׁטְרֵיכֶם כֹּל אִישׁ יִשְׂרָאֵל. טַפְּכֶם נְשֵׁיכֶם וְגֵרְךָ אֲשֶׁר בְּקֶרֶב מַחֲנֶיךָ מֵחֹטֵב עֵצֶיךָ עַד שֹׁאֵב מֵימֶיךָ. לְעָבְרְךָ בִּבְרִית ה' אֱלֹקֶיךָ וּבְאָלָתוֹ אֲשֶׁר ה' אֱלֹקֶיךָ כֹּרֵת עִמְּךָ הַיּוֹם. לְמַעַן הָקִים אֹתְךָ הַיּוֹם לוֹ לְעָם וְהוּא יִהְיֶה לְּךָ לֵאלֹקִים כַּאֲשֶׁר דִּבֶּר לָךְ וְכַאֲשֶׁר נִשְׁבַּע לַאֲבֹתֶיךָ לְאַבְרָהָם לְיִצְחָק וּלְיַעֲקֹב.

You are standing this day, all of you, before Hashem your G-d, the heads of your tribes, your elders and your officers, all the men of the *benei yisrael.* Your children, your wives, even the stranger within your camp, from woodchopper to water drawer, to enter into the covenant of Hashem your G-d, which Hashem your G-d is concluding with you this day, with its dread oath, so that He may establish you this day as His people and be your G-d, as He promised you and as He swore to your fathers, Avraham, Yitzchak, and Yaacov.

The Medrash Tanchuma comments

זה שאמר הכתוב הפוך רשעים ואינם, ובית צדיקים יעמוד (משלי י"ב ז')

This is as the *passuk* says (Mishlei 12.7)

הָפוֹךְ רְשָׁעִים וְאֵינָם וּבֵית צַדִּיקִים יַעֲמֹד

Overturn the *reshaim* (wicked) and they are gone, but the house of the *tzaddikim* (righteous) will endure.

- Why does the *passuk* refer to the house of *tzaddikim*, but not to the house of *reshaim*?

The sedrah continues (29.17)

פֶּן יֵשׁ בָּכֶם אִישׁ אוֹ אִשָּׁה אוֹ מִשְׁפָּחָה אוֹ שֵׁבֶט אֲשֶׁר לְבָבוֹ פֹנֶה הַיּוֹם מֵעִם ה' אֱלֹקֵינוּ לָלֶכֶת לַעֲבֹד אֶת אֱלֹקֵי הַגּוֹיִם הָהֵם פֶּן יֵשׁ בָּכֶם שֹׁרֶשׁ פֹּרֶה רֹאשׁ וְלַעֲנָה

Lest there is among you a man or a woman, or a family or a tribe, whose heart turns away today from Hashem our G-d to go and worship the gods of those nations, lest there is among you a root sprouting poison weed and wormwood.

Rashi explains:

אשר לבבו פונה היום: מלקבל עליו הברית

Whose heart turns away today: From accepting the covenant

- It would appear difficult to understand why Rashi explains that the *passuk* refers to someone who does not wish to accept the covenant at all. Maybe, the *passuk* refers to someone who was happy to accept the covenant, but nevertheless their heart would still stray after *avodah zarah*, as the *passuk* says אֲשֶׁר לְבָבוֹ פֹנֶה הַיּוֹם מֵעִם ה' אֱלֹקֵינוּ לָלֶכֶת לַעֲבֹד אֶת אֱלֹקֵי הַגּוֹיִם הָהֵם - "Whose heart turns away today from Hashem our G-d to go and worship the gods of those nations"?

The next *passuk* says (29.18)

וְהָיָה בְּשָׁמְעוֹ אֶת דִּבְרֵי הָאָלָה הַזֹּאת וְהִתְבָּרֵךְ בִּלְבָבוֹ לֵאמֹר שָׁלוֹם יִהְיֶה לִּי כִּי בִּשְׁרִרוּת לִבִּי אֵלֵךְ לְמַעַן סְפוֹת הָרָוָה אֶת הַצְּמֵאָה

And it will be when he hears the words of this dread oath and he will assure himself in his heart, saying, "Peace will be to me, though I follow the wilfulness of my heart," to add the drunkenness to the thirst.

Rashi explains

לְמַעַן סְפוֹת הָרָוָה: לפי שאוסיף לו פורענות על מה שעשה עד הנה בשוגג והייתי מעביר עליהם וגורם עתה שאצרפם עם המזיד ואפרע ממנו הכל

To add drunkenness [to the thirst]: In order that I may add punishment for him even for the sins he has committed until now inadvertently (for which the figurative expression is הרוה, drunkenness), and which I used to overlook, but now he causes Me to combine them with those committed with premeditation (for which the figurative expression is הצמאה – thirst, referring to those sins committed when sober) and to exact punishment from him for everything.

- Normally we have a rule that (Avodah Zara 3a) אין הקב"ה בא בטרוניא עם בריותיו, "Hashem does not judge his creations unreasonably." If so, why does the *passuk* say here that Hashem will give punishment for sins committed inadvertently as though they had been committed deliberately?

It would seem that we can explain as follows[47]:

The Yerushalmi says (Horayos, 3.5)

מה טעמא אַתֶּם נִצָּבִים הַיּוֹם כֻּלְּכֶם [לִפְנֵי ה' אֱלֹקֵיכֶם רָאשֵׁיכֶם שִׁבְטֵיכֶם זִקְנֵיכֶם וְשֹׁטְרֵיכֶם כֹּל אִישׁ יִשְׂרָאֵל] וכתיב וַיֶּאֱסֹף יְהוֹשֻׁעַ אֶת כָּל שִׁבְטֵי יִשְׂרָאֵל שְׁכֶמָה [וַיִּקְרָא לְזִקְנֵי יִשְׂרָאֵל וּלְרָאשָׁיו וּלְשֹׁפְטָיו וּלְשֹׁטְרָיו

---

[47] עיין בספר דברי יואל

וַיִּתְיַצְּבוּ לִפְנֵי הָאֱלֹקִים]. משה הקדים ראשים לזקינים יהושע הקדים זקינים לראשים וכו' ר' יהושע דסיכנן בשם רבי לוי משה ע"י שצפה ברוח הקודש שעתידין ישראל להסתכר במלכיות וראשיהן עומדין על גביהן הקדים ראשים לזקינים

Why is that Moshe put the heads of the tribes before the elders, as it says (Devarim 29.9), "You stand this day, all of you, before Hashem your G-d, the heads of your tribes, your elders." But Yehoshua put the elders before the heads of the tribes as it says (Yehoshua 24.1), "He summoned the elders of the *benei yisrael* and the heads of the tribes."

Rabbi Yehoshua of Sichnin said in the name of Rabbi Levy, "Moshe put the heads before the elders because he foresaw that the *benei yisrael* would be handed over into the hands of governments in *galus* and if their heads would not endeavour to represent the Jewish people favourable before the governments it would not be possible for the elders to sit and learn Torah. [Yehoshua, on the other hand, was talking to the generation that entered into Eretz Yisrael where the elders were at peace to be able to sit and learn Torah and therefore naturally came first.]"

It is evident from the Yerushalmi that when the *passuk* says אַתֶּם נִצָּבִים הַיּוֹם כֻּלְּכֶם – "You are standing this day, all of you," it does not mean that all of the *benei yisrael* happened to be standing together before Hashem. Rather it means that the *benei yisrael* can only stand before Hashem when every part of the *benei yisrael* assists all the others to stand before Hashem. Hence, when the *benei yisrael* will be in *galus*, the heads will enable the elders to stand before Hashem, and therefore they are placed first in the *passuk*.

That is why the Medrash Tanchuma quotes the *passuk* in Mishlei that says, "Overturn the *reshaim* (wicked) and they are gone, but the house of the *tzaddikim* (righteous) will endure." It is specifically because the *tzaddikim* form themselves into one united house that they stand before Hashem. And it is because the *reshaim* are never truly united into one house, but rather each one has his own best interests in mind, that they fall when tested.

The covenant into which the *benei yisrael* entered was that each would help the other to stand before Hashem. Subsequently, for one whose heart turns away from accepting the covenant, not only will they not help others stand before Hashem, but they will also not be aided by others to stand before Hashem.

Since it is only possible to stand before Hashem as a member of Hashem's *bris*, estrangement from the common willingness to assist and be assisted in one's service of Hashem, automatically implies that one's heart will wander after other gods. Hence Rashi explains that "whose heart turns," means, "Whose heart turns from accepting the covenant."

For such a person who abandons the *bris* to stand together before Hashem, the sins that they did inadvertently will in the end be considered as sins done deliberately.

Since it was only the surrounding aura of *avodas Hashem* that elevated that person to the level where at least their sins were inadvertent, once they abandon their allegiance to be part of assisting and being assisted in *avodas Hashem*, Hashem will consider all of their actions in the light of their not having been part of the *bris*, under which conditions their sin would indeed have been committed deliberately.

Vayelech

Moshe's legacy

It says in this week's *sedrah* (31.14)

וַיֹּאמֶר ה' אֶל מֹשֶׁה הֵן קָרְבוּ יָמֶיךָ לָמוּת קְרָא אֶת יְהוֹשֻׁעַ וְהִתְיַצְּבוּ בְּאֹהֶל מוֹעֵד וַאֲצַוֶּנּוּ וַיֵּלֶךְ מֹשֶׁה וִיהוֹשֻׁעַ וַיִּתְיַצְּבוּ בְּאֹהֶל מוֹעֵד

And Hashem said to Moshe, "The time is drawing near for you to die. Call Yehoshua and present yourselves in the Ohel Moed, that I may instruct him. Moshe and Yehoshua went and presented themselves in the Ohel Moed."

The Yalkut Shimoni (Devarim 31, 940) comments on this *passuk*

אמר רבי אייבו, אמר משה לפני הקב"ה, רבש"ע, בדבר שקלסתיך בתוך ששים רבוא מקדישי שמך, [שנאמר הן לה' אלקיך השמים וגו'] קנסת עלי מיתה, שנאמר הן קרבו ימיך למות, כל מדותיך מדה כנגד מדה שמא מדה רעה כנגד מדה טובה מדה חסרה כנגד מדה שלמה מדה צרה כנגד מדה טובה.

א"ל הקב"ה למשה, אף זו מדה טובה היא שאמרתי לך הן, שנאמר הנה אנכי שולח מלאך, הן צדיק בארץ ישולם, הנה אנכי שולח לכם את אליהו הנביא, כשם שהעלית אותי על ששים רבוא כך אני מעלה אותך לעתיד לבא על נ"ה צדיקים גמורים, שנאמר הן בגימטריא נ"ה

Rabbi Ayvu said, "Moshe said to Hashem, 'Master of the Universe, how is it that with the same word (הֵן) that I praised you in front of 600,000 people who sanctified Your name (as the *passuk* says (Devarim 10.14) הֵן לַה' אֱלֹקֶיךָ הַשָּׁמַיִם וּשְׁמֵי הַשָּׁמַיִם הָאָרֶץ וְכָל אֲשֶׁר בָּהּ), you decreed death on me, as the *passuk* says הֵן קָרְבוּ יָמֶיךָ לָמוּת?..

Hashem responded to Moshe, "That which I said to you the word הֵן, is also for your good, as the *passuk* says (Shemos 23.20), הִנֵּה אָנֹכִי שֹׁלֵחַ מַלְאָךְ לְפָנֶיךָ - "Behold I am sending an angel before you." And the *passuk* says (Mishlei 11.31), הֵן צַדִּיק בָּאָרֶץ יְשֻׁלָּם - "Behold even the righteous receive retribution on earth." And the *passuk* says (Malachi 3.23), הִנֵּה אָנֹכִי שֹׁלֵחַ לָכֶם אֵת אֵלִיָּה הַנָּבִיא - "Behold, I will send the prophet Eliyahu to you."

Just as you exalted me above 600,000, so too will I exalt you in the future over 55 perfect *tzadikim*. As the *passuk* says הֵן, and הֵן has the gematria of 55.

- In what way was Moshe comforted through the *passuk* of הִנֵּה אָנֹכִי שֹׁלֵחַ מַלְאָךְ לְפָנֶיךָ - "Behold I am sending an angel before you"?

Furthermore, Rashi (שמות כ"ג כ') comments on that *passuk* as follows:

> **הנה אנכי שולח מלאך**: כאן נתבשרו שעתידין לחטוא ושכינה אומרת להם (שמות ל"ג) כי לא אעלה בקרבך

> Here they were informed that they were going to sin and that the *shechinah* would have to tell them, "For I will not go up among you."

- Why was Moshe comforted with a *passuk* that foretold that the *benei yisrael* would sin?

Later in the *sedrah* it says (31.29)

> כִּי יָדַעְתִּי אַחֲרֵי מוֹתִי כִּי הַשְׁחֵת תַּשְׁחִתוּן וְסַרְתֶּם מִן הַדֶּרֶךְ אֲשֶׁר צִוִּיתִי אֶתְכֶם וְקָרָאת אֶתְכֶם הָרָעָה בְּאַחֲרִית הַיָּמִים כִּי תַעֲשׂוּ אֶת הָרַע בְּעֵינֵי ה' לְהַכְעִיסוֹ בְּמַעֲשֵׂה יְדֵיכֶם

> [Moshe said], "For I know that after my passing you will act wickedly and turn away from the path that I commanded you, and that in time to come misfortune will befall you for having done evil in the eyes of Hashem to anger him by the work of your hands."

Rashi comments

> **אחרי מותי כי השחת תשחיתון**: והרי כל ימות יהושוע לא השחיתו שנאמר ויעבדו ישראל את ה' כל ימי יהושוע מכאן שתלמידו של אדם חביב עליו כגופו כל זמן שיהושוע חי היה נראה למשה כאילו הוא חי

But you see that all the days of Yehoshua they did not become corrupt, for it states, (Shoftim 2:7) "And the people served Hashem all the days of Yehoshua"? Rather we derive from here that one's pupil is as dear to him as his own self. So long as Yehoshua was alive it appeared to Moshe it was as if he himself was alive.

- If Moshe meant that the *benei yisrael* were destined to sin after Yehoshua's lifetime, then why did he not say כִּי יָדַעְתִּי אַחֲרֵי מוֹת יְהוֹשֻׁעַ כִּי הַשְׁחֵת תַּשְׁחִתוּן – "For I know that after Yehoshua's passing you will act wickedly"?

It would seem that we can explain as follows:

The *sefer* Yismach Moshe (Mishpatim 22) explains that the word מלאך in the *passuk* of הִנֵּה אָנֹכִי שֹׁלֵחַ מַלְאָךְ does not mean an angel, instead it refers to either Moshe or Yehoshua. Had the *benei yisrael* not sinned, it would have referred to Moshe, once they did sin, it came to refer to Yehoshua.

הנה אנכי שולח מלאך (שמות כ"ג כ'). עיין באברבנאל שכתב בשם חכמי הקראים כי זה נאמר על יהושע וכו', מכל מקום נקבל את הטוב כי כמה מפרשים הלכו בדרך הזה שהנביא נקרא מלאך, עיין במעשה ה' (הובא להלן) וכו'.

והנה נאמר סתום, כי אם היו ישראל זוכים, היה קאי על משה, כי הכל נאמר למשה מילי ממסרי לשליח להגיד לעם ה', וכמו שאמרו רז"ל (ויק"ר א' א') וישלח מלאך ויוציאנו ממצרים (במדבר כ' ט"ז), זה משה, ואז היה קאי אל המקום אשר הכינותי, אל גן עדן כמ"ש בעשרה מאמרות, וכי שמי בקרבו, כי משה הוא השם א' מע"ב שמות.

The Abarbanel says that the word מלאך refers to Yehoshua, since we find that the word מלאך may refer to a *navi*... The *passuk* does not, however, explain which *navi* the word מלאך refers to. For had the *benei yisrael* been meritorious, then this word would have referred to Moshe, as we find that Moshe is described as a *malach* (Bamidbar 20.16), "And He sent a *malach* and he brought us out of *Mitzrayim*." [But since the *benei yisrael* sinned, the word *malach* came to refer to Yehoshua, who carried out the mission that had originally been given to Moshe.]

According to this explanation, we see from the *passuk* of הִנֵּה אָנֹכִי שֹׁלֵחַ מַלְאָךְ that Moshe's mission could be transparently handed over to Yehoshua. It made no difference to Moshe if he or Yehoshua would bring the *benei yisrael* into Eretz Yisrael, since both of them were simply acting as a *malach*, a messenger of Hashem. That is why one word, *malach*, could refer to either Moshe or Yehoshua, since they were synonymic purveyors of Hashem's word.

The reason that as long as Yehoshua was alive it was as if Moshe was alive is because the fiery motivation of Moshe's life, which was to bring the word of Hashem to the *benei yisrael*, burnt equally within Yehoshua. Therefore, as long as Yehoshua was alive, it was as if Moshe's spirit was still present.

Furthermore, כל זמן שיהושוע חי היה נראה למשה כאילו הוא חי - "As long as Yehoshua was alive it appeared to Moshe as if he was alive." There is no reason to think that it could only have been "as if Moshe was alive" during the lifetime of Yehoshua, so that we should say that it was inevitable that the *benei yisrael* would sin after the passing of Yehoshua. Rather it would seem that it is always possible to make it "as if Moshe is alive". So long as the passion to observe the word of Hashem burns equally brightly as it did when Moshe was alive, then it is as if Moshe is alive, and the *benei yisrael* will endure.

According to this explanation, when Moshe said כִּי יָדַעְתִּי אַחֲרֵי מוֹתִי כִּי הַשְׁחֵת תַּשְׁחִתוּן – "For I know that after my passing you will act wickedly," Moshe did not mean that the *benei yisrael* would inevitably sin after Yehoshua's passing. Rather he meant that if the *benei yisrael* would allow his message to fade so that it would be as if he was no longer alive, then they would be liable to fall into sin.

Thus Hashem said to Moshe, "That which I said to you the word הֵן, is also for your good, as the *passuk* says (Shemos 23.20), הִנֵּה אָנֹכִי שֹׁלֵחַ מַלְאָךְ לְפָנֶיךָ – "Behold I am sending an angel before you." And the *passuk* says (Mishlei 11.31), הֵן צַדִּיק בָּאָרֶץ יְשֻׁלָּם – "Behold even the righteous receive retribution on earth." And the *passuk* says (Malachi 3.23), הִנֵּה אָנֹכִי שֹׁלֵחַ לָכֶם אֵת אֵלִיָּה הַנָּבִיא – "Behold, I will send the prophet Eliyahu to you."

Meaning to say, do not be concerned that I have said הֵן קָרְבוּ יָמֶיךָ לָמוּת, "The time is drawing near for you to die," because it is exactly the presence of the spirit of your illuminated message to the *benei yisrael* that will preserve their integrity through all the ages, until the final bearer of your message, Eliyahu *ha'navi*, makes himself known to the *benei yisrael*.

Ha'azinu

The dedication of the *avos*

It says in this week's *sedrah* (32.10)

יִמְצָאֵהוּ בְּאֶרֶץ מִדְבָּר וּבְתֹהוּ יְלֵל יְשִׁמֹן יְסֹבְבֶנְהוּ יְבוֹנְנֵהוּ יִצְּרֶנְהוּ כְּאִישׁוֹן עֵינוֹ

He found him in a desert land, and in a wasteland, howling and desolate. He encircled him, watched over him, guarded him as the pupil of His eye.

The Sifri comments on this *passuk*

> ימצאהו בארץ מדבר, זה אברהם אבינו. משל למלך שיצא הוא וחיילותיו למדבר, הניחוהו חיילותיו במקום הצרות ובמקום הגייסות ובמקום ליסטות והלכו להם. נתמנה לו גבור אחד. אמר לו מלך אל יפול לבך עליך, ואל יהי עליך אימה של כלום, חייך שאיני מניחך עד שתיכנס לפלטורין שלך ותישן על מטתך, כענין שנאמר (בראשית ט"ו) ויאמר אליו אני ה' אשר הוצאתיך מאור כשדים...

> יצרנהו כאישון עינו, אפילו בקש המקום מאבינו אברהם גלגל עינו היה נותן לו. ולא גלגל עינו בלבד אלא אף נפשו הוא נותן לו, שחביבה עליו מן הכל שנאמר (בראשית כ"ב) ויאמר קח נא את בנך את יחידך אשר אהבת את יצחק, והלא בידוע שהוא בנו יחידו, אלא זו נפש שנקראת יחידה, שנאמר (תהלים כ"ב) הצילה מחרב נפשי מיד כלב יחידתי.

"He found him in a desert land," this refers to Avraham

Avinu. It is analogous to a king and his soldiers who went out to the wilderness, his soldiers abandoned him in a place of affliction, armed bands and robbers. A mighty warrior chanced upon him and said, "King, do not despair and fear naught. I swear not to leave you until you are able to return to your palace and sleep in your bed." Similarly, Hashem said to Avraham, "I am Hashem, who brought you out of Ur Kasdim…"

"He guarded Him like the apple of his eye". Even had Hashem asked Avraham Avinu for his eyeball, he would have given it to Him. And not his eyeball alone, but even his soul he gave to Him, that was dearer to him than anything else, as it says, "And He said, 'Please take your son, your only one, whom you love, Yitzchak." Is it not obvious that Yitzchak is his only son? Rather we understand that "your only one" refers to the soul, which is called "the only one" as it says in Tehillim (22:21) [that Esther said,] "Save my life from the sword; from the hand of the dog, יחידתי – my soul."

It is interesting to note that in Tanach, the following terms are used to refer to the soul – נפש, רוח, נשמה, חיה, יחידה. As the medrash says (Bereishis Rabbah, 14.9)

חמישה שמות נקראו לה: נפש, רוח, נשמה, חיה, יחידה

The soul is called by five names: *nephesh, ruach, neshama, chaya, yechidah.*

- If so, why does the *passuk* refer to the soul as יחידה, specifically, at the Akeidah?

It would seem we can explain as follows[48]:

The Sifri quotes the following *passuk* in Tehillim (22.21)

הַצִּילָה מֵחֶרֶב נַפְשִׁי מִיַּד כֶּלֶב יְחִידָתִי

Save my life from the sword; from the hand of the dog, יחידתי - my soul.

The gemara in Megillah (15b) explains that this *passuk* was said by Esther when she went to Achashverosh to plead for the life of the Jewish nation.

This *passuk* uses the word יחידה to refer to the soul. According to the *sefer* Etz Chaim (שער דרושי אבי"ע פרק א'), the יחידה is the highest part of the soul

יש ניצוץ קטן מאד שהוא בחי' אלקות נמשך ממדרגה האחרונה שבבורא, וזהו הניצוץ מתלבשת בכח ניצוץ אחד נברא . . הנקרא יחידה

There is a very small godly spark which comes from the lowest level that we can understand of Hashem, and this spark is clothed with the creation of life… and it is called the יחידה.

---

[48] עיין בספר גבול בנימין, חלק ג', דרוש ל'

According to this explanation, a difficulty arises in understanding the *passuk* in Tehillim. Since the יחידה is the highest part of the soul, from which other perspective did Esther say this *tefillah*? Or in other words, which other part of Esther could have referred to her own יחידה objectively, given that there is no other part of the soul that can exist independently of the יחידה.

To answer this question, it appears that we have to say that when Esther spoke of herself in her *tefillah* on approaching Achashverosh, she was not referring to the danger to her life, rather she was talking about her role in a historical perspective, and about the initial purpose of her creation.

That means to say, Esther was not worried about the possibility of her mission being a failure, rather she was concerned about the possibility of her mission being a success.

Esther had previously said to Mordechai (Megillas Esther 4.16)

לֵךְ כְּנוֹס אֶת כָּל הַיְּהוּדִים הַנִּמְצְאִים בְּשׁוּשָׁן וְצוּמוּ עָלַי וְאַל תֹּאכְלוּ וְאַל תִּשְׁתּוּ שְׁלֹשֶׁת יָמִים לַיְלָה וָיוֹם גַּם אֲנִי וְנַעֲרֹתַי אָצוּם כֵּן וּבְכֵן אָבוֹא אֶל הַמֶּלֶךְ אֲשֶׁר לֹא כַדָּת וְכַאֲשֶׁר אָבַדְתִּי אָבָדְתִּי

Go, assemble all the Jews who live in Shushan, and fast in my behalf; do not eat or drink for three days, night or day. I and my maidens will observe the same fast. Then I shall go to the king, though it is contrary to the law; and if I am to perish, I shall perish!"

The gemara in Megillah (15a) explains that Esther meant:

וכאשר אבדתי אבדתי כשם שאבדתי מבית אבא כך אובד ממך

[And Esther further said:] "And if I perish, I perish" (Esther 4:16). What she meant was: Just as I was lost to my father's house ever since I was brought here, so too, shall I be lost to you, for after I have entered voluntarily to Ahasuerus, I will become forbidden to you.[49]

Esther's role in being created was to be part of the Jewish people, and now if she went to Achashverosh willingly, she would become lost to the Jewish people altogether.

Her *tefillah* to Hashem therefore was from an objective perspective of her own creation, altogether. Esther asked Hashem that she should not lose her part in His plan for creation, although she would no longer be able to fulfill the role originally intended for her. This level of *tefillah* was at an even higher level than the יחידה, it was a *tefillah* from the perspective of Hashem's plan for the world and for her, before she was created at all.

Similarly, when Avraham was asked to bring Yitzchak as a *korban*, it could have seemed to him that his entire purpose of being was to be surrendered to Hashem as a part of this *korban*, seeing as he would now no longer have any children capable of continuing his message of *emunah* to the world.

---

[49] The gemara explains that Esther was Mordechai's wife. Until now, her forced marriage to Achashverosh did not cause her to become forbidden to Mordechai, since she had been coerced into becoming the queen. But now that she would enter into Achashverosh's chamber willingly, she would become forbidden to Mordechai.

The Sifri continues:

> ד"א ימצאהו בארץ מדבר, אלו ישראל, כענין שנאמר (הושע ט', י')
> כַּעֲנָבִים בַּמִּדְבָּר מָצָאתִי יִשְׂרָאֵל, ובתוהו ילל ישימון, במקום הצרות
> במקום הגייסות במקום ליסטות

> Alternatively, "He found them in a desert land," this refers to the *benei yisrael*, as it is written (Hoshea 9:10) "As grapes in the desert, I found the *benei yisrael*." "And in a wasteland, howling and desolate", in a place of afflictions, armed bands and robbers.

According to the alternative explanation of the Sifri, the *passuk* of יִמְצָאֵהוּ בְּאֶרֶץ מִדְבָּר refers to the *benei yisrael*. Hashem, as if it were, expresses surprise that He found the *benei yisrael* so pleasing and good, like a traveller who finds grapes in the desert.

Avraham was prepared to sacrifice the apple of his eye, meaning, everything that he perceived was meaningful to him, to Hashem. Even concerning his mission to bring the knowledge of Hashem to the world, he did not assume that that what was had to be, according to his own understanding.

Because he sacrificed himself in this manner, the purity and devotion that he achieved at the akeidah was able to jump through the passage of time, and be acquired directly by his descendants, the *benei yisrael*, when they came out of Mitzrayim.

Thus Hashem found the *benei yisrael* unsullied by their slavery and surprisingly good and pleasant, after He brought them out of Mitzrayim.

Ve'zos he' berachah

Finding Hashem in *galus*

It says in this week's *sedrah* (33.5)

וַיְהִי בִישֻׁרוּן מֶלֶךְ בְּהִתְאַסֵּף רָאשֵׁי עָם יַחַד שִׁבְטֵי יִשְׂרָאֵל

Then He became King in Yeshurun, when the heads of the people assembled, when the tribes of the *benei yisrael* are together.

The Sifri comments on this *passuk* as follows

יחד שבטי ישראל, כשהם עשוים אגודה אחת, ולא כשהם עשוים אגודות אגודות. וכן הוא אומר (עמוס ט') הבונה בשמים מעלותיו ואגדתו על ארץ יסדה. ר' שמעון בן יוחי אומר, משל לאדם שהביא שתי ספינות וקשרם בעוגגים ובעשתות, והעמידן על גביהם ובנה עליהם פלטירים. כל זמן שהספינות קשורות פלטורין קיימים. פרשו ספינות אין פלטורים קיימים. כך ישראל כשעושים רצונו של מקום עליותם בשמים. וכשאין עושים רצונו של מקום ואגודתו על ארץ יסדה.

"When the tribes of the *benei yisrael* are together." When they form one group, and not when they are split into different groups. And so too it says in the *passuk* in Amos, "Who built His chambers in heaven and founded the group of His people on the earth." Rabbi Shimon bar Yochai said, "It is analogous to a man who brought two ships and tied them together with anchors and iron bars, and then he placed a platform on top of the bars and he built a palace on top of the platforms. As long as the ships are tied together, the palace can survive. If the ships separate, then the palace will fall. So too is it with the *benei yisrael*, when they do the will of Hashem, then their chambers are in the heavens. And when they do not do the will of Hashem, then their groups can rise no higher than the earth."

- Why does the Sifri compare the *benei yisrael* to ships, that tend to naturally drift apart?

- Also, the Sifri starts by saying that the palace (representing a high *madregah* of the *benei yisrael*) can only survive when the benei *yisrael* come together. But then the Sifri concludes that the *benei yisrael* reach a high *madregah* simply by doing the will of Hashem. It would seem from this that it is only possible for the *benei yisrael* to do the will of Hashem when they all come together. Why is this so?

The *passuk* in Vayelech (31.16-18) says:

וַיֹּאמֶר ה' אֶל מֹשֶׁה הִנְּךָ שֹׁכֵב עִם אֲבֹתֶיךָ וְקָם הָעָם הַזֶּה וְזָנָה אַחֲרֵי אֱלֹהֵי נֵכַר הָאָרֶץ אֲשֶׁר הוּא בָא שָׁמָּה בְּקִרְבּוֹ וַעֲזָבַנִי וְהֵפֵר אֶת בְּרִיתִי אֲשֶׁר כָּרַתִּי אִתּוֹ. וְחָרָה אַפִּי בוֹ בַיּוֹם הַהוּא וַעֲזַבְתִּים וְהִסְתַּרְתִּי פָנַי מֵהֶם וְהָיָה לֶאֱכֹל וּמְצָאֻהוּ רָעוֹת רַבּוֹת וְצָרוֹת וְאָמַר בַּיּוֹם הַהוּא הֲלֹא עַל כִּי אֵין אֱלֹקַי בְּקִרְבִּי מְצָאוּנִי הָרָעוֹת הָאֵלֶּה. וְאָנֹכִי הַסְתֵּר אַסְתִּיר פָּנַי בַּיּוֹם הַהוּא עַל כָּל הָרָעָה אֲשֶׁר עָשָׂה כִּי פָנָה אֶל אֱלֹהִים אֲחֵרִים.

And Hashem said to Moshe, "Behold you are soon to lie with your fathers. This people will thereupon go astray after the alien gods in their midst, in the land that they are about to enter; they will forsake Me and break My covenant that I made with them. Then My anger will flare up against them, and I will abandon them and hide My countenance from them. They shall be ready prey, and many evils and troubles shall befall them. And they shall say on that day, "Surely it is because my G-d is not in my midst that these evils have befallen me." And I will surely hide My face on that day, because of all the evil they have done in turning to other gods.

It would seem difficult to understand why the *passuk* says וְאָנֹכִי הַסְתֵּר אַסְתִּיר פָּנַי – "And I will surely hide My face," after the *passuk* says וְאָמַר בַּיּוֹם הַהוּא הֲלֹא עַל כִּי אֵין אֱלֹקַי בְּקִרְבִּי מְצָאוּנִי הָרָעוֹת הָאֵלֶּה – "Surely it is because my G-d is not in my midst that these evils have befallen me."

- If the *benei yisrael* acknowledged that evil has befallen them because Hashem was not in their midst, then surely they are repentant, in which case Hashem should return His presence?

It would seem that we can explain as follows[50]:

The *passuk* in Ki Savo'u (Devarim 28.47) explains that the reason for *galus* is:

---

[50] עיין בספר אמרי נועם

תַּחַת אֲשֶׁר לֹא עָבַדְתָּ אֶת ה' אֱלֹקֶיךָ בְּשִׂמְחָה וּבְטוּב לֵבָב מֵרֹב כֹּל

Because you did not serve Hashem your G-d in joy and gladness from an abundance of everything.

It follows from this *passuk*, that in order to do complete *teshuvah*, the *benei yisrael* have to serve Hashem with joy in a situation of abundance, in *galus*[51]. If they turn to Hashem from a desperate situation, that does not rectify that which they turned away from Hashem despite their comforts. Therefore, when the *benei yisrael* say, "Surely it is because my G-d is not in my midst that these evils have befallen me," this is not a complete *teshuvah*.

Subsequently it would seem then that it should never be possible for the *benei yisrael* to do complete *teshuvah* in *galus*, because their situation in *galus* will never be as luxurious as it was in Eretz Yisrael.

This is why the *passuk* says

וְאָנֹכִי הַסְתֵּר אַסְתִּיר פָּנַי בַּיּוֹם הַהוּא

---

[51] See Rambam, Hilchos Teshuva (2.1)

> אֵי זוֹ הִיא תְּשׁוּבָה גְּמוּרָה. זֶה שֶׁבָּא לְיָדוֹ דָּבָר שֶׁעָבַר בּוֹ וְאֶפְשָׁר בְּיָדוֹ לַעֲשׂוֹתוֹ וּפֵרַשׁ וְלֹא עָשָׂה מִפְּנֵי הַתְּשׁוּבָה.
>
> What is complete repentance? He who once more had in it in his power to repeat a violation, but separated himself therefrom, and did not do it because of repentance, not out of fear or lack of strength.

It is evident from the Rambam that in order to do *teshuvah* it is necessary for the person to be presented with the same situation in which they sinned, and not sin.

And I will surely hide My face on that day.

The expression הַסְתֵּר אַסְתִּיר implies that there will be many different types of hiddenness of Hashem. This is because the *benei yisrael* will be spread amongst many nations, and in each place that they are, they will be treated well in one way but treated badly in a different way. In the way that the *benei yisrael* are treated well by one nation, they will be treated badly by another nation, and vice versa. (Thus there are many different hiddennesses, because the way in which the *benei yisrael* are treated badly is a hiddenness of Hashem.)

Subsequently, the *benei yisrael* in one country, will be able to do complete *teshuva* regarding the aspect in which they are treated well in that country, and the *benei yisrael* in a different country will be able to do complete *teshuva* regarding the aspect in which they are treated well in that country. Altogether, the joint *teshuvah* of the *benei yisrael* across the world will be one in which all the *mitzvos* are kept with gladness from amidst abundance.

In order for the teshuvah of the *benei yisrael* to be considered as a complete whole, the *benei yisrael* must unite and support each other, so that each group will be able to share their perfect level of *teshuva* that relates to the way in which they are treated well, with the rest of the *benei yisrael*. In this way, all will be on the *madregah* of keeping the entire Torah from a situation of abundance, and their *teshuvah* will be complete.

The *passuk* says at the beginning of Ve'zos Ha'berachah (Devarim 33.3)

אַף חֹבֵב עַמִּים כָּל קְדֹשָׁיו בְּיָדֶךָ וְהֵם תֻּכּוּ לְרַגְלֶךָ יִשָּׂא מִדַּבְּרֹתֶיךָ

Even when He loved the peoples, all his holy ones are in Your hand. And they followed in Your steps, accepting Your pronouncements.

Rashi comments

> דבר אחר, אף חובב עמים אף בשעת חיבתן של האומות שהראית להם פנים שוחקות ומסרת את ישראל בידם. כל קדושיו בידך: כל צדיקיהם וטוביהם דבקו בך ולא משו מאחריך ואתה שומרם

Another explanation: Even at the time that He shows love towards the nations and He hands the *benei yisrael* into their hands. Nevertheless, all His holy ones are in Your hands. This means that all of their *tzadikim* cleave to You and did not move away from you and You guard them.

According to this explanation, the *pessukim* at the beginning of Ve'zos Ha'berachah are talking about a time when the *benei yisrael* will be in *galus*.

If so, the Sifri that gives the *mashal* of the palace on the platform between the two ships is also talking about when the *benei yisrael* are in the sea of *galus*. Hence, we can understand why the Sifri implies that it is only possible for the *benei yisrael* to keep the Torah completely when they come together.

Since each section of the *benei yisrael* can only do complete *teshuvah* regarding the way in which they are treated well in their place in *galus*, it is only possible for the *benei yisrael* to keep the whole of the Torah when they are combined, since then each part of the *benei yisrael* can share the area in which they have achieved perfect *teshuvah*, with the rest of *klal yisrael*.

Without unity, the *benei yisrael* in *galus* will drift apart so that the palace[52] that seek to rebuild will fall into the sea, since each will excel in only one approach of *avodas Hashem*. But with unity, the *benei yisrael* can do complete *teshuvah* and merit the rebuilding of the *beis ha'mikdash* in Eretz Yisrael.

---

[52] Maybe for this reason the Sifri uses the analogy of a palace, since a palace represents luxuriousness and ease of living.

Simchas Torah

Completing the Torah

The *passuk* says in Melachim Alef (3.5 – 15)

בְּגִבְעוֹן נִרְאָה ה' אֶל שְׁלֹמֹה בַּחֲלוֹם הַלָּיְלָה וַיֹּאמֶר אֱלֹקִים שְׁאַל מָה אֶתֶּן לָךְ... וְנָתַתָּ לְעַבְדְּךָ לֵב שֹׁמֵעַ לִשְׁפֹּט אֶת עַמְּךָ לְהָבִין בֵּין טוֹב לְרָע כִּי מִי יוּכַל לִשְׁפֹּט אֶת עַמְּךָ הַכָּבֵד הַזֶּה. וַיִּיטַב הַדָּבָר בְּעֵינֵי ה' כִּי שָׁאַל שְׁלֹמֹה אֶת הַדָּבָר הַזֶּה.

וַיֹּאמֶר אֱלֹקִים אֵלָיו יַעַן אֲשֶׁר שָׁאַלְתָּ אֶת הַדָּבָר הַזֶּה... הִנֵּה עָשִׂיתִי כִּדְבָרֶיךָ הִנֵּה נָתַתִּי לְךָ לֵב חָכָם וְנָבוֹן אֲשֶׁר כָּמוֹךָ לֹא הָיָה לְפָנֶיךָ וְאַחֲרֶיךָ לֹא יָקוּם כָּמוֹךָ... וַיִּקַץ שְׁלֹמֹה וְהִנֵּה חֲלוֹם וַיָּבוֹא יְרוּשָׁלַם וַיַּעֲמֹד לִפְנֵי אֲרוֹן בְּרִית ה' וַיַּעַל עֹלוֹת וַיַּעַשׂ שְׁלָמִים וַיַּעַשׂ מִשְׁתֶּה לְכָל עֲבָדָיו.

Hashem appeared to Shlomo in Givon in a dream by night and Hashem said, "Ask, what shall I grant you?"

Shlomo said, "...Grant then, your servant, an understanding mind to judge your people, to distinguish between good and bad, for who can judge this vast people of yours?"

Hashem was pleased that Shlomo had asked for this and Hashem said to him, "Because you asked for this, you did not ask for long life, you did not ask for riches, you did not ask for the life of your enemies, but you asked for discernment in dispensing justice, I now do as you have spoken. I grant you a wise and discerning mind; there has never been anyone like you before, nor will anyone like you arise again…"

Then Shlomo awoke and behold it was a dream. He went to Yerushalayim, stood before the Aron of the Covenant of Hashem, and sacrificed *olos* and presented *shelamim* and he made a banquet for all his servants.

The medrash (Koheles Rabbah 1.1) comments on these *pessukim* as follows:

וַיֹּאמֶר אֱלֹקִים שְׁאַל מָה אֶתֶּן לָךְ, אָמַר שְׁלֹמֹה אִם אֲנִי שׁוֹאֵל כֶּסֶף וְזָהָב וּמַרְגָּלִיּוֹת הוּא נוֹתֵן לִי, אֶלָּא הֲרֵינִי שׁוֹאֵל אֶת הַחָכְמָה וְהַכֹּל בִּכְלָל... אָמַר לוֹ הַקָּדוֹשׁ בָּרוּךְ הוּא הַחָכְמָה שָׁאַלְתָּ וְלֹא שָׁאַלְתָּ לְךָ עֹשֶׁר וְכָבוֹד וְנֶפֶשׁ אוֹיְבֶיךָ, לְפִיכָךְ הַחָכְמָה וְהַמַּדָּע נָתוּן לָךְ, וְעַל יְדֵי כֵן גַּם עֹשֶׁר וּנְכָסִים וְכָבוֹד אֶתֶּן לָךְ, מִיָּד (מלכים א' ג', ט"ו) וַיִּקַץ שְׁלֹמֹה וְהִנֵּה חֲלוֹם. אָמַר רַבִּי יִצְחָק חֲלוֹם עוֹמֵד עַל כַּנּוֹ, צִפּוֹר מְצוֹיֵץ וְיוֹדֵעַ עַל מָה מְצוֹיֵץ, חֲמוֹר נוֹהֵק וְיוֹדֵעַ עַל מָה נוֹהֵק, מִיָּד (מלכים א' ג', ט"ו) וַיָּבוֹא יְרוּשָׁלַיִם וַיַּעֲמֹד לִפְנֵי [אֲרוֹן בְּרִית ה' וַיַּעַל עֹלוֹת וַיַּעַשׂ שְׁלָמִים] וַיַּעַשׂ מִשְׁתֶּה לְכָל עֲבָדָיו, אָמַר רַבִּי יִצְחָק מִכָּאן שֶׁעוֹשִׂין סְעוּדָה לִגְמָרָהּ שֶׁל תּוֹרָה.

And Hashem said, "Ask that which I should grant you." Shlomo said, "If I ask for silver and gold and pearls He will give them to me. But instead I will ask for wisdom and everything else is included. Hashem said to him, "You asked for wisdom and you did not ask for wealth and honour and the lives of your enemies, therefore wisdom and understanding is given to you, and thereby I will also give you wealth and belongings and honour."⁵³

Immediately, "And Shlomo woke up and behold it was a dream."

Rabbi Yitzchak said, "The dream was immediately proven to be true. When Shlomo heard a bird chirping, he now knew what it was saying. When he heard a donkey braying, he now knew what it was saying."

Immediately, "And Shlomo came to Yerushalayim and he stood before the Aron of the covenant of Hashem and he brought *olos* and he sacrificed *shelamim* and he made a banquet for all of this servants."

Said Rabbi Yitzchak, "From here we learn that we make a *seudah* when we complete [a section of] the Torah."

- There appears to be no hint in the *pessukim* that the *seudah* that Shlomo made was a *siyum* for the completion of the Torah. If so, why does the medrash say that one can see from here that there is an obligation to make a *siyum* on completion of the Torah?

---

⁵³ It is intriguing to note that in the list of things that Hashem praised Shlomo for not requesting, we find wealth, honour and the lives of Shlomo's enemies. However, the lives of his enemies was not one of the things that Hashem said He would give Shlomo anyway, "Therefore wisdom and understanding is given to you, and thereby I will also give you wealth and belongings and honour."

See subsequent footnote.

It would appear that we can explain as follows[54]:

We find two people in Tenach who were able to understand the language of dinkeys, Shlomo and Bilam.

However, the difference was that Shlomo was able to simultaneously understand the language of a donkey and also stand before the *Aron Ha'kodesh*. On the other hand, although Bilam was able to talk to his donkey, he also descended to its level (Bamidbar 22.30)

וַתֹּאמֶר הָאָתוֹן אֶל בִּלְעָם הֲלוֹא אָנֹכִי אֲתֹנְךָ אֲשֶׁר רָכַבְתָּ עָלַי מֵעוֹדְךָ עַד הַיּוֹם הַזֶּה הַהַסְכֵּן הִסְכַּנְתִּי לַעֲשׂוֹת לְךָ כֹּה וַיֹּאמֶר לֹא

The donkey said to Balaam, "Am I not the donkey that you have been riding all along until this day? Have I been in the habit of doing thus to you?" And he answered, "No."

The gemara comments (Avodah Zarah 4b)

(במדבר כ"ד, ט"ז) ויודע דעת עליון אפשר דעת בהמתו לא הוה ידע דעת עליון מי הוה ידע

---

[54] עיין בספר יד יוסף

מאי דעת בהמתו לא הוה ידע בעידנא דחזו ליה דהוה רכיב אחמריה אמרו ליה מאי טעמא לא רכבתא אסוסיא אמר להו ברטיבא שדאי ליה מיד ותאמר האתון הלא אנכי אתונך אמר לה לטעינא בעלמא אמרה ליה אשר רכבת עלי אמר לה אקראי בעלמא אמרה ליה מעודך ועד היום הזה ולא עוד אלא שאני עושה לך רכיבות ביום ואישות בלילה כתיב הכא ההסכן הסכנתי וכתיב התם (מלכים א' א', ב') ותהי לו סוכנת

"And knows the knowledge of the Most High" (Bamidbar 24:16). Now, this should not be understood to mean that Bilam knew the thoughts of Hashem, as is it possible that Bilam did not know the mind of his animal, and yet he did know the mind of the Hashem?

[What is meant by the statement that Bilam did not know the mind of his animal?] When the princes of Moav saw that Bilam was riding on his donkey, they said to him, "What is the reason that you do not ride upon a horse, which is more fitting for you?" Bilam said to them, "I am riding on a donkey because I left my horse in a meadow to graze." Immediately, "And the donkey said to Bilam, 'Am not I your donkey?'" This means, the donkey you always use. Bilam said to it, "For carrying burdens only, not for riding."

The donkey further said to Bilam, "Upon which you have ridden." Bilam said to it, "Merely at irregular occurrences." The donkey said to him, "All your life until this day". The donkey added, "And moreover, I perform for you riding during the day, and intimacy during the night."

The gemara explains that this is derived from the following comparison. It is written here that Bilam's donkey said: "Was

I ever wont (*hahasken hiskanti*) to do so to you?" And it is written there, with regard to Avishag the Shunammite and King David, "And be a companion (*sochenes*) unto him." This teaches that the term *hiskanti* alludes to marital relations.

In other words, Shlomo was able to understand the message of Hashem that is present in all facets of creation, from the donkey and the bird to the *aron ha'kodesh*[55]. Bilam, on the other hand, was only able to understand the language of a donkey by descending, himself, to the level of a donkey. Therefore he was unable to both understand the language of the donkey and also be honoured before Hashem (Bamidbar 24.11)

וְעַתָּה בְּרַח לְךָ אֶל מְקוֹמֶךָ אָמַרְתִּי כַּבֵּד אֲכַבֶּדְךָ וְהִנֵּה מְנָעֲךָ ה' מִכָּבוֹד

And now flee back to your place. I said I would reward you greatly, but behold Hashem has withheld you from honour.

---

[55] With this explanation, it is possible to answer the question raised in the previous footnote.

Since the wisdom that was granted to Shlomo incorporated the entire creation, from the speech of the donkey to the message of the *Aron ha'kodesh*, it was no longer necessary for him to ask for the lives of his enemies, because his enemies were now included in the range of Shlomo's wisdom, and therefore automatically fell under his dominion.

The proof that Shlomo completed the Torah (so that we should say that the *seudah* that he made was in honour of the completion of the Torah) is that he acquired the ability to perceive the message and the glory of Hashem in all aspects of creation, from the donkey to the *aron ha'kodesh*.

Only through a complete understanding of the Torah is it possible to perceive the message of Hashem that emanates from the totality of creation, in such divergent and multi-faceted ways.

Glossary of Hebrew terms

Term	Meaning
aggadata	homiletical sections of the Talmud
aron ha'kodesh	ark of the covenant that contains the tablets on which were inscribed the Ten Commandments
avodah	service - namely an individual's service of Hashem or the order of the service in the *beis ha'mikdash*
avodas Hashem	service of Hashem
avos	patriarchs
ayin ha'ra	evil eye
beis din	legal court
beis ha'mikdash	temple in Yerushalayim (Jerusalem)
benei yisrael	literally Children of Israel, i.e. the Jewish nation
beracha	blessing
berachos	blessings
bikkurim	first fruits that are brought to the *beis ha'mikdash* and presented to the *cohen*
birchas cohanim	blessing given by the *cohanim*
bitachon	trust in Hashem
bitul	nullification
bris	covenant
chametz	leavened bread which may not be eaten or owned on Pesach
chayav misah	culpable of the death penalty
chilul Hashem	desecration of Hashem's name which is caused by a Jew displaying undesirable behaviour
cohen	member of the priestly family, i.e. a patrilineal descendant of Aharon

Term	Meaning
cohen gadol	high priest
David ha'melech	King David
derasha	derivation of the intended meaning of a *passuk* through careful analysis of wording and grammar
derush	homiletical interpretation of a verse
din	judgement
divrei Torah	Torah thoughts. Plural of *dvar Torah,* literally, words of Torah.
dvar Torah	Torah thought, literally a word of Torah.
edus	testimony
Elokim	G-d
emunah	belief in Hashem
galus	exile
geulah	redemption
gezera	decree
hakhel	a *mitzva* to come to the *beis ha'mikdash* to hear the king reading Devarim (the fifth section of the Torah), on Succos in the year of *shemitah*
halacha	religious law
halachos	religious laws (plural of *halacha*)
ha'navi	the prophet
hashgachah pratis	Divine providence
heh	fifth letter of the Hebrew alphabet
heilige	holy (Yiddish)
hekesh	a method of deriving the *halachah*, wherein the *halachic* details of two different *mitzvos* that are mentioned in the same *passuk* are derived from each other
issur	religious injunction that prohibits an action or that prohibits eating or benefiting from an object
kapparah	atonement or means of attaining atonement
kedushah	sanctity or holiness
kehunah	priesthood

Term	Meaning
ketores	incense
kiddush Hashem	sanctification of Hashem's name which is caused by a Jew displaying meritorious and praiseworthy behaviour
klal	generality or group
klal yisrael	nation of Israel
kodesh ha'kedashim	Holy of Holies (inner sanctum in the Beis Ha'mikdash)
korban	sacrifice in the beis ha'mikdash
korbanos	sacrifices in the beis ha'mikdash (plural of korban)
krias ha'torah	public torah reading from a Torah scroll in the synagogue
krias yam suf	splitting of the Reed Sea
lashon ha'kodesh	Hebrew. Literally, the holy tongue.
le'asid lavo	in the future. Normally a reference to the days of the messiah.
lechem oni	bread of affliction or bread of poverty, a reference to matza eaten on Pesach
lishmah	something done for its own sake and for no ulterior motive
ma'aseh bereishis	creation
machlokess	argument or dispute
madregah	literally "level", refers to a spiritual level
malach	angel
malachim	angels (plural of malach)
mashal	parable
mashiach	messiah
matzah	unleavened bread eaten on Pesach
medrash	a rabbinic commentary on the scriptures dating from the period of the Talmud
meraglim	spies (normally refers to the spies sent by Moshe to spy out Eretz Yisrael)
merkavah	the Divine chariot
mesorah	tradition

Term	Meaning
midbar	Desert (normally refers to the desert in which the Jews wandered for 40 years after the Exodus)
middah	measure, attribute or character trait
middas ha'din	Divine attribute of strict justice
middas ha'rachamim	Divine attribute of mercy
mincha	afternoon prayer
minhag	custom
mishkan	tabernacle built by the Jews in the *midbar*
Mitzrayim	Egypt
Mitzri	Egyptian
mitzva	commandment
mitzvos	commandments (plural of *mitzva*)
neshama	soul
nesi'im	princes of the tribes of Israel
nevuah	prophecy
nisayon	test (normally refers to a test given by Hashem)
nissim	miracles
olah	burnt offering, a sacrifice that is completely burnt (except for the hide)
olam ha'bah	world to come (normally understood to be a spiritual world)
olam hazeh	this (corporeal) world
olos	plural of *olah*
parshah	portion of the Torah. May refer to the section read in the weekly Torah reading.
Passuk	verse in the scriptures
passul	invalidated by the *halacha*
pesak	legal decision
peshat	simple meaning (of a verse)
pessukim	many verses (plural of *passuk*)
petirah	passing away of a person

Term	Meaning
rashi	an acronym for Rabbi Shlomo Yitzchaki (22 February 1040 – 13 July 1105). A medieval French rabbi and author of a comprehensive commentary on the gemara and commentary on Tenach.
reshaim	evil people
ruach ha'kodesh	spirit of Divine inspiration
sedrah	weekly Torah portion
sefer	book
seforim	books (plural of *sefer*)
seudah	celebratory feast
shamayim	heavens
shechinah	divine presence
shelamim	peace offering, a sacrifice that is brought to denote that all is well with the person who brings it
shemitah	seventh year of the agricultural cycle in Eretz Yisrael in which it is forbidden to cultivate the land
shevatim	Tribes of Israel
shirah	song
shivas ha'minim	seven types of fruits and grain whereby Eretz Yisrael is praised
shul	synagogue (Yiddish)
siyum	celebration of the completion of a section of the Torah
taharah	purity
tahor	ritually pure (opposite of *tameh*)
talmid chacham	a sage knowledgeable in the Torah
tameh	ritually unpure (opposite of *tahor*)
tefillah	prayer
tefillos	prayers (plural of *tefillah*)
tenach	scriptures (the word *tenach* is an acronym of Torah, Nevi'im and Kesuvim)
tevah	nature
teshuvah	repentance

Term	Meaning
tosafos	medieval commentaries on the gemara. (Critical and explanatory glosses, printed on the outer margin and opposite Rashi's notes.)
tumah	impurity
tzadik	righteous person
tzaddikim	righteous people (plural of *tzaddik*)
tzara'as	commonly translated as leprosy, however this word appears to refer to a physical disease representative of an inner spiritual malaise, which is not currently extant
umos ha'olam	nations of the world
vav	sixth letter of the Hebrew alphabet
yam suf	Reed Sea
yeshiva	educational institution dedicated to study of the Torah
yetzer ha'ra	evil inclination
yetzias mitzrayim	exodus from Egypt
yisrael	Jew
yud	tenth letter of the Hebrew alphabet

Bibliography

The following is a bibliography of the rare and out-of-print *sefarim* that are quoted in this *sefer*.

Ben Heh-heh

- **Author**: Rabbi Dovid ben Aharon ha'cohen
- **Printed**: Livorno (Italy), 1820

Chesed Shmuel

- **Author**: Rabbi Shmuel Auerbach
- **Printed**: Amsterdam, 1698

בחסד ואמת יכופר עון

ספר

חסד שמו אל

ראה זה חדש אשר לא היה לעולמים · והוא ספר
מעט הכמות ורב האיכות על ספר בראשית ובו
פשטים רמזים דרשות סודות נפלאות שהיו
נפלאים מעינינו וגם יש בו קצרת תוכחה חברו ונם
יסדו אחד מבני עליה המועטים חסיד ופרוש אחד
מן החסידים הפרושים שבדור הזה ושמו מהרי"ר
שמואל בן הקדוש הר"ר דוד הי"ד
משפחת אויערבך מק"ק לובלין עיר
ואם בישראל אי"ע

נדפס

באמשטרדם

בבית ובמצות הבחור הנחמד והיקר כמ"ר
משה בן הישיש הנכבד החסיד ועניו כבוד
אברהם מינדיס קויטינייו זצ"ל·

ובהשגחת עין פרטית
הגביר שמואל טישיירה יצ"ו

Divrei Shmuel

- **Author**: Rabbi Shmuel Zanvil ben Chanoch

- **Printed**: Amsterdam, 1678

ספר

(הוא עיט לי״ס

דברי שמואל

על שם המקרא

טלם חיים בזולהים עגון עד יךעינך ה'

ויהי דברי שמואל לכל ישראל׃ ראה זה דבר
חדש אשר לא היה לעולם׃ והוא ביאור חדש׃
דרושים נחמדים על התורה׃ עם מדרשים
נפלאים׃ וחידושים ישנים׃ וגם חדשים׃
בפלפולא חריפתא׃ ורזי אורייתא׃ אשר לא
נשמע מעולם׃ דיחכמתא׃ וגבורתא׃
כאשר עיני כל תחזינה משרים׃ ויגל וישמח
לבו עם שאר כל אברים׃ ויאמרו דברים אלו
ראויס לאמרם לדוד דורים׃ חברו הרב
המופלא׃ כשמו׃ כן תהילתו׃ כבור מהדר
שמואל זנוויל במהדר חנוך זצ״ל מלובלין
אשר היה תקע אהלו ואור תורתו בק״ק יאס״
וגם היה סוף ימיו אב״ד בק״ק סעניץ׃

Gevul Binyamin

- **Author**: Rabbi Binyamin ben Eliezer ha'cohen Vitale of Reggio (1651–1730)

- **Printed**: Amsterdam 1727

ספר
גבול בנימין

יסדתי בהררי קדש אשר יאמר היום בהר ה' יראה ול"ו ימצא ז"ה או"ר בכל גבולי לאפני חפץ חפצי שמים החדשים והאר"יש החדשה עתה הצמח בחבור הגדול הזה מדרושים מחודשים ונפלאות מהרותיו על כל **פרשיות התורה והפטרות · ולחדשים ולשבתות ולמועדים · וארבע פרשיות ובין המצרים ·** ועוד דרושים נפלאים **להספד ולנשואין ולברית מילה ·** כלם גבוהים וישרים

וחרשוות הוא מגיד מישרים לישר בלבותם ואבנים טובות ומרגליות קבועות בו בשרשרית גבלות ובהקדמות העליונות ממעונות אריות בנו"יות ברמ"ה דברים העומרים ברומו של עולם ואת ישרים סודו כו"ד וסב"ד בגבולו סביב סביב קדש קדשים מאישי"ה וכלל לאישי"ם והלך הגבו"ל אל הים"ין ויביאם אל גב"ול קדשו ה"ר ז"ה קנתה ימי"נו הורועו ואוד פני יש"ל הרב המחבר הכהן הגדול מופת הדור והדרו ראשון לכל דבר שבקדושה נאה דורש ונאה מקיים ככוש"ר של קיימא ברדישה ופרישה המביאה לד"י טהרה וקדושה ה"ה החכם הכולל החסיד והענו המקובל האקי נ"י מרנא ורבנא כמוה"ר **בנימין הכהן** נר"ו:

באמשטרדם

בדפוס ובבית
כהר"ר שלמה בן כהר"ר **יוסף** כ"ץ זצ"ל **פרופס**

מוכר ספרים

בשנת אשר **מלאתיו** רוח חכמה לפ"ק:

Imrei Shefer

- **Author**: Rabbi Naftali Ashkenazi
- **Printed**: Venice 1601

ספר
אמרי שפר

יסדו וגם חקרו החכם השלם כמ"הרר נפתלי אשכנזי נר"ו תושב צפת תוב"ב שבנו ליל העליון חכו ממתקים כב'אור מאמרי רז"ל ופשטים נאים ומתוקים מדבש ונופת צופי' בלקוטי קצת פסוקי' בררן ותלח רחים בצוארו וטחנך זו בזו והוציא קמחן סולת נקי'ה מנופה ב'ג נפה כאשר עין הקורא תחזינה
מ'שרים:

ותהי התחלת המלאכה מלאכת שמים על יד נחמן להכת המחבר המ' הצעיר נסים שושן לנו בשנת ישמח ח"ר צ'ון לפ"ק

פה ויניציאה

במצות דכ"אל זכ'טי ו בני'תו
Con licentia dei Superiori.

Kesef Nivchar

- **Author**: Rabbi Aviezri Zelig Margolies. Rabbi in Kalish, Prague and Halberstadt.

- **Printed**: Livorno (Italy), 1794

Yad Yosef

- **Author**: Rabbi Yosef Tzarfati. Born Adrianople (Edirne), Turkey. Died 4th Cheshvan, 5400 (1640).

- **Printed**: Venice (1616), Amsterdam (1700)

ספר
יד יוסף

והוא אוצר מלא החמדה להשקות מים לעדה אין מים אלא תורה ארבע׳ או חמשה
דרושים מתוקים מדב״ש בכל פרשה ופרשה ודרוש׳ לחופה ולמילה ודרושים לנדבת שלם פעמים
ולשבת הגדול ולחג הפסח ולחג השבועות ולר״ה וי״ה ולסוכות ודרושי׳ לשבת דברי ולשבת שמעו
ולשבת איכה ולשבת נחמו ולתשובה ולשבת בנתים **בשפע ותיפעה כמה מאמרי**
חז״ל מהגמרא והמדרשי׳ והילקוט ופסיקתא ומכילת׳ וספר׳
וספרי מבוארים באר היטב בדרך הדש ממש ממה
שפירש וישן מפני חדש תוציאו וכמ׳ מילי
מעלית בכל פרשה ופרשה לזרות
ולחבר בטעמא דמסתבר
ופשטים נחמדים מן התורה מן הנביאים מן הכתובים בקיצור האפשרי:

סכינו ונס חקרו הסכם הסלם הסמופלא סיני ועוקר הרים כמה״רר

יוסף צרפתי זלה״ה

אשר אור תורתו זרח יהאיר לכל בני דורו
מעיר

אנדרינופולי :

Yakar Mipaz

- **Author**: Rabbi Alexander Zusha ha'Cohen
- **Printed**: 1932

Printed in Poland

www.ingramcontent.com/pod-product-compliance
Lightning Source LLC
Chambersburg PA
CBHW032029150426
43194CB00006B/203